CURRY KITCHEN

CURRY KITCHEN

Jacki Passmore

VIKING

an imprint of

PENGUIN BOOKS

A note on serving sizes

The serving size suggested for each recipe is based on that dish being served as a main course with rice and/or bread. But in the curry-eating countries, curry is rarely served on its own: menus are planned to provide a spectrum of flavours, textures and colours, with at least two main curries and a variety of side dishes. A recipe marked 'Serves 4' would therefore extend to 6–8, or even more, when served with one or more other curries. Adjust the quantities in recipes accordingly, or save leftovers for another meal (most curries freeze well).

Contents

Introduction — 1

Basic recipes — 9

Vegetable & egg curries — 25

Seafood curries — 93

Chicken & duck curries — 157

Meat curries — 209

Accompaniments & side dishes — 279

Curry spices & special ingredients — 295

Conversions — 303

Index — 304

Introduction

Curries can easily become an obsession. With myriad different flavours and textures, and jewel-bright colours, they are evocative cameos of a region's history and culture.

In this book you'll find inspiring curries from India, Pakistan and Sri Lanka, and all corners of Southeast Asia. There are also recipes for curry pastes, powders and spice mixes, and for traditional accompaniments such as flatbreads, rice, sambals and chutnies. And there are helpful hints on garnish and presentation, and even practical tips on stocking up the curry kitchen.

Indian curries are a showcase for spices – used whole, ground into curry pastes and powders, or fried in bubbling oil to splash over a dish as a final, aromatic flourish. In the north and in picturesque Kashmir, curries are predominantly mild, often deliciously creamy. Further south, where rice takes over from wheat breads and seafood and coconuts play key roles, curries become a complex blending of sweet, spicy and fiery-hot, with sour flavour notes from tamarind and citrus.

Other curry styles, such as Goan and Nonya, reflect the fusion of a number of cultures and cuisines.

In Indonesia and Thailand, fresh local herbs and plants such as kaffir lime often take centre stage. The curries of Burma and Malaysia straddle the two cooking styles, using both spices and herbs lavishly.

India, Pakistan & Sri Lanka

North Indian curries include elegant classics handed down from palace kitchens of the lavish Moghul era of the sixteenth to the eighteenth centuries. India's southern vegetarian cuisine is an inventive collaboration between fresh local ingredients, legumes, chillies and spices.

In India slow cooking often produces meltingly tender meat curries with complex spicy flavours and thick, creamy sauces enriched with yoghurt, cream, ground cashews and almonds. Seafood curries are luscious, and often fiercely hot. For the vegetarian there is endless choice and variation.

Pakistani, Bangladeshi and the curry cuisine popularised in Britain as 'Balti' are boldly flavoured variants of the north Indian theme, integrated with influences from western and eastern neighbours Iran, Afghanistan and Burma (Myanmar). Then there's the teardrop-shaped island of Sri Lanka, separated from southern India by a narrow stretch of ocean, where curries are given potent appeal from dark and smoky roasted chillies and spices.

As with most curry cuisines, you can feature just one curry, or make up a menu with several.

Typical garnishes for these curries include roasted or fried whole almonds, silver-wrapped almonds, crushed roasted cashews and chopped pistachios; wedges of hard-boiled egg; sprinkled lines of powdered spices and saffron; raw onion rings and fried onion; whole spices and curry leaves fried in oil or ghee; and mint sprigs.

Traditional accompaniments are cooling yoghurt, often flavoured (see raita, page 286); chutneys and pickles (hot with sweet curries, sweet with hot curries, tangy with mild curries); fresh chutneys and relishes (see the fresh mint chutney, page 286); breads (such as flat rotis and chapatis, puffy naans, buttery parathas); and basmati rice in all sorts of guises (see page 280).

Thailand & Burma (Myanmar)

Southeast Asian curries rely less on spices and more on fresh herbs for their wonderful fragrance and distinctive flavour, although spices do play a role in some blends. In Thailand fresh is definitely best, with vibrantly flavoured curry pastes featuring red and green chillies, coriander, fresh kaffir limes and lemongrass. The unique array of local eggplants, fresh peppercorns, bamboo shoots and mushrooms are showcased also in the golden, turmeric-flavoured curry sauces of Burma.

Plan to serve at least two curries or more, to fully enjoy the spectrum of flavours and textures.

Jasmine rice is the centrepiece of most Thai meals, with sticky rice and softened rice vermicelli also popular. Typical garnishes include chilli flowers; spring-onion curls; shredded fresh red and green chilli; chopped roasted peanuts; banana flower slices; torch ginger flowers; crushed roasted rice; fried onions or shallots; and fresh herbs (basil, mint, coriander, dill). You can serve these curries with pickled garlic, salted duck eggs (from Asian food stores), and sliced cucumber and other salad ingredients.

Indonesia, Malaysia & Singapore

Spices and fresh herbs create the intense, complex flavours typical of Indonesian and Malaysian curries.

Although much of the world's spices are exported from Indonesia, curries there start with a rempah of pounded fresh local herbs and the root spices galangal, ginger and turmeric in rich and creamy coconut-milk curry sauces. The curry cuisine of Malaysia and Singapore reflects both India and Indonesia in its lavish, boldly flavoured sauces fragrant with whole and ground spices, and creamy, nutty coconut.

Garnish these curries with fresh herbs (Vietnamese mint, coriander, dill); fried onions and garlic; toasted shredded coconut; roasted or fried cashews; chilli flowers; spring-onion curls; and shredded fresh red and green chilli. Serve them with rotis and other flat or Indian breads; hot and spicy, fresh or purchased sambals; steamed white rice or some variation; sticky (glutinous) rice compressed into blocks.

Setting up the curry kitchen

Curries require little in the way of specialist cooking equipment, except for a good mortar and pestle and/or electric spice (coffee) grinder for grinding spices and herbs.

A couple of saucepans with good heavy bases, a wok, and for rice a heavy saucepan with a tight-fitting lid (or an electric rice cooker, which frees up a hotplate for other pans) provide the basics. Of course, once you're hooked on curries, you might want to add a compartmented spice box, a chapati-rolling board, a Balti pan, and some of those dinky little mini woks and clay pots for serving.

Fresh herbs are indispensable for curry-making. If you can grow your own, so much the better. The most common herbs used in curries are: basil (including Thai or holy basil), coriander (common and sawtooth), dill, kaffir lime, lemongrass and mint (common and Vietnamese).

For the pantry

- bamboo shoots, canned sliced
- besan (chickpea) flour
- bread (ready-to-eat Indian breads)
- chickpeas, canned or dried
- coconut, desiccated/shredded
- coconut milk/cream, canned, powdered, block
- curry pastes
- curry powders
- dried shrimp
- fish sauce
- kecap manis (sweet soy sauce)
- lentils and split peas
- mushrooms, canned and dried (enoki, oyster, straw, shiitake)
- nuts (almonds, cashews, candlenuts, macadamias, peanuts, pistachios)
- oil (peanut, sunflower, vegetable)
- rice (basmati, jasmine, long-grain white, medium-grain white)
- shrimp paste
- sugar (palm, soft brown, white)
- tomatoes, canned

For fridge or freezer

- chillies, various sizes, red and green
- eggplant
- galangal
- garlic
- ghee (clarified butter, see recipe page 10)
- ginger
- kaffir lime leaves (can be frozen)
- kaffir limes (can be frozen)
- lemongrass
- lemons
- limes
- okra (frozen)
- onions (shallots, onions, spring onions)
- peas (frozen)
- potatoes
- sambal ulek (chilli paste)
- spinach (frozen)
- tomatoes

Basic recipes

These days you can buy good-quality curry basics such as pastes, powders and stocks, in most supermarkets as well as Asian food stores. But making your own doesn't take much time or effort and it definitely gives you a fresher, more flavourful result. Indeed, for many cooks much of the joy of curry cooking comes with starting from scratch: selecting and roasting spices, and the fragrance of freshly pounded herbs.

Home-made curry pastes may not be as intensely hot as purchased ones. If using a bought paste, add only half of the suggested quantity at first, taste the curry halfway through the cooking time and add more if required. If using a home-made curry paste use the quantity suggested, but you can add more to taste.

Pastes in particular keep well: store in an airtight container (such as a small storage bag) for up to a week in the fridge or up to 1 year in the freezer.

Ghee (clarified butter)

Place a block of butter in a small saucepan and heat gently until the yellow pure butter fat floats above the white milk solids. This can be strained off to make pure ghee, which is bright yellow and will keep for months, even without refrigeration.

By continuing to cook the butter until the liquid in the milk solids has cooked away and the solids have integrated with the butter fat, you have a whiter product with a 'milkier' taste, which many curry cooks prefer. It must be refrigerated.

Curry pastes & powders

There are possibly as many curry pastes and powders as there are cooks to use them. Family recipes are passed down over generations, though they are not set in stone.

In principal, curry pastes are a mixture of spices and fresh herbs, aromatic roots and other flavouring ingredients, combined with oil or other moistening agents. Curry powders are simply that – a mix of dried, ground spices. These mixtures provide the base flavour and colour of a curry sauce, which are accentuated by cooking the paste or powder to draw out and develop the flavours before adding the main ingredients. Some spice mixes, such as garam masala, are also sprinkled over finished dishes for a final burst of flavour.

When buying Indian curry mixes, the label usually specifies the degree of heat. In general, and for your reference when making your own pastes or powders, korma-style curries are milder than madras-style, while vindaloo is hottest. Most Indian curry pastes can be used for Balti-style curries.

Vindaloo paste

1 tablespoon coriander seeds
1 teaspoon cumin seeds
1 teaspoon fenugreek seeds
1 teaspoon brown mustard seeds
½ teaspoon black peppercorns
a 5-cm cinnamon stick
3 whole cloves

1 teaspoon sugar
½ teaspoon ground turmeric
5–6 large dried chillies, deseeded and soaked in hot water for 20 minutes
4 tablespoons white vinegar
2 tablespoons vegetable oil or mustard oil

In a small pan, dry-roast the coriander, cumin, fenugreek, mustard and peppercorns for about 1½ minutes, until fragrant. Transfer to a spice grinder, add cinnamon stick, cloves and sugar, and grind to a fine powder. Add turmeric, drained chillies, vinegar and oil, and continue to grind until reduced to a paste.

Use at once, or store in a small airtight container in the refrigerator for up to 3 weeks.

MAKES ABOUT ½ CUP (ENOUGH FOR 3–5 CURRIES)

BASIC RECIPES

Tandoori paste

You can store this paste in the refrigerator for up to 1 week.

2–3 cloves garlic, peeled
1 small onion, roughly chopped
a 2-cm piece fresh ginger, roughly chopped
1 tablespoon ground coriander
2 teaspoons ground cumin
1 teaspoon salt
1 teaspoon ground chilli (hot or mild, to taste)
2 teaspoons ground sweet paprika
1 tablespoon creamy yoghurt
1 tablespoon oil
1 tablespoon freshly squeezed lemon juice
a few drops red (or red and yellow) food colouring (optional)

Grind garlic, onion and ginger to a smooth paste and press through a sieve, discarding the solids. Add the ground spices, yoghurt, oil, lemon juice and food colouring (if using), mixing well.

When ready to use, mix with an extra ¼–½ cup creamy yoghurt.

MAKES ABOUT ½ CUP (ENOUGH FOR 3–4 CURRIES)

Hot Indian curry paste (Balti curry paste)

½ teaspoon fenugreek seeds
1½ teaspoons brown mustard seeds
1 quantity garam masala (page 16)
1½ teaspoons ground turmeric
2–2½ teaspoons ground chilli
2–3 tablespoons vegetable oil or mustard oil

Dry-roast fenugreek and mustard seeds in a small pan until they pop (about 1 minute). Grind to a fine powder and mix with the garam masala, turmeric and chilli.

Heat oil, pour it over the spices and mix well. Leave to cool, and use at once or store in a small jar (it will keep for 2–3 months in the refrigerator).

MAKES ½ CUP (ENOUGH FOR 3–4 CURRIES)

BASIC RECIPES

Mild Indian (korma) curry paste

1 quantity garam masala (page 16)
seeds from 3 cardamom pods,
 finely ground
½ teaspoon ground cinnamon
½ teaspoon grated nutmeg
2 tablespoons vegetable oil

Heat oil and add spices. Warm through, and use at once (or store in a small container in the refrigerator).

MAKES ¼ CUP (ENOUGH FOR 2–4 CURRIES)

Roasted curry spices ›

For Sri Lankan roasted curry powder, roast the spices until very dark.

1 teaspoon brown mustard seeds
¼ cup coriander seeds
1 tablespoon cumin seeds
1 teaspoon cardamom seeds
2 whole cloves
a 2-cm cinnamon stick

Heat a small pan or wok over medium heat. Add the spices and dry-roast until browned, shaking the pan from time to time. Transfer spices to a spice grinder or mortar and grind to a fine powder. Shake through a sieve onto a plate to remove coarse bits, and when cool store in a small airtight jar.

MAKES ⅓ CUP (ENOUGH FOR 4–6 CURRIES)

Garam masala

1 tablespoon coriander seeds
2½ teaspoons cumin seeds
2 teaspoons black peppercorns
3 whole cloves
seeds from 3 cardamom pods
a 2-cm cinnamon stick
a few gratings of nutmeg (optional)
½ teaspoon fennel seeds (optional)

In a small pan dry-roast the coriander, cumin and peppercorns over moderate heat for about 1½ minutes. They will begin to smell very fragrant. Transfer to a spice grinder or mortar, add the cloves, cardamom seeds and cinnamon, and grind to a fine powder. Add nutmeg and fennel (if using), pulse briefly, then tip into a sieve and shake onto a plate.

When cool, store in a small airtight jar.

MAKES ¼ CUP (ENOUGH FOR 2–4 CURRIES)

Basic curry powder

There are endless spice combinations for curry powders. This is a good standard mix, which can be adjusted with more or less of the listed spices, according to taste.

2 tablespoons coriander seeds
3 teaspoons cumin seeds
½ teaspoon caraway or fennel seeds
½ teaspoon brown mustard seeds
½ teaspoon black peppercorns

a 3-cm cinnamon stick
2 whole cloves
½ teaspoon ground chilli
½ teaspoon ground turmeric

Place the whole spices in a spice grinder or mortar and grind to a fine powder. Shake through a sieve onto a plate, and add the chilli and turmeric.

Transfer mixture to a spice jar and store in a cool, dry place for up to 3 months.

MAKES ⅓ CUP (ENOUGH FOR 2–4 CURRIES)

Thai red curry paste

1½ teaspoons shrimp paste
1½ tablespoons coriander seeds
2 teaspoons white peppercorns
3 teaspoons ground sweet paprika
1 stem lemongrass, roughly chopped
⅓ cup chopped shallots or onions
a 2-cm piece fresh ginger, peeled
   and thickly sliced
5 cloves garlic, peeled
6 fresh hot red chillies, deseeded
   and coarsely chopped
vegetable oil
salt

Wrap shrimp paste in a square of aluminium foil and place in a small frying pan without oil. Cook over moderate heat for 30 seconds, turning once.

Add the coriander seeds and peppercorns to the pan and cook for a further 1½ minutes, shaking the pan from time to time. Tip these spices into a spice grinder and grind to a fine powder, then add the paprika.

Unwrap shrimp paste and allow to cool. In a blender or food processor chop the lemongrass, shallots or onions, ginger, garlic and chillies, adding as much oil as needed to produce a thick, reasonably smooth paste. Add shrimp paste and spices, and pulse to mix evenly.

Use at once, or keep for 5–6 days in the refrigerator. (To keep longer, cook in a non-stick pan with salt and 1–2 tablespoons extra oil for 3–4 minutes, and then store.)

MAKES ABOUT 1 CUP (ENOUGH FOR 2–4 CURRIES)

Thai green curry paste

1½ teaspoons shrimp paste
2 teaspoons coriander seeds
½ teaspoon black peppercorns
4 spring onions, chopped
4–6 large fresh green chillies, deseeded and chopped
2 stems lemongrass, roughly chopped
¾ cup (loosely packed) coriander leaves
4 cloves garlic, peeled
a 3-cm piece fresh ginger or galangal, peeled and thickly sliced
grated zest of 1 lime
½ teaspoon ground turmeric
1½ teaspoons salt
vegetable oil

Wrap shrimp paste in a small square of aluminium foil, place in a small frying pan and dry-roast for 30 seconds, turning once. Add coriander seeds and peppercorns to pan and roast for a further 1½ minutes, shaking the pan from time to time. Transfer spices to a spice grinder and grind to a powder.

Unwrap shrimp paste and allow to cool. Place spring onions, chillies, lemongrass, coriander leaves, garlic, ginger (or galangal) and lime zest in a blender or food processor and chop finely. Add the shrimp paste, ground spices, salt and enough oil to assist the process, and grind to a smooth paste. Press through a sieve to remove any large bits.

Use the paste at once, or keep for 5–6 days in the refrigerator in an airtight container. (To keep for longer, cook in a non-stick pan with 1–2 tablespoons extra oil for 3–4 minutes, and then store.)

MAKES ABOUT 1 CUP (ENOUGH FOR 2–4 CURRIES)

Thai Mussaman curry paste

3 teaspoons shrimp paste
2 tablespoons coriander seeds
2 teaspoons cumin seeds
½ teaspoon cardamom seeds
a 10-cm cinnamon stick
4 whole cloves
½ teaspoon black peppercorns
½ teaspoon grated nutmeg
4–5 large dried chillies, deseeded and soaked in hot water for 20 minutes
2 tablespoons chopped lemongrass
8 cloves garlic, peeled
5 shallots or 1 small onion
5–6 thin slices fresh galangal or ginger
grated zest of ½ lime
1¼ teaspoons salt
2–3 tablespoons oil

Wrap shrimp paste in a small square of aluminium foil, place in a small frying pan or wok without oil, and cook for 1 minute, turning twice. Add coriander, cumin, cardamom, cinnamon, cloves and peppercorns to pan, and dry-roast for about 1½ minutes, shaking the pan from time to time.

Unwrap shrimp paste and set aside to cool. Transfer spices to a spice grinder or mortar and grind to a fine powder, then add the nutmeg.

In a blender or food processor, grind chillies, lemongrass, garlic, shallots or onion, lime zest and galangal or ginger to a paste, adding salt and a little oil to assist the process. Add ground spices and shrimp paste, and pulse to combine.

Use the paste at once, or store in the refrigerator for up to 1 week. (To keep longer, fry for 2–3 minutes in the remaining oil before storing.)

MAKES ½ CUP (ENOUGH FOR 2–3 CURRIES)

BASIC RECIPES   19

Thai yellow curry paste

This paste is used mainly with fish and seafood.

6 dried red chillies, deseeded and soaked in hot water for 20 minutes
a 10-cm stem lemongrass, chopped
3 cloves garlic, peeled
4 shallots, peeled
4–5 slices fresh galangal or ginger, peeled
2 teaspoons grated lime zest

2–3 tablespoons oil
2 teaspoons ground coriander
1 teaspoon ground cumin
¾ teaspoon ground cinnamon
⅓ teaspoon ground mace
1 teaspoon ground turmeric
¼ teaspoon ground cardamom
1½ teaspoons salt

Drain chillies and place in a food processor. Add lemongrass, garlic, shallots, galangal or ginger, and the lime zest, and grind to a smooth paste, adding oil to assist the process. Stir in the ground spices and the salt.

Use at once, or refrigerate for up to 1 week. (To keep longer, fry for a few minutes and cool before refrigerating.)

MAKES ABOUT ½ CUP (ENOUGH FOR 2–3 CURRIES)

Thai jungle curry paste

3 teaspoons shrimp paste
3–4 hot green chillies, deseeded and chopped
3 shallots, peeled
4 cloves garlic, peeled
1 stem lemongrass, roughly chopped
7–8 slices fresh galangal or ginger, peeled

2 sprigs fresh coriander, including roots
2 teaspoons grated lime zest
½ teaspoon ground white pepper
1 teaspoon salt
1 tablespoon oil

Wrap shrimp paste in a square of foil and cook in a pan without oil for 1½ minutes, turning several times. Unwrap and leave to cool. In a blender or food processor grind the chillies, shallots, garlic, lemongrass, galangal (or ginger) and coriander until smooth and pasty. Add lime zest, pepper, salt and oil, and grind again until smooth.

Use paste at once or refrigerate for up to 1 week. (To store for longer, fry with extra oil for 3–4 minutes, and refrigerate in a small jar.)

MAKES ABOUT ½ CUP (ENOUGH FOR 2–3 CURRIES)

Stocks

Fresh stock is easy to make, and definitely worth the effort, when time allows. But ready-to-use stock from delicatessens and supermarkets is of acceptably good quality. If you are using stock powder or cubes, do not add salt until you taste the finished dish, to avoid over-seasoning.

Vegetable stock

handful of parsley or coriander stems
1 small onion, sliced
1 spring onion, roughly chopped
2 cups chopped vegetables (celery, choko, white radish)

Place all the ingredients in a large saucepan with 6 cups water. Bring barely to the boil, reduce heat, and simmer gently for about 20 minutes. Strain.

Refrigerate for up to 3 days (or freeze).

MAKES 4–5 CUPS

Fish stock

bones and heads from 1–2 fish
1 small onion, cut in half
1 stick celery, roughly chopped
⅓ teaspoon fennel seeds

Place all ingredients in a large saucepan with 6 cups water and bring barely to the boil. Reduce heat, then simmer gently for about 18 minutes, skimming the surface from time to time.

Strain and refrigerate for 1–2 days (or freeze).

MAKES 4–5 CUPS

Chicken stock

1 chicken carcass (or 1 kg chicken necks)
1 small onion, cut in half
a 3-cm piece fresh ginger or galangal, cut into chunks
½ stem lemongrass, bruised (optional)
a few black peppercorns

Rinse the chicken parts and place in a deep saucepan. Add 7 cups water, the onion, ginger, lemongrass and peppercorns, bring to the boil and then immediately reduce heat to a simmer. Skim off any froth and impurities which rise to the surface, and simmer for about 25 minutes, skimming every few minutes.

Strain well. Use at once, or keep in the refrigerator for up to 2 days (or freeze).

MAKES ABOUT 3½ CUPS

Lamb or beef stock

1 kg lamb, mutton or beef (or goat) bones
2 tablespoons ghee or oil
1 medium-sized onion, chopped
2 cloves garlic, peeled
a 1-cm piece fresh ginger
5 whole cloves

In a heavy saucepan brown the bones in the ghee or oil until very well coloured. Add the onion, garlic, ginger and cloves, and fry briefly, then pour in about 8 cups of water and bring to the boil. Reduce heat and simmer for 1–1¾ hours, skimming occasionally, to obtain a richly flavoured broth. Strain into a bowl.

Use at once, or keep in the fridge for up to 4 days (or freeze).

MAKES ABOUT 3½ CUPS

Vegetable & egg curries

Indian vegetarian cuisine is a flamboyant celebration of deliciously healthy ingredients, offering limitless scope for culinary invention. Vegetables soak up curry sauces without sacrificing their own character, and are often cooked simply with grated coconut, herbs and spices. Many vegetable dishes are sent to the table sparkling with a 'tempering' of crunchy spices and/or curry leaves fried in ghee and oil.

To a lesser extent, other cuisines include vegetarian curries. In Thailand, these dishes will feature root vegetables, bamboo shoots and exotic mushrooms. Gourds, pumpkins and melons, bean sprouts and fresh fruit (such as pineapple, jackfruit and bananas) are enriched by spicy Burmese, Indonesian and Malaysian curry sauces.

Even humble vegetables like pumpkin, potato, peas and tomatoes make lively, mouth-teasing curries. Most of the exotic varieties suggested in these recipes are available in Asian food stores or supermarkets these days. And what's not sold fresh may be found in the freezer.

Enjoy these curries on their own with rice or bread, or follow Asian tradition and serve several together. Or you can team them with your favourite grills and roasts.

Green-bean, tomato & coconut dry curry

- 2 tablespoons oil or ghee
- 1 teaspoon cumin seeds
- 1 teaspoon brown mustard seeds
- ½ teaspoon asafoetida powder
- 4–5 curry leaves (optional)
- ½–1 fresh hot red chilli, deseeded and chopped
- 250 g green beans or snake beans, sliced
- 2 tomatoes, deseeded and diced
- salt
- ¼ cup desiccated or shredded coconut

Heat the oil or ghee in a saucepan and fry the cumin and mustard seeds until they pop and sputter (about 40 seconds). Add asafoetida, curry leaves and chilli, and fry briefly, then add the beans and tomatoes with ½ cup water and ½ teaspoon salt. Cover, and simmer for about 6 minutes, until beans are tender. Stir in the coconut, check seasoning and serve.

SERVES 4–6

Thai green-bean, cauliflower & peanut curry

1 small onion, chopped
a 10-cm stem lemongrass, chopped
1 fresh hot green chilli, deseeded
a 1-cm piece fresh ginger, peeled
3 cloves garlic, peeled
2 tablespoons peanut or other oil
½ cup coconut cream
1 teaspoon palm or brown sugar
250 g green or snake beans, cut into 4-cm pieces
¼ head cauliflower (250–300 g), separated into small florets
2–4 tablespoons crunchy peanut butter or crushed roasted peanuts
1 cup coconut milk
fish sauce

In a food processor grind the onion, lemongrass, chilli, ginger and garlic to a paste.

Heat the oil and fry prepared paste for about 2 minutes, stirring well. Add coconut cream and sugar, and simmer for 3–4 minutes. Add the beans and cauliflower, and cover. Bring to the boil and simmer for 5–6 minutes.

Mix peanut butter or crushed peanuts into the coconut milk and add 1 tablespoon fish sauce. Pour over the vegetables and cook for a further 5 minutes or until the vegetables are tender.

Check seasoning, adding salt or extra fish sauce if needed, and serve.

SERVES 3–4

Cauliflower, tomato & pea curry

- 1 medium-sized onion, cut into chunks
- 3 cloves garlic, peeled
- a 1.5-cm piece fresh ginger, peeled
- 1–2 fresh hot red chillies, deseeded
- 2–3 tablespoons ghee or oil
- 3 teaspoons ground coriander
- 1 teaspoon ground cumin
- ½ teaspoon ground black pepper
- 1 small cinnamon stick
- 2 cloves
- 2 cardamom pods, cracked
- ¼ head cauliflower (250–300 g), separated into florets
- 2 large tomatoes, deseeded and roughly chopped
- ¼ cup creamy yoghurt
- 2 tablespoons desiccated coconut or coconut powder
- salt
- 1 cup peas

Place the onion in a food processor or blender with the garlic, ginger and chillies. Grind to a paste.

Heat the ghee or oil in a heavy saucepan and fry the prepared paste for about 3 minutes, stirring. Add the ground and whole spices, the cauliflower and the tomatoes, and stir over medium heat for 1 minute until vegetables are coated with the seasonings.

Stir in the yoghurt, ¼ cup water, the coconut and ¾ teaspoon salt. Cover, and simmer over low heat for about 5 minutes until the vegetables are almost tender, stirring several times.

Add peas and cook for a further 3–4 minutes, or until tender. Check seasoning and serve.

SERVES 4

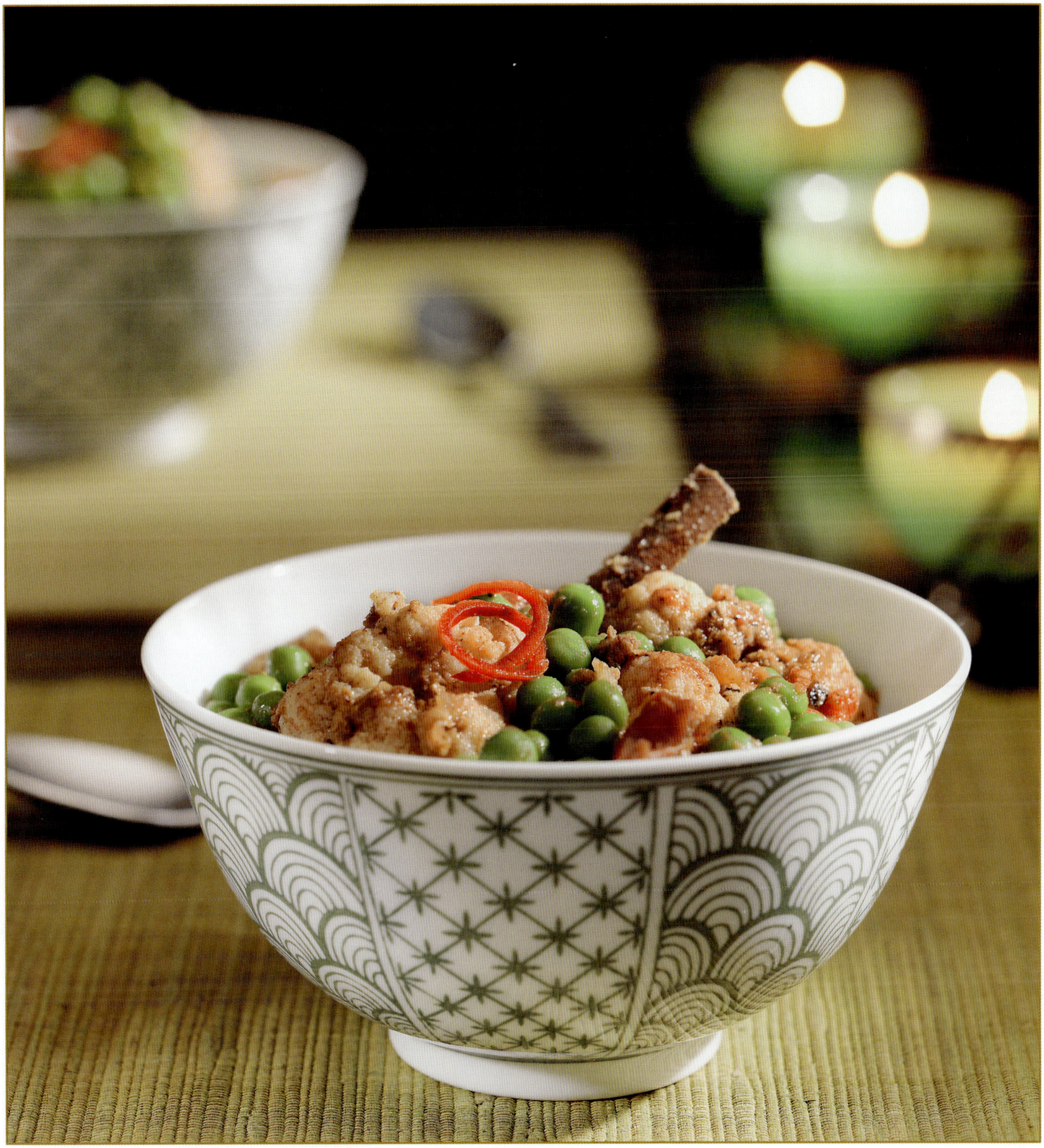

Kashmiri okra & cauliflower curry

Fresh okra is increasingly seen in produce markets and Asian food stores. If you can't find baby okra, use sliced larger ones instead. You can use frozen okra pieces (also available from Asian food stores) for this recipe: defrost before using and add just before the final steam-cooking.

250 g okra
250 g cauliflower, separated into very small florets
¼ cup oil or ghee
2 teaspoons grated fresh ginger
1 fresh hot green chilli, deseeded and chopped
¼ teaspoon fenugreek seeds
¼ teaspoon nigella seeds
½ teaspoon asafoetida powder
1 teaspoon ground sweet paprika
1 teaspoon ground coriander
½ teaspoon ground turmeric
1 teaspoon salt
3–4 tablespoons chopped fresh coriander

Trim stem ends and tips of fresh okra, if using, and cut each into 3–5 pieces. Heat the oil in a small heavy pan and fry okra and cauliflower over medium heat until lightly golden (3–4 minutes). Remove to a plate using a slotted spoon, and pour off all but 2 tablespoons of the oil.

Reheat the pan and fry ginger and chilli for 30 seconds. Add the whole and ground spices, and the salt. Stir well.

Return the cauliflower and okra to the pan (add defrosted frozen okra now, if using) and add ½ cup water. Cover tightly and steam-cook until tender (6–8 minutes), stirring once or twice.

Stir in the coriander and check for salt before serving.

SERVES 4

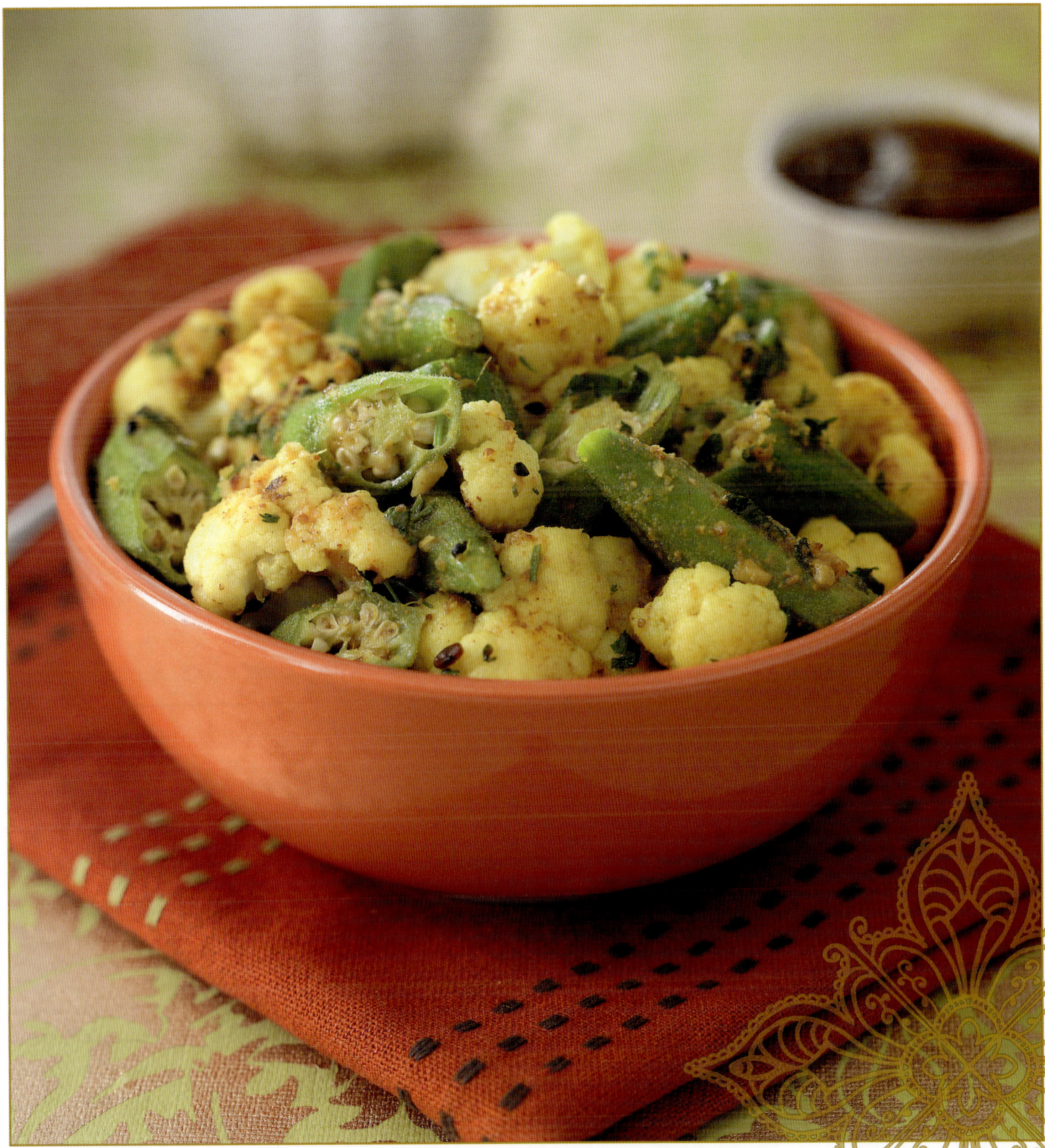

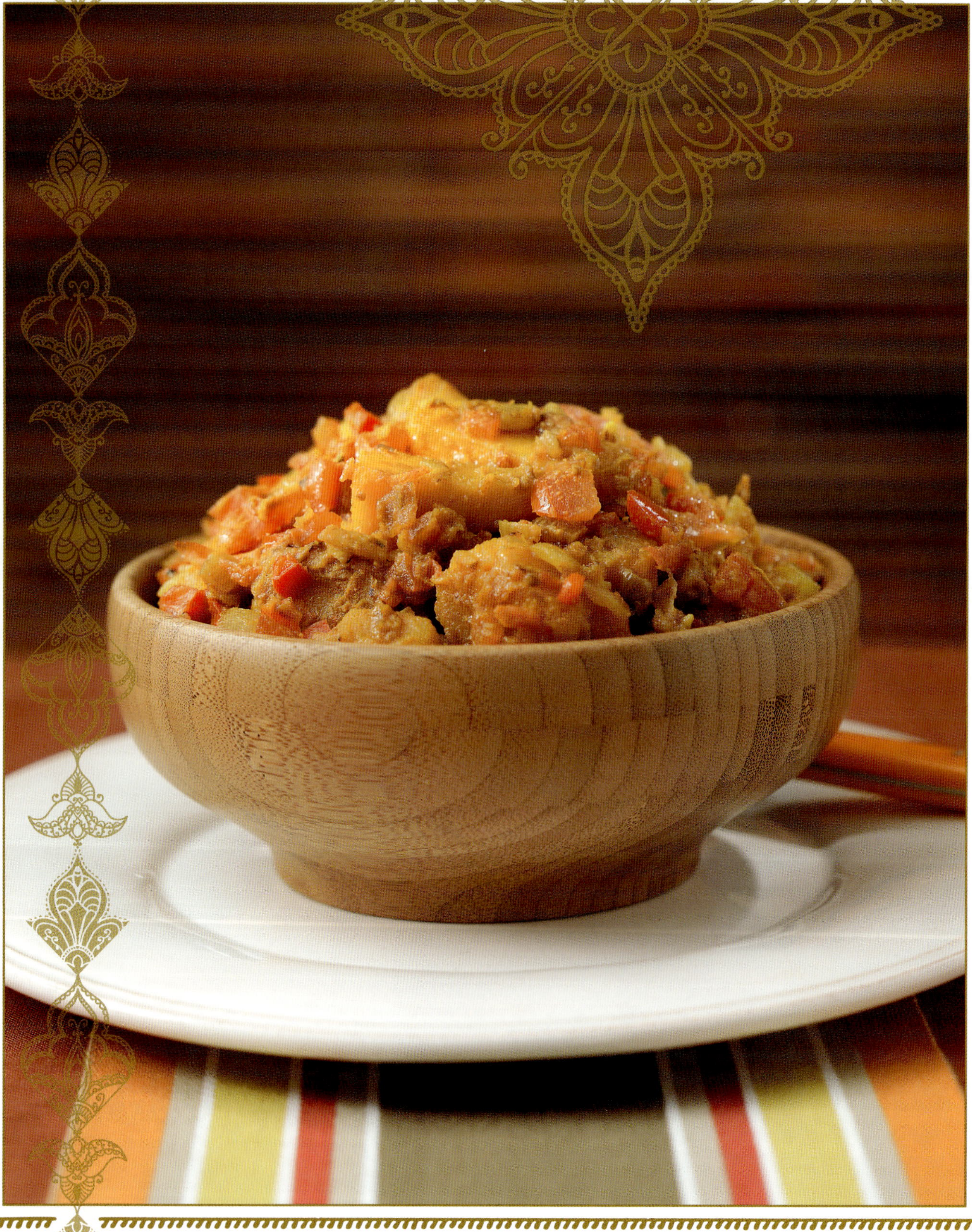

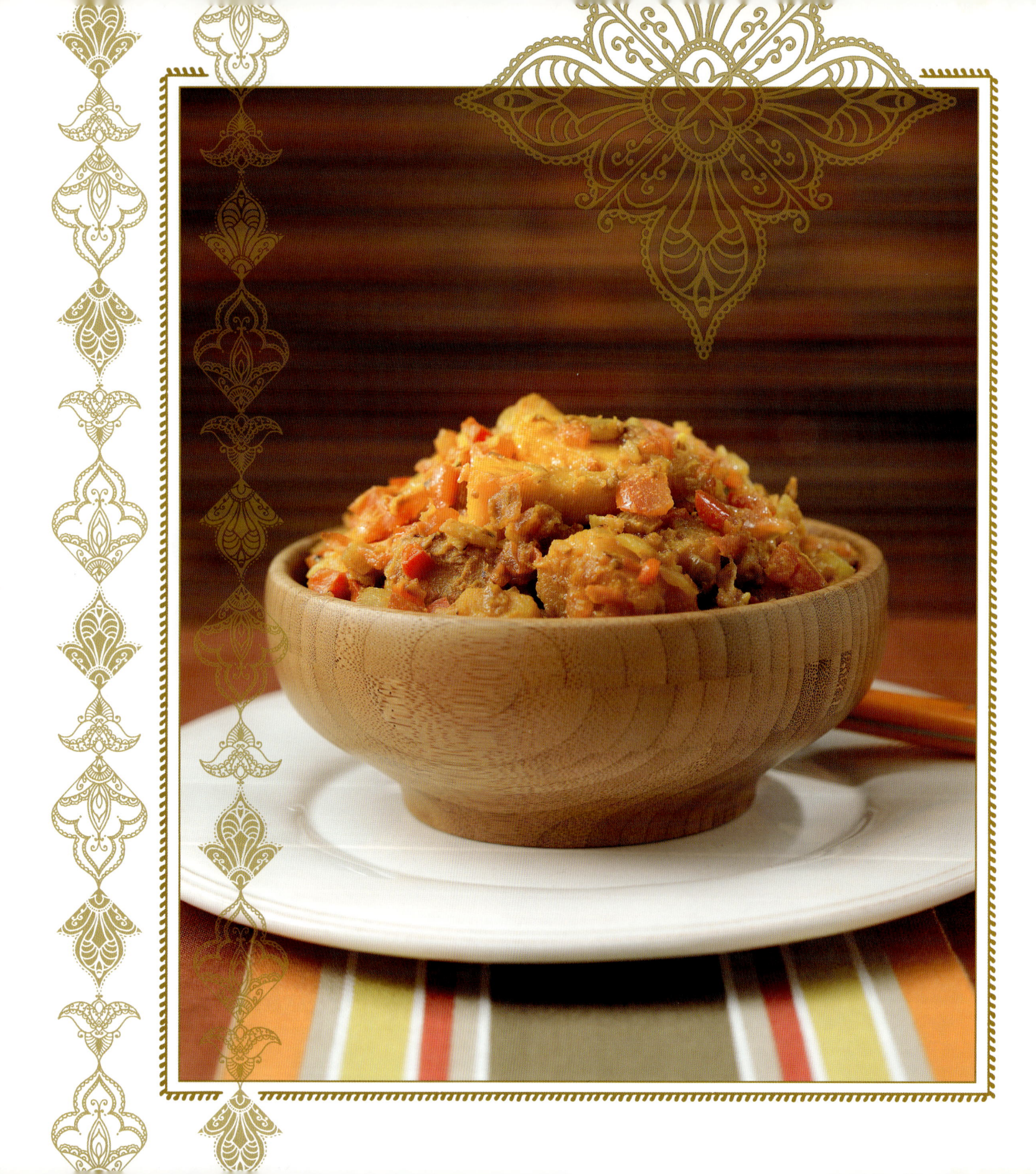

Curried pumpkin

- 2–3 tablespoons ghee or oil
- 1 medium-sized onion, finely chopped
- 600 g pumpkin, peeled and cut into 3-cm cubes
- 2 cloves garlic, finely chopped
- 3 teaspoons grated fresh ginger
- ½ teaspoon ground turmeric
- 1½ teaspoons ground cumin
- 1 fresh hot red chilli, deseeded and chopped
- juice of ½ large lemon
- 1 teaspoon salt
- ½ teaspoon sugar
- 2 tomatoes, deseeded and diced
- 2 tablespoons chopped fresh coriander or mint

Heat the ghee or oil in a non-stick pan and fry the onion over medium heat until becoming translucent (about 2 minutes). Add the pumpkin and stir over higher heat for about 2 minutes, or until caramelised.

Add the garlic, ginger, turmeric, cumin and chilli to the pan, mix well and cook for 30 seconds. Stir in the lemon juice, salt and sugar. Add tomatoes and 2–3 tablespoons water, cover tightly and steam-cook over low heat for 7–10 minutes, until the pumpkin is tender. Check seasoning, adding more salt if needed, and stir in chopped herbs before serving.

SERVES 4–6

Creamy mashed pumpkin payesh

400 g diced pumpkin
2½ tablespoons ghee
⅓ teaspoon ground turmeric
1 teaspoon ground cumin
¾ cup full-cream milk
1 small fresh hot red chilli, deseeded and finely chopped
2 tablespoons thick cream (optional)
salt
½ teaspoon brown mustard seeds
5–6 curry leaves

In a medium-sized saucepan fry the pumpkin in 1½ tablespoons of the ghee until lightly caramelised (about 2 minutes). Add turmeric and cumin, and stir to coat pumpkin with the spices.

Pour the milk into the pan and add the chilli. Cover tightly and cook over low heat until the pumpkin is tender enough to mash (about 10 minutes). Uncover, then simmer to boil off any remaining milk, and add salt to taste. Stir in the cream, if using, and mash smoothly. Spread pumpkin in a shallow serving dish.

In a small pan heat the remaining ghee and fry the mustard seeds and curry leaves until sputtering. Pour spices and butter over the pumpkin, and serve at once.

SERVES 3–4

Cumin-spiced sweet potato with asparagus

- 1 large orange-fleshed sweet potato (about 650 g), peeled and cubed
- 2 tablespoons ghee or oil
- 2 teaspoons grated fresh ginger
- 1 teaspoon crushed garlic
- 1 large fresh, hot red chilli, deseeded and chopped
- 1½ teaspoons cumin seeds, lightly crushed
- ½ teaspoon fennel seeds, lightly crushed
- salt and pepper
- 8 asparagus spears, sliced

Place sweet potato in a saucepan with the ghee or oil and brown over medium heat, turning often. Add the ginger, garlic, chilli, cumin and fennel seeds, salt and pepper, and stir to coat the sweet potato.

Add ½ cup water to pan and cover tightly. Cook for about 7 minutes, then add the asparagus and cook covered for a further 4–5 minutes, shaking the pan occasionally.

Check seasonings, and serve.

SERVES 4–6

Indonesian spinach & pumpkin curry

3 tablespoons oil
1 kg pumpkin, peeled and cut into 2-cm cubes
2 cloves garlic, finely chopped
1 teaspoon grated fresh ginger
¾ teaspoon sambal ulek or red chilli paste
1 tablespoon ground coriander
½ teaspoon ground nutmeg
⅓ teaspoon black pepper
1 × 400-ml can coconut milk
120 g baby spinach leaves
salt

Heat the oil in a saucepan or wok and sauté the pumpkin for about 2 minutes, until browned. Add garlic, ginger, sambal ulek (or chilli paste) and spices, cook together briefly, then add the coconut milk. Bring to the boil, immediately reduce heat and simmer, covered, for about 5 minutes. Add the spinach, season with salt to taste, and serve.

SERVES 4

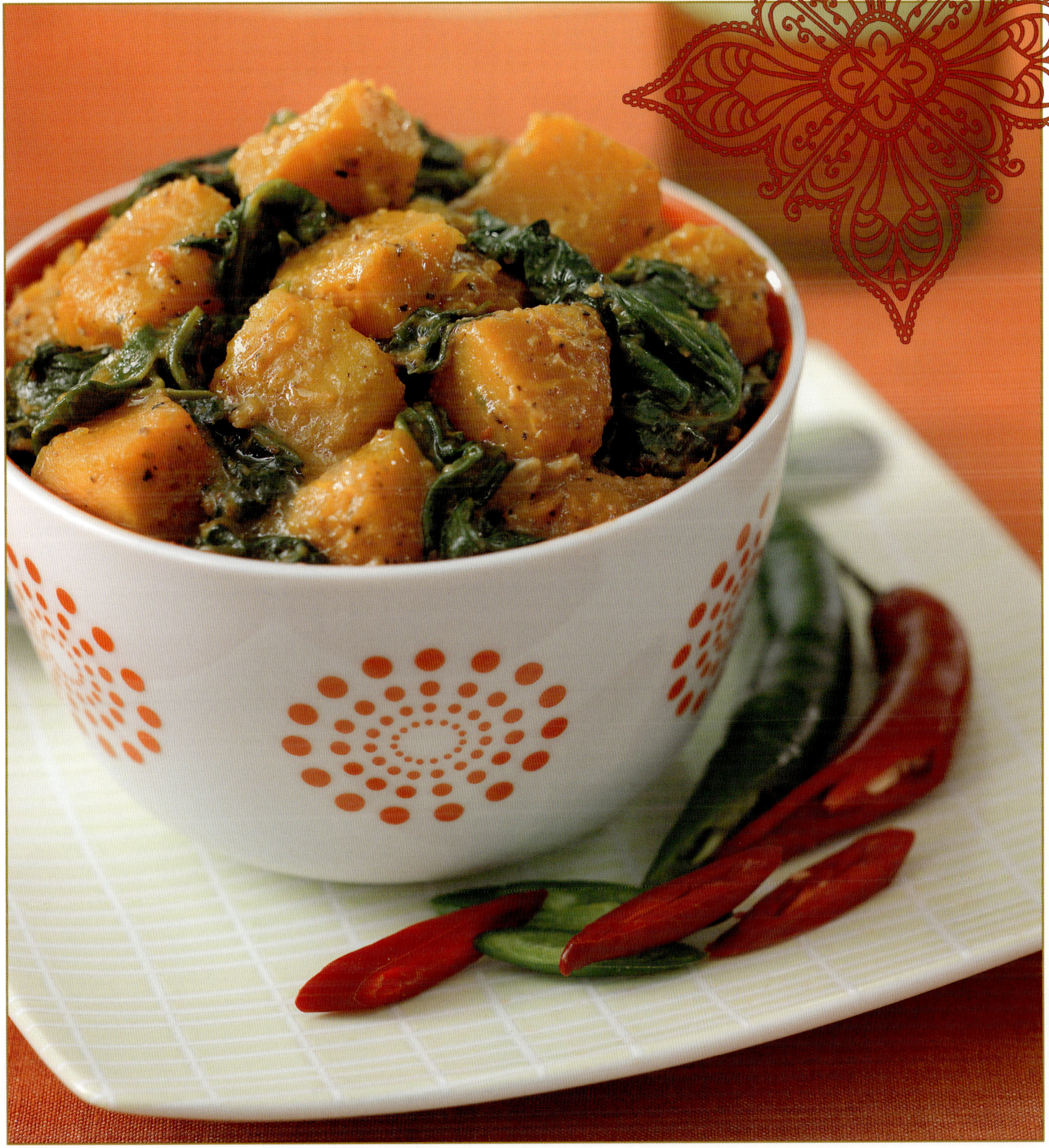

Peas with paneer in mild curry sauce (mattar paneer)

450 g frozen peas
salt
5 tablespoons ghee or oil
200–250 g paneer cheese, cut into bite-sized slices or cubes
2 large onions, roughly chopped
a 2-cm piece fresh ginger, peeled
2 teaspoons ground coriander
1½ teaspoons garam masala (page 16)
1 teaspoon ground turmeric
½ teaspoon ground chilli

Bring a saucepan of lightly salted water to the boil, add peas and boil for 4–5 minutes, until tender but not soft. Strain off hot water and at once cover peas with cold water to stop them cooking and to retain the bright-green colour.

Heat ghee or oil in a non-stick pan and fry paneer until lightly golden (about 1½ minutes), remove to a plate using a slotted spoon, and set aside.

In a food processor or blender, grind the onions and ginger to a paste. Tip into a strainer over a bowl and reserve the juice.

Pour off all but 2 tablespoons of the ghee or oil from the pan, and fry the onion and ginger pulp over medium heat for about 6 minutes, stirring frequently. Sprinkle the spices in and stir to mix. Season with about 1 teaspoon salt, add the reserved onion and ginger juice, and simmer for 1–2 minutes, stirring now and then.

Add peas and paneer, and simmer gently for another 2–3 minutes.

SERVES 4–5

Green vegetables in coconut

For the greens, use a combination of spinach, water spinach, bok choy, green beans, choko, zucchini and broccoli

2 teaspoons dried shrimp
2 tablespoons oil
1 large onion, finely chopped
1–2 fresh hot green chillies, slit lengthways and deseeded
500 g mixed green vegetables, chopped or diced
¾ cup desiccated coconut
¾ teaspoon ground turmeric
6–8 curry leaves
1 teaspoon salt
1–2 teaspoons freshly squeezed lemon juice

In a blender or spice grinder, whiz the dried shrimp to a fluffy powder and set aside.

Heat oil in a saucepan and fry the onion and chillies for about 2½ minutes, until onion is translucent. Add vegetables, dried shrimp, coconut, turmeric, curry leaves and salt, and stir to mix well. Now stir in about ½ cup water, cover the saucepan tightly and cook over low–medium heat for about 12 minutes: don't open the pan during this time but shake it occasionally to turn the vegetables and prevent sticking.

Check if vegetables are tender, and cook a little longer if necessary. Before serving, season with lemon juice and extra salt if needed.

SERVES 3–4

Cabbage with chilli & coconut

⅓ cup shredded coconut

¾ cup coconut milk

2 tablespoons oil

½ teaspoon brown mustard seeds

½ teaspoon cumin seeds

⅓ teaspoon fennel seeds

7–8 cups (about 500 g) shredded cabbage

2 fresh hot green chillies, deseeded and chopped

salt and pepper

Soak the coconut in the coconut milk.

Meanwhile, heat the oil and fry the mustard, cumin and fennel seeds until they pop and sputter. Add the cabbage and chillies, and stir to coat with the oil. Add the coconut and soaking milk with at least 1 teaspoon salt and a few twists of the pepper mill.

Cover pan tightly and cook gently for about 10 minutes, shaking the pan from time to time to turn the cabbage, until tender. Check seasonings, then serve.

SERVES 4–6

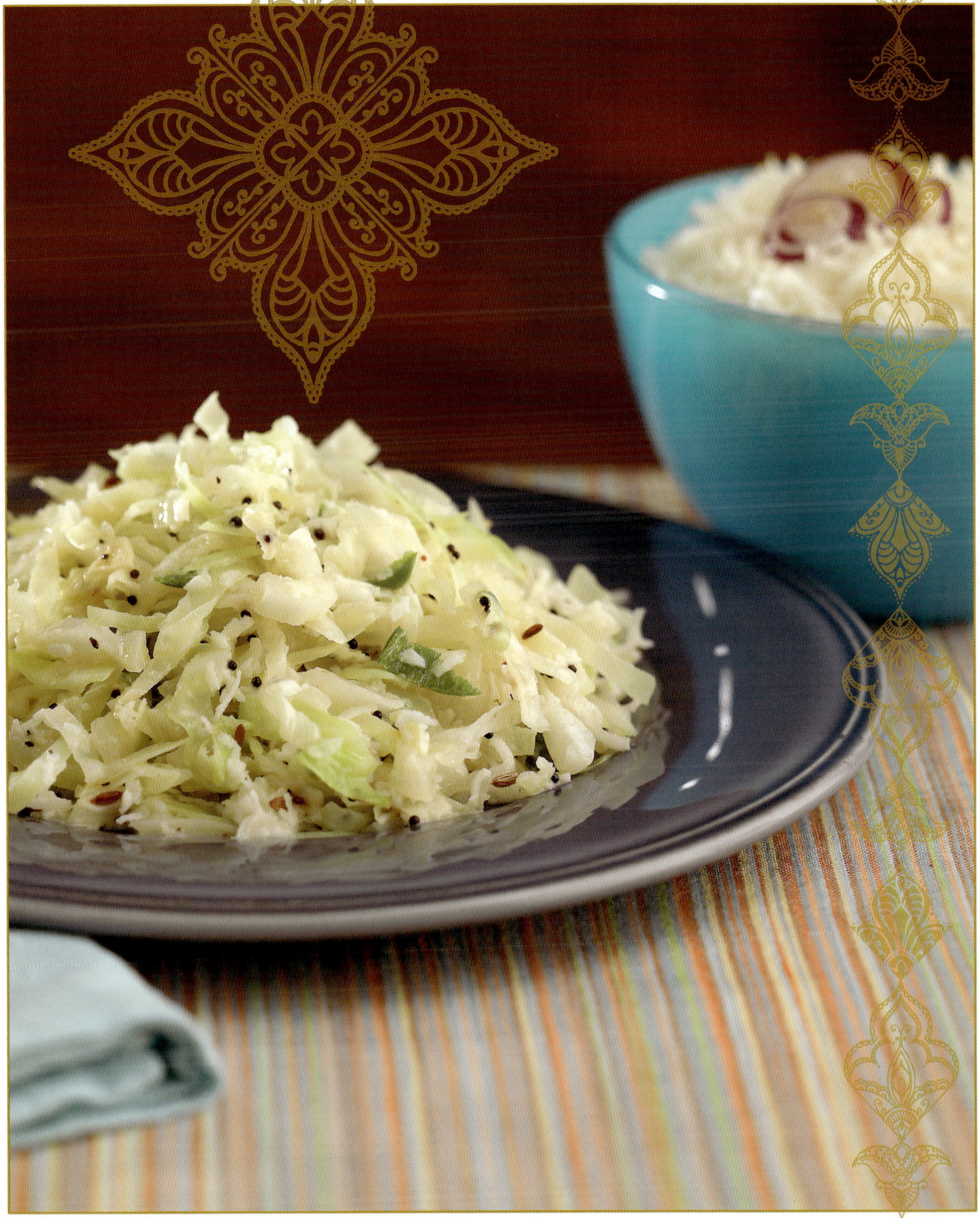

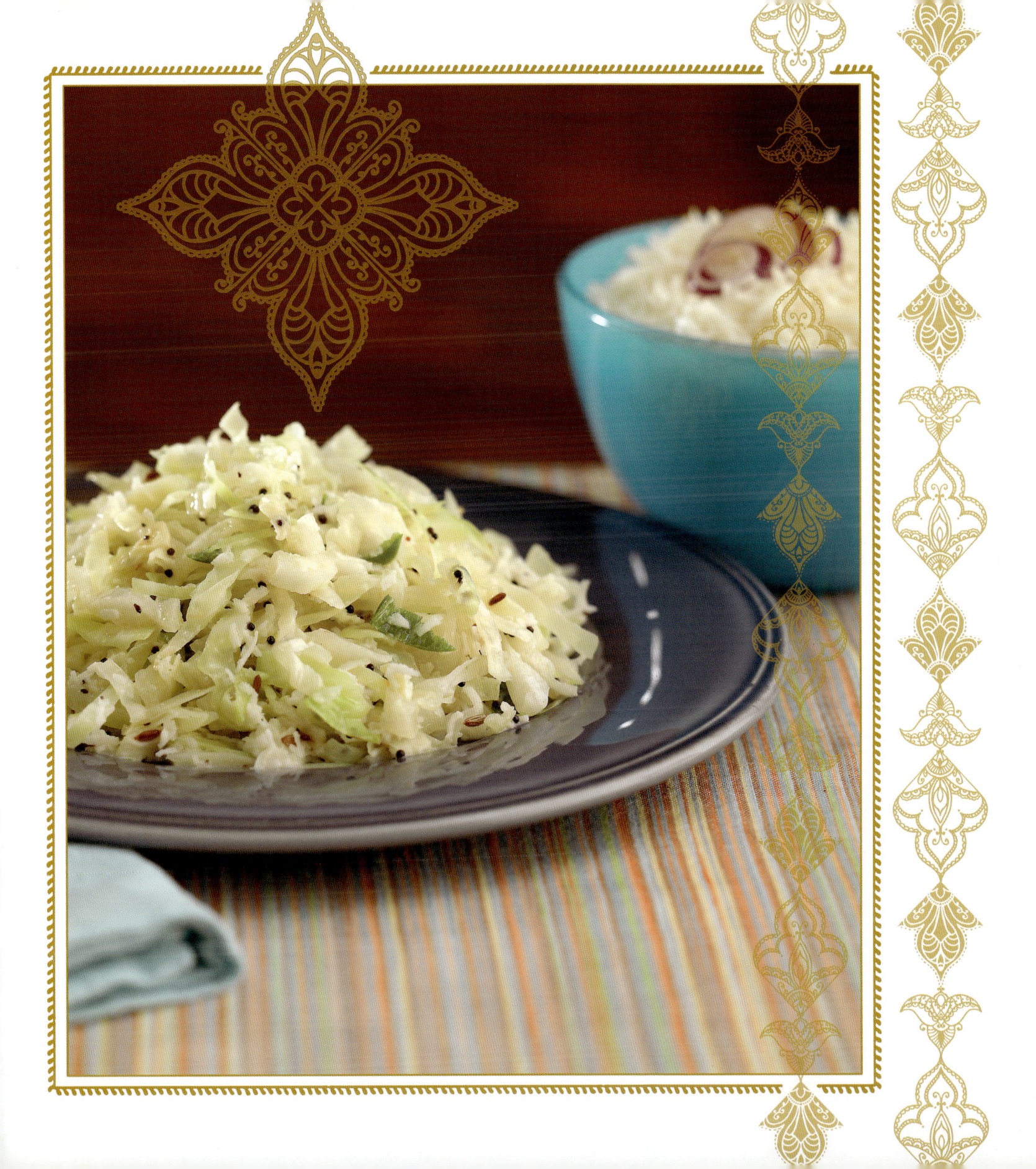

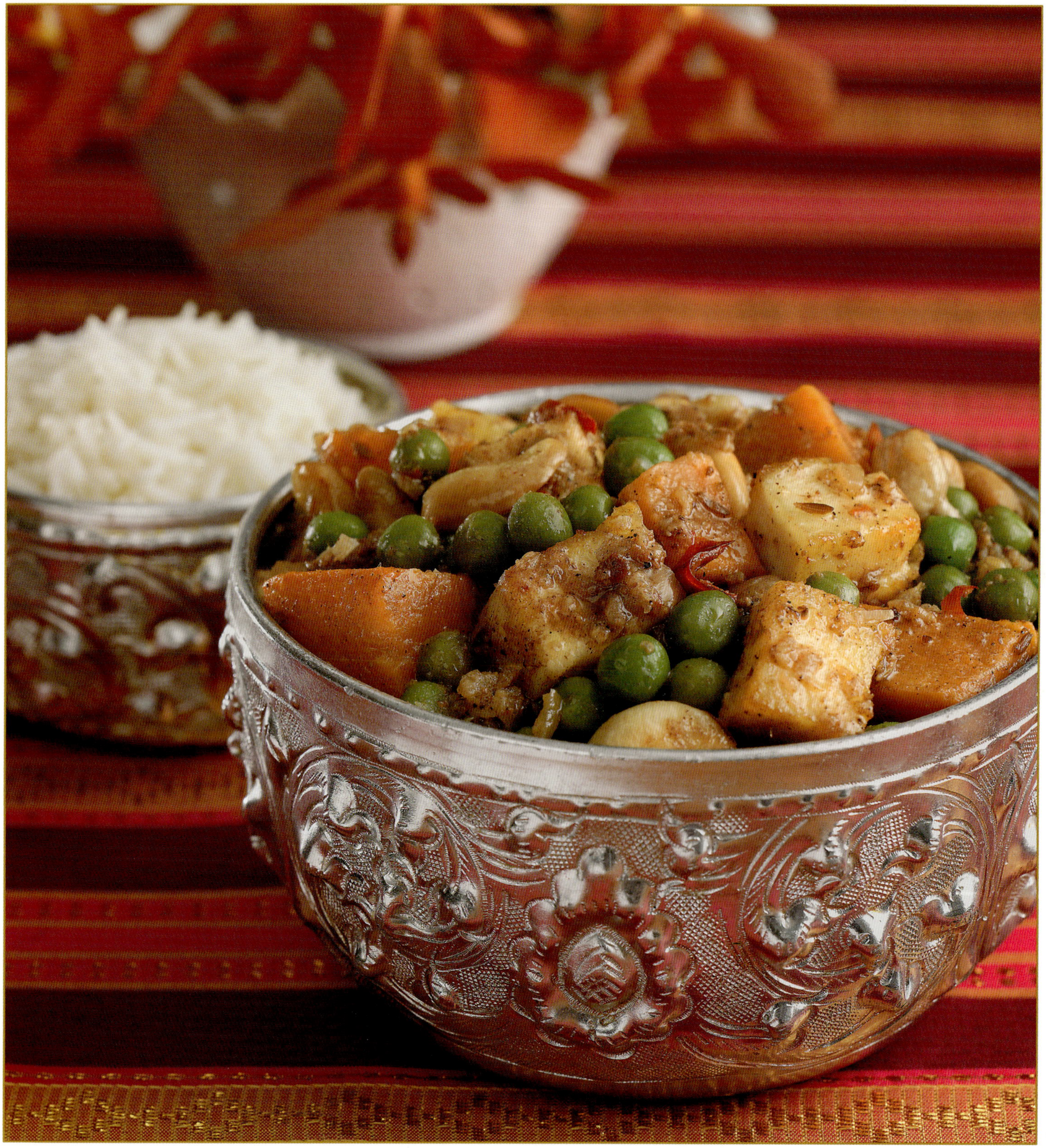

Sweet potato, paneer, pea & cashew curry

Cashews are an important crop in many parts of southern India and Sri Lanka, and often feature in curries, sometimes even as the main ingredient.

4 tablespoons ghee
250 g paneer cheese, cubed
1 medium-sized onion, diced
2 teaspoons grated fresh ginger
1–2 fresh hot red chillies, deseeded and chopped
1 tablespoon ground coriander
1½ teaspoons cumin seeds
½ teaspoon fennel seeds, lightly crushed
1 tablespoon garam masala (page 16)
500 g sweet potato, chopped
1 cup raw cashew nuts
1½ cups peas
salt

Heat the ghee in a non-stick pan and fry paneer over medium heat until golden (about 1½ minutes). Remove to a plate using a slotted spoon, and set aside.

In the same pan fry the onion, ginger and chillies for about 3 minutes until lightly coloured, stirring frequently. Sprinkle in the coriander, the cumin and fennel seeds and half the garam masala, and fry for 30 seconds, stirring.

Stir sweet potato and cashews into the pan, then pour in 1 cup water. Cover tightly, bring to the boil and simmer for 8–10 minutes. Add peas and paneer, with salt to taste, and continue to simmer gently until the vegetables are tender, adding a little extra water if needed.

Season to taste and sprinkle on remaining garam masala before serving.

SERVES 6

VEGETABLE & EGG CURRIES

Paneer in spiced tomato sauce (khadai paneer)

1 cup oil or ghee
200–250 g paneer cheese, cut into 2-cm cubes
2 medium-sized onions, one finely chopped and the other roughly chopped
4 cloves garlic, peeled
a 1.5-cm piece fresh ginger, peeled
2 teaspoons garam masala (page 16)
1 teaspoon ground cumin
¾ teaspoon fennel seeds, lightly crushed
¼ teaspoon ground turmeric
½–1 teaspoon ground hot chilli
1 × 425-g can tomato purée or diced tomatoes
salt and pepper
2–3 tablespoons chopped fresh mint, coriander, dill or spring-onion greens

Heat oil or ghee in a wok or saucepan and fry paneer till golden-brown. Remove to a bowl, cover with water and set aside. Pour off all but 2 tablespoons of the ghee or oil.

Place roughly chopped onion in a food processor or blender with the garlic and ginger. Grind to a paste.

Reheat the pan and fry finely chopped onion over medium heat for about 2½ minutes. Add the onion paste and continue to cook, stirring often, until lightly browned. Add the garam masala, cumin, fennel seeds, turmeric and chilli, and mix well, cooking for 30 seconds.

Rinse out the food processor or blender with 1 cup water, pour into the pan and bring to the boil. Reduce heat and simmer for 5–6 minutes, stirring occasionally. Stir in tomato purée or diced tomatoes and 1 teaspoon salt. Bring to the boil, reduce the heat and simmer for 5–6 minutes. Check seasoning, adding pepper to taste.

Add fried paneer and chopped herbs to the sauce and heat gently for 2–3 minutes.

SERVES 4

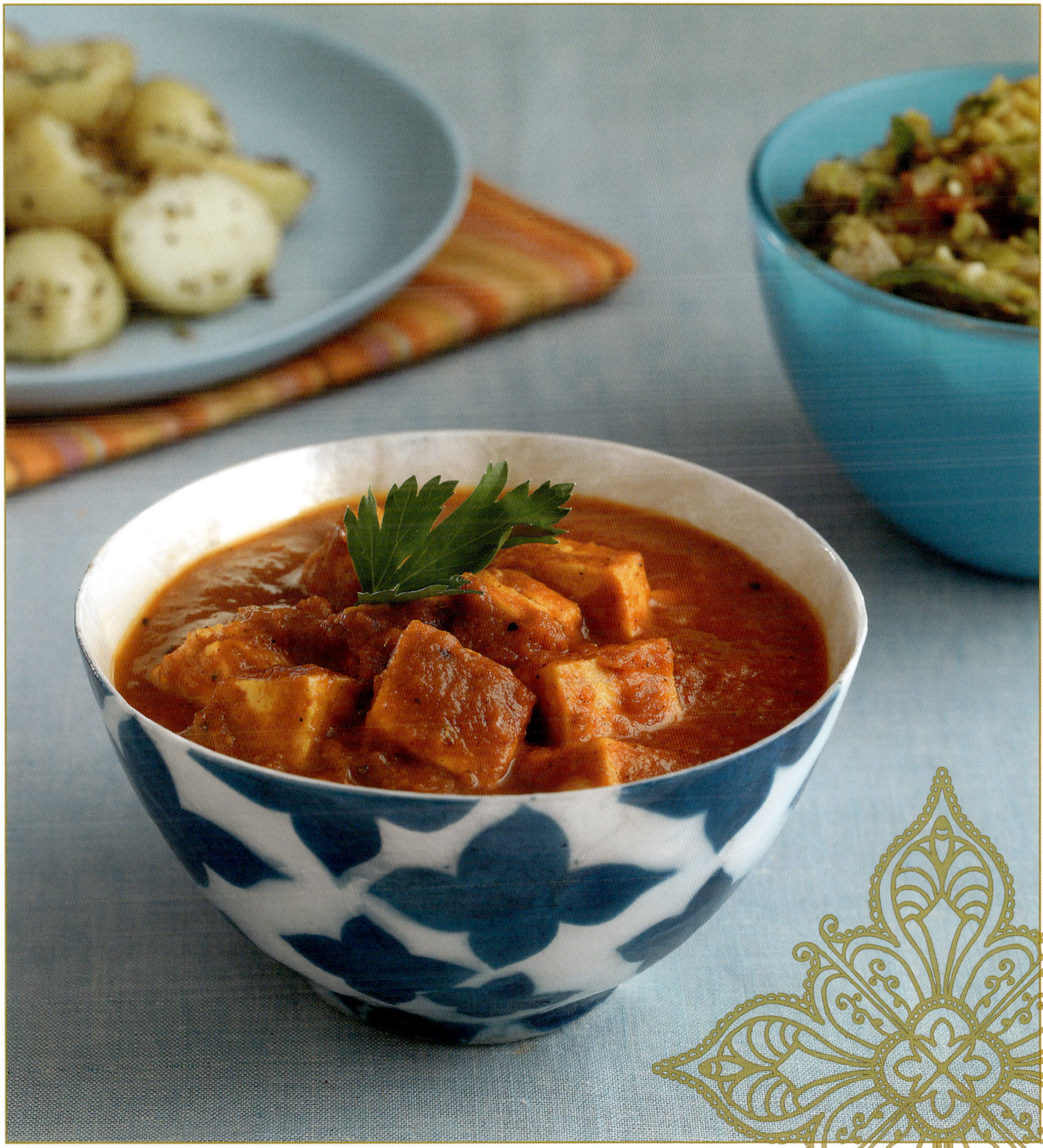

Burmese curry of potato, cabbage & onion

1 large potato, cubed
1 medium-sized carrot, thickly sliced
salt
2 tablespoons oil or ghee
1 large onion, finely sliced
3½ cups chopped cabbage
1–2 cloves garlic, crushed
¾ teaspoon ground turmeric
1 teaspoon cumin seeds
½ teaspoon ground black pepper
¼–½ teaspoon ground hot chilli (or chilli flakes)
freshly squeezed lemon juice
chopped fresh dill or coriander

Boil potatoes and carrot in enough lightly salted water to barely cover, for about 8 minutes, until partly cooked.

In a sauté pan heat the oil or ghee and fry onion over medium heat until tender and lightly coloured (about 4 minutes). Add cabbage and garlic, and sauté until lightly browned (about 3 minutes). Season with the turmeric, cumin, pepper and chilli.

Stir onion mixture into the potatoes and carrots, cover and simmer for about 7 minutes, until the potatoes and carrots are tender but still holding their shape, and the cabbage and onion are very tender.

Check and adjust seasonings, adding salt if needed, and a squeeze of lemon juice. Transfer to a serving dish and garnish with the chopped herbs.

SERVES 4

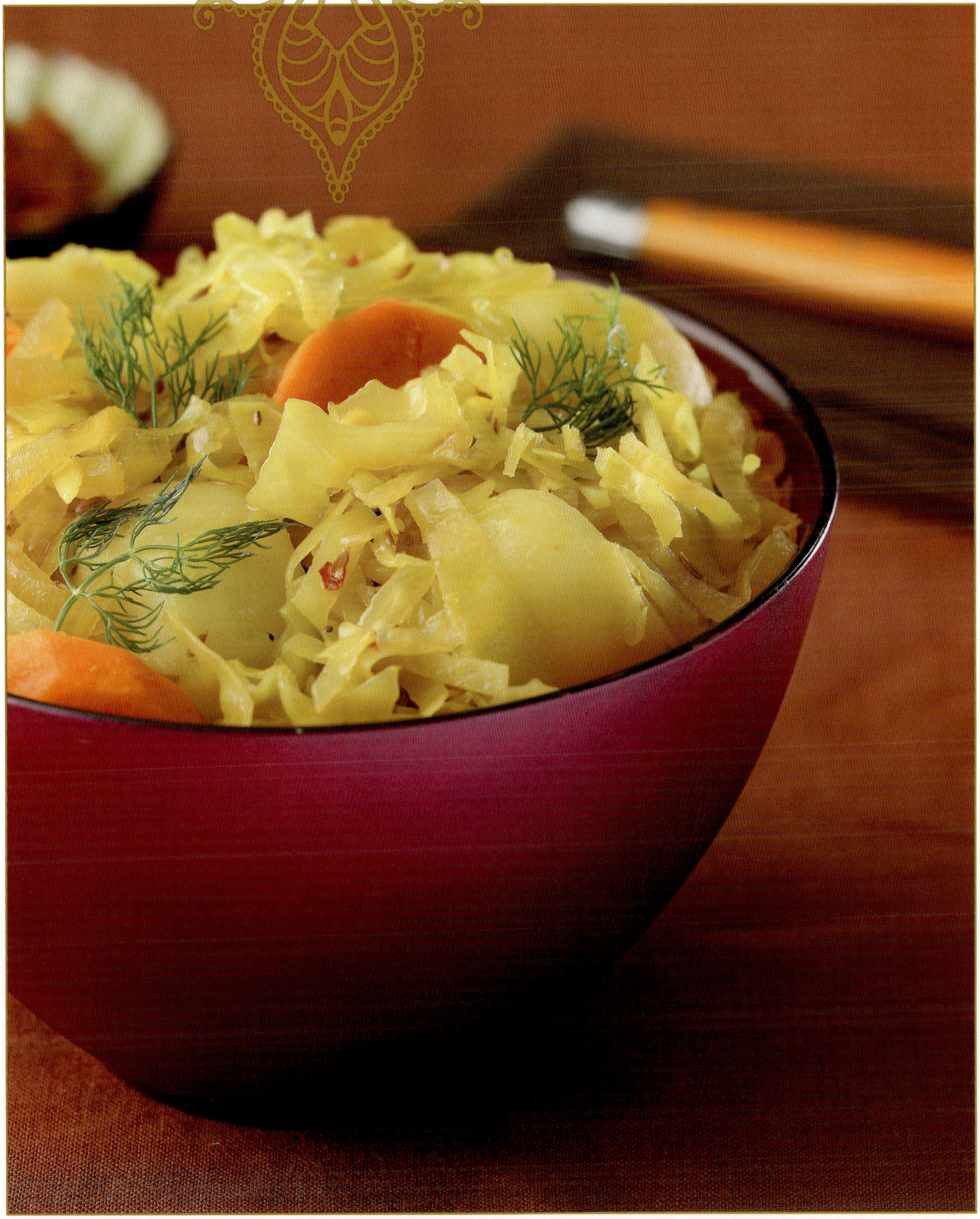

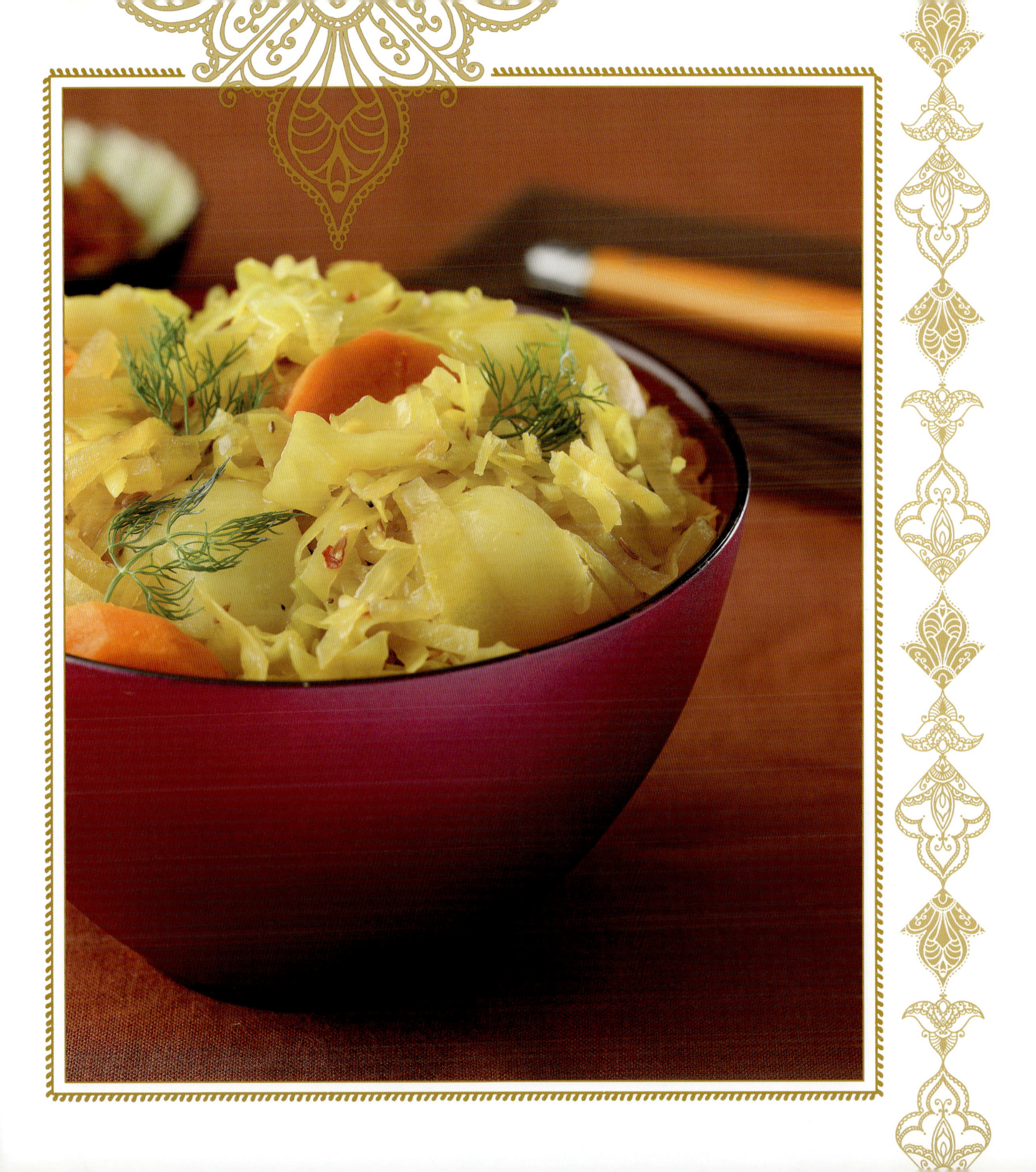

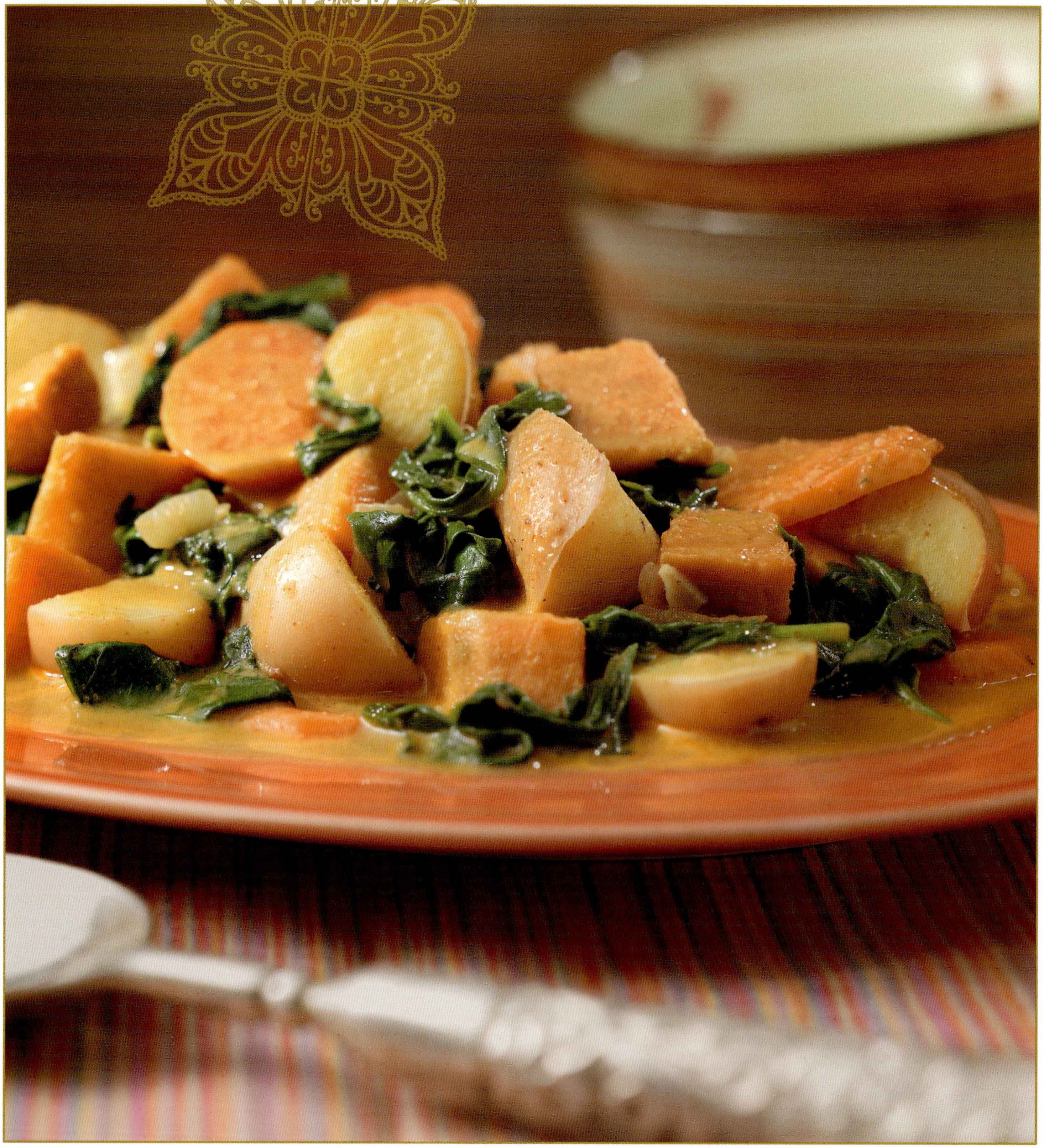

Red curry of vegetables

3 tablespoons oil
1 large onion, chopped
3 cloves garlic, chopped
3–5 teaspoons Thai red curry paste (page 17)
300 g sweet potato, peeled and cubed
300 g pink-skinned potatoes, cubed
300 g carrots, sliced
1 × 400-ml can coconut cream
salt and black pepper
120 g baby spinach leaves
1 tablespoon fish sauce or light soy sauce
freshly squeezed lemon or lime juice

Heat the oil in a heavy saucepan and fry onion until lightly coloured (about 3 minutes). Add the garlic and curry paste, and fry briefly, mixing well. Mix in the sweet potato, potatoes and carrots and cook for about 4 minutes until lightly browned, stirring frequently.

Add coconut cream and 1½ cups water with 1 teaspoon salt and a couple of twists of the pepper mill. Cover, bring to the boil, then reduce heat and simmer over low heat for about 12 minutes, or until the vegetables are barely tender.

Stir in spinach, add fish sauce or soy sauce and cook gently for a further 1–2 minutes, until spinach is tender. Finish with a squeeze of lemon or lime juice, and transfer to a serving dish.

SERVES 4–6

Balinese vegetables

2 medium-sized potatoes, cut into 2-cm cubes
1 thick wedge pumpkin or sweet potato (about 250 g), cut into 3-cm cubes
1 × 400-ml can coconut milk
1 teaspoon grated fresh ginger
½ teaspoon sambal ulek or 1 teaspoon ground hot chilli
¾ teaspoon ground turmeric
1 tablespoon ground coriander
1 teaspoon salt
1 cup sliced green or snake beans
1 cup fresh bean sprouts
120 g fresh water spinach or baby spinach leaves
1 teaspoon palm sugar or soft brown sugar (optional)
pepper

Place potatoes and pumpkin or sweet potato in a saucepan with the coconut milk, ⅓ cup water, and the ginger, sambal ulek or chilli, turmeric, coriander and salt. Bring to the boil, reduce heat and simmer, partially covered, for 10–12 minutes, until vegetables are cooked but holding their shape.

Add the beans to the pan and cook for 3 minutes, then stir in the bean sprouts and water spinach or baby spinach. Cook just long enough for the leaves to wilt, stir in sugar and pepper to taste, and check for salt.

SERVES 4–6

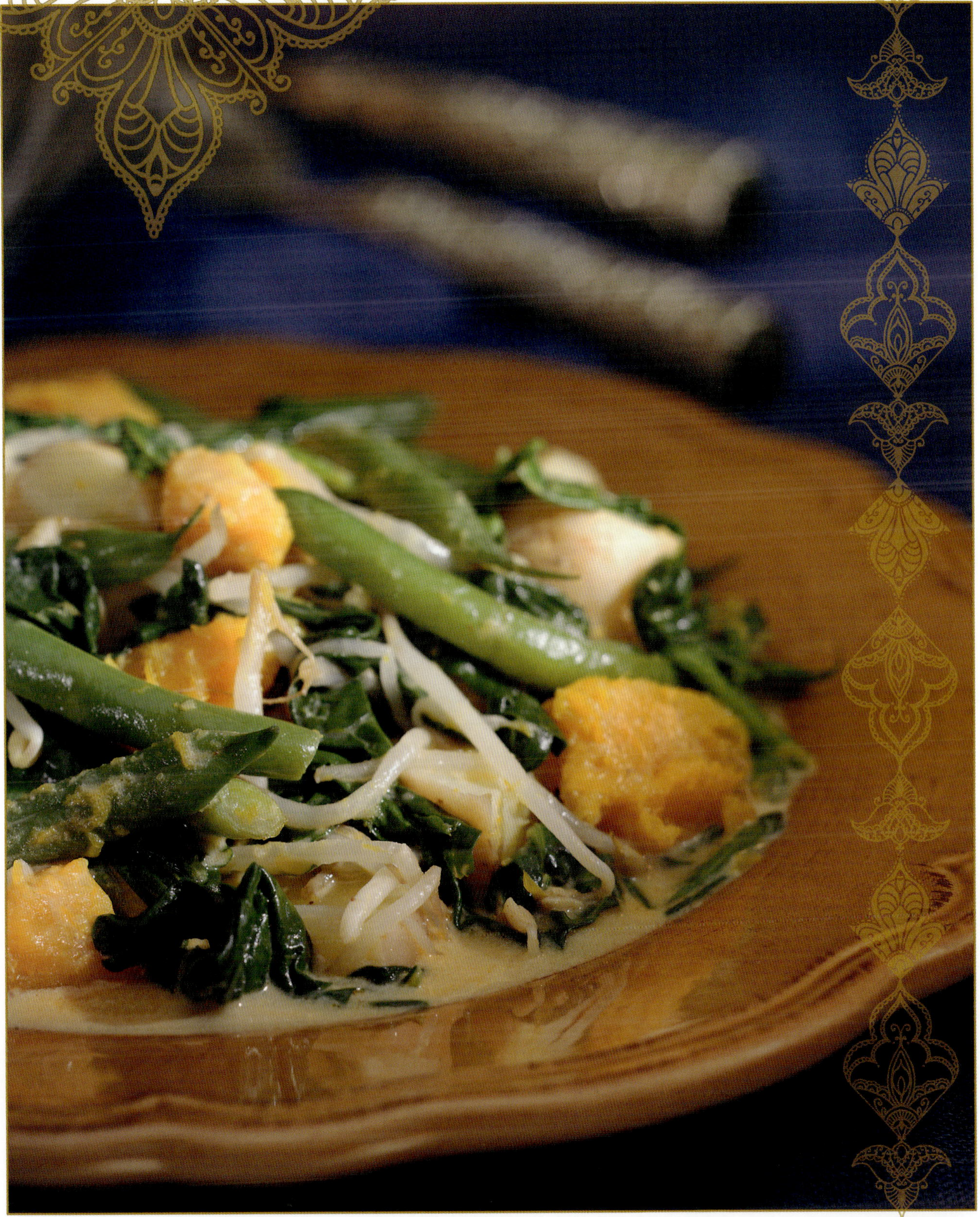

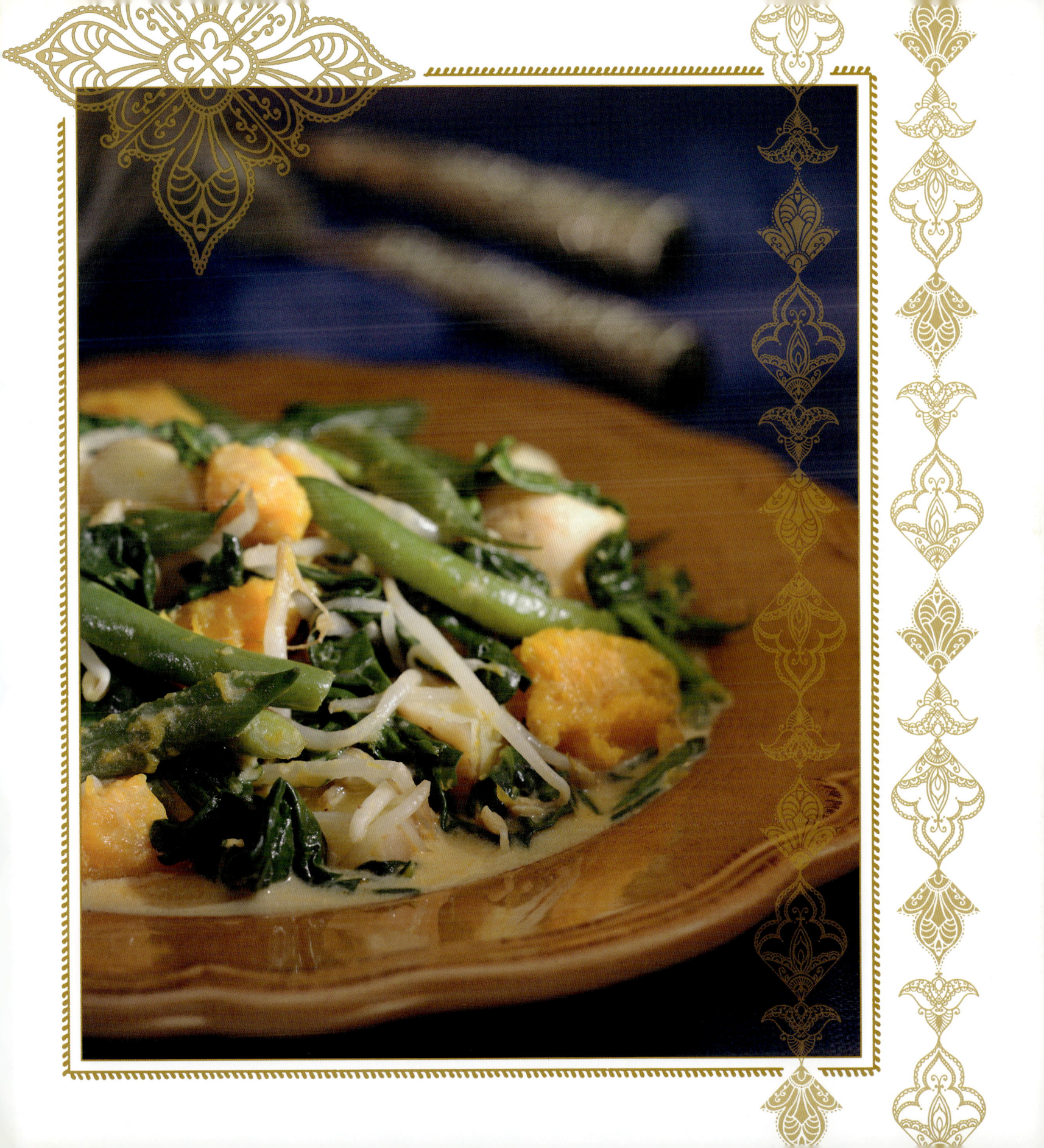

Mussaman potato & peanut curry

3 tablespoons oil
1 large onion, finely chopped
1 clove garlic, crushed
1 tablespoon Thai Mussaman curry paste (page 19)
1 kg potatoes, cut into 3-cm cubes
¾ cup unsalted roasted peanuts, skinned
1 tablespoon ground coriander
2 cloves
½ cinnamon stick
2 bay leaves
½ teaspoon fennel or caraway seeds
1 × 400-ml can coconut milk
1½ tablespoons fish sauce
3–4 teaspoons freshly squeezed lime juice
salt and pepper
chopped fresh coriander, mint or basil

In a heavy saucepan heat the oil over medium–high heat and brown the onion. Stir in garlic and curry paste, and cook for 1 minute, stirring constantly. Add the potatoes, peanuts (save a few for garnish), spices and coconut milk, and ½ cup water. Bring to the boil, reduce heat and simmer for 15–20 minutes, or until the potatoes are tender.

Season with fish sauce and lime juice, and add salt and pepper to taste. Transfer to a serving dish and garnish with reserved peanuts and chopped herbs.

SERVES 4–6

Penang curry of eggplant, cabbage & beans

6 shallots or 1 medium-sized onion, peeled
2 cloves garlic, peeled
a 2-cm piece fresh turmeric, peeled
2–3 fresh red chillies, deseeded (or ¾ teaspoon ground chilli)
½ teaspoon shrimp paste
3 tablespoons oil
1 × 400-ml can coconut cream
¼ cup dried shrimp
2 slender Asian eggplants, cut into 1.5-cm slices
1¼ cups chopped cabbage
4 snake beans (or 12 green beans), cut into 5-cm lengths
salt

In a blender or mortar grind the shallots or onion, garlic, turmeric, chillies and shrimp paste to a reasonably smooth paste. Heat the oil in a heavy-based pan and fry the paste for 1–2 minutes, stirring. Add half the coconut cream with the dried shrimp, and simmer for about 3 minutes.

Add the remaining coconut cream and 1½ cups water, and bring to the boil. Add the eggplant, with salt to taste, and simmer for about 5 minutes. Last, add the cabbage and beans, and cook for 10–15 minutes until vegetables are very tender and the sauce slightly reduced. Check seasoning and serve.

SERVES 4–6

Singapore potato curry

1½ tablespoons coriander seeds
1 teaspoon cumin seeds
½ teaspoon brown mustard seeds
2 dried red chillies, deseeded
3 tablespoons oil
1 medium-sized onion, sliced
4 cloves garlic, finely chopped
2 teaspoons grated fresh ginger
3 large potatoes, cut into 3-cm cubes
2 cardamom pods, cracked
2 whole cloves
1 cinnamon stick (or a piece of cassia bark)
1 sprig curry leaves
salt and black pepper
freshly squeezed juice of ½ lemon
½ cup creamy yoghurt or sour cream
chopped fresh mint or coriander

In a wok or saucepan dry-roast the coriander, cumin and mustard seeds with the chillies, stirring, until fragrant (about 2 minutes). Transfer to a spice grinder and grind to a fine powder. Set aside to cool.

In the same pan heat the oil and then fry the onion for about 2½ minutes, until lightly browned. Add garlic and ginger, fry briefly and then add the potatoes with the ground spices, the cardamom, cloves, cinnamon, curry leaves, 1 teaspoon salt and a few twists of the pepper mill. Stir around until the potatoes are coated, then add water to not quite cover them. Bring to the boil, reduce heat and simmer until potatoes are tender (about 18 minutes).

Check seasonings, adding additional salt and pepper if needed, and stir in the lemon juice and yoghurt or sour cream. Serve in a bowl, garnished with chopped herbs.

SERVES 4–5

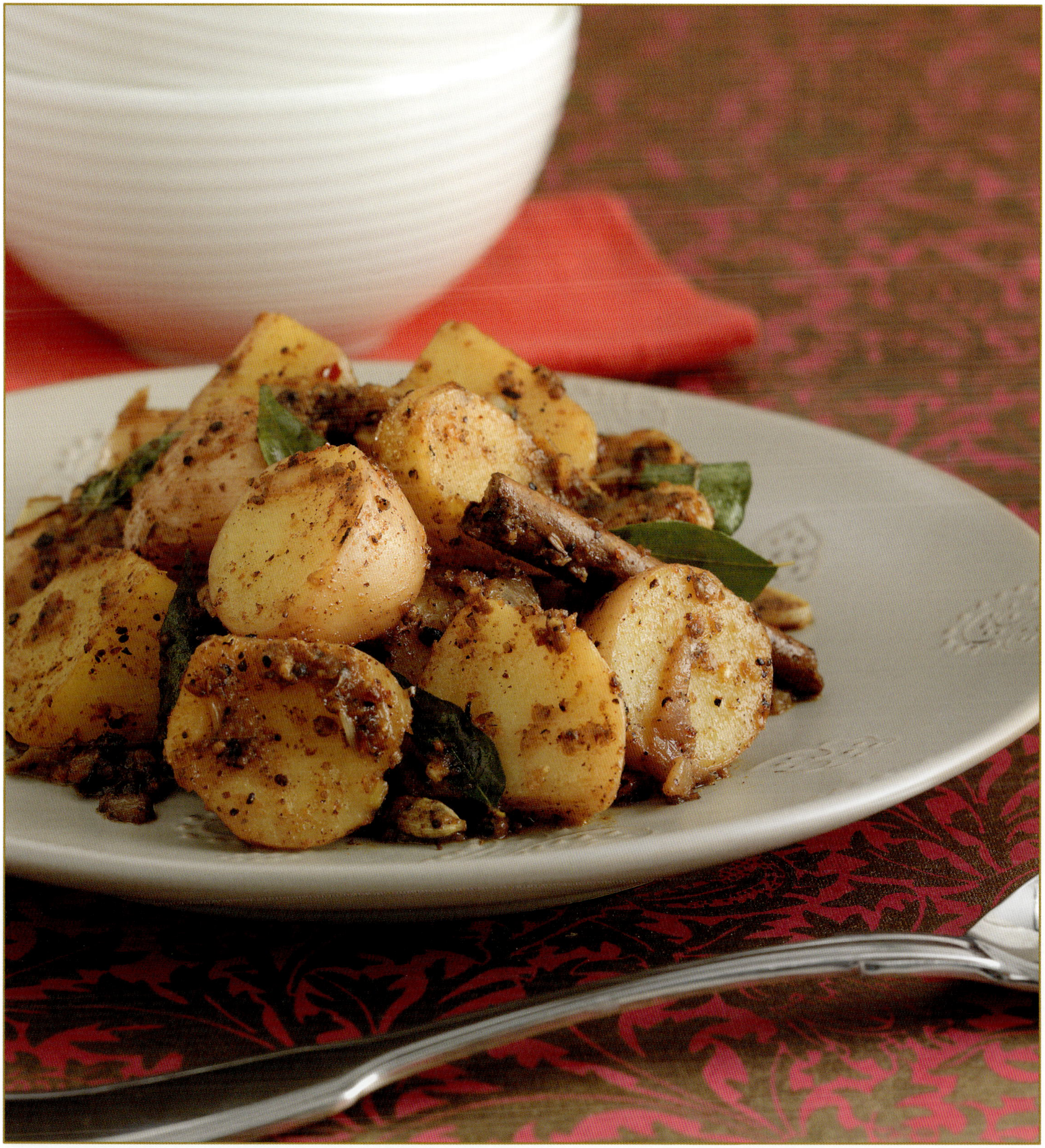

Vegetables in mildly spiced coconut sauce

1 large potato, peeled and sliced
5 cups shredded cabbage
250 g broccoli, cut into florets
200 g pumpkin, peeled and sliced
1 medium-sized carrot, thinly sliced
1½ cups sliced green or snake beans
1 × 400-ml can coconut milk
¾ teaspoon ground turmeric
2 teaspoons ground coriander
½ teaspoon cumin seeds
1 teaspoon grated fresh ginger
1 fresh hot green chilli, slit and deseeded
salt and pepper
freshly squeezed lemon juice

Combine all the ingredients, except the lemon juice, in a saucepan. Add ¾ cup water, cover tightly, then bring to the boil, reduce heat and simmer-steam until the vegetables are tender.

Before serving, check seasonings, adding extra salt, pepper and lemon juice to taste.

SERVES 4–5

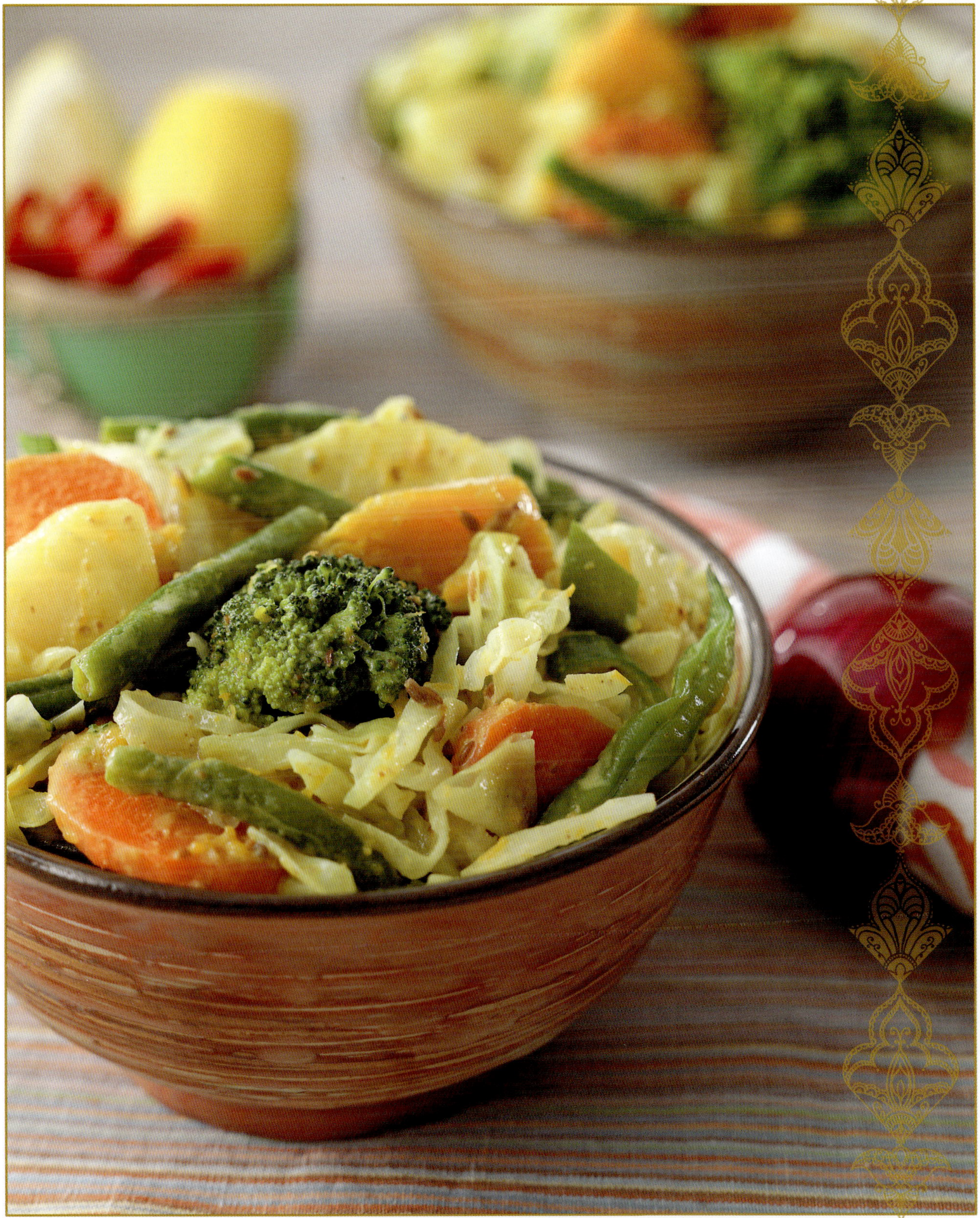

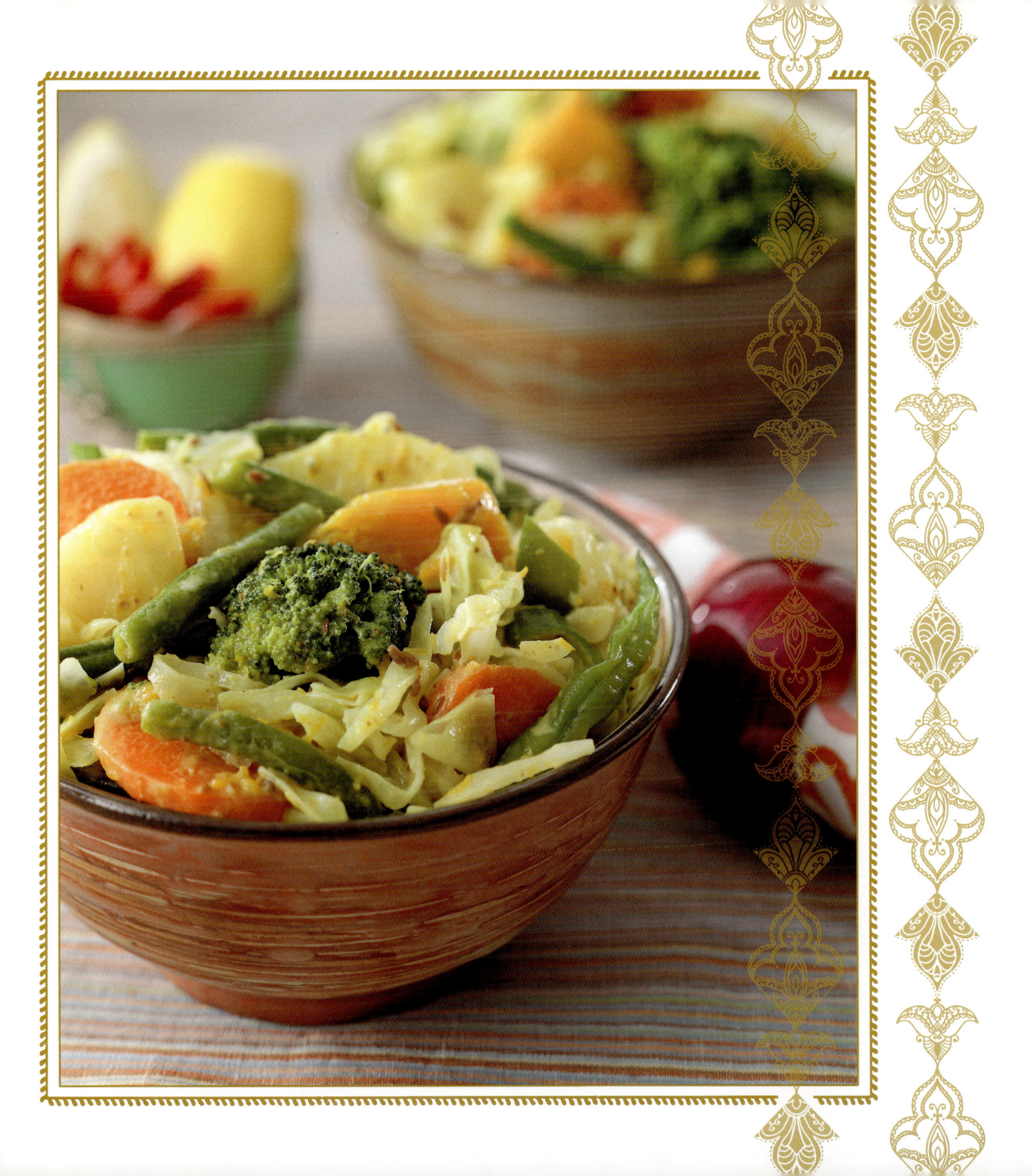

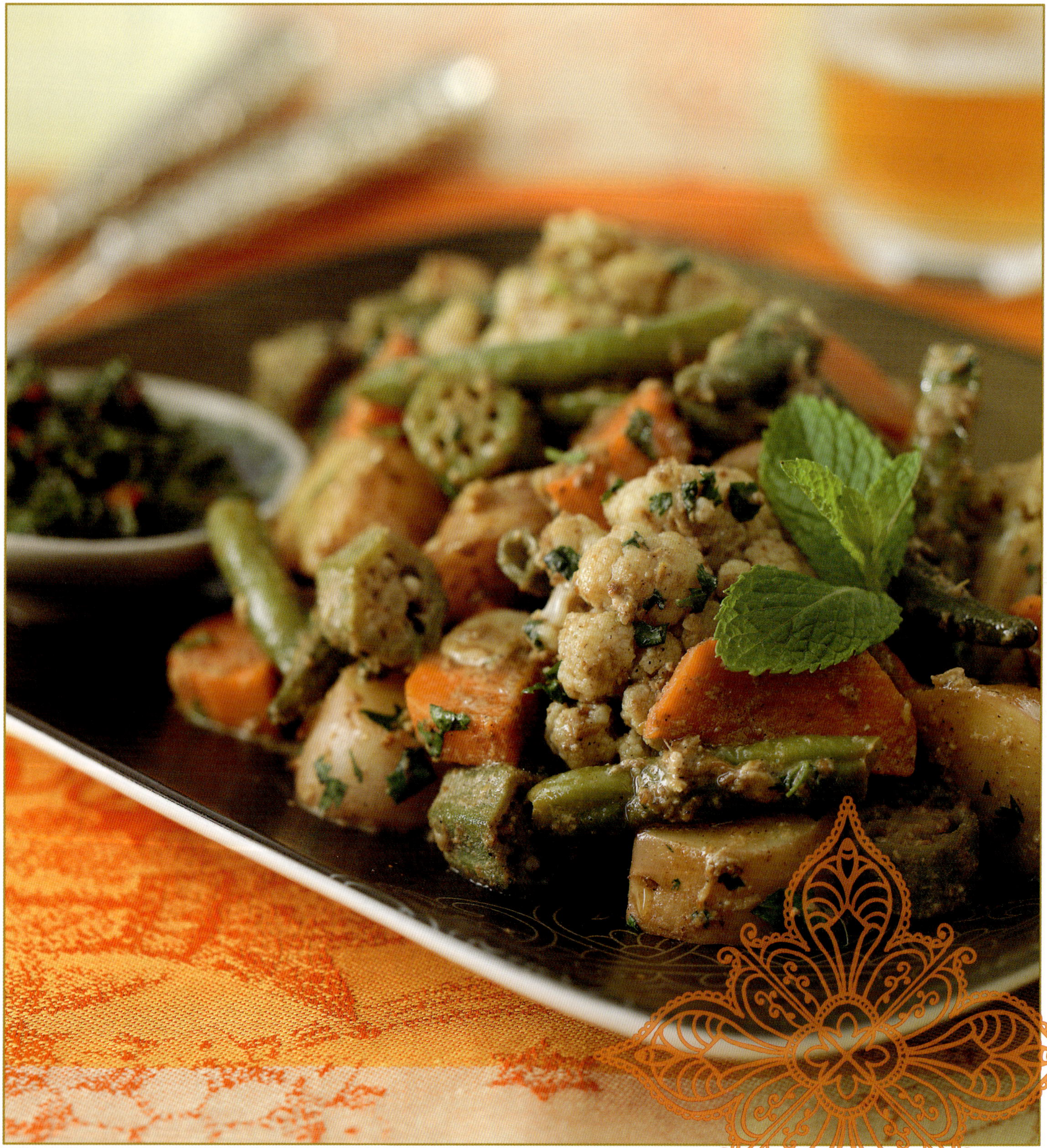

Mixed vegetable curry

2½ tablespoons ghee or oil
1 large potato, cut into 2-cm cubes
1 medium-sized carrot, peeled and sliced
1 medium-sized onion, cut into slim wedges
250 g cauliflower, divided into florets
2 teaspoons garam masala (page 16)
1 tablespoon ground coriander
1 teaspoon ground cumin
150 g fresh or frozen baby okra
8 green beans, cut in half
2 teaspoons grated fresh ginger
1–2 cloves garlic, crushed
½ cup creamy yoghurt
1½ teaspoons salt
chopped fresh coriander or mint

Heat the ghee or oil in a saucepan and brown the potato, carrot and onion for about 3 minutes. Add the cauliflower and cook for a further 2 minutes.

Sprinkle the spices over the vegetables, add the okra and beans, ginger and garlic, and mix well. Add the yoghurt, 1 cup water and the salt. Cover and cook for 10–15 minutes, stirring occasionally.

Add the chopped herbs, taste and add more salt if needed, then transfer to a serving bowl.

SERVES 4–6

VEGETABLE & EGG CURRIES

Thai vegetable yellow curry

This refreshingly tart curry goes well with plain rice for a light and healthy meal. Or you can serve it as a side dish with grilled meat or other curries.

- 1½ cups vegetable stock
- 1 tablespoon Thai yellow curry paste (page 20)
- 3 teaspoons tamarind concentrate
- 1½ teaspoons sugar
- 1 tablespoon fish sauce
- 3–4 snake beans, cut into 5-cm pieces
- 250 g cauliflower, cut into florets
- 1 young choko (weighing about 200 g) cut into 2-cm cubes
- 2 tomatoes, quartered
- 2 large cabbage leaves, shredded

Bring stock to the boil in a large saucepan and stir in the curry paste, tamarind, sugar and fish sauce. Add the vegetables and simmer gently until tender (8–10 minutes). Check seasonings and adjust to taste, then serve.

SERVES 4

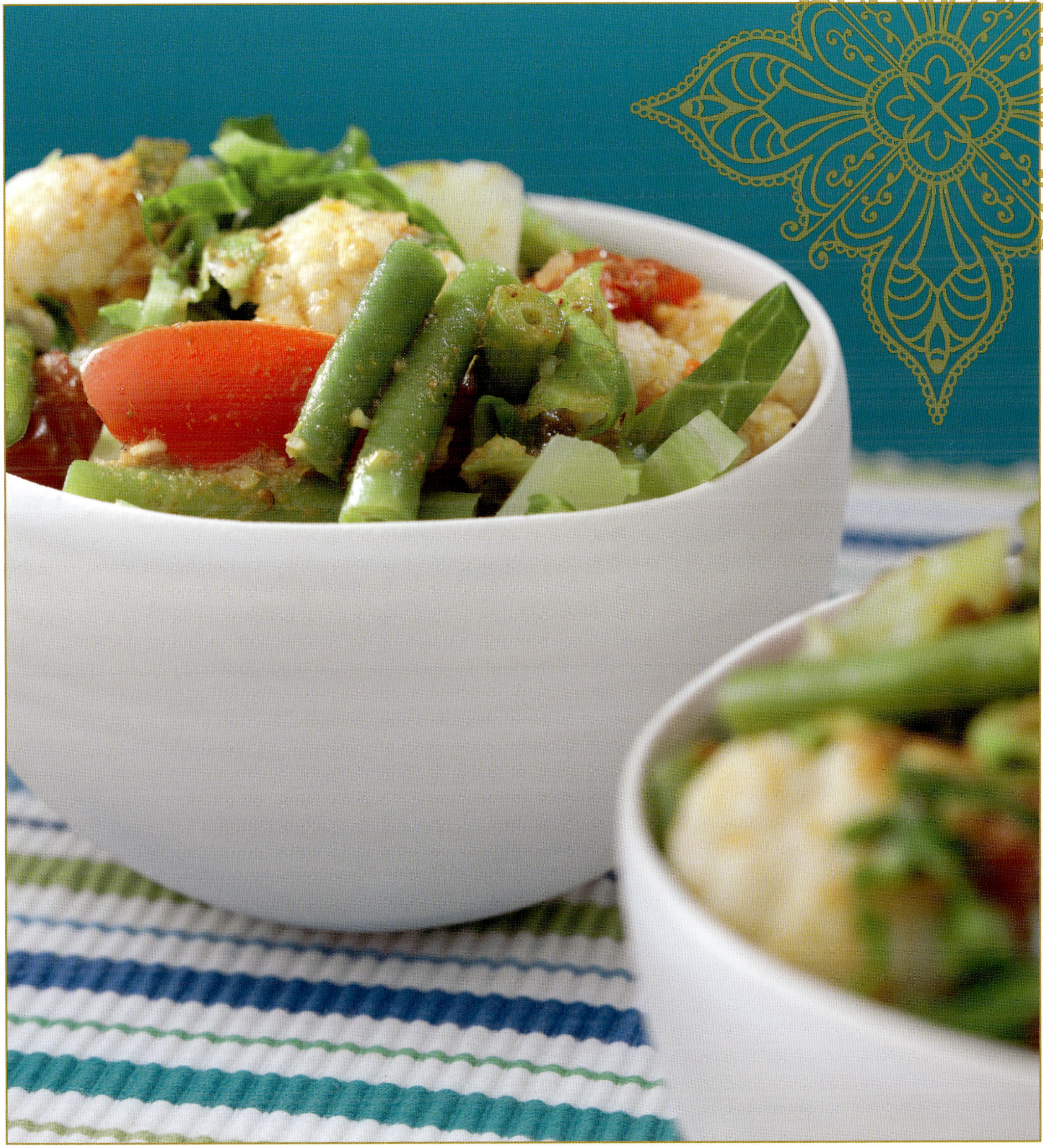

Tomato curry

2 large onions
3 cloves garlic, peeled
a 2-cm piece fresh ginger, peeled
1 fresh hot red chilli, deseeded and chopped
2 tablespoons ghee or oil
2 whole cloves
2 cardamom pods, cracked
2 bay leaves, crumbled
1½ teaspoons ground coriander
⅓ teaspoon ground turmeric
½–1 teaspoon ground hot chilli
1 teaspoon ground sweet paprika
1 cup creamy yoghurt
500 g tomatoes, halved, deseeded and roughly chopped
1½ teaspoons salt
1 teaspoon sugar
2–3 tablespoons chopped fresh mint, basil or coriander

Finely slice one of the onions and set aside. Roughly chop the other onion, place in a food processor or blender with the garlic, ginger and chilli, and grind to a paste.

In a heavy saucepan heat the ghee or oil and fry the cloves, cardamom and bay leaves for 30 seconds over medium heat. Add the sliced onion and fry for about 3 minutes, until golden-brown. Stir in the prepared onion paste and fry, stirring constantly, for about 2½ minutes. Add the ground spices and cook briefly, stirring, then mix in the yoghurt.

Rinse out the food processor or blender with ⅓ cup water and pour into the pan.

Simmer over medium heat until the mixture is thick and oily (about 5 minutes), add the tomatoes, salt and sugar, and cook for 4–5 minutes until the tomatoes are soft but not collapsing. Stir in chopped herbs just before serving.

SERVES 3–4

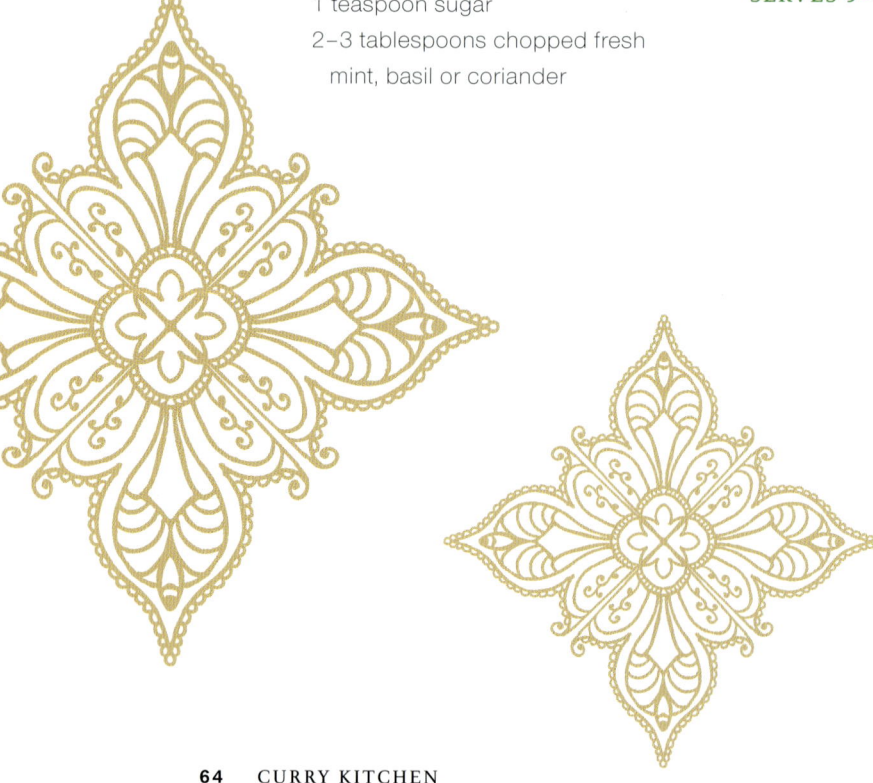

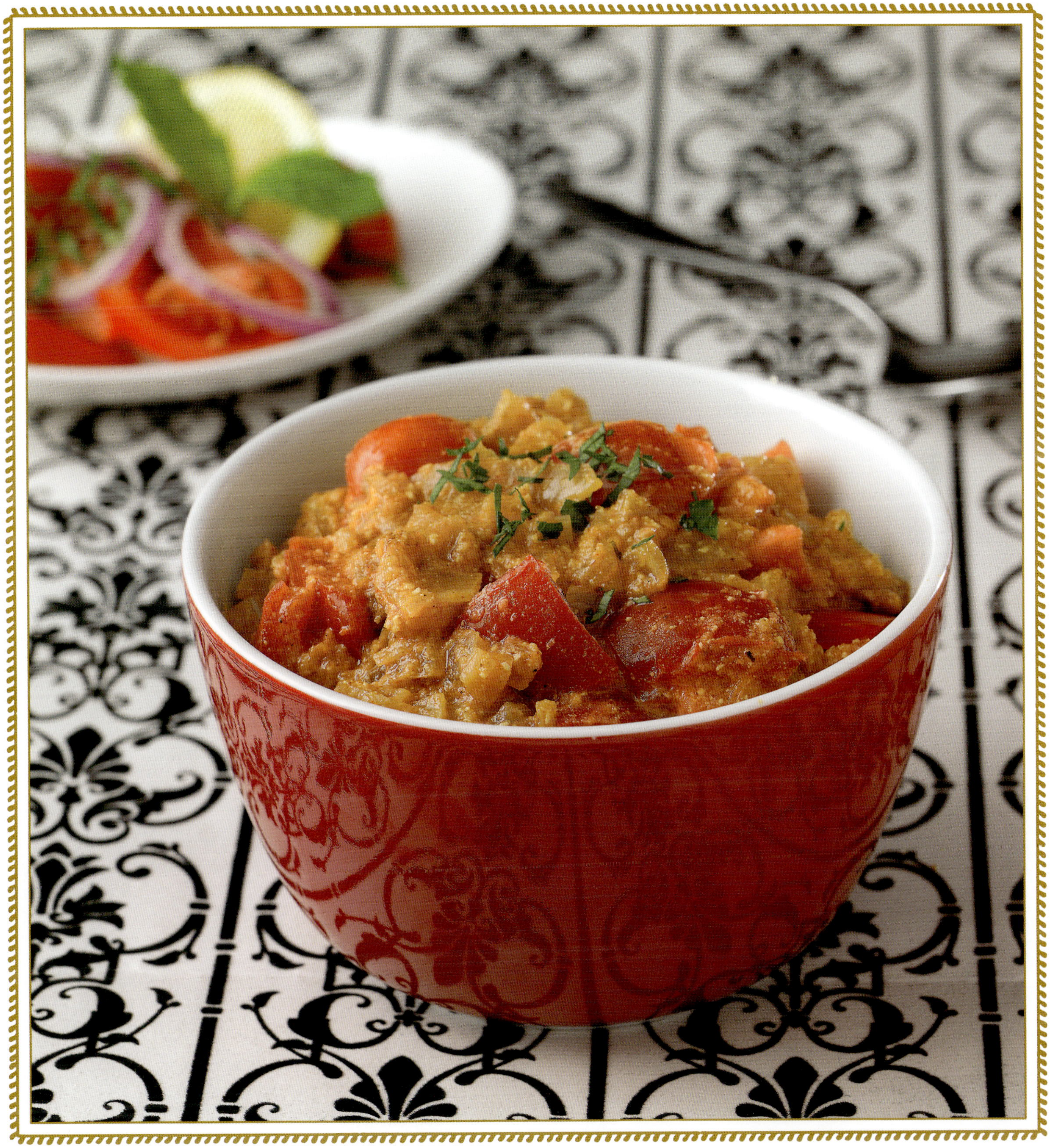

Mushrooms & peas in mild curry

You can make this into a tasty super-fast meal by serving it with microwaved rice and bought chapatis or rotis.

1 cup frozen peas
100 g button or oyster mushrooms, sliced
2 firm tomatoes, cut into wedges
3 spring onions, chopped
1½ tablespoons ghee or oil
2 teaspoons ground coriander
¾ teaspoon garam masala (page 16)
salt and pepper
2 tablespoons cream (optional)
1 tablespoon chopped fresh coriander or mint (optional)

Mix the vegetables, spring onions and ghee or oil in a small saucepan, cover tightly and cook over low heat for about 4 minutes, shaking the pan occasionally to turn the contents and prevent sticking.

Stir in the spices, salt and pepper, and ¼ cup water, and simmer, stirring occasionally, for 2–3 minutes. Add the cream and chopped herbs (if using), before serving.

SERVES 2–3

Eggplant, onion & pea curry

3 tablespoons oil or ghee
½ large eggplant (300–350 g), cut into 2-cm cubes
2 medium-sized onions, sliced
3 cloves garlic, chopped
1 teaspoon brown mustard seeds
1 teaspoon cumin seeds
½ teaspoon ground turmeric
1½ teaspoons salt
1½ cups crushed tomatoes
¾–1 cup water
½ teaspoon sugar
1 teaspoon tamarind concentrate or lemon juice
1 cup peas
2 tablespoons chopped fresh mint (optional)

Heat oil or ghee in a non-stick pan and fry eggplant and onions over high heat for about 4 minutes, until lightly browned. Add garlic, mustard, cumin and turmeric, and stir to coat the vegetables.

Stir salt, tomatoes and water into the pan and bring to the boil. Reduce to a simmer and cook for 6–7 minutes. Add sugar, tamarind and peas and simmer for a further 4–5 minutes, adding extra water if needed (though the curry should be quite thick).

Stir in chopped mint, and serve.

SERVES 3–4

Green Thai curry of mushrooms, peppers & zucchini

1 red capsicum, cut into 2-cm squares
1 fresh hot green chilli, slit and deseeded
1 stem lemongrass, cut into 3-cm lengths
2 tablespoons oil
1 large zucchini, sliced
8 button mushrooms (or half a 425-g can straw mushrooms), sliced
4 spring onions, chopped
2 cloves garlic, crushed
2–3 teaspoons Thai green curry paste (page 18)
1 × 400-ml can coconut milk
fish sauce and sugar to taste
salt and pepper
freshly squeezed lime juice
chopped fresh coriander (optional)

In a wok or frying pan sauté the capsicum, chilli and lemongrass in the oil until capsicum softens slightly (about 1½ minutes). Add zucchini, mushrooms, spring onions and garlic, and stir-fry for 1 minute.

Stir in the curry paste, fry briefly and then add the coconut milk. Bring to the boil, reduce heat and simmer for about 6 minutes, until the vegetables are tender. Season to taste with fish sauce, sugar, salt and pepper, and 2–3 teaspoons of lime juice – the flavours should be fresh and very slightly tart. Stir in the coriander (if using) and serve.

SERVES 4

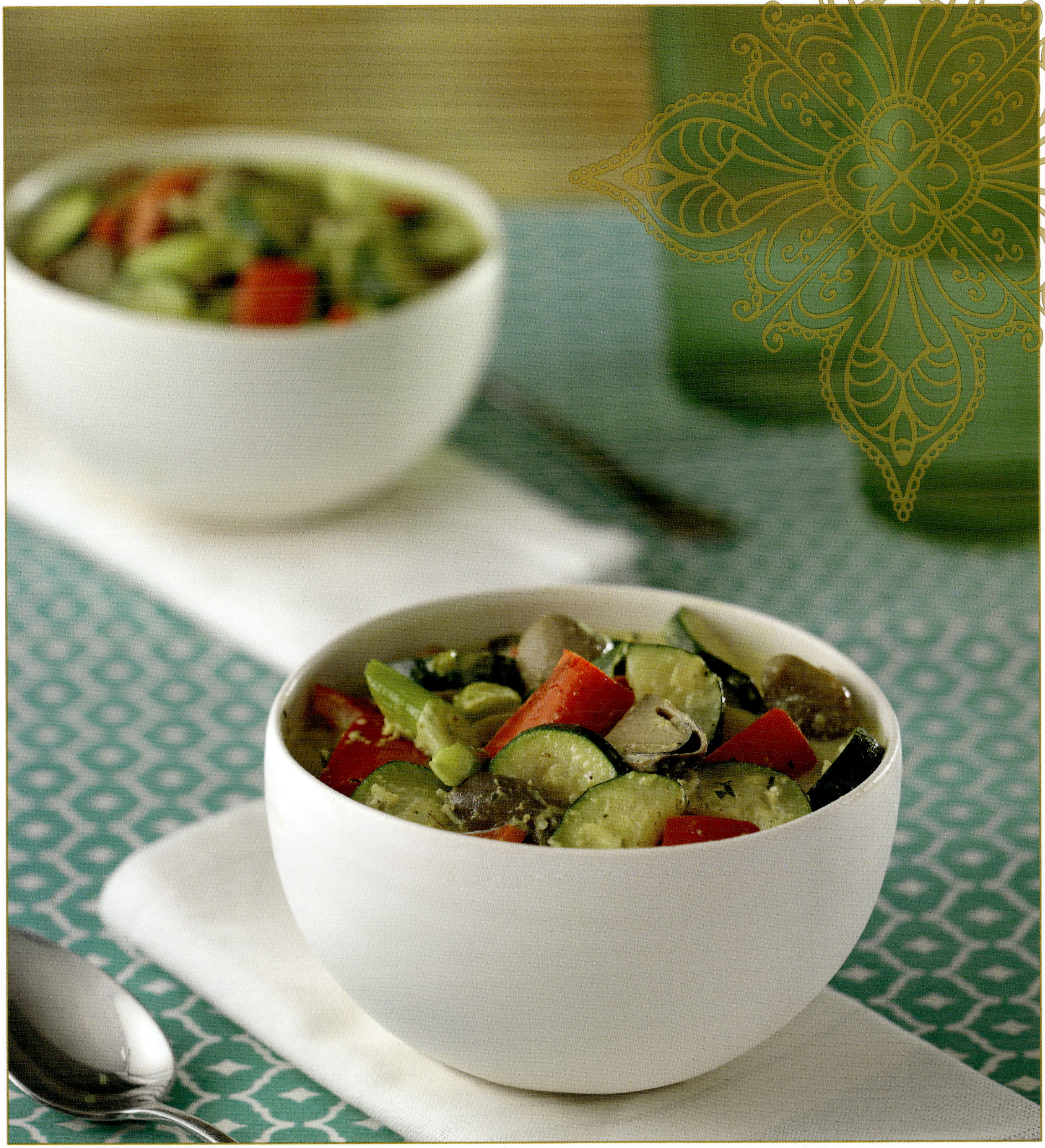

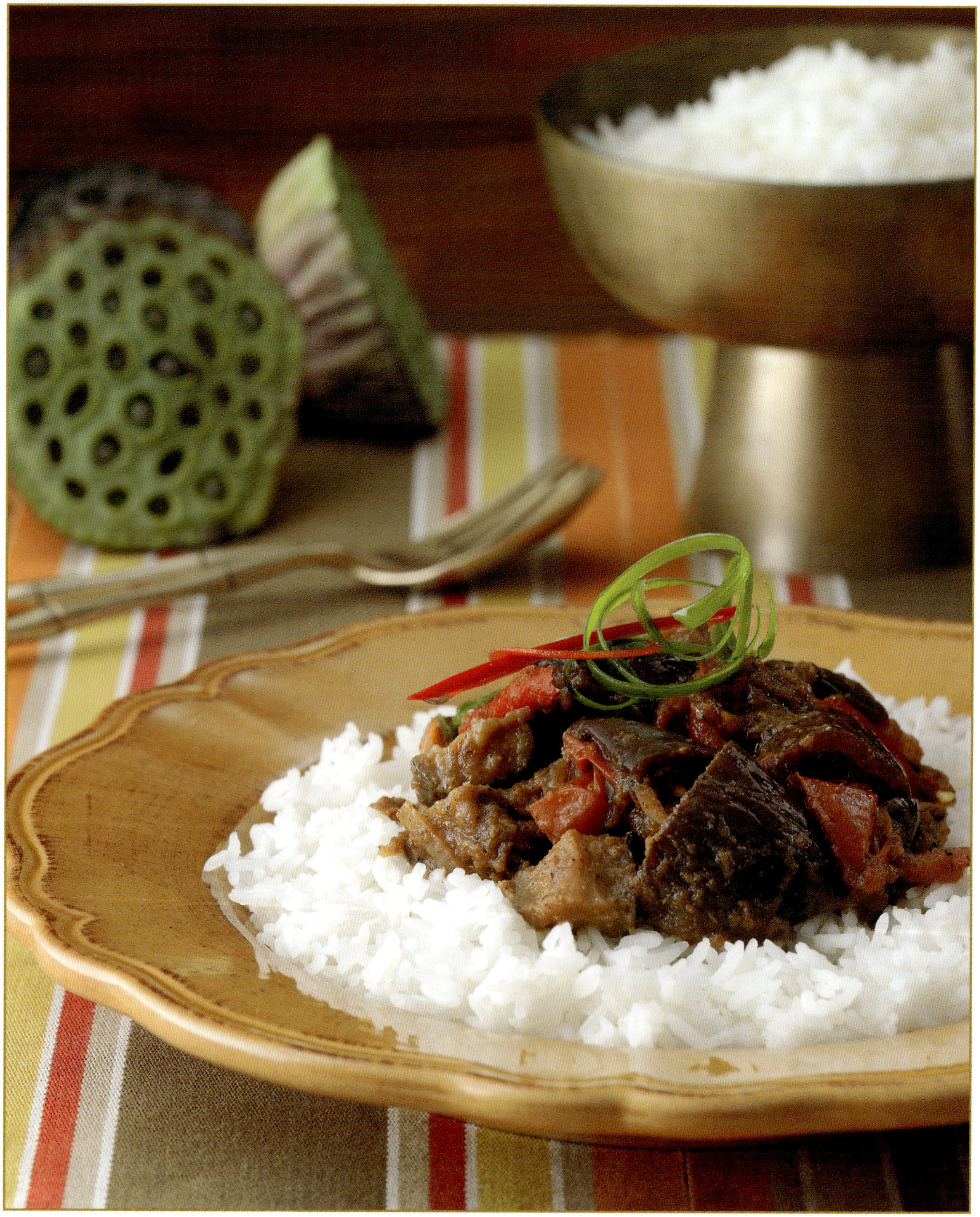

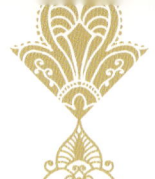

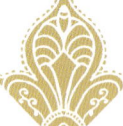

Spicy Sri Lankan eggplant

Lashings of rice will balance the intense richness of this curry if you are serving it as a main course. You can also offer it as a side dish with grilled or roasted meat. Sri Lankan curries are invariably hot, but you can vary the number of chillies according to your preference.

1 tablespoon coriander seeds
1 teaspoon cumin seeds
½ teaspoon black peppercorns
1 whole clove
2 cardamom pods, cracked
2 large onions
2–4 fresh hot red chillies, deseeded
4 cloves garlic, peeled
a 2-cm piece fresh ginger, peeled
5 tablespoons ghee or oil
800 g eggplant, cut into 3-cm cubes
1–2 cinnamon sticks
2 large red tomatoes, deseeded and diced
2 teaspoons palm sugar or soft brown sugar
2 teaspoons tamarind concentrate
salt

In a small pan dry-roast the coriander and cumin seeds, peppercorns, clove and cardamom until the spices are reasonably dark and giving off a roasted aroma. Pick out and discard cardamom pods and transfer the other spices to a spice grinder. Grind to a fine powder and set aside.

Roughly chop one onion, place in a food processor with the chillies, garlic and ginger, and grind to a paste.

Slice the remaining onion. Heat half the ghee or oil in a heavy pan and fry the sliced onion until well browned. Add the eggplant and cinnamon, and stir over medium–high heat until well browned (about 4 minutes), adding extra ghee or oil if needed.

Sprinkle in the ground spices, stir, then add the onion–garlic paste and the tomatoes. Cook over medium–high heat for about 5 minutes, until the tomatoes are soft and pulpy.

Mix the sugar and tamarind with ½ cup water and pour into the pan. Cover, and simmer gently for 10–15 minutes until eggplant is tender. Season to taste before serving.

SERVES 5–6

Eggplant in hot curry sauce

A sublimely fragrant last-minute addition of aromatics fried in ghee or oil makes this dish a sensation.

3 tablespoons ghee or oil
400 g slender Asian eggplants, thickly sliced
1 large onion, finely chopped
2 cloves garlic, crushed
2 teaspoons grated fresh ginger
1–2 tablespoons hot Indian curry paste (page 13)
3 tablespoons chopped fresh coriander
salt
extra 2 tablespoons oil
½ teaspoon each of brown mustard, fennel and fenugreek seeds
6–8 curry leaves

Heat the ghee or oil and fry eggplants and onion together for about 5 minutes, stirring frequently. Add garlic, ginger and curry paste, and stir over high heat for about 40 seconds.

Add 1 cup water to the pan and bring to the boil. Reduce heat and simmer for about 12 minutes or until the eggplant is tender and has absorbed most of the liquid. Season to taste with salt, and stir in the coriander.

Heat the extra oil in a small pan and fry the spice seeds and curry leaves for 1–2 minutes, until they pop and sputter. Transfer eggplant to a bowl and pour spicy oil over before serving.

SERVES 4

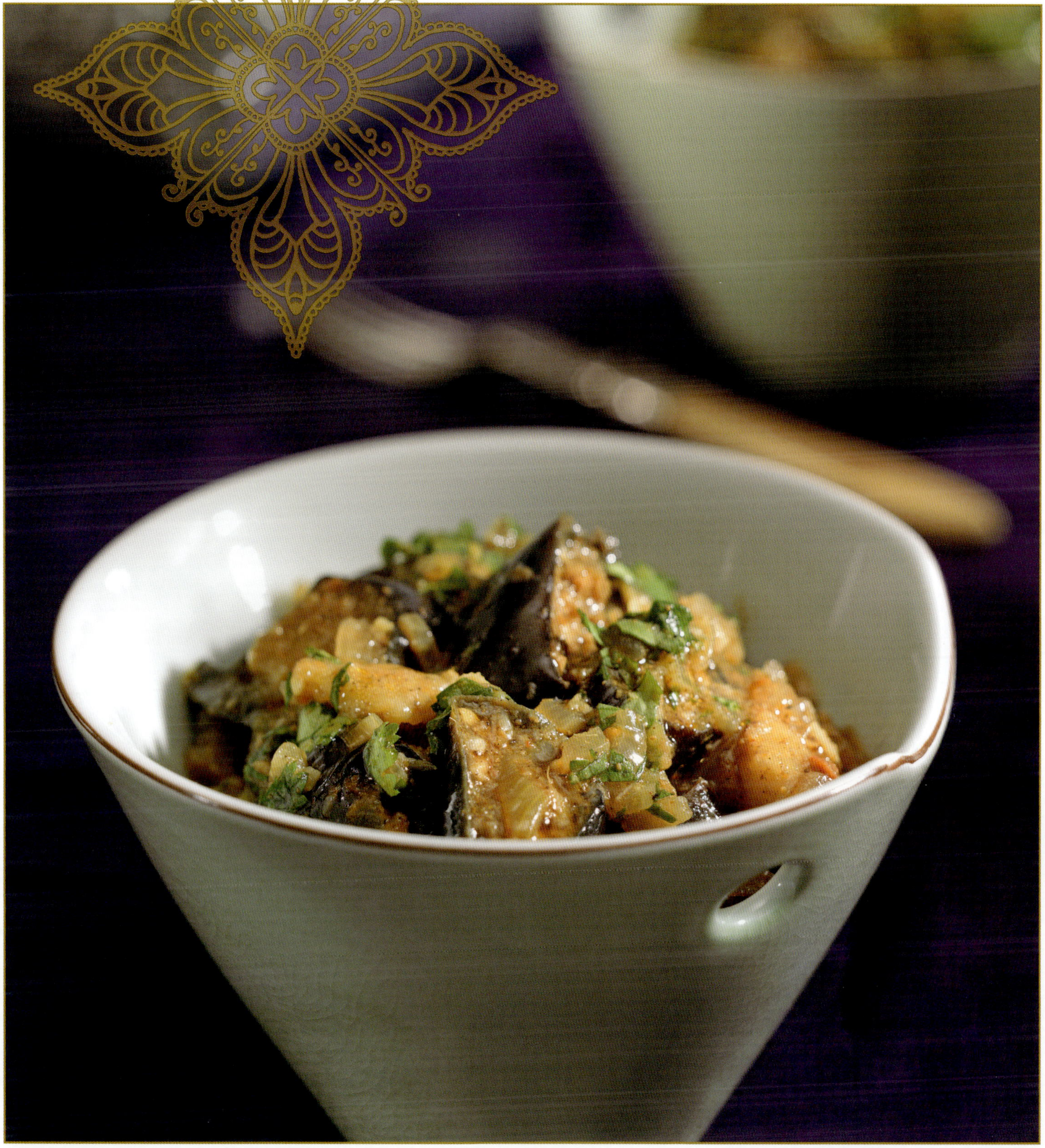

Smoky eggplant yellow curry

1 large eggplant (about 650 g), cut into 3-cm cubes
salt
2–3 tablespoons oil
1 large onion, roughly chopped
5 shallots
4 cloves garlic, peeled
a 2-cm piece fresh ginger, peeled
2 large hot red chillies, deseeded
1 tablespoon Thai yellow curry paste (page 20)
½ teaspoon ground turmeric
2–3 kaffir lime leaves
1 × 400-ml can coconut milk
Vietnamese mint or coriander leaves, for garnish

Place eggplant cubes in a colander, sprinkle generously with salt and leave for 10 minutes. Rinse, drain and dry.

Heat a wok or iron grill plate over high heat and moisten with some of the oil. Sprinkle eggplant with a little more of the oil and cook, stirring and turning frequently, until well browned. Remove and set aside.

In a food processor or blender grind the onion, shallots, garlic, ginger and chillies to a reasonably smooth purée. Heat the wok or a heavy saucepan and add remaining oil. Stir-fry the onion purée for about 4 minutes, stirring fairly constantly, until fragrant and almost dry. Add curry paste and turmeric, and fry briefly.

Stir grilled eggplant through the curry mixture and add lime leaves, coconut milk and about ¾ cup water. Bring to the boil, reduce heat and simmer for 12–15 minutes until the sauce is thick and the eggplant soft. Season with salt to taste. Serve garnished with mint or coriander leaves.

SERVES 3–4

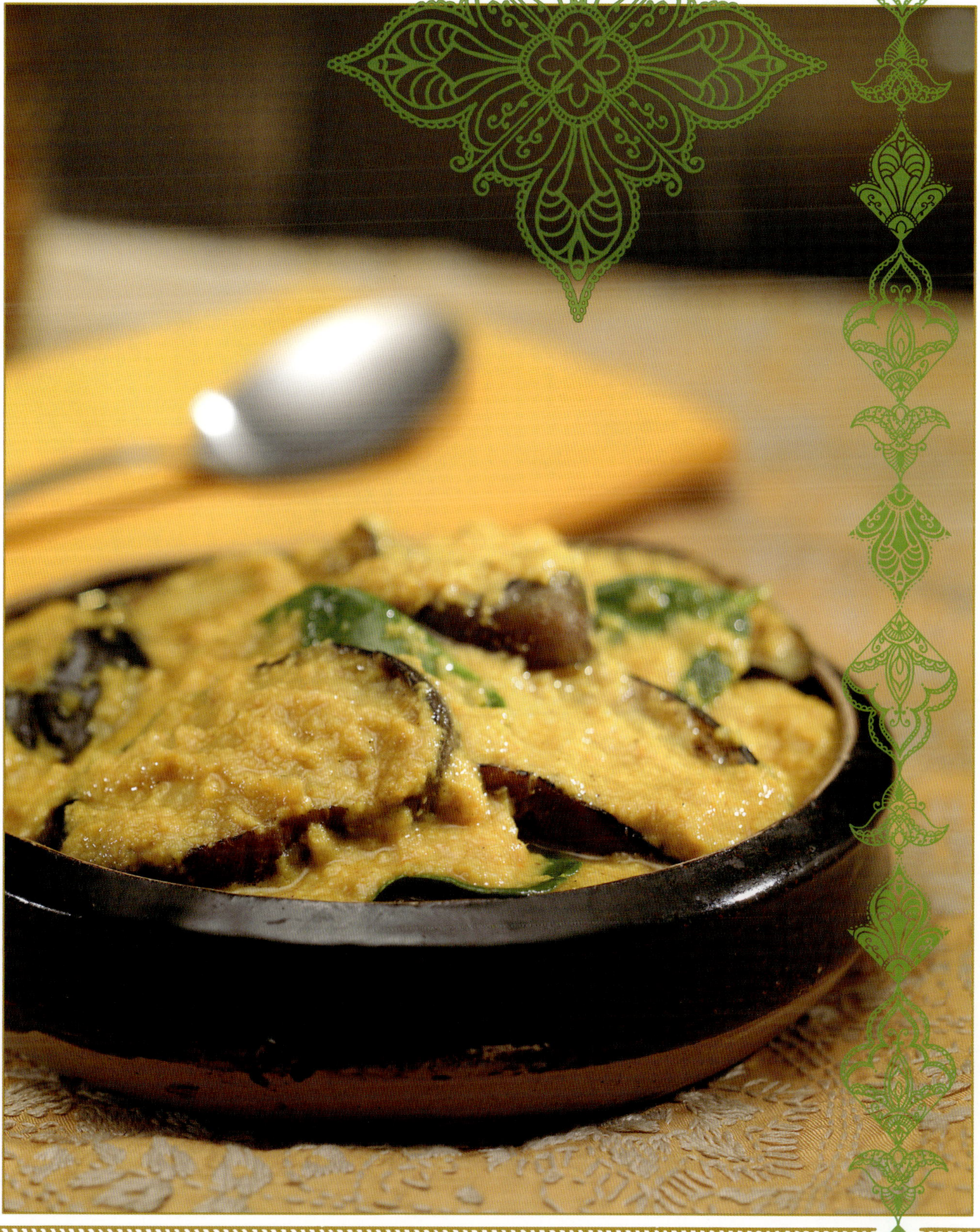

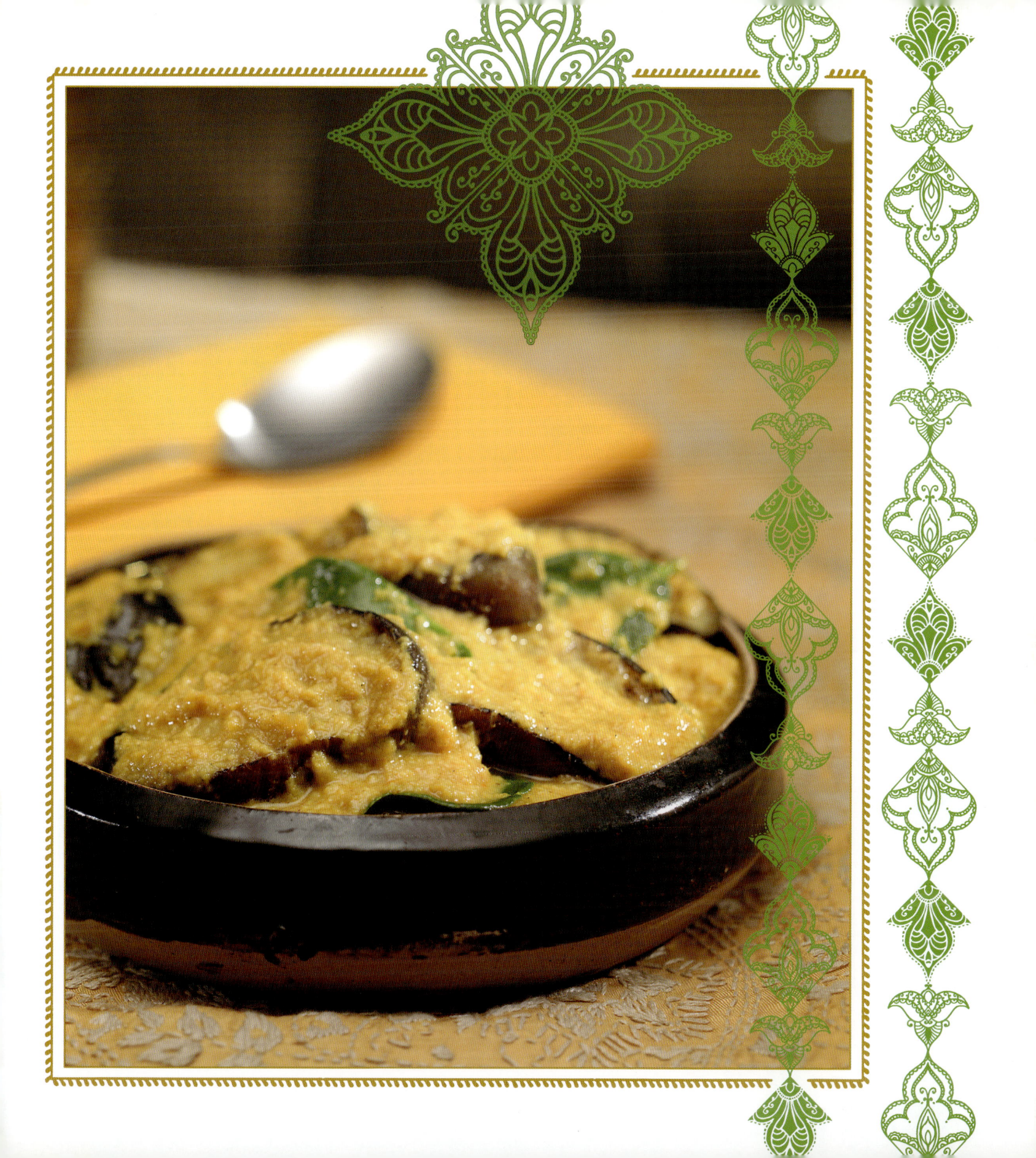

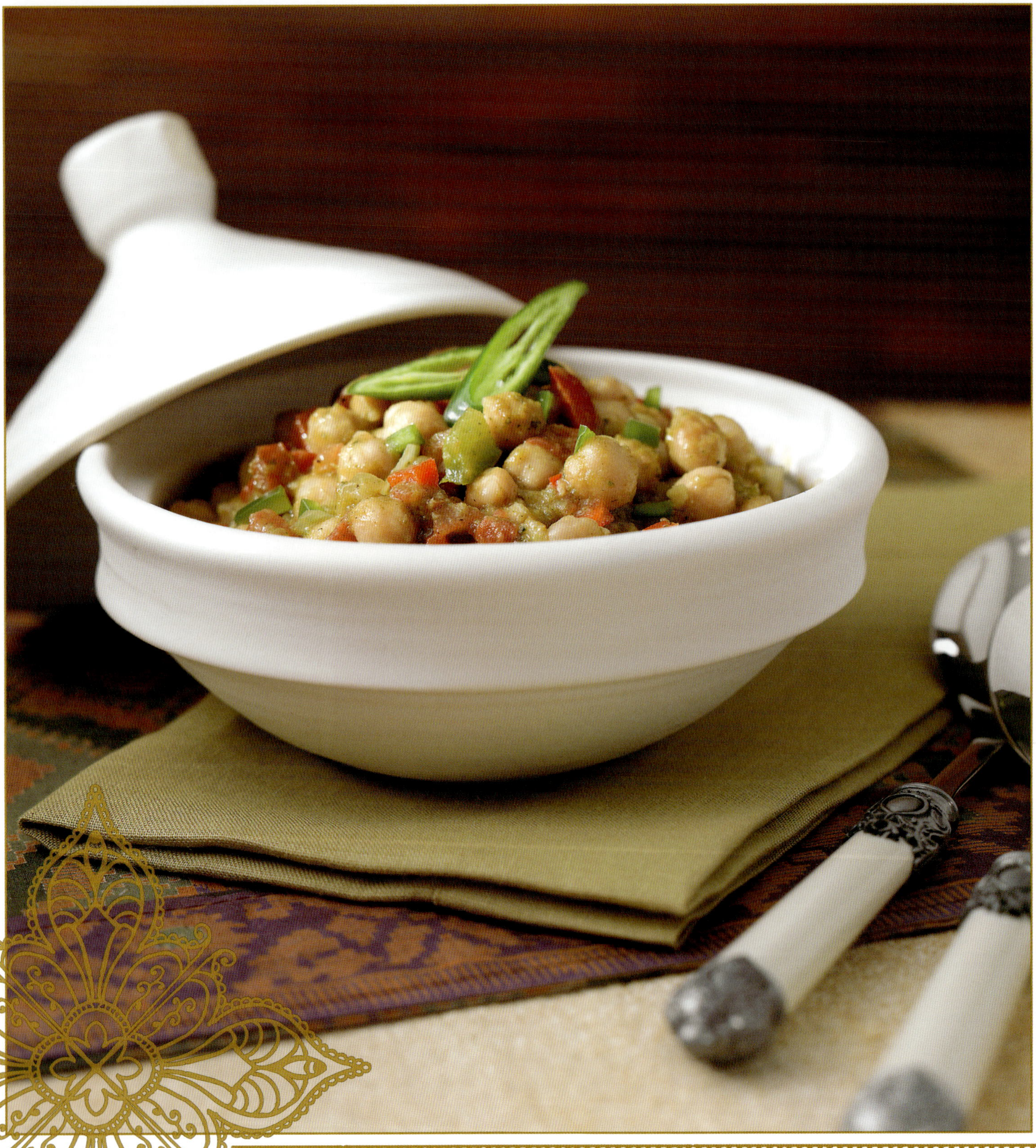

Chickpeas with green chillies & tomatoes

2 fresh hot green chillies, deseeded and chopped
a 2-cm piece fresh ginger, peeled
1 clove garlic, peeled
4 sprigs fresh coriander
2 tablespoons ghee or oil
1 small onion, diced
¼ green capsicum, diced
¼ red capsicum, diced
2 tomatoes, deseeded and chopped
salt and pepper
3½ cups canned or cooked chickpeas, drained
sugar and freshly squeezed lemon juice, to taste

In a food processor or blender grind the chillies, ginger, garlic and coriander to a paste.

Heat the ghee or oil in a saucepan and fry the onion and the prepared chilli paste over medium heat for 2 minutes. Add the capsicums and cook, stirring, for another 2 minutes. Add tomatoes, salt, pepper and ½ cup water, and bring to the boil. Pour in the chickpeas and cook, uncovered, until most of the liquid has evaporated.

Check seasonings, adding salt and pepper, sugar and a squeeze of lemon juice to taste.

SERVES 4

VEGETABLE & EGG CURRIES

Curried chickpeas with tomatoes & coriander

1 small onion, finely chopped
2 tablespoons ghee or oil
2 tomatoes, chopped (or ¾ cup canned crushed tomatoes)
1 teaspoon grated fresh ginger
1 clove garlic, crushed
1 tablespoon ground coriander
½ teaspoon ground black pepper
¾ teaspoon salt
1¾ cups canned or cooked chickpeas, drained
1½ teaspoons garam masala (page 16)
2 tablespoons chopped fresh coriander
grated zest and juice of ½ lemon

In a medium-sized saucepan sauté the onion in ghee or oil until translucent. Add tomatoes, ginger and garlic, and sauté for 2 minutes, stirring.

Add coriander, pepper, salt, chickpeas and 1 teaspoon of the garam masala, pour in ½ cup water, cover, and simmer for 5 minutes.

Remove the lid and simmer for a further 5 minutes. Stir in remaining garam masala, the coriander, lemon zest and juice, and heat briefly.

SERVES 2–3

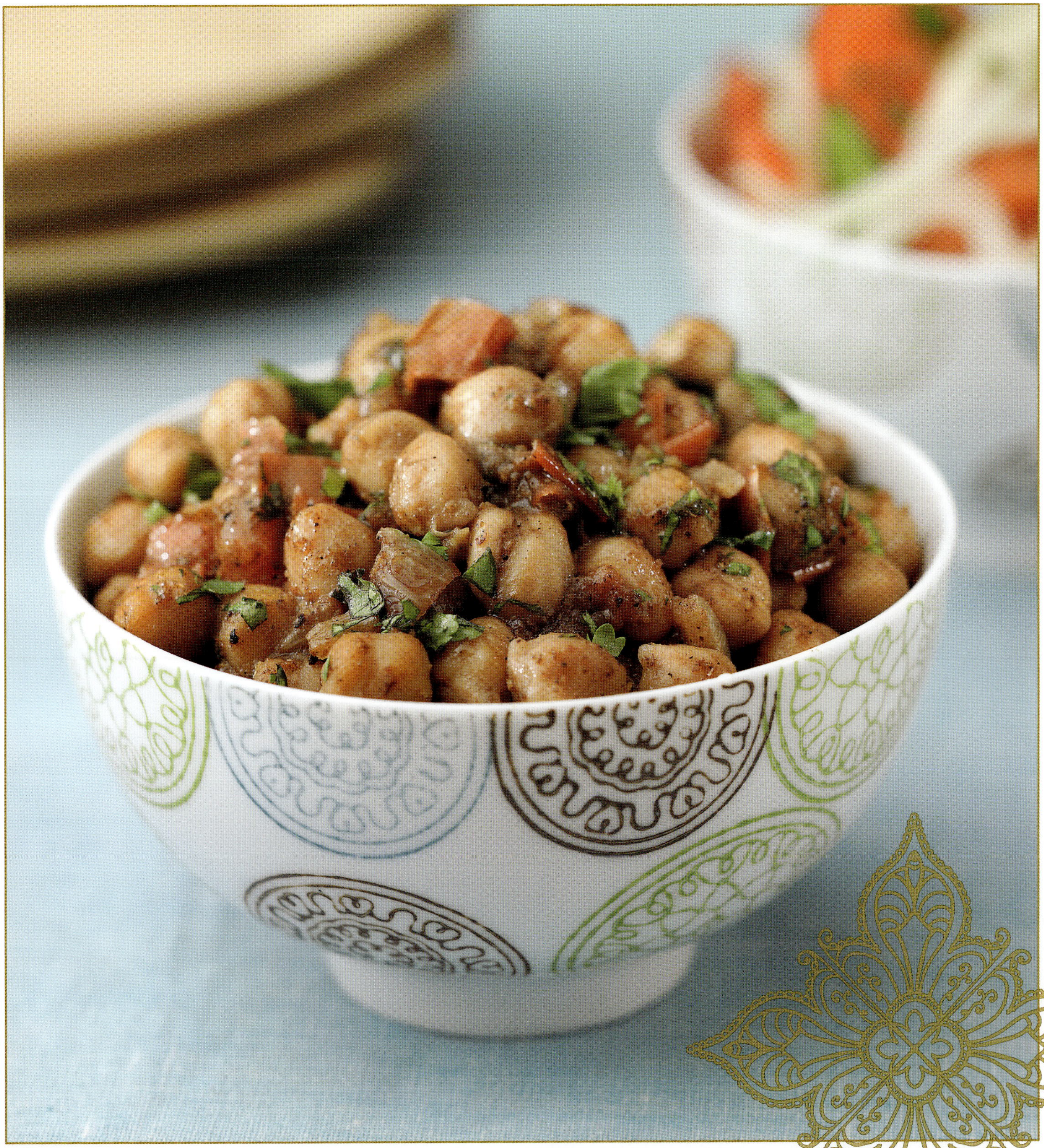

Red curry of tofu & water spinach

The crunchy hollow stems of water spinach are usually eaten as well as the leaves. You can substitute English spinach for water spinach in most recipes.

2–3 tablespoons oil
1 medium-sized onion, cut into narrow wedges and layers separated
4 cloves garlic, chopped
2 teaspoons grated fresh ginger
1 tablespoon Thai red curry paste (page 17)
1 × 400-ml can coconut milk
650 g firm tofu, cut into 2.5-cm cubes
8 small button mushrooms, halved
½ cup sliced bamboo shoots
1 bunch fresh water spinach (or English spinach)
3–5 teaspoons fish sauce
1 teaspoon grated palm sugar or soft brown sugar

Heat oil in a wok or medium-sized saucepan and sauté the onion until lightly browned (about 2½ minutes). Add garlic, ginger and curry paste, and stir over medium–high heat for 1 minute. Pour in half the coconut milk and simmer for 2–3 minutes, stirring often.

Add tofu and mushrooms to the pan and simmer for 1 minute. Pour in the remaining coconut milk, ½ cup water, and add the bamboo shoots and spinach. Simmer just long enough for the spinach leaves to wilt.

Season with fish sauce and sugar, and serve.

SERVES 4–6

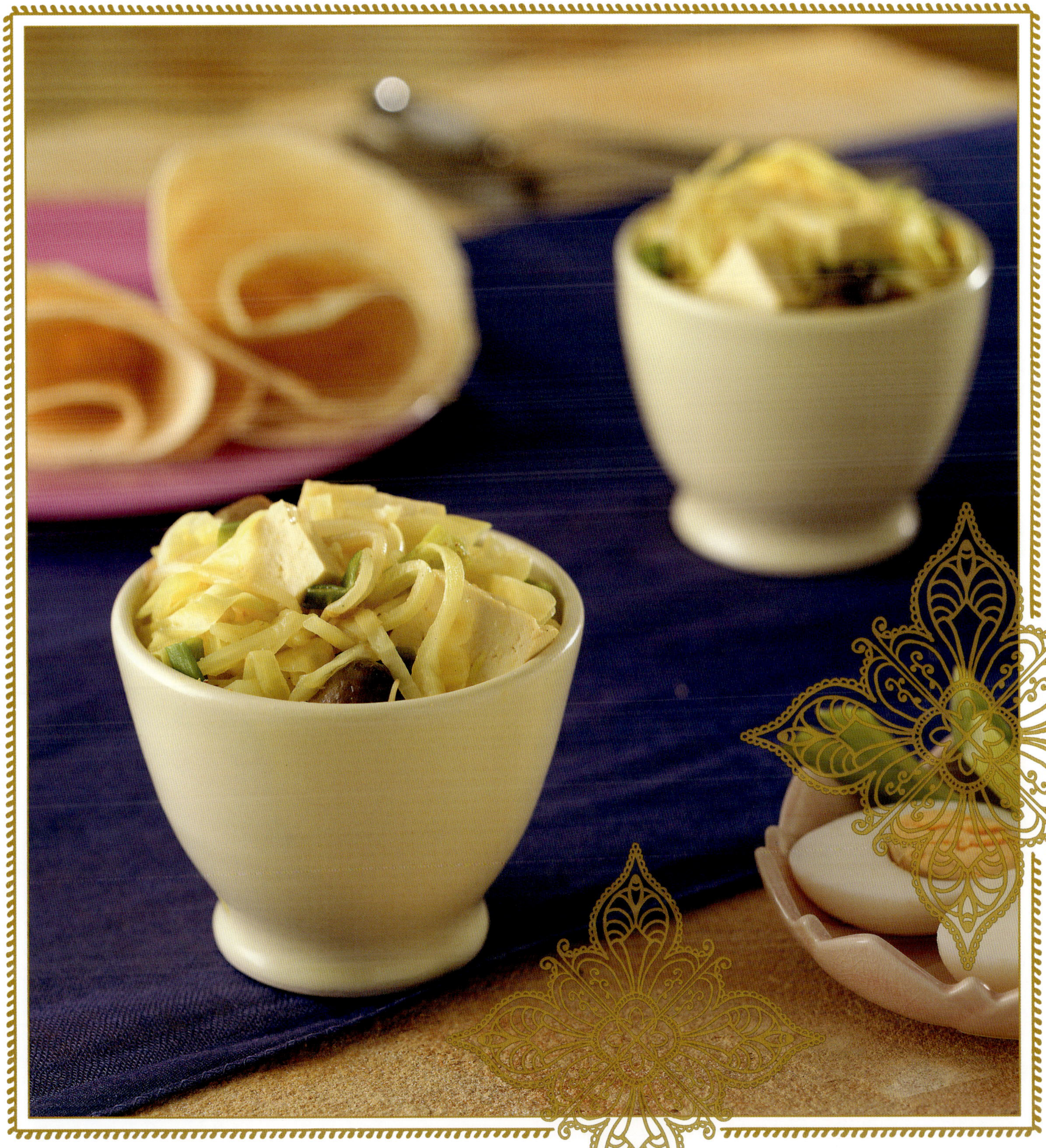

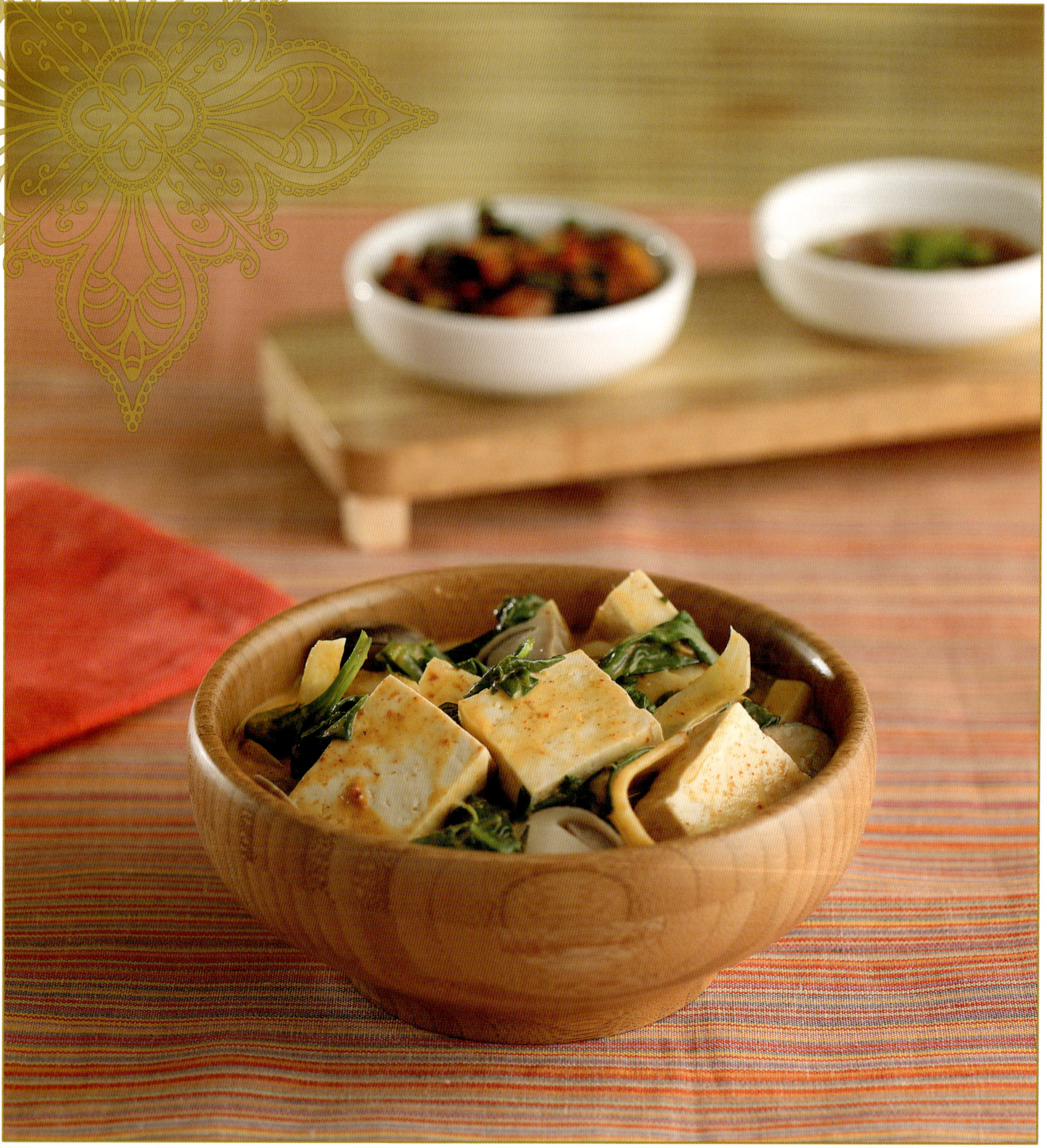

Tofu & Chinese cabbage in coconut curry

half a 425-g can straw mushrooms, drained
3 cups chopped Chinese cabbage (wombok)
1 cup bean sprouts, rinsed and drained
2 spring onions, chopped
½ teaspoon ground turmeric
2 teaspoons ground coriander
1 clove garlic, crushed
1 teaspoon grated fresh ginger
¼–¾ teaspoon sambal ulek or hot chilli paste
1 × 400-ml can coconut milk
salt and pepper
250 g firm tofu, cut into cubes

Place all the ingredients, except the tofu, in a saucepan and bring to the boil. Reduce heat, cover and simmer-steam for 8–10 minutes, until the cabbage is very tender.

Check seasonings, add tofu and warm through gently, then transfer to a serving bowl.

SERVES 3–4

Split-pea dal with spices

1½ cups yellow or green split peas (or a mixture of both)
3 tomatoes, chopped
leaves from 1 small bunch coriander, chopped
salt and pepper
2–3 tablespoons oil or ghee
1 medium-sized onion, finely chopped
1½ teaspoons grated fresh ginger
3 cloves garlic, finely chopped
½ teaspoon cumin seeds
½ teaspoon brown mustard seeds
8–10 curry leaves

Boil split peas in plenty of unsalted water for 35–40 minutes, until cooked. Add the tomatoes, cook until pulpy (5–6 minutes), and then stir in the chopped coriander and season to taste with salt and pepper.

Heat the oil or ghee in a small pan and fry onion until well browned (about 2 minutes). Add ginger, garlic, cumin and mustard seeds, and the curry leaves, and cook for about a minute until fragrant and the spices are sputtering and popping.

Serve peas in a bowl, with the hot dressing poured over them (including all of the oil or ghee).

SERVES 4–6

Red lentil dal

1⅓ cups red lentils
2 teaspoons salt
1–2 fresh green chillies, slit and deseeded
1 teaspoon ground turmeric
1 large onion, roughly chopped
a 2-cm piece fresh ginger, peeled
3 cloves garlic, peeled
2 tablespoons ghee or oil
2 small tomatoes, deseeded and chopped
2 teaspoons garam masala (page 16)
fresh coriander leaves, for garnish

Rinse lentils and place in a saucepan with the salt, chillies, turmeric and 1 litre water. Bring to the boil, cover and simmer for about 9 minutes, or until lentils are soft but holding their shape. Drain, reserving the liquid.

In a food processor grind the onion, ginger and garlic to a paste. Heat the ghee or oil in a frying pan or saucepan and fry the paste for about 5 minutes, stirring, until the liquid evaporates and onion is lightly browned. Add tomatoes and cook for another 2 minutes over medium heat, stirring occasionally.

Stir lentils into the onion–tomato mixture and add the garam masala. Add enough of the reserved cooking liquid to make a smooth purée, and bring to a simmer. Cook for 2–3 minutes, then serve garnished with the coriander.

SERVES 5

Lentil dal with tamarind & coriander

1 cup green or red lentils
½ teaspoon asafoetida powder
1½ tablespoons tamarind concentrate
2 fresh hot green chillies, deseeded and chopped
¾ teaspoon ground turmeric
salt and pepper
½ cup chopped fresh coriander (leaves and stems)

Rinse and drain the lentils. Transfer to a heavy saucepan and add 2½ cups water, bring to the boil, cover partially and simmer for 9–10 minutes, or until just tender, stirring occasionally.

Add asafoetida, tamarind, chillies, turmeric, salt and pepper to the pan and cook for another 8–10 minutes, stirring. Check seasoning and stir in the coriander before serving.

SERVES 4

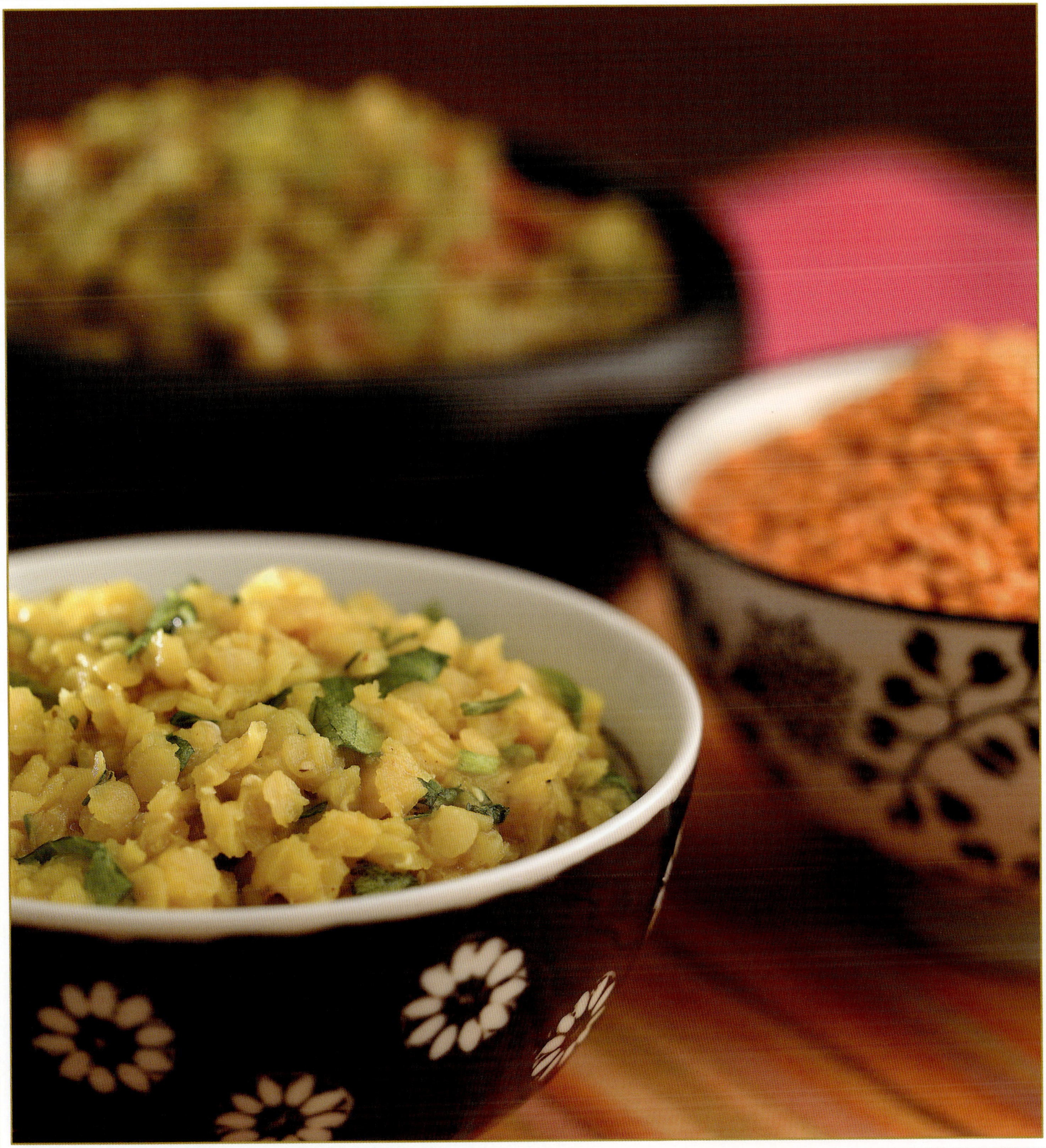

Sambal eggs

Sambals are intensely flavoured small dishes often served with Indonesian and Malaysian curries, although they can be eaten on their own with rice. In this recipe, sun-dried tomatoes add colour and concentrated flavour that would usually come from chillies.

4–6 eggs, at room temperature
1 tablespoon dried shrimp
2 tablespoons fried onions (page 284)
1 teaspoon sambal ulek or other red chilli paste
2 cloves garlic, crushed
1–2 tablespoons oil
1 tablespoon ground coriander
2 teaspoons finely chopped sun-dried tomatoes
1 teaspoon sugar
2 teaspoons smooth peanut butter or macadamia butter
2 teaspoons kecap manis (sweet soy sauce)

Place the eggs in a saucepan of cold water and bring to the boil. Reduce heat and simmer for 8–9 minutes to hard-boil eggs.

In another small saucepan sauté the dried shrimp, fried onions, sambal ulek (or chilli paste) and garlic in the oil for 2 minutes, stirring constantly. Add coriander, sun-dried tomatoes, sugar and ¾ cup water and simmer for 3–5 minutes, until the tomatoes are pulpy and the liquid reduced. Blitz to a purée with a stick mixer, then stir in the nut butter and kecap manis.

Drain the eggs, shell them and cut each lengthways in half. Arrange eggs, cut side up, in a serving dish and cover with the sauce.

SERVES 4–8

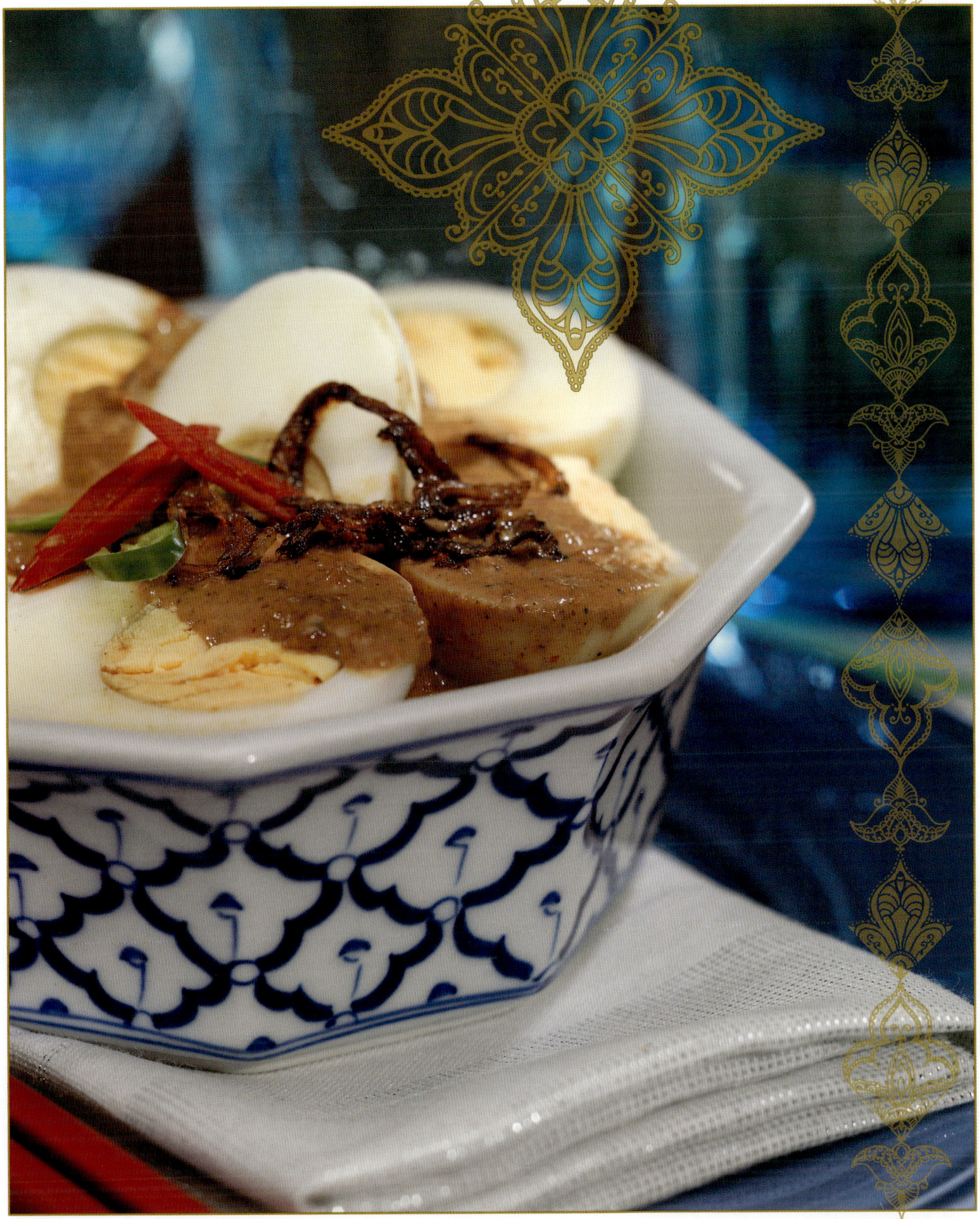

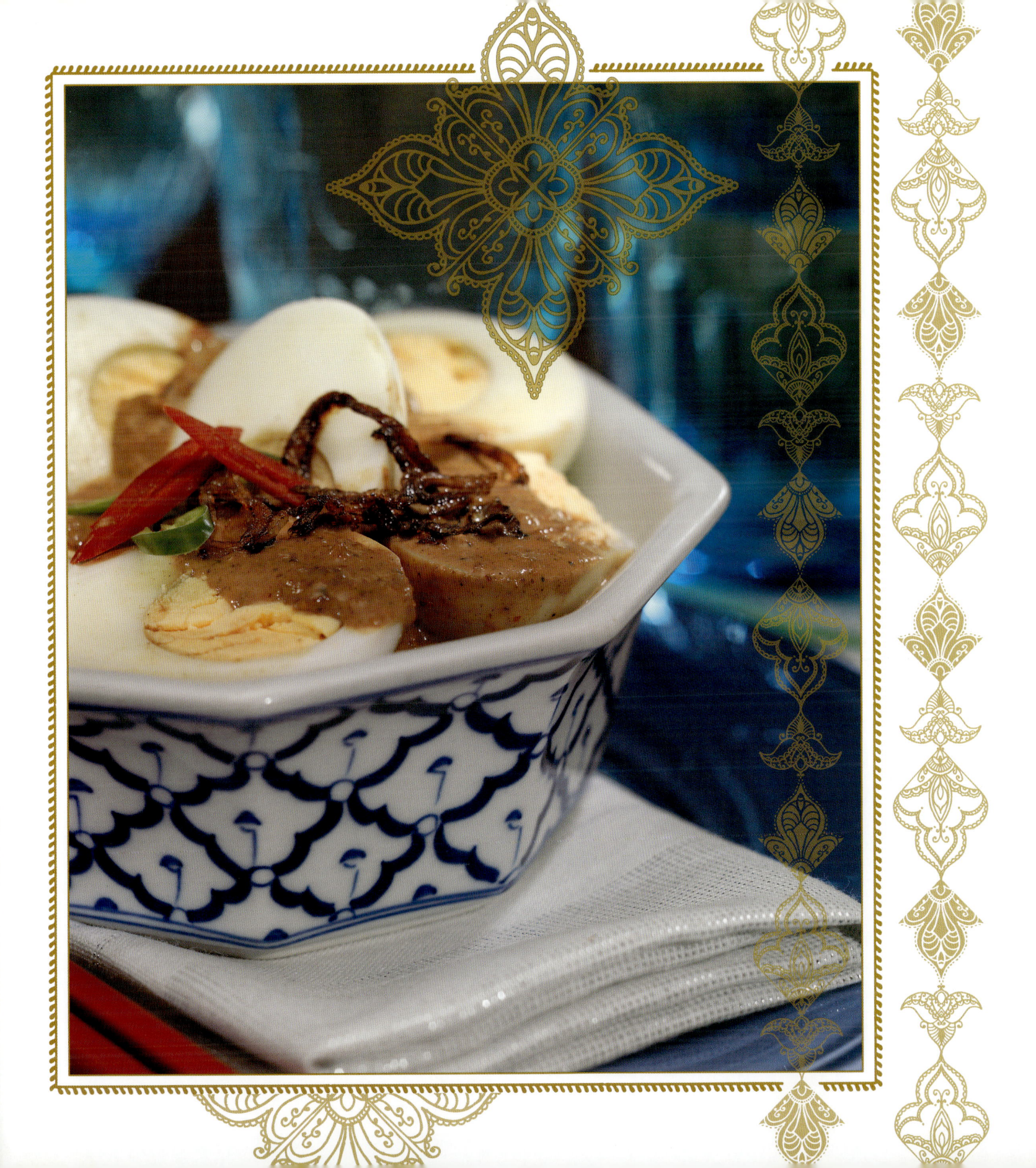

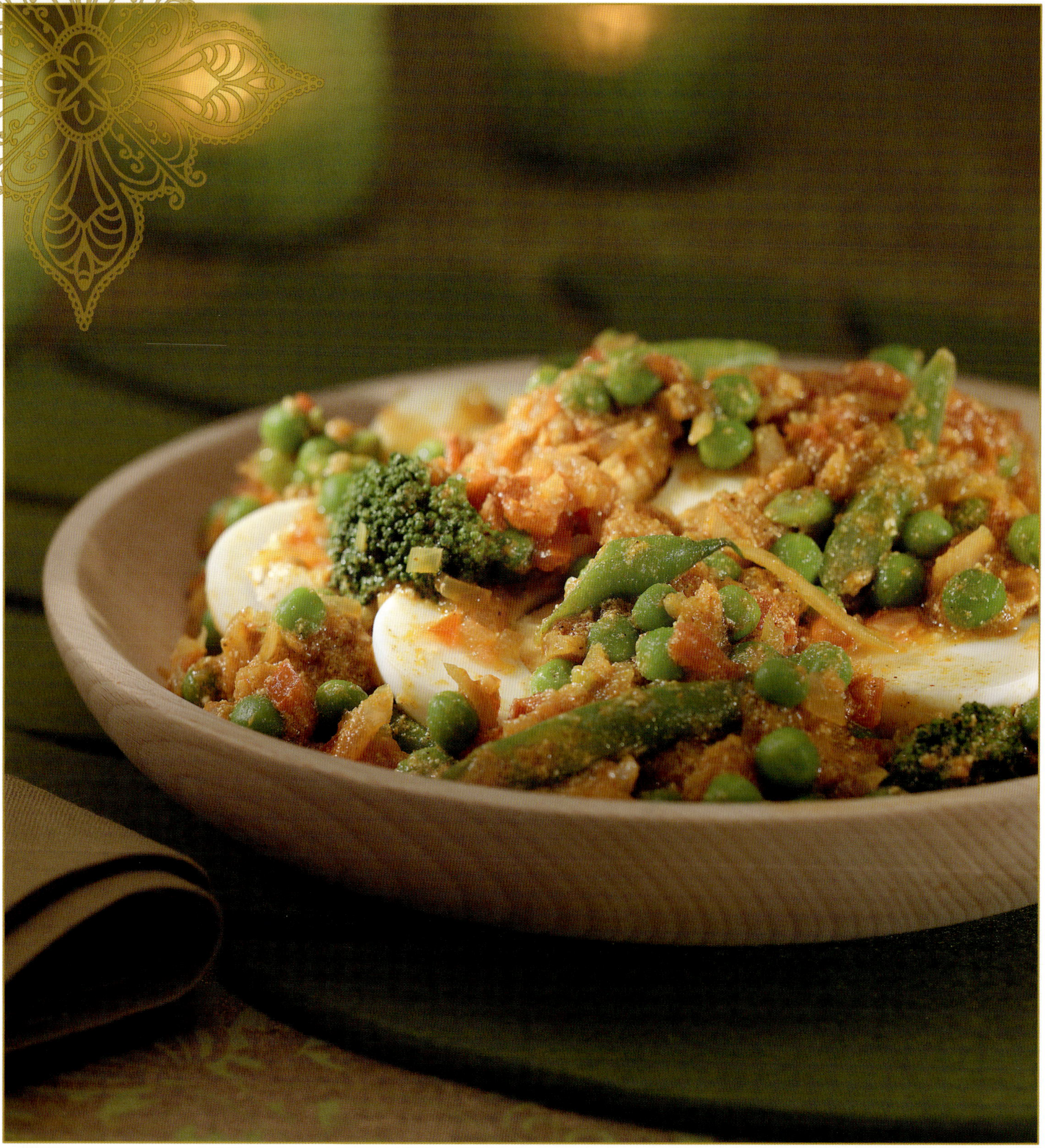

Egg & green vegetable vindaloo

A curry in the time it takes to boil an egg. Fantastic.

6 eggs, preferably at room temperature
1 cup frozen sliced green beans, peas and/or small broccoli florets
1½ tablespoons oil or ghee
1 large onion, very finely chopped
3 teaspoons vindaloo paste (page 11)
1 vine-ripened tomato, deseeded and chopped
1 teaspoon tomato paste
½ cup creamy yoghurt or sour cream
chopped fresh mint
fried onions (page 284)

Place the eggs in a saucepan of cold water and bring slowly to the boil. Reduce heat marginally and simmer for 8–9 minutes to hard-boil. Drain, cool and then shell them, cut in half, and set aside. Meanwhile steam or microwave the vegetables until cooked.

In a pan heat oil or ghee and fry the onion until soft and lightly browned (about 4 minutes). Stir in vindaloo paste and cook for 30 seconds, then add the tomato, tomato paste and yoghurt or sour cream and cook, stirring, until the onion is well browned and the liquid has almost evaporated (about 4 minutes).

Add ½ cup water to the pan and bring to the boil, simmering briefly. Stir in the cooked vegetables, then add the eggs and simmer in the sauce for 2 minutes.

Transfer to a serving dish and garnish with mint and fried onions.

SERVES 4 (OR UP TO 12 AS A SIDE DISH)

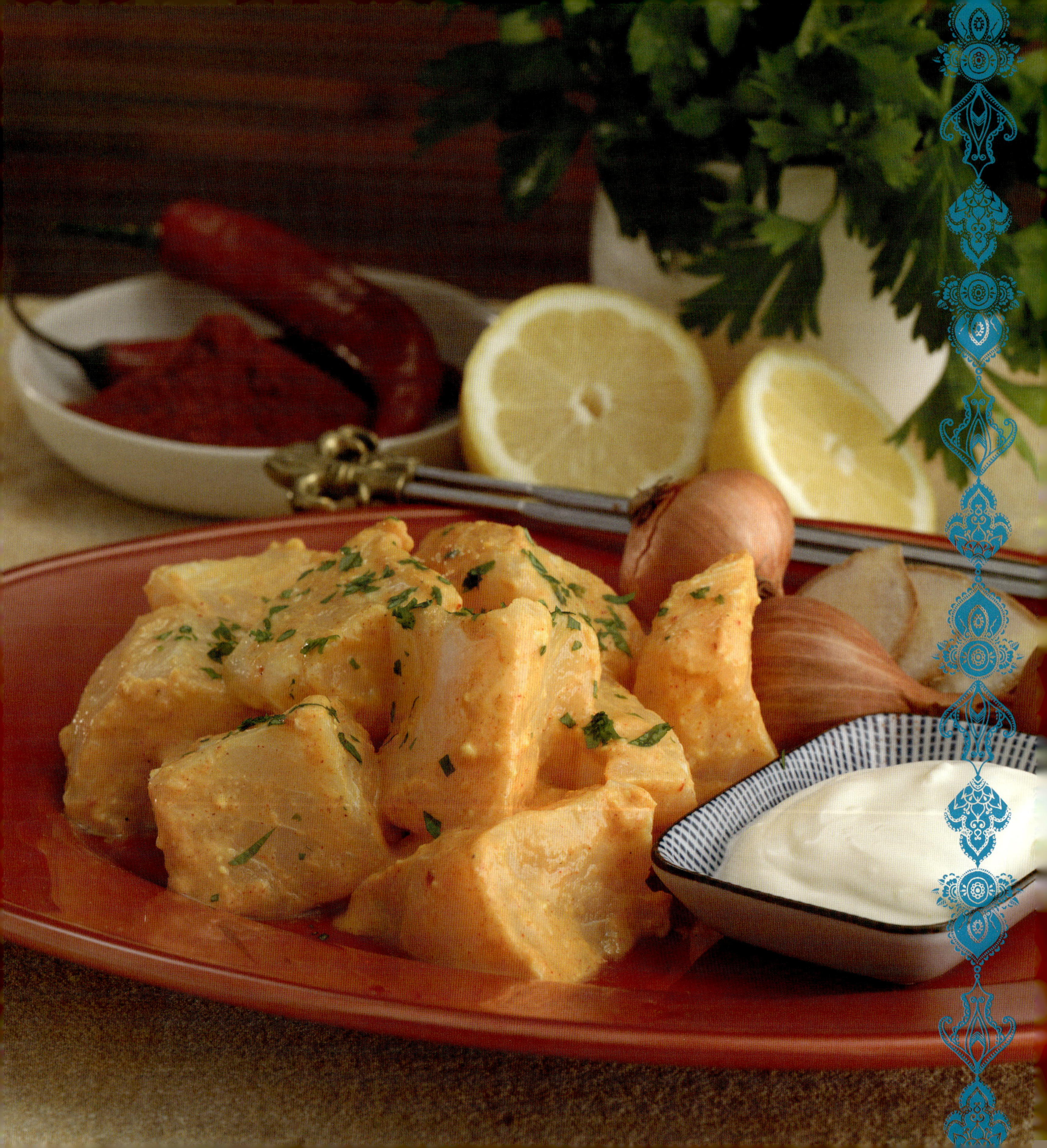

Seafood curries

The sweet succulence of shellfish teams superbly with curry spices and sauces, from fiery hot vindaloos and Thai green curries exploding with chilli heat, to luscious mild kormas, creamy-rich and tinted golden with saffron. Curry spices enhance the briny, fresh-from-the-sea taste of fish, and its firm yet delicate flesh is wonderfully complemented by sauces based on tomatoes and tangy tamarind, or on coriander, and with the citrus of lemongrass and lime. The correct cooking time is crucial for seafood: just long enough to imbue them with flavour, short enough to retain moisture and soft texture.

Squid and cuttlefish also go well in curry sauces, gentle slow simmering bringing them to melting tenderness. The all-important rule with seafood – for best results, always use the freshest available.

Tandoori fish skewers

Indian bread, raw onion rings and lemon wedges are the usual accompaniments to tandoori fish. To grill rather than barbecue, line a grill tray with aluminium foil or baking paper and set a rack over it. Brush rack with oil or ghee, heat grill to hot, and grill the skewers until done.

600 g firm white fish (e.g. rockling), cut into 4-cm cubes
salt and pepper
1 small onion, peeled
a 1-cm piece fresh ginger
1 clove garlic, peeled
½ cup creamy yoghurt
1 tablespoon freshly squeezed lemon juice
½–1 teaspoon ground chilli
1 teaspoon ground sweet paprika
1 tablespoon ground coriander
⅓ teaspoon ground turmeric
red (or yellow and red) food colouring (optional)
oil or ghee
1 teaspoon lightly crushed fennel or ajwain seeds

Soak bamboo skewers in water for at least 15 minutes. Thread fish cubes onto the skewers, season well with salt and pepper, and place in a flat dish.

Grind onion, ginger and garlic to a paste in a food processor. Place a fine strainer over a bowl, tip in paste and press with a wooden spoon to push through the juice and fine solids (discard the rest). Stir in the yoghurt, lemon juice and ground spices, mixing well, and add food colouring (if using).

Spread the yoghurt mixture over the fish and turn each skewer several times to coat evenly. Cover with plastic wrap and refrigerate for 1 hour.

Heat a barbecue to medium–hot, moistening the grid or hotplate with oil or ghee. Arrange the skewers side by side (allow space between them) and grill for about 6 minutes, turning several times, until the fish is tender and the surface well seared.

Sprinkle cooked skewers with fennel or ajwain, and serve at once.

SERVES 4

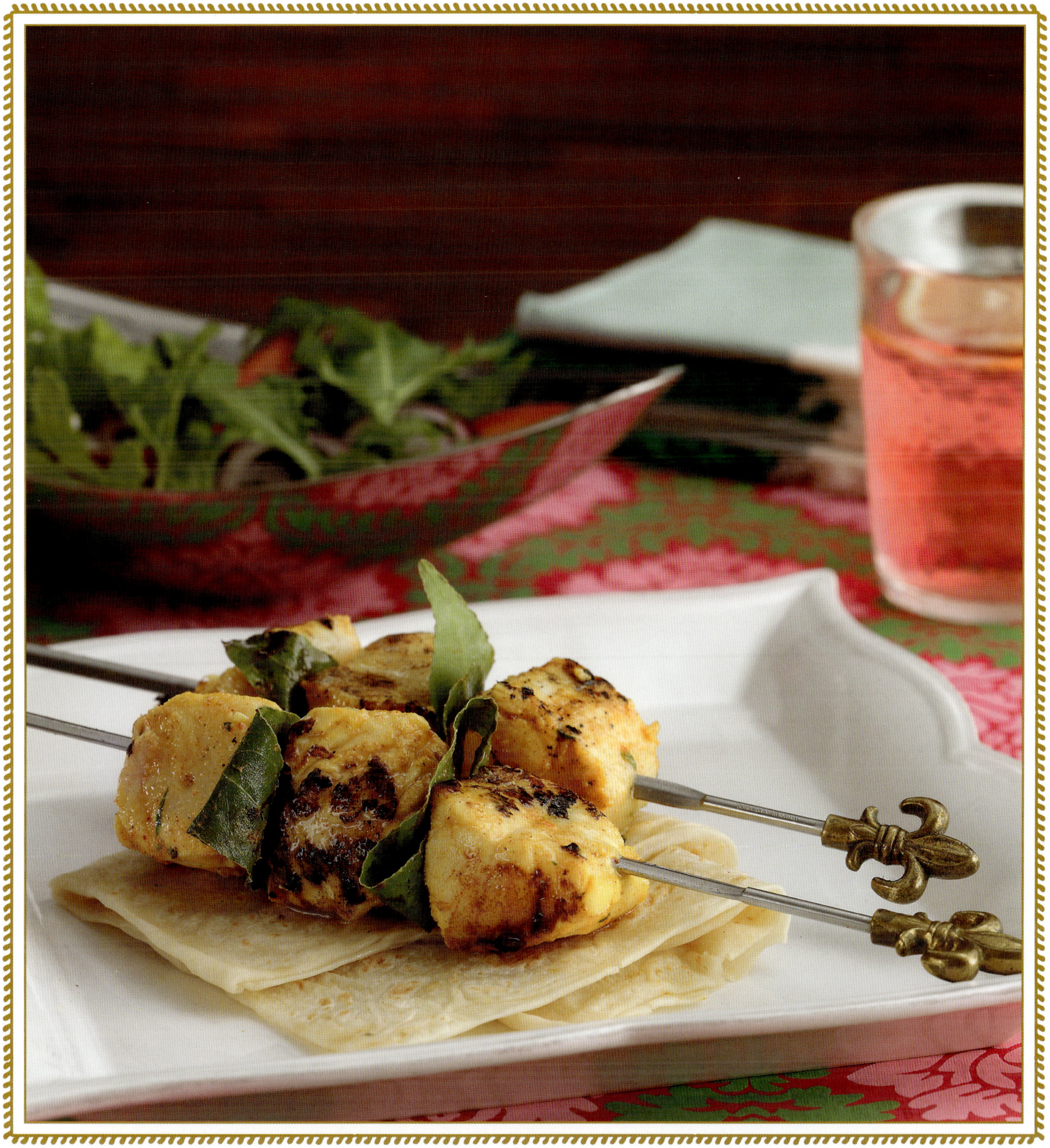

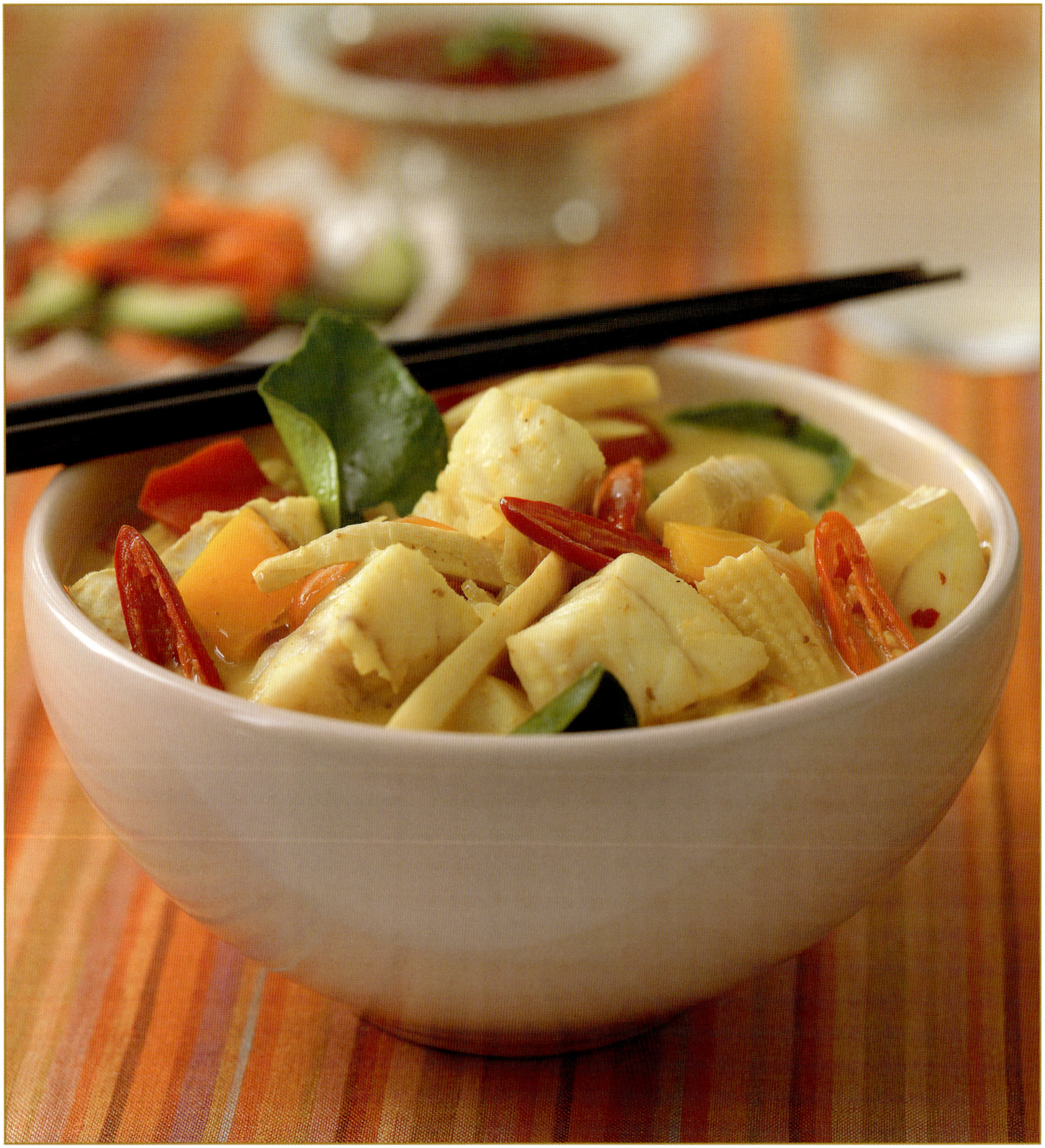

Yellow curry of fish with baby bamboo shoots

1–1½ tablespoons Thai yellow curry paste (page 20)
2 tablespoons oil
2 tablespoons fish sauce
1 small onion, finely chopped
1–2 fresh hot red chillies, cut in half and deseeded
3 kaffir lime leaves
1 × 400-ml can coconut cream
½ red or yellow capsicum, cut into small squares
5–6 baby bamboo shoots, diagonally sliced (or ¼ cup canned sliced bamboo shoots)
5–6 pieces baby corn, diagonally sliced
300 g firm white fish, cut into 3-cm cubes
3 yellow or red cherry tomatoes, cut in half
small sprigs of fresh coriander, to serve

In a wok or medium saucepan, sauté the curry paste in the oil for 1–2 minutes, stirring continually. Stir in half the fish sauce, add onion, chillies and lime leaves, and cook for 1 minute. Pour in ½ cup of the coconut cream and ½ cup water, and bring to the boil. Add capsicum, bamboo shoots and corn and simmer for about 5 minutes

Stir in remaining coconut cream and increase heat to bring almost to the boil. Add fish, reduce heat and simmer for 4–5 minutes until the fish is tender (but not breaking up). Stir in the tomatoes, remaining fish sauce, coriander sprigs, and add a little extra water to increase the sauce, if desired. Warm through, and transfer to a serving bowl.

SERVES 4

Goan mackerel in hot curry sauce

Goa, on India's central west coast, was a busy Portugese trading port for centuries, and one of the first cuisines to adopt that perky import from 'the New world' – chillies. Flathead fillets could replace the mackerel in this recipe.

1 medium-sized onion, roughly chopped
1 clove garlic, peeled
1 fresh hot red chilli, cut in half and deseeded (optional)
½ cup plain flour
salt and pepper
4 mackerel cutlets
1 cup oil
2 tablespoons vindaloo or other hot curry paste (page 11)
½ teaspoon ground turmeric
1 teaspoon cumin seeds
1½ cups canned or fresh diced tomatoes
2 teaspoons tamarind concentrate
2 teaspoons ground sweet paprika
1½ teaspoons sugar

Purée the onion, garlic and chilli in a blender or food processor.

Mix flour, salt and pepper in a shallow bowl and coat fish lightly and evenly. Heat the oil in a large non-stick pan and fry fish until lightly browned. Remove and set aside on a plate.

Pour off oil (reserve it), rinse and dry the pan, and return 2 tablespoons of the oil. Fry onion paste for about 3 minutes, stirring over medium heat, then add the curry paste, turmeric and cumin, and stir for 1 minute. Add tomatoes, tamarind, paprika and sugar with ½ cup water and simmer, stirring occasionally, for about 8 minutes, until sauce has thickened and the flavours are mellow and balanced. (For a smooth sauce, purée in a blender or blitz with a stick mixer, and strain.) Season with salt to taste.

Transfer the fish to the sauce and simmer gently for about 5 minutes, turning once, until tender.

SERVES 4

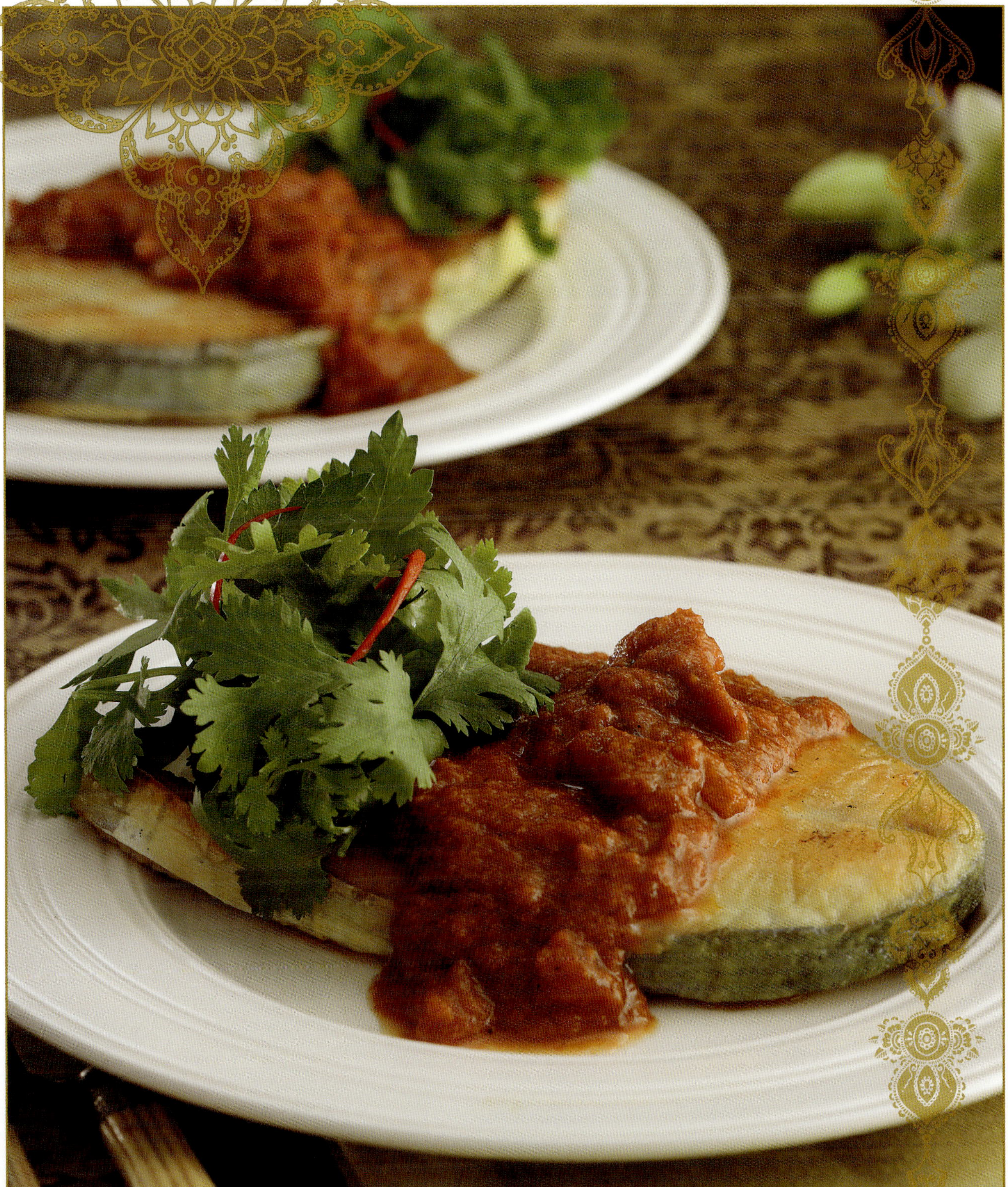

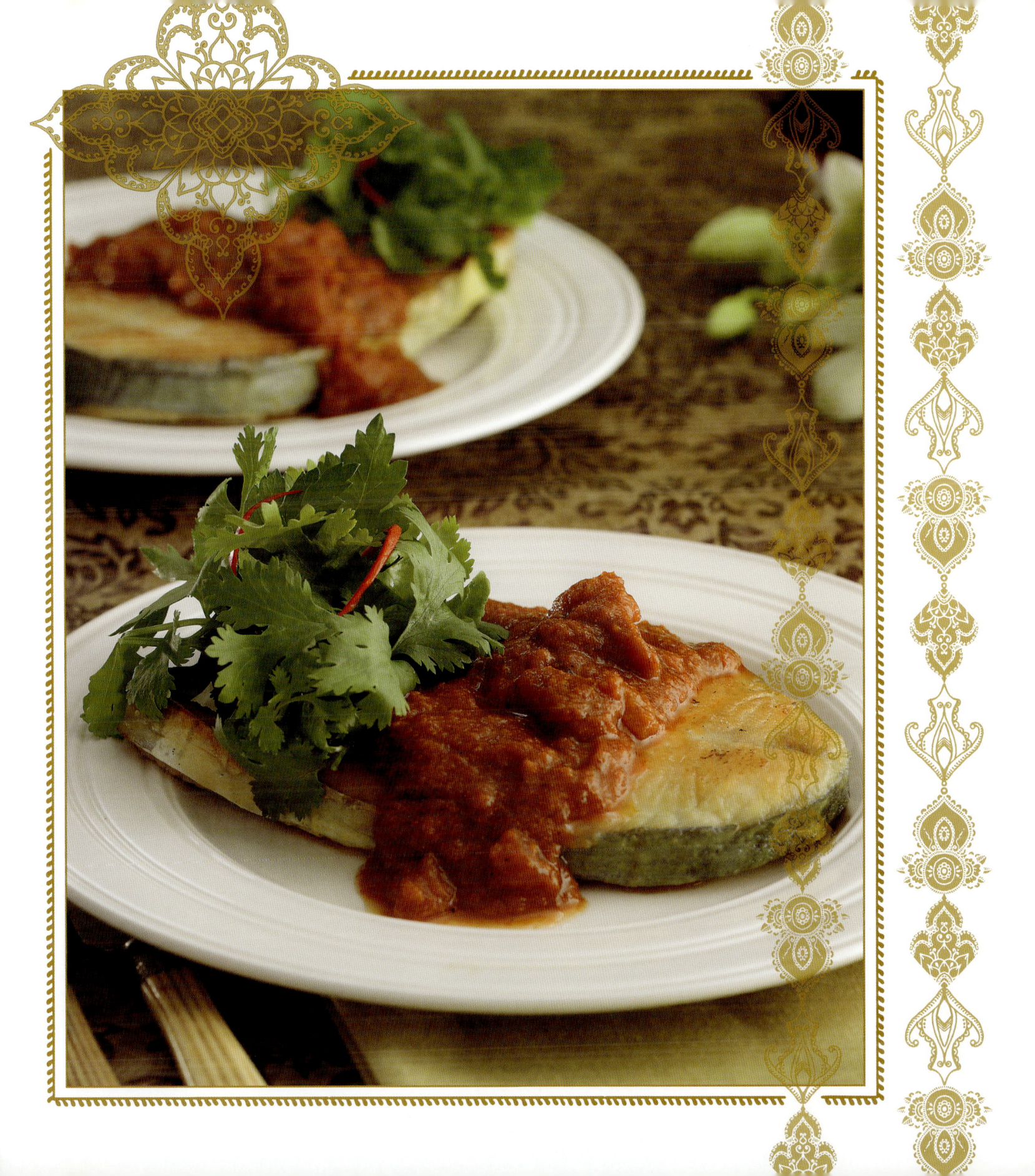

Kerala green curry of fish

Bright-green and fresh-flavoured, this popular dish is a specialty of Kerala on India's southern coast.

1 large onion, quartered
2 cloves garlic, peeled
a 2-cm piece fresh ginger, peeled
1 teaspoon fennel seeds
1 tablespoon coriander seeds
⅓ teaspoon black peppercorns
2 tablespoons oil
salt and pepper
¾ teaspoon ground turmeric
2 fresh hot green chillies, deseeded
leaves from 2 large bunches fresh coriander, finely chopped
1 × 400-ml can coconut milk
80 g finely ground cashew or macadamia nuts
400–500 g thick fish fillets, skinned and cut into 3-cm cubes

Grind onion, garlic and ginger to a paste in a food processor or blender. Dry-roast the fennel and coriander seeds with the peppercorns in a small pan. Tip into a spice grinder and grind to a fine powder.

Heat oil in a frying pan or saucepan over medium heat and fry onion paste for 3–4 minutes, stirring almost continually. Stir in the spice powder, salt, pepper and turmeric, and cook briefly before adding the chillies, coriander, coconut milk, 1 cup water and the ground nuts. Bring to boil, reduce heat and simmer for 5–6 minutes, stirring occasionally.

Check seasoning, add fish and simmer gently for about another 5 minutes, until tender.

SERVES 4–5

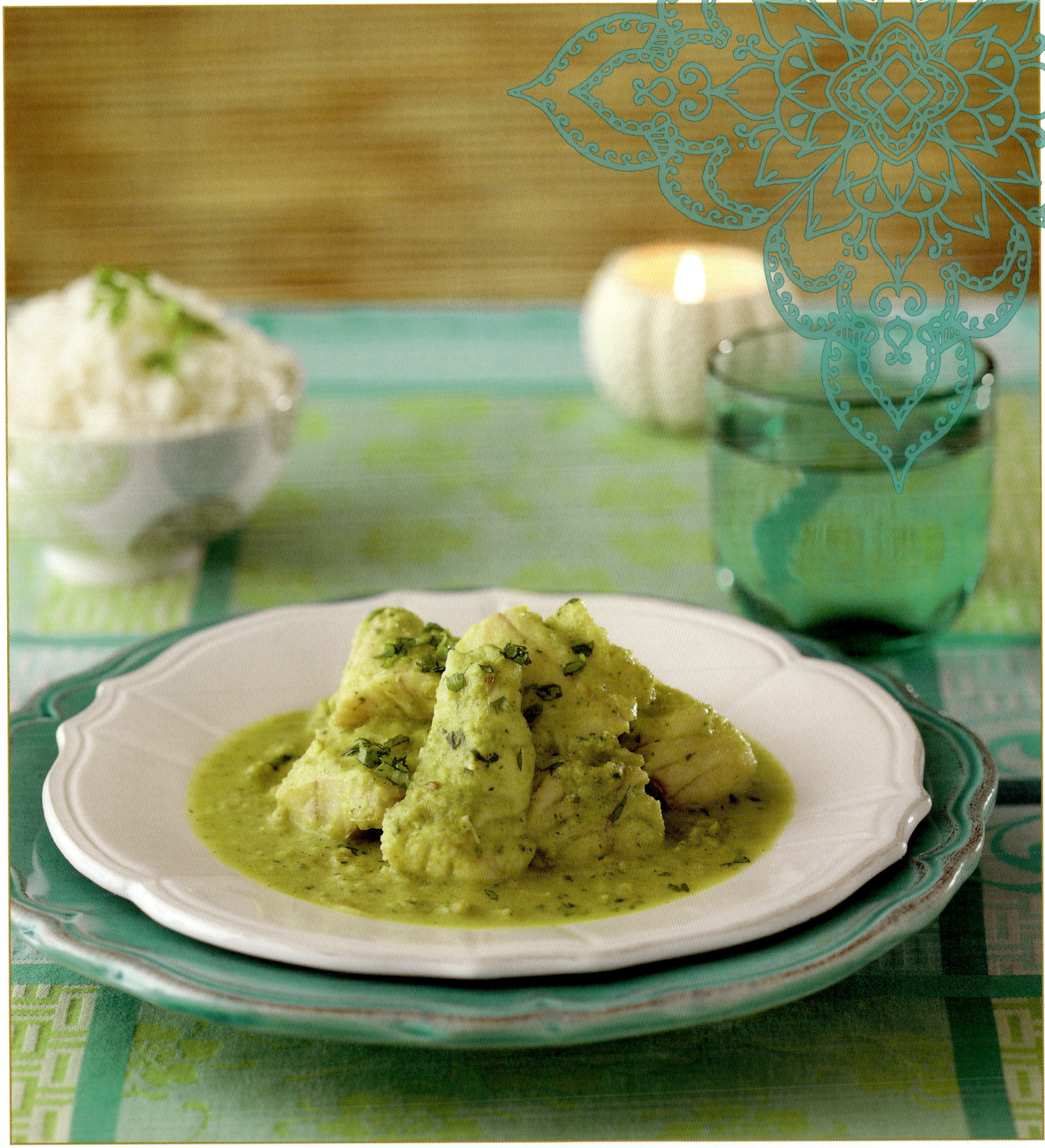

Spicy Malaysian fish curry

¾ cup light coconut milk
2–3 cloves garlic, crushed
2 teaspoons grated fresh ginger
½ teaspoon sambal ulek or hot chilli paste
4 firm white fish steaks or fillets
1 large onion, finely chopped
2 tablespoons oil
1½ tablespoons Malaysian hot curry paste
200 ml canned crushed tomatoes
salt and black pepper
½ cup frozen peas, or sliced green beans
⅓ teaspoon dill or fennel seeds, lightly crushed
chopped fresh coriander, or small sprigs fresh dill

In a small dish combine the coconut milk, garlic, ginger and sambal ulek or chilli paste, and mix well. Add the fish, turn several times to coat, and set aside.

In a pan sauté the onion in the oil for about 5 minutes until browned, stirring frequently. Add curry paste and stir for 40 seconds, then add tomatoes, the fish marinade liquid and ¾ cup water. Bring to the boil, reduce heat and simmer for 8–10 minutes, stirring from time to time.

Season sauce with salt and pepper, then add the fish, the peas and the dill or fennel seeds. Simmer gently for about 8 minutes, until the fish is tender.

Stir in the herbs, and serve.

SERVES 4

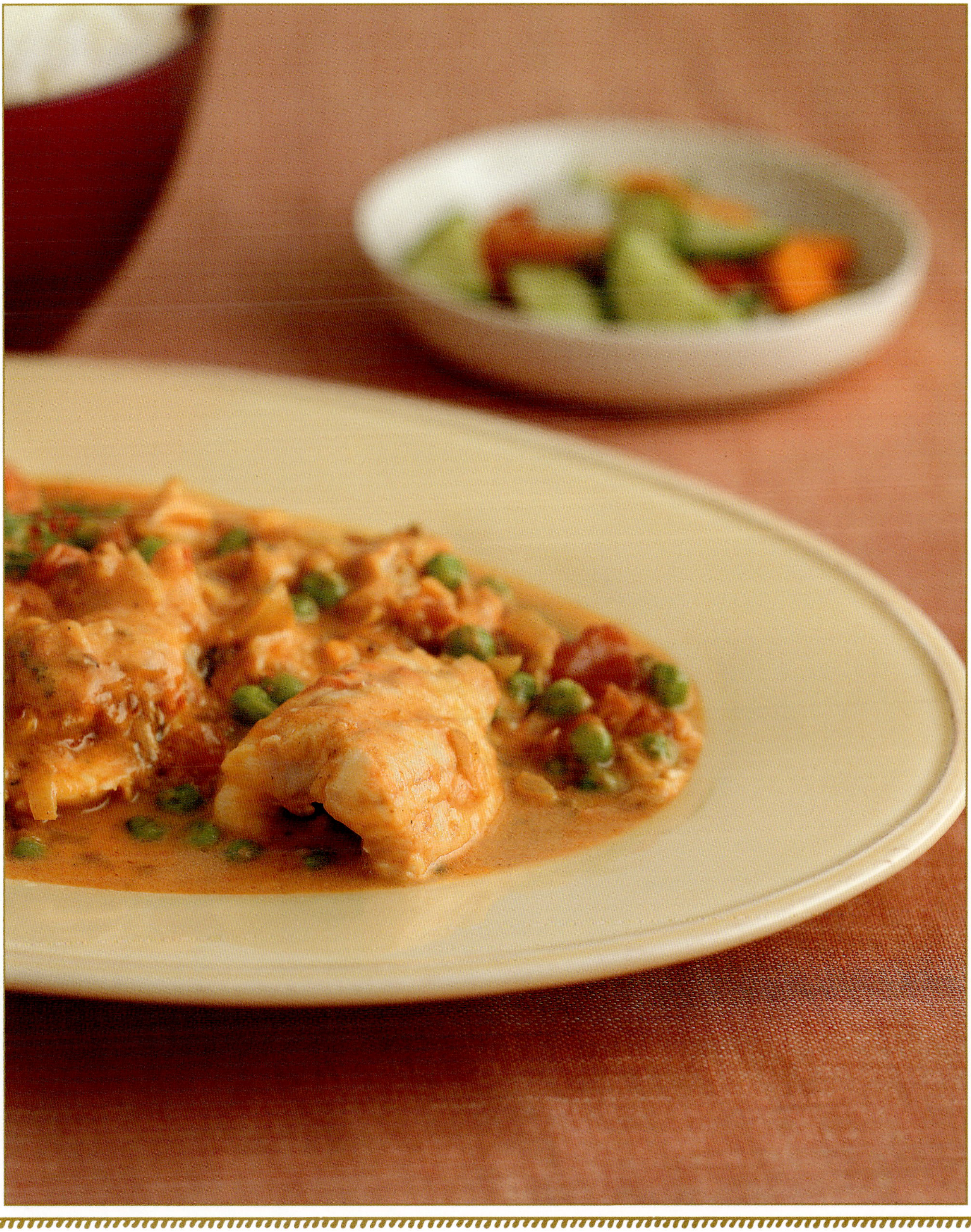

Malaccan pepper fish

The food of Malacca, which lies on the southern Malay peninsula, reflects the passing parade of settlers, traders and migrants who traversed or settled there over centuries. Remnants of its past glory as a strategic Portuguese port can still be found in elegant architecture and cuisine.

4–6 mackerel cutlets
1½ teaspoons ground turmeric
3 tablespoons plain flour
1 teaspoon salt
1 cup oil
6 candlenuts or 12 macadamia nuts
1 large onion, roughly chopped
3–4 cloves garlic, peeled
a 2-cm piece fresh ginger, peeled
1 fresh hot red chilli, deseeded and chopped
1 teaspoon shrimp paste
2½ teaspoons ground black pepper
2 large very ripe tomatoes, deseeded and chopped
2 teaspoons tamarind concentrate
1 × 400-ml can coconut milk
1 teaspoon grated palm sugar or soft brown sugar
2–3 tablespoons chopped fresh mint, coriander or dill

Pat the fish dry with paper towels. In a plastic bag combine the turmeric, flour and salt, and shake to mix well. Add the fish, close the bag and shake to coat evenly.

Heat oil in a large pan and fry the fish until golden-brown on both sides. Remove to a plate. Pour off the oil (reserve for later) and rinse out the pan.

Grind the nuts in a food processor or blender. Separately grind the onion, garlic, ginger and chilli to a paste. Wrap shrimp paste in a small square of aluminium foil and dry-roast in the pan for about 1 minute over medium-high heat, turning often. Remove and set aside.

Return about 2½ tablespoons of the frying oil to the pan and fry the ground nuts, onion paste and shrimp paste together for about 2½ minutes, until fragrant and thick. Add tomatoes and tamarind, and cook for 1–2 minutes, stirring often. Pour in the coconut milk, add sugar and bring to the boil, then reduce heat and simmer gently for 6–8 minutes, until creamy.

Add the fried fish to the pan and simmer gently in the sauce for about 6 minutes, seasoning with salt to taste. Stir in the chopped herbs, and serve.

SERVES 4–6

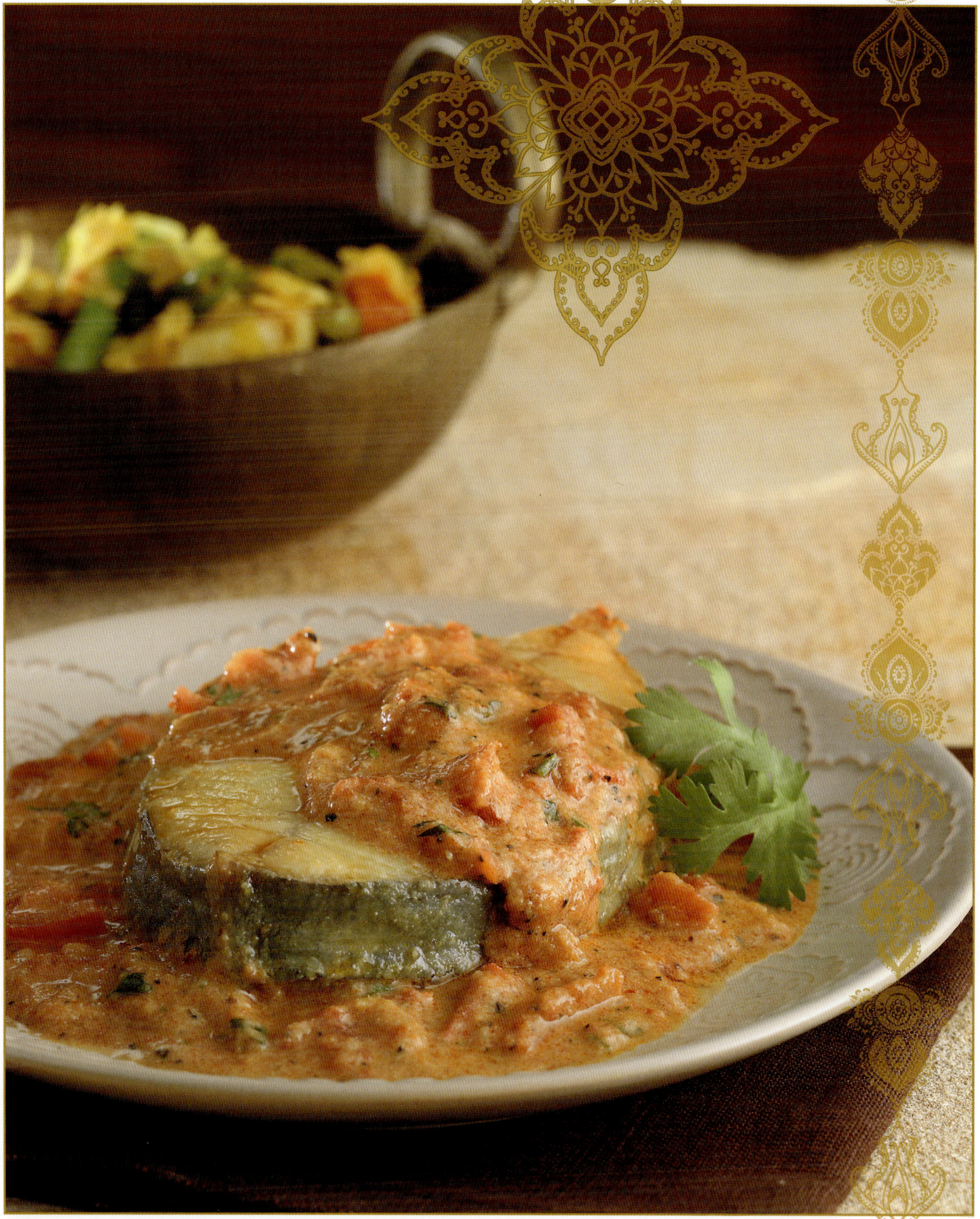

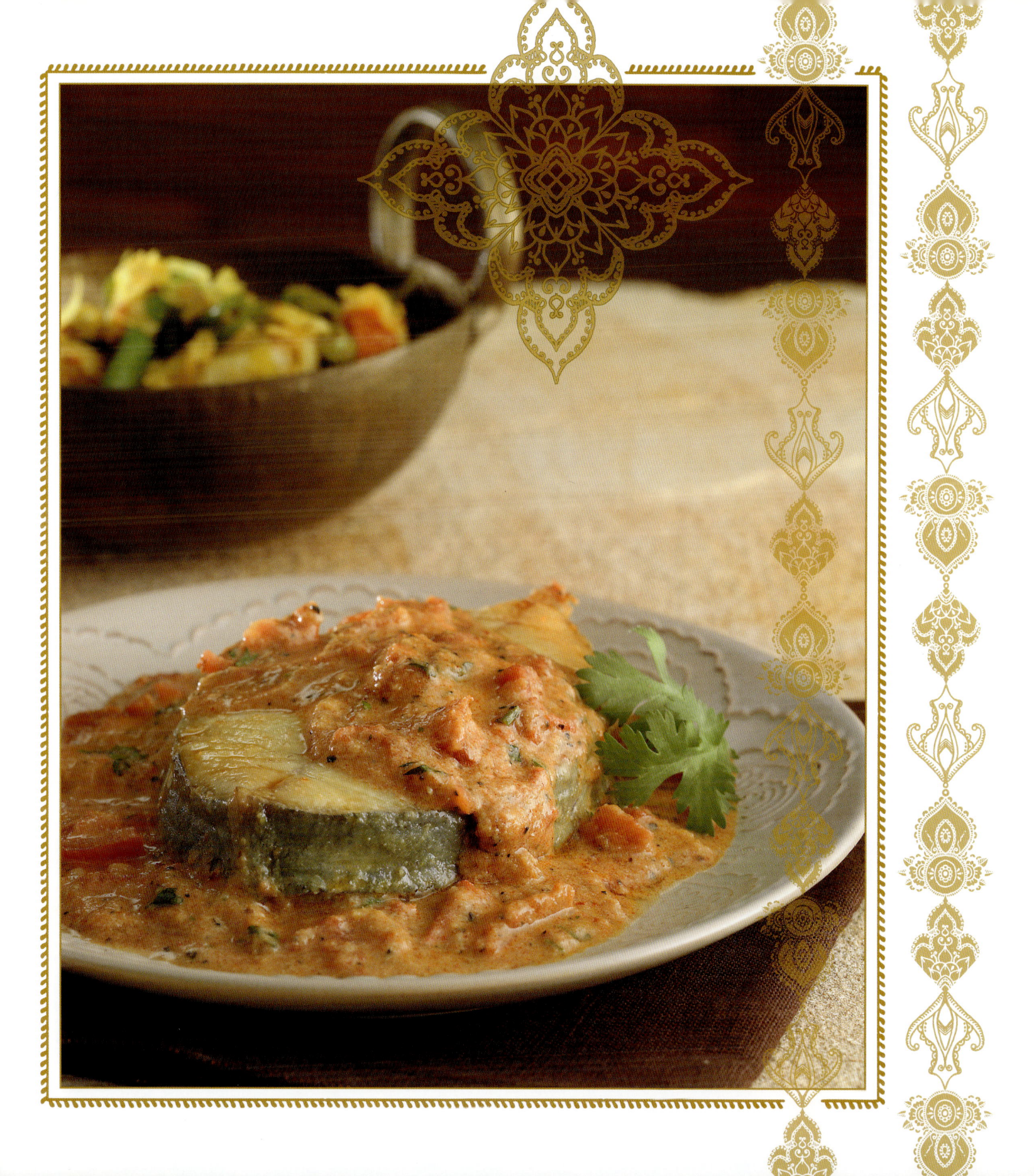

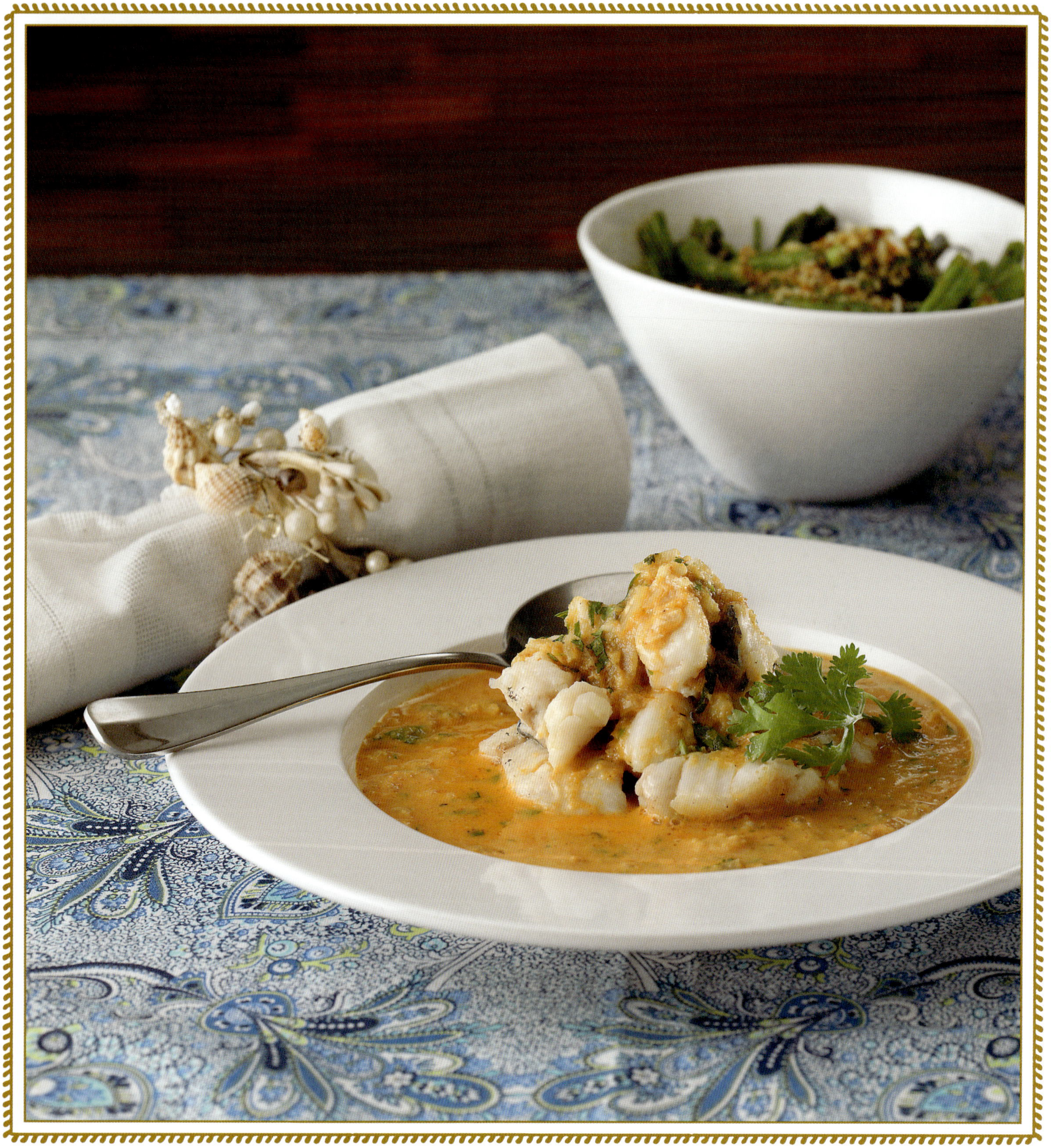

Indonesian fish in tangy curry spices

In the Indonesian kitchen, coconut oil is a preferred cooking oil as it imparts luscious flavour and fragrance. If coconut oil sets hard in the bottle, microwave for a few seconds or stand it in a pan of hot water, until it is liquid enough to pour (do not overheat).

1 large onion, roughly chopped
3 cloves garlic, peeled
a 3-cm piece fresh ginger, peeled
about ½ cup coconut oil
1 teaspoon shrimp paste
2 teaspoons hot ground chilli, sambal ulek or chilli paste
2 teaspoons tamarind concentrate or 1½ tablespoons freshly squeezed lemon juice
1 × 400-ml can coconut cream or milk
salt and pepper
600 g oily fish such as mackerel (skin on), cut into 2-cm slices
sprigs or leaves of fresh basil, dill or coriander
fried onions or shallots (page 284)

Place onion, garlic and ginger in a food processor or blender and grind to a paste.

Heat 2 tablespoons of the oil in a wok or pan and fry paste over medium heat, stirring slowly, for about 3½ minutes until onion is lightly coloured and almost cooked. Add shrimp paste, mashing it against the side of the pan.

Stir in chilli powder or paste, tamarind or lemon juice, and coconut cream or milk, and bring to the boil, stirring continually. Season to taste with salt and pepper, and leave to simmer gently while you prepare the fish.

Heat the remaining oil in a non-stick pan and fry the fish slices in batches until lightly coloured on both sides. Gently slide cooked fish into the curry sauce and simmer for 2–3 minutes without stirring. Transfer to a serving dish and garnish with herbs and crisp shallots.

SERVES 4–6

Spicy barbecued fish

8 flathead fillets (or 4 tuna steaks) skin on
salt
⅓ teaspoon fennel seeds
1 teaspoon cumin seeds
⅓ teaspoon black peppercorns
1–2 cloves garlic, crushed
1½ teaspoons grated fresh ginger
½ teaspoon sambal ulek or red chilli paste
2 teaspoons grated lemon zest
¼ cup creamy yoghurt
lemon wedges, onion rings and fresh coriander, mint or dill, for garnish

If using tuna steaks, cut each lengthways in half. Season fish with salt.

Dry-roast the fennel and cumin seeds with the peppercorns in a small pan for about 1 minute, then grind finely.

In a bowl combine the garlic, ginger, chilli, lemon zest and yoghurt. Add the ground spices, and mix well. Spread over the fish, coating evenly, cover, and refrigerate for 20 minutes.

Heat a barbecue grill or hotplate, or a large non-stick pan, and brush with oil. Grill the fish, turning several times, for about 6 minutes, until cooked and well browned on the surface.

Transfer to a serving plate and garnish with lemon wedges, onion rings and herbs.

SERVES 4

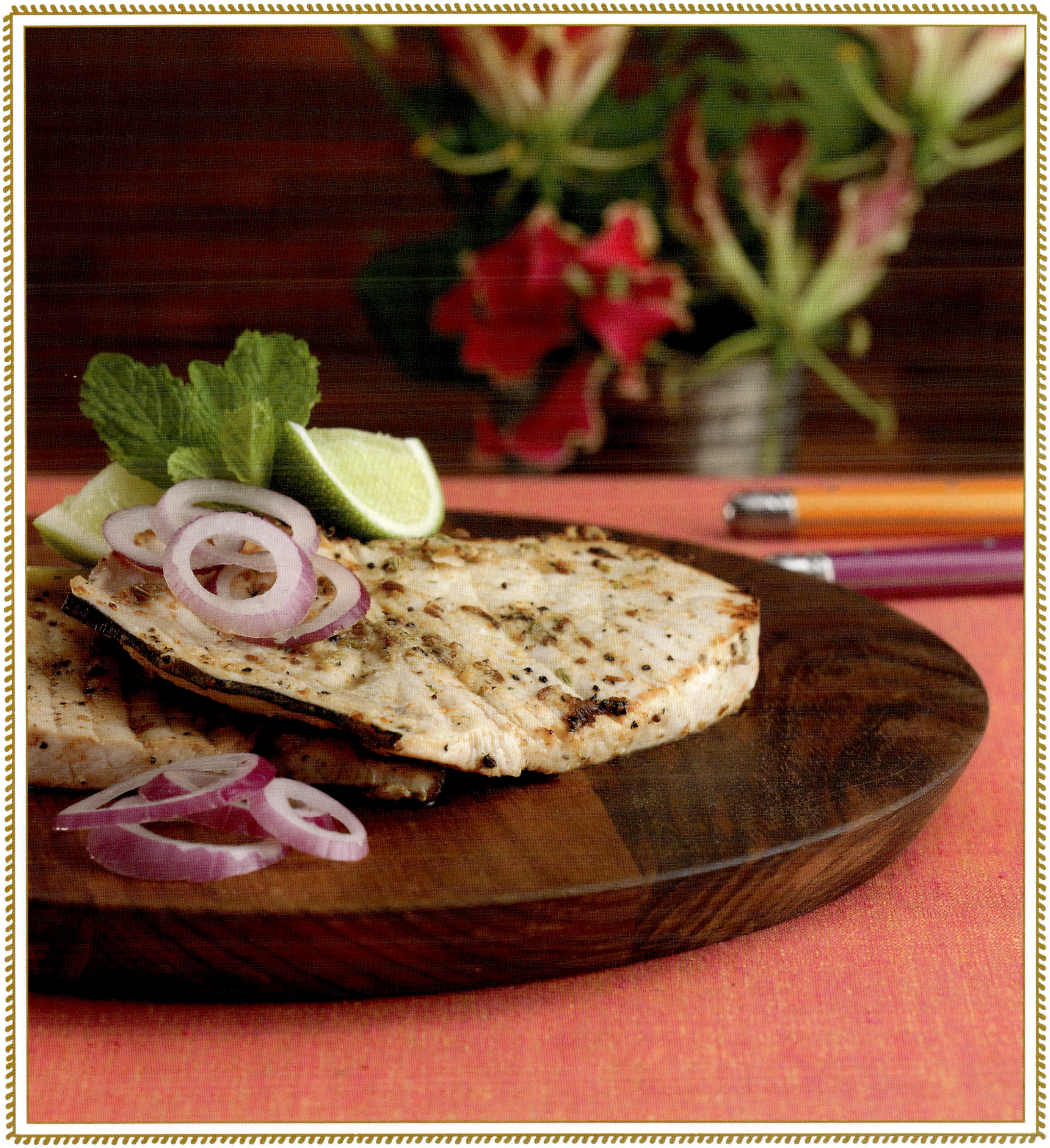

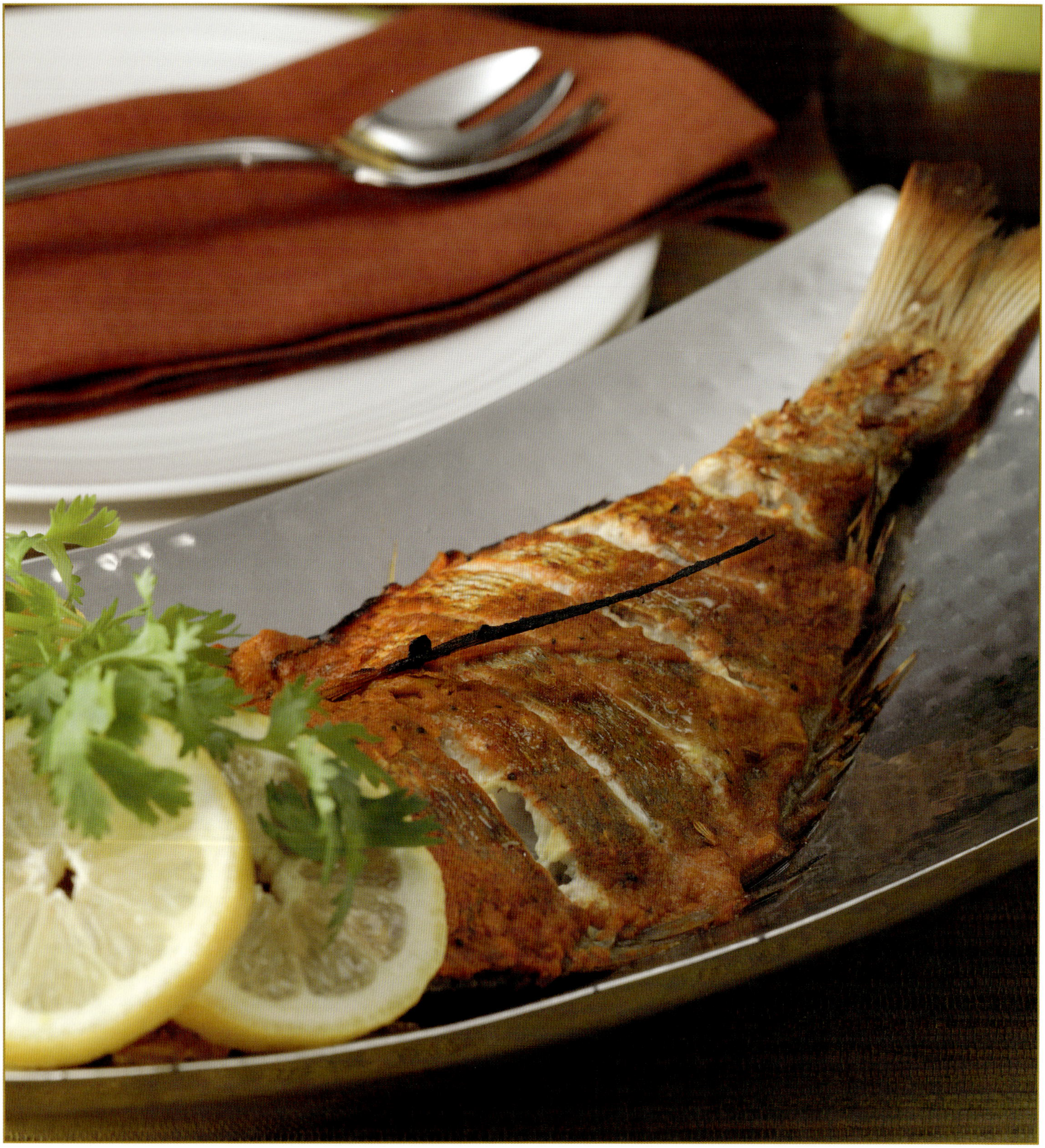

Tandoori-baked whole fish

- 1 large whole reef fish or snapper (about 1.3 kg)
- 1 cup natural yoghurt
- 1 medium-sized onion
- a 3-cm piece fresh ginger
- 3 cloves garlic, crushed
- ½-1 teaspoon red chilli paste or sambal ulek
- 1 tablespoon freshly squeezed lemon juice
- 2 teaspoons ground sweet paprika
- 2 tablespoons ground coriander
- 1 teaspoon ground turmeric
- 1 teaspoon fennel seeds, lightly crushed
- ½ teaspoon ground black pepper
- 1½ teaspoons salt
- red (or red and yellow) food colouring (optional)
- 1 lemon

Rinse the fish under running cold water, drain, and pat dry with paper towels. With a sharp knife make deep slashes across each side, at 2-cm intervals.

Tip yoghurt into a bowl. Grate the onion and ginger into a fine strainer over another bowl, press out as much juice as possible, and discard the solids. Add this juice, the garlic, chilli paste, lemon juice, spices, salt and pepper to the yoghurt and mix well. Add food colouring if you like, for an authentic look.

Smear yoghurt mixture thickly over the fish, cover, and marinate in the refrigerator for at least 4 hours, or overnight.

To cook, heat a covered barbecue to hot, or preheat oven to 200°C. Scrape excess marinade from the fish, and place the lemon in the cavity, folding the cavity flaps outwards so the fish can stand upright as it cooks. Cook for about 25 minutes, beginning to check for doneness after about 20 minutes. (When it's ready, the point of a knife should be easily able to separate layers of flesh at the thickest part, just behind the head.)

Carefully lift fish onto a serving platter, garnish and serve.

SERVES 6–8

Baked fish with spicy coconut crust

oil

2 tablespoons mild curry paste (page 14)

1½ cups desiccated coconut

1 × 400-ml can coconut cream

2 teaspoons tamarind concentrate

1½ teaspoons salt

1 teaspoon ground black pepper

6 fillets white fish (each about 150 g)

Heat the oven to 190°C. Brush a baking dish with oil.

In a bowl combine all the ingredients except the fish, and spread half in the oven dish. Arrange the fish fillets evenly on top, without overlapping if possible. Pour on the remaining spicy mixture, cover with aluminium foil and place dish in the oven. Cook for about 12 minutes, then increase the oven heat to 240°C and remove the foil.

Cook for a few more minutes to brown the top, then serve.

SERVES 6

Nonya fish curry with eggplant, tomatoes & cabbage

2 tablespoons hot curry paste or Thai Mussaman curry paste (page 19)
½ teaspoon shrimp paste
1 × 400-ml can coconut cream
500 g firm white fish, sliced
2 tablespoons oil
1 small red onion, finely sliced
3 cloves garlic, finely sliced
3–4 slices fresh ginger, finely shredded
1 tablespoon tamarind concentrate
2 slender Asian eggplants, cut into 1.5-cm slices
1–2 fresh hot green chillies, slit lengthways and deseeded
2 roma tomatoes, cut into small wedges and deseeded
2 cups finely shredded white or Chinese cabbage (wombok)
salt, pepper and sugar to taste
chopped fresh mint, dill, basil or coriander

In a bowl mix the curry paste, shrimp paste and ½ cup of the coconut cream. Add the fish slices, mix well, cover, and marinate for 20 minutes.

Heat the oil in a wok or saucepan and fry the onion, garlic and ginger for about 2 minutes over medium heat, until lightly coloured. Stir in the tamarind and 1 cup water, the eggplant and chillies, and simmer for about 8 minutes (add extra water if needed).

Add tomatoes, cabbage and remaining coconut cream to the pan with salt and pepper, and a pinch of sugar to balance the tartness of the tamarind, and simmer gently for about 7 minutes. Fold marinated fish into the curry and cook gently for about 5 minutes.

Check seasoning, add chopped herbs, and serve.

SERVES 4–6

Thai green prawn curry

- 1 snake bean or 4–6 green beans, cut into 4-cm diagonal slices
- 1 small carrot, thinly sliced
- ¼ cup peas
- ½ cup sliced bamboo shoots (optional)
- 2 tablespoons vegetable oil
- 1½ tablespoons Thai green curry paste (page 18)
- 4 kaffir lime leaves, bruised a little to release flavour
- 1 stem lemongrass, cut into 4-cm diagonal slices
- 1–1½ tablespoons fish sauce
- 2 cups coconut milk
- 24 medium-sized green (raw) prawns, butterflied
- ½ cup fresh basil leaves

Bring a small saucepan of lightly salted water to the boil and cook beans, carrot, peas and bamboo shoots (if using) until barely tender. Drain, refresh in cold water and set aside.

Heat oil in a medium-sized saucepan and fry curry paste for 4–6 minutes, stirring, until fragrant. Add lime leaves, lemongrass, fish sauce and ¾ cup water, and simmer for 3 minutes.

Add coconut milk to pan and bring to a gentle boil, then reduce heat and simmer briefly. Add cooked vegetables and prepared prawns, and cook gently for 3–4 minutes, until prawns are pink. Stir in basil leaves, check seasoning and add extra fish sauce or salt if needed.

SERVES 4

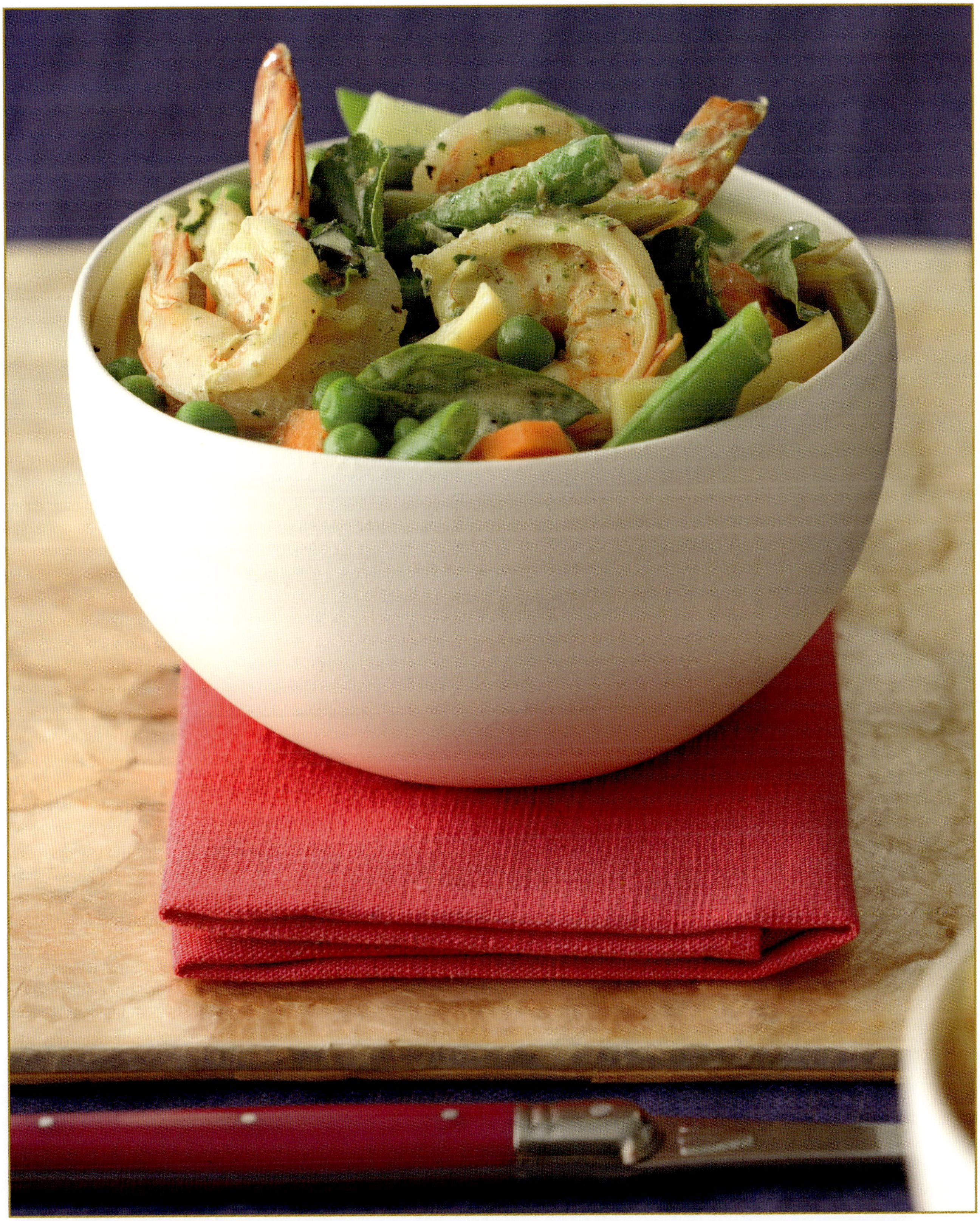

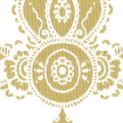

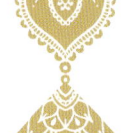

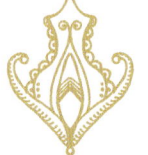

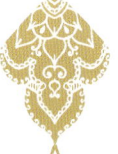

Red curry of prawns

600 g large green (raw) prawns in the shell
1½ tablespoons oil
1–1½ tablespoons Thai red curry paste (page 17)
½ stem lemongrass, bruised
½ cup coconut cream
3 kaffir lime leaves
1 fresh mild red chilli, slit lengthways and deseeded
1 × 400-ml can coconut milk
1½ tablespoons fish sauce
1½ teaspoons palm sugar or soft brown sugar
freshly squeezed lime juice, to taste

Use a sharp knife to cut along the centre back of each prawn, and devein.

Heat the oil in a saucepan and fry the curry paste for 1 minute, stirring. Add lemongrass and coconut cream, and simmer for about 3 minutes, stirring. Add lime leaves, chilli, coconut milk, fish sauce and palm sugar, and bring to the boil, stirring. Simmer for 1 minute, then add the prawns and cook over low heat until the shells are bright pink and the prawns cooked (about 12 minutes). Squeeze lime juice over the prawns, and serve at once.

SERVES 4

Prawns in mild cream curry

Keep a pack of peeled, uncooked prawns on hand in the freezer for deliciously quick and easy meals – like this creamy curry.

1 small red onion, finely chopped
1 clove garlic, crushed
2½ tablespoons butter
3 teaspoons mild curry powder (or 2 teaspoons Thai Mussaman curry paste – page 19)
¼ teaspoon ground turmeric
½ teaspoon fennel seeds, lightly crushed
1 small red apple, peeled and grated
1 tablespoon chopped raisins or toasted almonds
¾ cup fish stock
18 medium-sized shelled green (raw) prawns, deveined
⅔ cup cream
salt and pepper

Sauté the onion and garlic in the butter until softened (about 3 minutes). Sprinkle on the curry powder or paste, turmeric and fennel seeds, add the apple and raisins or almonds, then stir over medium heat for about 3 minutes until apple has softened.

Pour fish stock into pan and simmer for 5 minutes. Add prawns and cream, salt and pepper, and simmer gently for about 5 minutes until the sauce thickens and the prawns are tender.

SERVES 2

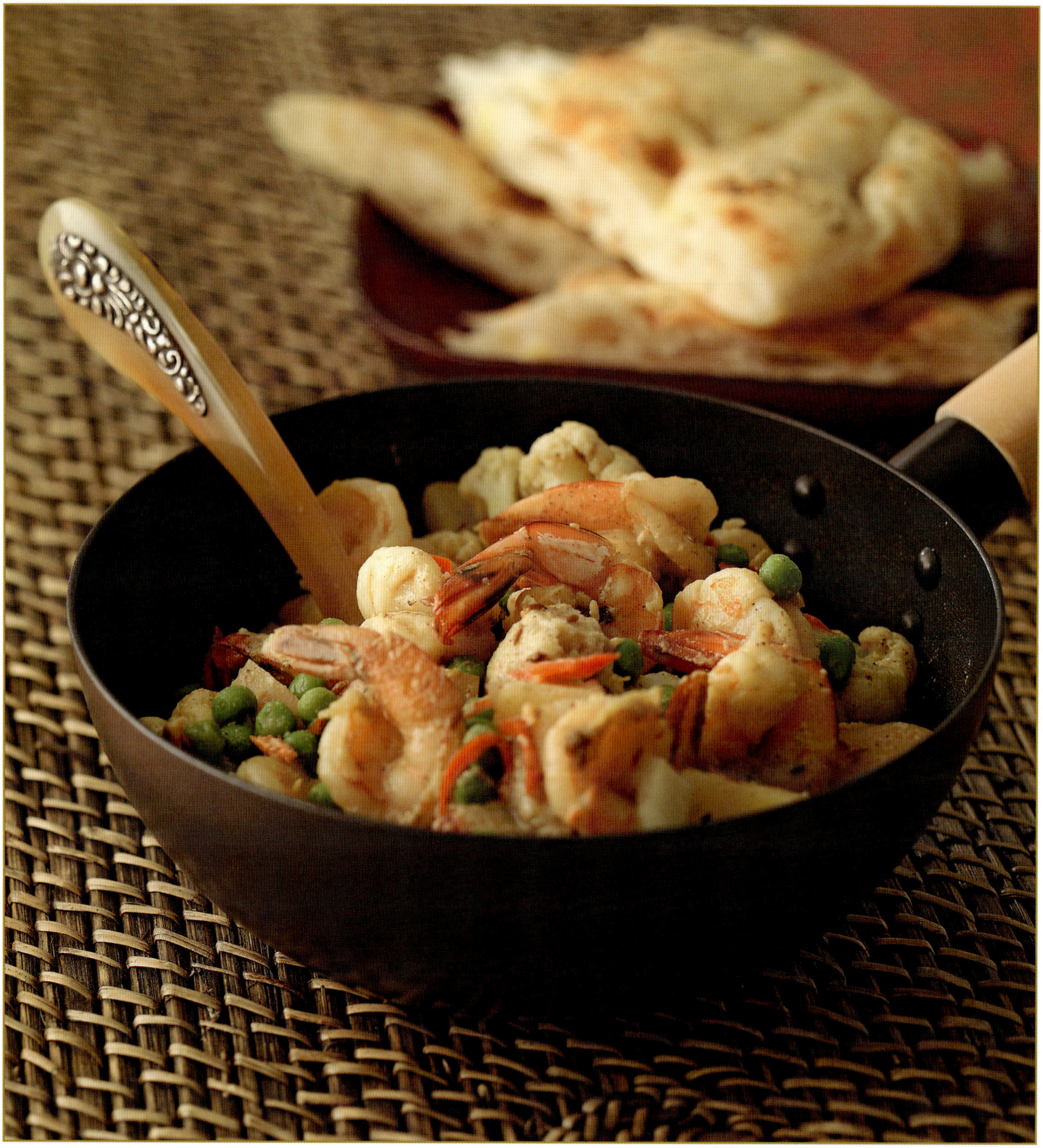

Prawn korma

500 g green (raw) prawns, shelled and deveined

1/3 teaspoon ground turmeric

about 1/2 teaspoon salt

1 tablespoon freshly squeezed lemon juice

1 teaspoon cumin seeds

2 tablespoons ghee or oil

2 teaspoons grated fresh ginger

1 mild fresh red chilli, deseeded and finely chopped

150 g cauliflower, broken into small florets

1 medium-sized potato, diced

1/2 cup creamy yoghurt

1/2 cup peas

1 1/2 teaspoons garam masala (page 16)

Rinse and dry the prawns and place in a bowl with the turmeric, salt and lemon juice. Mix, and leave for 10 minutes to marinate.

In a frying pan or saucepan without oil, dry-roast the cumin seeds over medium heat for about 1 minute, until fragrant. Add ghee or oil, ginger and chilli, and fry for 1 minute, then stir in the prawns and their marinade and stir over high heat for about 2 minutes, until the prawns are pink and firm. Transfer the prawns to a plate and set aside.

Add cauliflower and potato to pan and stir until coated with oil. Add yoghurt, a little more salt, and water to almost cover the vegetables. Bring to the boil, reduce heat and simmer for about 10 minutes, until potatoes are almost tender. Add peas and cook for a further 3 minutes.

Return the prawns to the pan, stir in garam masala and simmer gently for a few more minutes. Check seasoning, and serve.

SERVES 4

Prawn & onion vindaloo

Vindaloos are usually fiercely hot and slightly tart, although the sweetness of the onions tempers this version a little.

500 g shelled green (raw) prawns
2 teaspoons grated fresh ginger
1½–2 tablespoons vindaloo paste (page 11)
2 teaspoons white vinegar
1 teaspoon tamarind concentrate
2 tablespoons ghee or oil
2 medium-sized onions, thinly sliced
½ teaspoon fennel seeds, lightly crushed
salt
2 tablespoons chopped fresh coriander

Place prawns in a bowl and add the ginger, vindaloo paste, vinegar, tamarind and 2–3 tablespoons water. Mix well and set aside.

Heat the ghee or oil in a saucepan and cook the onions until well browned (about 12 minutes), stirring frequently. Remove to a plate.

Add fennel seeds, prawns and marinade to the pan and cook over high heat for about 2 minutes, stirring and turning continually, until prawns have changed colour and begun to firm.

Return onions to pan, add water to barely cover and simmer for about 8 minutes, until thickened, seasoning to taste with salt. Stir in the coriander just before serving.

SERVES 4

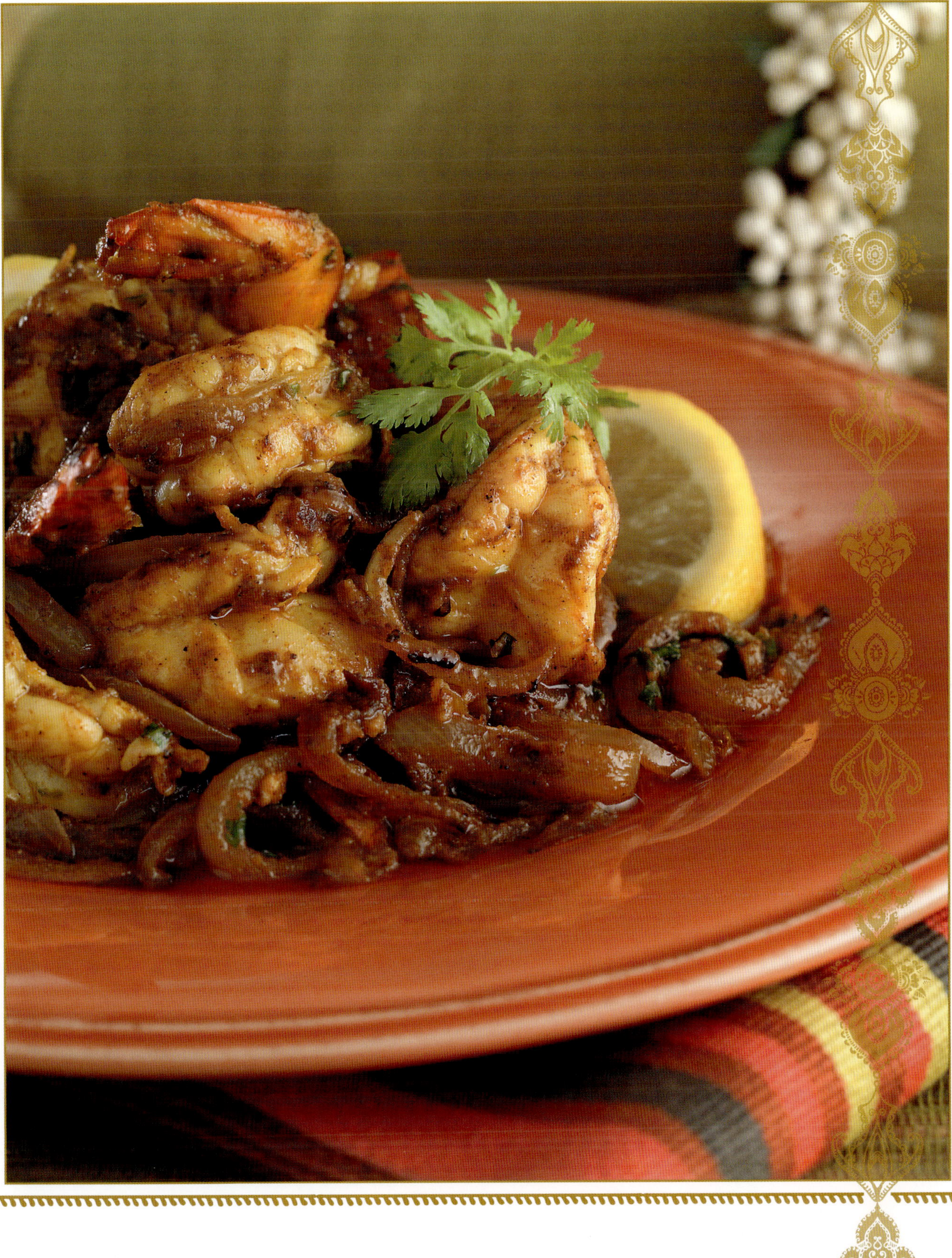

Prawn & vegetable Balti stir-fry

Balti curries are quick-cook dishes, so have all the ingredients measured and ready before you begin. These curries can be served with rice, but are best enjoyed with a piece of hot, spongy naan bread.

1½ tablespoons oil
12–16 green (raw) prawn cutlets
2 spring onions, sliced
¼ red capsicum, cut into small squares
¼ green capsicum, cut into small squares
1 small zucchini, sliced
2–3 thin slices fresh ginger, shredded
3 teaspoons Balti curry paste (page 13)
½ cup water or coconut milk
salt and pepper
freshly squeezed lemon juice, to taste

Heat the oil in a sauté pan or wok. When hot, stir-fry the prawns, vegetables and ginger for about 3 minutes, until the prawns have changed colour and curled up, and the vegetables have softened.

Add the curry paste to the pan and cook briefly, then add water or coconut milk, salt and pepper to taste, and a squeeze of lemon juice and simmer for 3–4 minutes.

SERVES 2

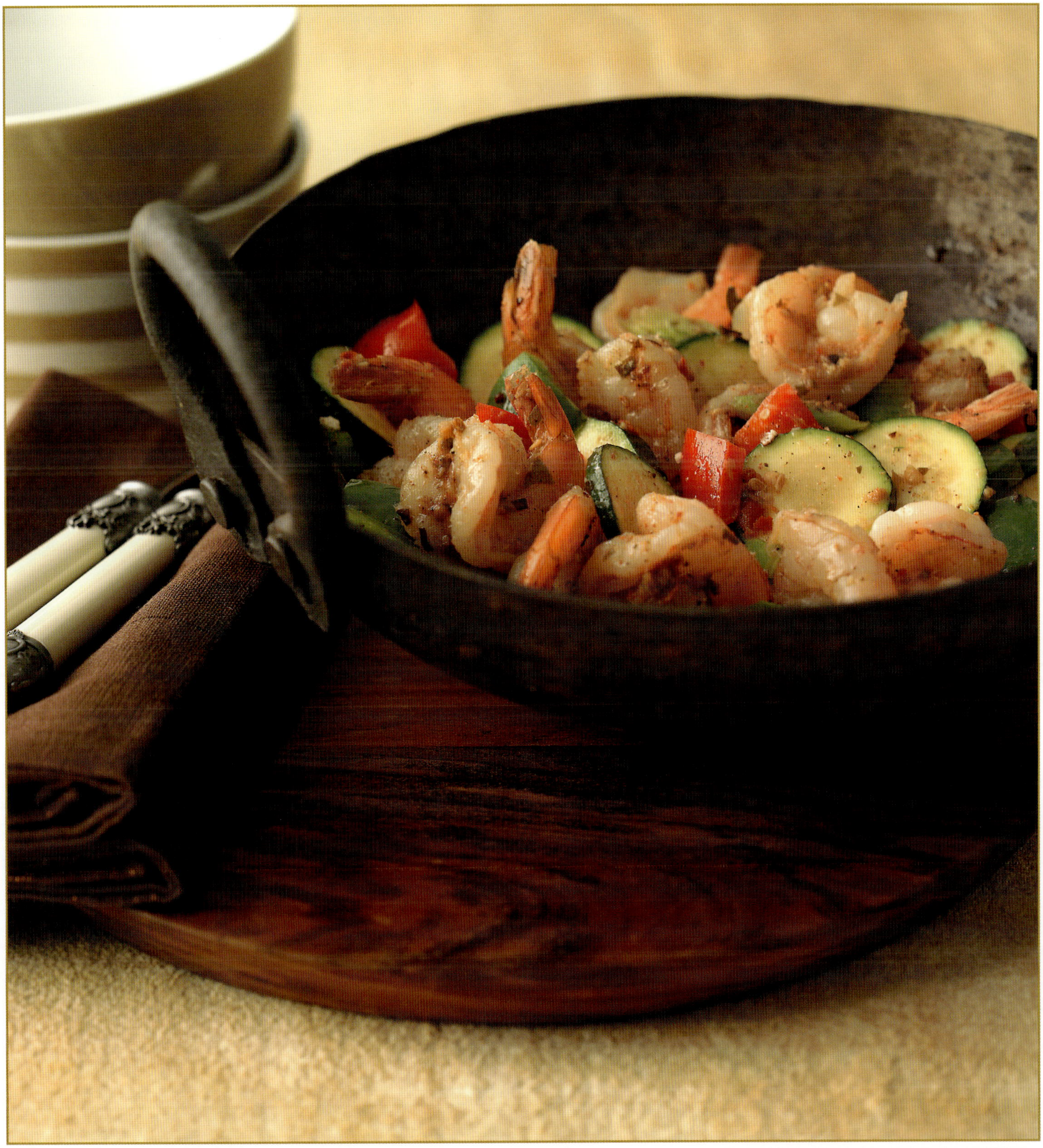

Prawns & Chinese cabbage in coconut milk

20 good-sized prawns, shelled but tails left on
½ cup sliced straw, button or oyster mushrooms
2 cups sliced Chinese cabbage (wombok)
2 spring onions, finely chopped
¾ teaspoon ground turmeric
1 clove garlic, crushed
1 teaspoon grated fresh ginger
¼–½ teaspoon sambal ulek or hot chilli paste
1 × 400-ml can coconut milk
salt and pepper
1 tablespoon oil
½ teaspoon fennel seeds
½ teaspoon cumin seeds

Combine all the ingredients, except the oil and spice seeds, in a saucepan and bring to the boil. Reduce to a simmer and cook gently for about 8 minutes. Check seasoning, adjusting salt and pepper to taste, then transfer to a serving dish.

In a small pan fry the spice seeds in the oil until they begin to pop and sputter. Pour quickly over the curry, and serve.

SERVES 4

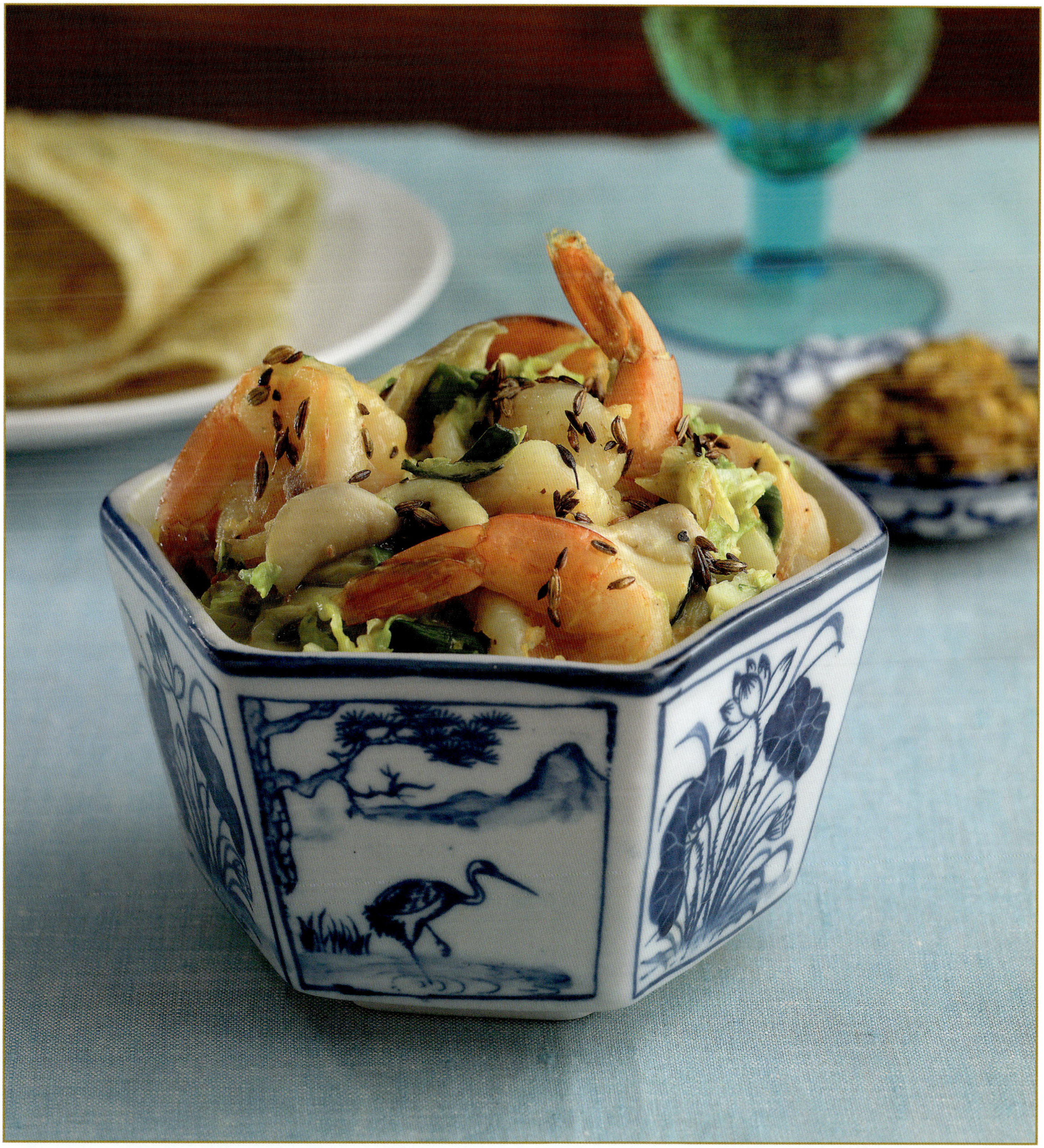

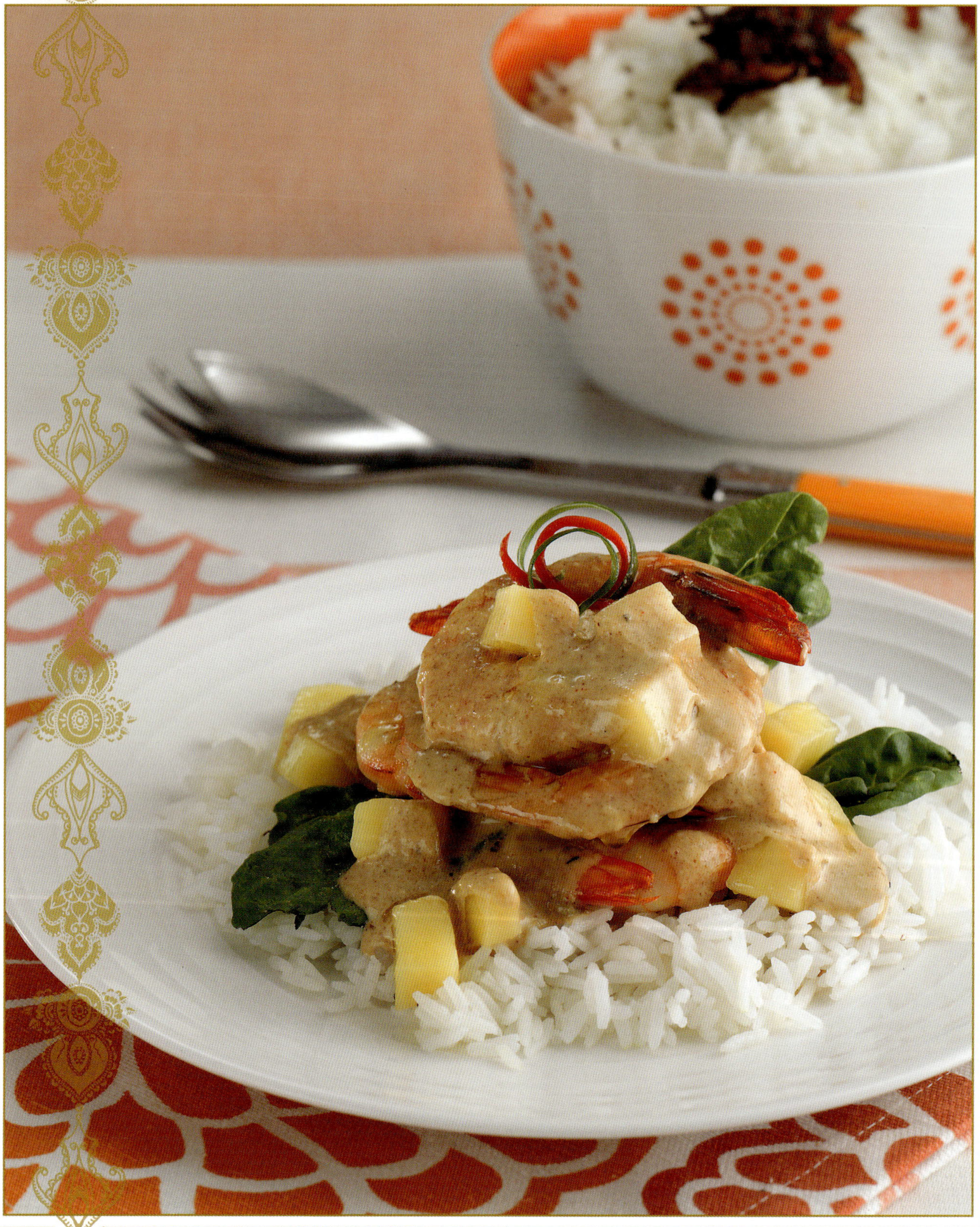

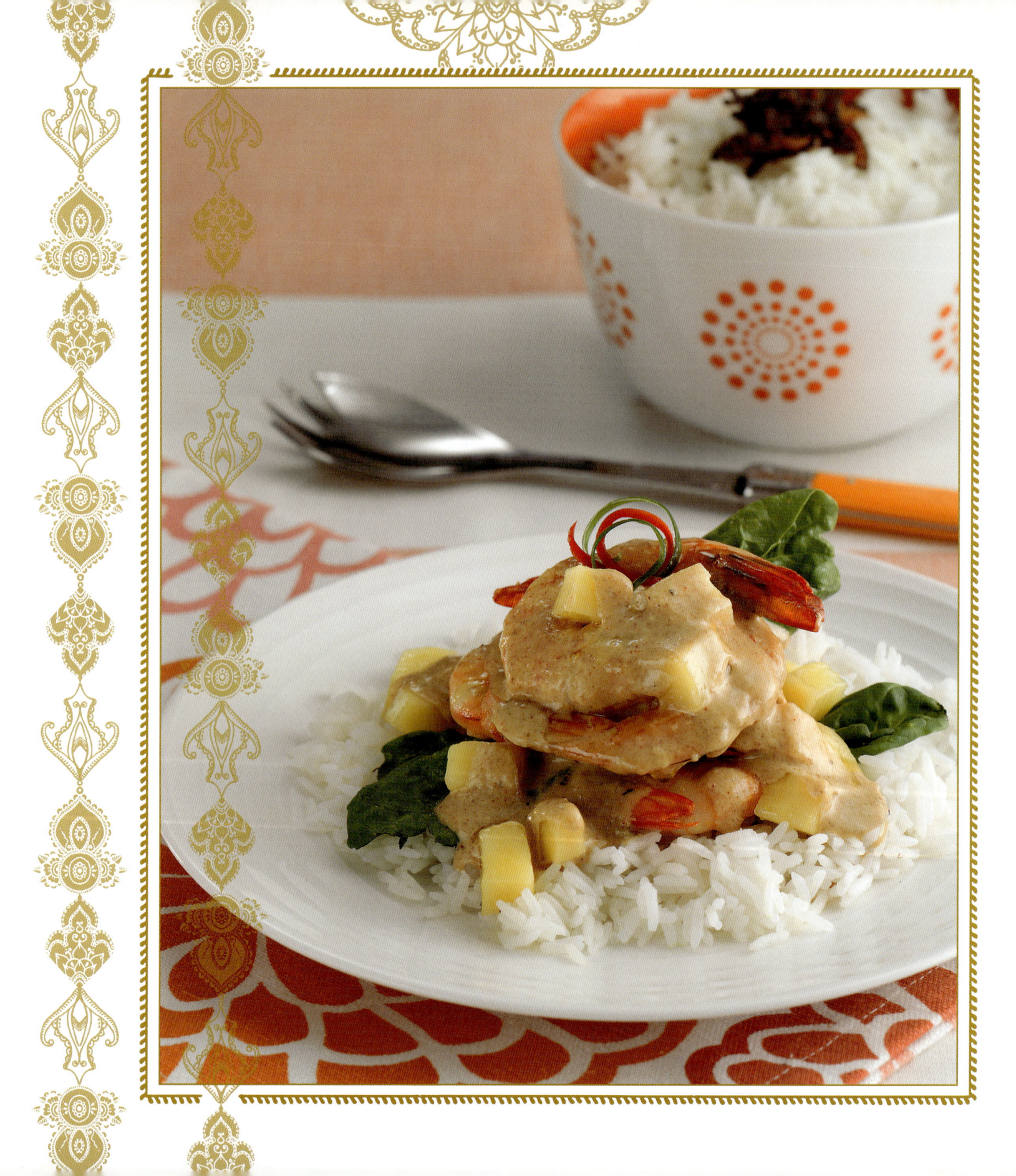

Prawn & mango curry

1 cup desiccated coconut
1 tablespoon ground coriander
1 teaspoon ground cumin
1 teaspoon hot curry powder
1 teaspoon ground sweet paprika
¾ teaspoon ground turmeric
1 large onion, roughly chopped
2½ tablespoons ghee or oil
8–10 curry leaves
salt and white pepper
500 g green (raw) prawn cutlets
1 large, slightly under-ripe mango, flesh cut into 1.5-cm cubes
½ cup coconut cream
fresh coriander leaves for garnish

In a food processor or blender, grind the coconut to a powder. Add the coriander, cumin, curry powder, paprika and turmeric, mix well, and transfer to a bowl.

Purée onion in food processor, and strain liquid into the coconut and spices, adding enough cold water to make a thick paste. Reserve the onion pulp.

Heat a medium-sized saucepan and sauté the onion pulp in the ghee or oil for about 3 minutes. Add curry leaves and coconut spice paste and fry, stirring, for about 2 minutes, until fragrant. Add 1¾ cups water and bring to the boil. Season to taste with salt and pepper, and simmer for 5–6 minutes.

Add the prawns and mango to the pan and simmer gently for a further 5–6 minutes.

Check and adjust seasoning, stir in half the coconut cream and heat gently. Transfer to a serving bowl and garnish with the remaining coconut cream and the coriander leaves.

SERVES 4

Green prawn curry from south-western India

You can buy prepared prawn cutlets which have already been butterflied.

1 large bunch fresh coriander, rinsed and dried
3 spring onions, roughly chopped
1 clove garlic
a 1-cm piece fresh ginger
1 large hot green chilli, deseeded and roughly chopped
a 4-cm piece lemongrass, roughly chopped
1 × 400-ml can coconut milk or cream
3 tablespoons oil
16–24 butterflied green (raw) prawns
salt and pepper
sugar and freshly squeezed lemon juice, to taste

Chop the coriander roughly and place in a blender or food processor with the spring onions, garlic, ginger, chilli and lemongrass. Grind to a paste, moistening with 2–3 tablespoons of the coconut milk or cream.

Heat the oil in a non-stick pan and fry the prawns for about 3 minutes, until pink and firm. Remove to a plate using a slotted spoon, and set aside.

Add the herb paste to the pan and fry, stirring, for 2 minutes. Add the remaining coconut milk or cream and simmer for another 5 minutes or so. Season to taste with salt and pepper, a pinch of sugar and a generous squeeze of lemon juice, and then return the prawns to gently warm in the sauce.

SERVES 3–4

Sri Lankan prawn curry

16 large prawns in the shell
1 large onion, roughly chopped
3 cloves garlic, peeled
1 large fresh hot red chilli, deseeded and roughly chopped
4 tablespoons coconut oil or vegetable oil
8 curry leaves
⅓ teaspoon fenugreek seeds
4 teaspoons ground coriander
2 teaspoons ground cumin
1 teaspoon ground chilli
2 teaspoons Sri Lankan roasted curry spices (page 14)
¾ teaspoon salt
1½ teaspoons ground sweet paprika
½ teaspoon ground turmeric
¾ cup coconut cream
fresh dill sprigs

Shell the prawns (leave tails on) and devein them. Nestle two prawns together, curving into each other to form a round shape. Do this with the remaining prawns to make 8 pairs, then set aside.

Place prawn shells in a food processor or blender with 1 cup water and process until well puréed. Pass through a sieve into a bowl, pressing through as much of the pink-grey juice as possible, and set aside.

Grind onion, garlic and chilli in the food processor or blender until very well chopped.

Heat 2 tablespoons of the oil in a heavy pan and fry curry leaves and fenugreek seeds for 1 minute, stirring. Add the onion purée and cook, stirring almost continually, until the liquid has dried up and the onion is lightly golden (about 3 minutes). Stir in the ground coriander, cumin and chilli, and mix well, frying for a few minutes. Add the prawn-shell liquid to the pan and bring to the boil. Simmer for about 5 minutes, stirring occasionally, and then add the coconut cream.

In another pan heat the remaining oil. Fry the prawn pairs for about 2 minutes on each side, until cooked. Pour the coconut sauce over and simmer for a few minutes, then carefully lift out the prawns in their pairs. Stack two pairs together on each plate, layered with a few sprigs of dill. Spoon some sauce over, and serve.

SERVES 4

Scallops in red curry sauce

- 1 × 400-ml can coconut cream
- 1 tablespoon Thai red curry paste (page 17)
- 4 teaspoons palm sugar or soft brown sugar
- 1½–2 tablespoons fish sauce
- 6 kaffir lime leaves
- 400 g large scallops
- 1–2 tablespoons oil
- 20 basil leaves
- 1 fresh red chilli, deseeded and shredded

Pour ½ cup of the coconut cream into a saucepan and bring to the boil, reduce heat and simmer for about 5 minutes until oil begins to separate out. Add curry paste and stir together until very fragrant (about 2 minutes), then add the sugar, fish sauce, lime leaves and remaining coconut cream with ½ cup water. Simmer gently for 5–6 minutes.

Heat a non-stick pan and add the oil. Fry scallops briefly over high heat, turning once or twice, until well browned on the surface and almost cooked. Transfer them to the curry sauce and simmer for just a few minutes. Check seasonings, stir in basil leaves and chilli, and serve at once.

SERVES 4

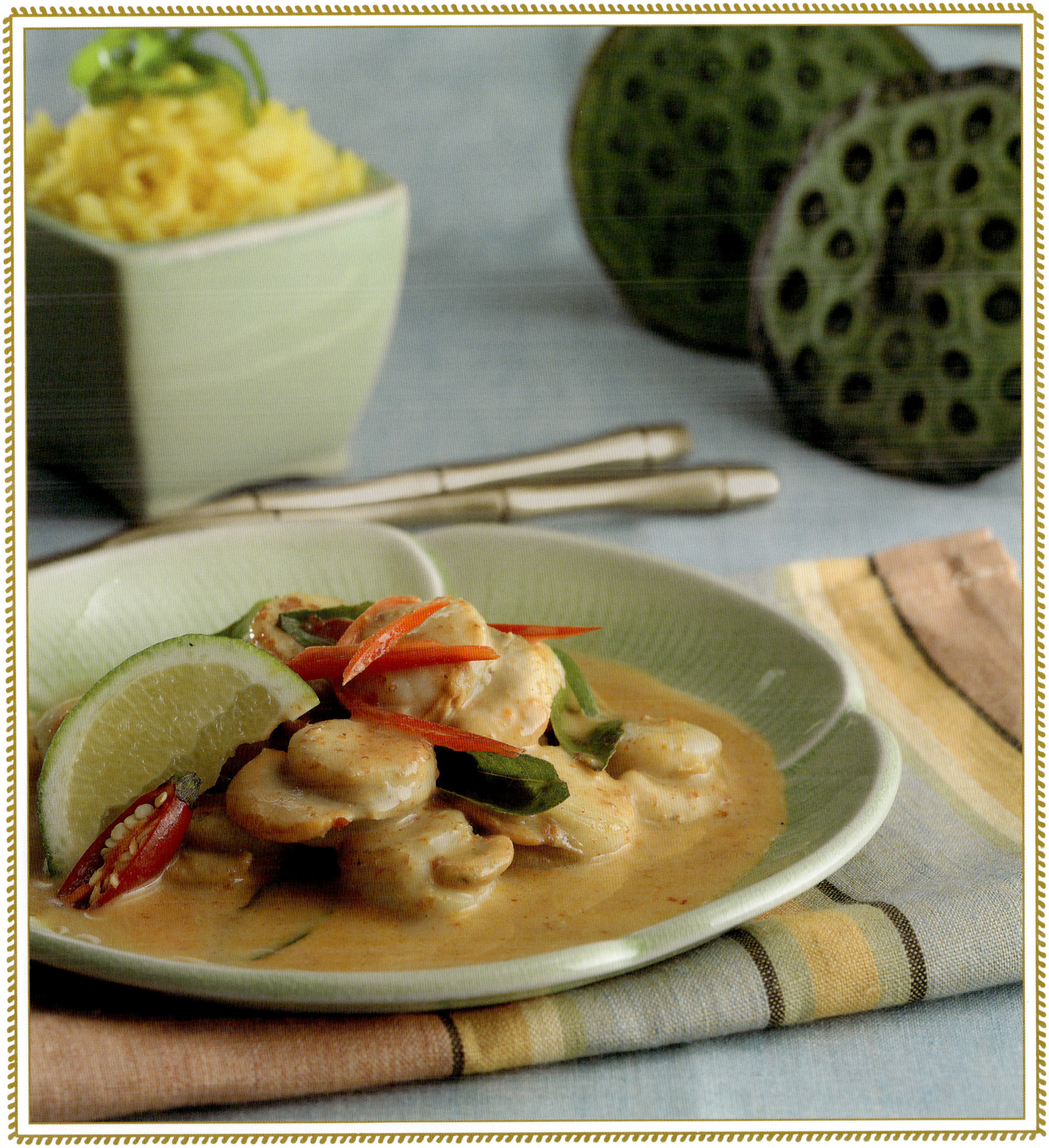

Scallops in creamy masala

400 g large scallops, preferably with roe on
1 small onion, finely chopped
½ teaspoon grated fresh ginger
1 large garlic clove, crushed
2½ tablespoons ghee
1 teaspoon garam masala (page 16)
1 teaspoon sweet paprika
½ cup pouring cream
chopped fresh coriander or dill

Rinse and drain the scallops and set aside.

In a non-stick pan heat the ghee and sauté onions, ginger and garlic for 3 minutes on medium heat, stirring often.

Add paprika and garam masala and the scallops and cook gently, turning several times, until the scallops firm up and turn white, about 2 minutes.

Add the cream with salt and pepper to taste and simmer gently for a few minutes, and then stir in coriander or dill.

SERVES 4–5

Tangy curry of scallops, prawns & fish balls with spinach

½ onion, finely chopped
1 large clove garlic, crushed
1½ teaspoons grated fresh ginger
2 tablespoons oil
2–4 teaspoons Thai green curry paste (page 18)
500 g mixed seafood (scallops, shelled prawns, fish or squid balls)
¾ cup tomato pasta sauce
400 ml coconut cream (or cream)
2 cups chopped fresh spinach or silverbeet leaves
½ teaspoon lightly crushed fennel seeds
salt and black pepper
fish sauce and freshly squeezed lemon juice to taste

Sauté the onion, garlic and ginger in the oil for 2–3 minutes until lightly coloured. Add curry paste and cook briefly, and then add the seafood and sauté for 1–2 minutes, stirring gently.

Add the tomato sauce, coconut cream or cream, spinach or silverbeet, fennel, salt and pepper, and cook gently for about 8 minutes, stirring from time to time. Season to taste with fish sauce and lemon juice.

Serve with steamed jasmine rice.

SERVES 3–4

Thai yellow seafood curry

1 × 400-ml can coconut cream
1 stem lemongrass, cut lengthways in half
3 very thin slices fresh ginger
1 fresh hot red or green chilli, deseeded and cut in half
2 teaspoons mild curry powder or paste
3 teaspoons Thai yellow curry paste (page 20)
½ red capsicum, cut into thin strips
2 spring onions, cut into 3-cm lengths
220 g firm white fish, cut into cubes
12 medium-sized green (raw) prawns, butterflied
12 small squid rings
fish sauce, salt and white pepper
freshly squeezed lime juice

In a medium-sized saucepan bring half the coconut cream to the boil. Reduce heat, add lemongrass, ginger, chilli and curry powder or paste, and simmer for about 3 minutes, stirring occasionally.

Add the remaining coconut cream to the pan with ½ cup water and the capsicum and spring onions. Bring to the boil, reduce heat to medium and simmer for 2 minutes.

Add the fish and prawns, and simmer for about 4 minutes, until barely tender. Stir in the squid rings, season to taste with fish sauce, salt, pepper and lime juice, and cook for about 1 minute.

SERVES 4

Quick creamy curried crab meat

A versatile creamy curry to serve as a main course over rice, or as a snack on toast or in a bread roll. It also makes a delicious filling for vol-au-vents, or a dip with crackers or toast. You can substitute canned tuna for the crab meat.

2 eggs
200 g canned or cooked fresh crab meat
1 small onion, finely chopped
2 tablespoons butter
1 clove garlic, crushed
2 teaspoons mild curry powder
1 tablespoon plain flour
salt and pepper
1⅓ cups milk (or use half milk, half cream)
chopped fresh dill, chervil or parsley
squeeze of lemon juice

Place eggs in a saucepan of cold water to cover and bring slowly to the boil. Reduce heat and simmer for 8 minutes to hard-boil.

Pick over the crab meat to remove any fragments of shell and break up any clumps.

In a small pan sweat the onion in butter over lowish heat for about 5 minutes, until soft but not coloured. Add the garlic, and sprinkle curry powder and flour evenly over the onions. Season with salt and pepper, and stir over medium heat for about 1½ minutes, until lightly cooked. Pour in half the milk (or milk and cream) and stir slowly until the sauce thickens and comes to the boil, then add the remaining milk and simmer gently for about 4 minutes, stirring occasionally.

Shell the eggs and chop finely. Stir eggs and crab meat into sauce and heat gently, stirring. Fold in the herbs, check seasonings, add a squeeze of fresh lemon juice, and serve.

SERVES 2–3

Crab stir-fried with curry spices

In many of Thailand's outdoor food markets, you can choose your own live fish and shellfish from huge, bubbling tanks stocked from local fish farms in the Andaman Ocean. The seafood is usually cooked simply, as in this recipe. Bugs split down the centre, or big fresh prawns in their shells, are also terrific done this way.

2 sand or spanner crabs, or 1 mud crab
1½ tablespoons oil
1 clove garlic, chopped
1 tablespoon mild curry powder
4 spring onions (white parts and half of the greens), chopped
salt and fish sauce

Use a cleaver or heavy knife to quarter the crabs. Trim off and rinse out the inedible bits, then drain well.

Heat the oil in a wok until smoking, add crab and garlic, and toss energetically over a high flame for a few minutes. The crab shells will redden, and the meat turn white and firm up. Sprinkle with curry powder and cook briefly, then lift crabs onto a serving plate.

Add spring onions to the hot pan and move them around to gather up the spices. Add just enough water to make a drizzle of sauce, and season with salt and/or fish sauce. Return the crabs to the wok to coat them with the sauce, and serve.

SERVES 2–4

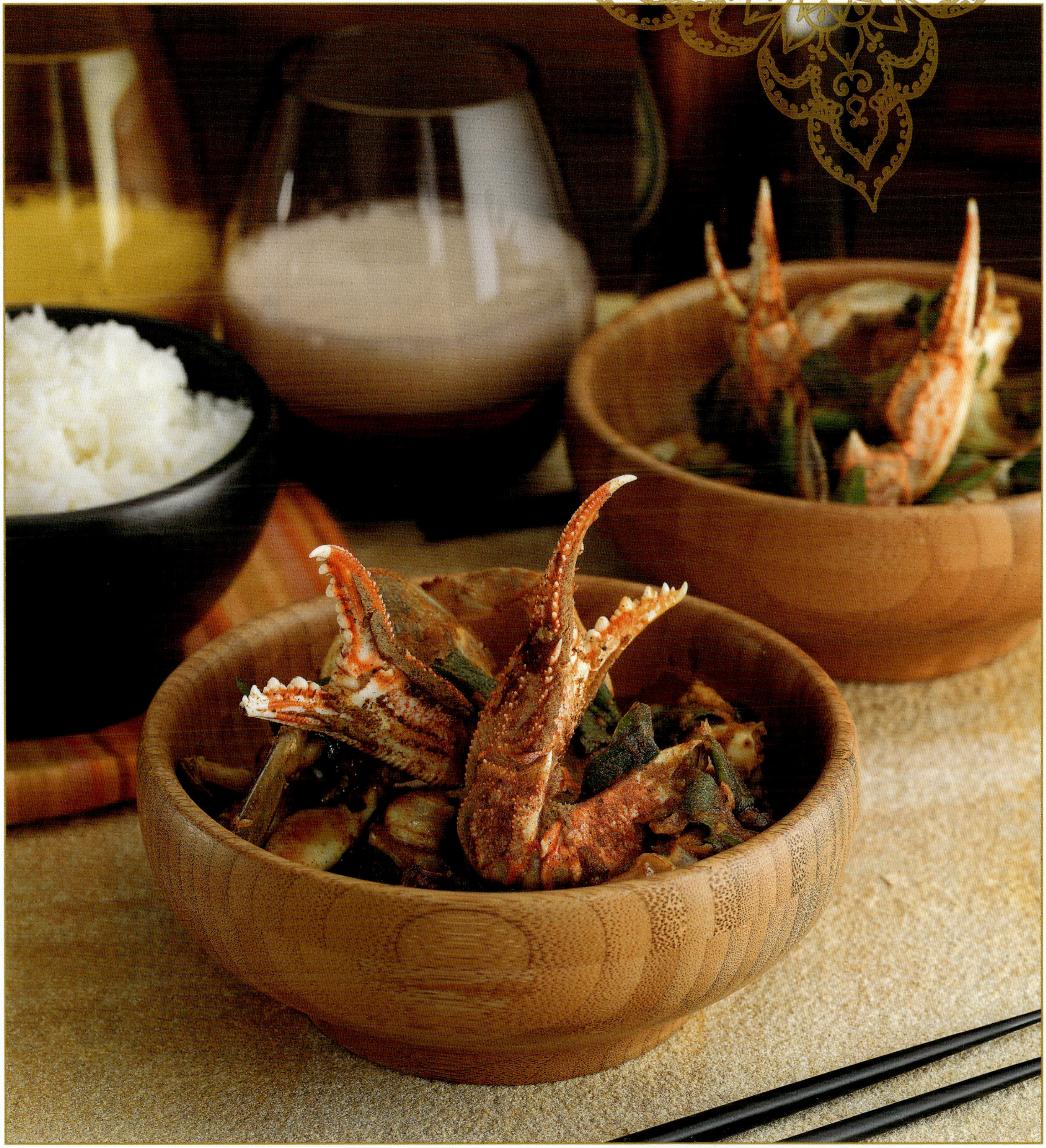

Crayfish in a creamy curry

Crayfish is a luxury for most of us, so when we indulge we want to make the most of it. This mildly spiced but rich curry sauce accentuates its succulence.

2 medium-sized fresh crayfish tails
3 tablespoons butter or oil
1 leek (white part only), very finely chopped
½ cup finely chopped bulb fennel or celery
2–3 teaspoons mild curry powder
½ teaspoon fennel seeds, lightly crushed
1 tablespoon plain flour
¾ cup fish stock
½ cup thick cream
1 small tomato, deseeded and diced
salt and white pepper
chopped fresh dill

Cut the crayfish into 1.5-cm thick medallions and lightly brown in 2 tablespoons of the butter or oil. Remove to a plate.

Add the remaining butter to the pan and gently sauté the leek and fennel or celery for about 3½ minutes, until softened and only very lightly coloured. Sprinkle curry powder, fennel seeds and flour evenly over the vegetables and stir to absorb the butter. Cook, stirring, for 1 minute, then add the stock and simmer for about 5 minutes, stirring often.

Stir in the cream and tomato, season to taste with salt and pepper, and add the crayfish. Simmer very gently until crayfish is cooked (about 3 minutes). Check seasoning, and add chopped dill just before serving.

SERVES 2–4

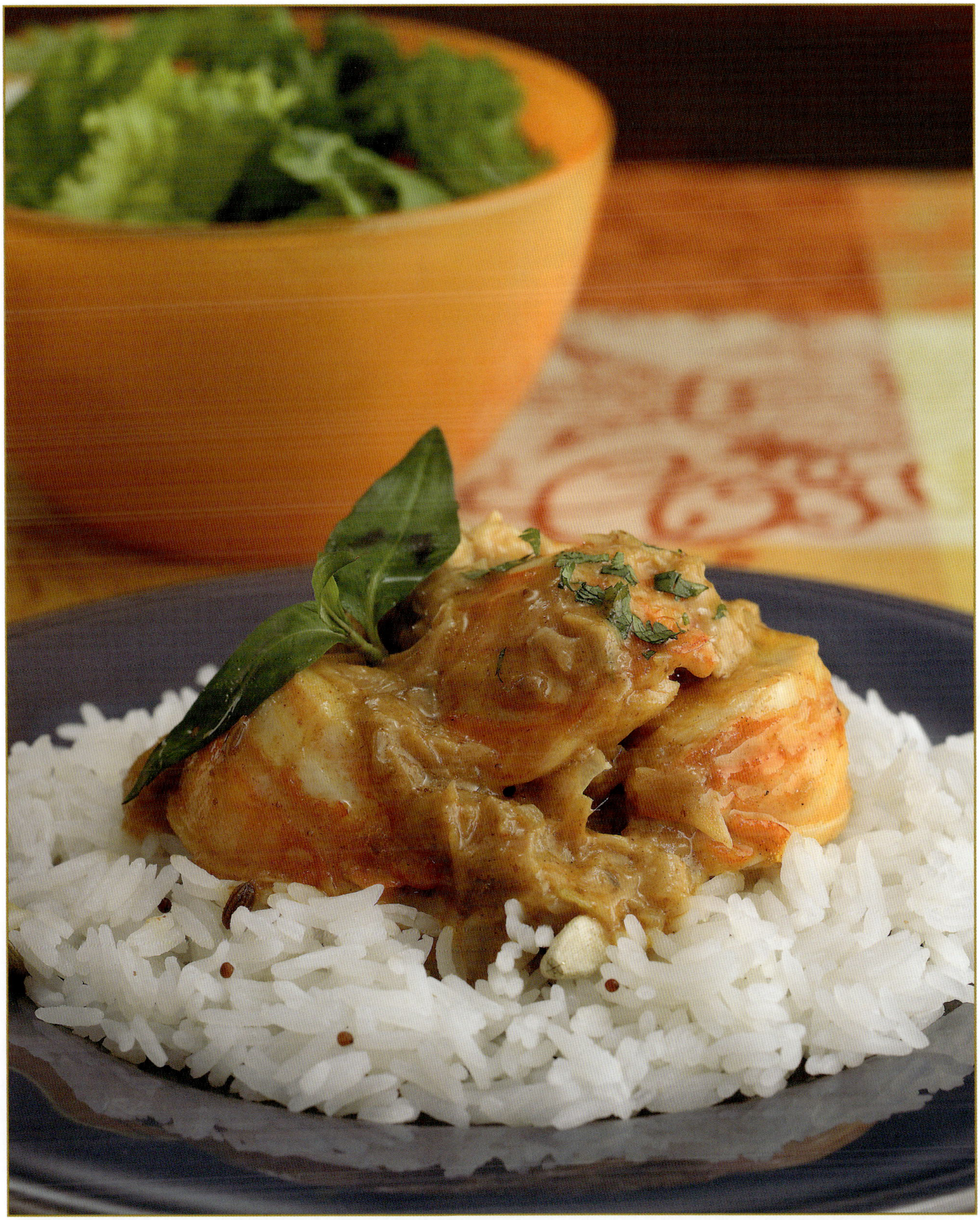

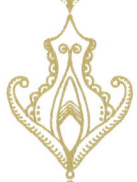

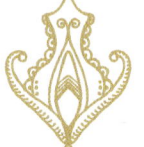

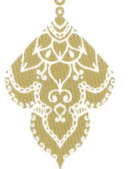

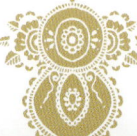

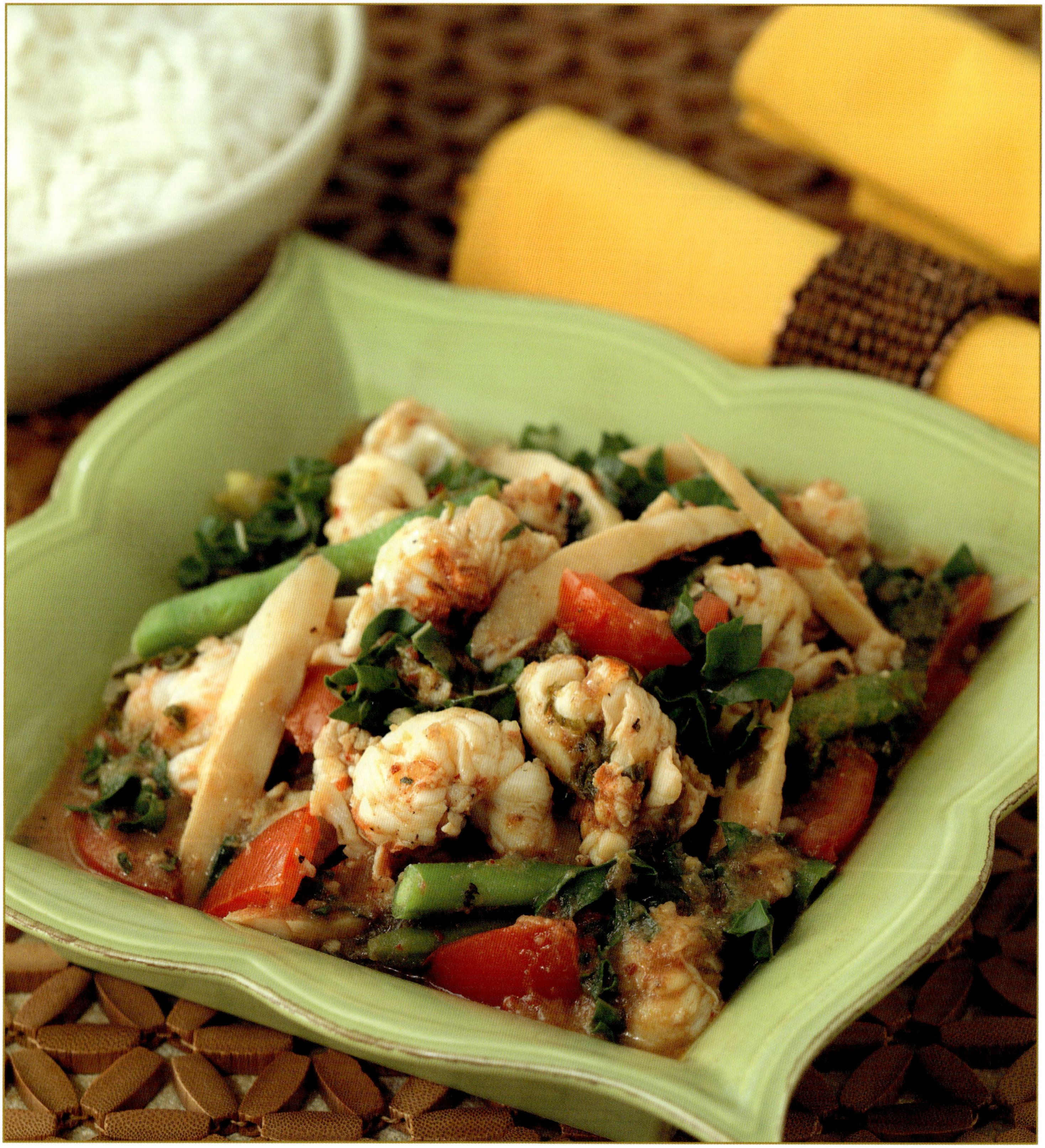

Thai sour orange curry of bug tails & vegetables

Tart curry sauces based on tamarind suit seafood of all kinds. Mussels in the shell, large prawns or chunks of fresh white or pink fish, could replace the bug tails in this recipe.

- 6–8 Moreton Bay or Balmain bug tails
- 2 tablespoons finely chopped shallots
- 3 dried red chillies, deseeded and soaked in hot water for 20 minutes
- 1½ teaspoons shrimp paste
- 3 teaspoons grated fresh galangal (or use ginger)
- 1 tablespoon tamarind concentrate
- 1 teaspoon white sugar or palm sugar
- 2 cups fish stock
- 2 tomatoes, deseeded and diced
- 1 large silverbeet leaf (white stem included), finely shredded
- 6 baby bamboo shoots, diagonally sliced
- 6 green beans or 2 snake beans, diagonally sliced
- 2 spring onions, diagonally sliced
- ½ choko, peeled and cut into julienne strips (optional)
- fish sauce and/or salt to taste

Cut the bug tails in half lengthways. (If using prawns, shell them but leave the tails on.)

In a blender, food processor or mortar grind the shallots, chillies, shrimp paste and galangal or ginger to a paste, then mix in the tamarind and sugar.

Bring the stock to the boil in a wok or saucepan, stir in the shallot paste and simmer for 5 minutes. Add vegetables and simmer for 3–4 minutes, stirring occasionally.

Add bug tails to the sauce, with fish sauce and/or salt to taste, and simmer gently until all the ingredients are tender.

SERVES 2–4

Mussels in hot red curry

Mussels are wonderfully accepting of the intense flavours that characterise most Asian cuisines, particularly the spectacular citrusy, chilli-hot tastes of Thailand.

1 cup coconut cream
3 teaspoons Thai red curry paste (page 17)
¾ cup peas or sliced green beans
2 teaspoons finely shredded fresh ginger
2 fresh hot red or green chillies, deseeded and sliced
2 spring onions, chopped
4–6 cherry tomatoes, cut in half
600 g mussels on the half shell or 400 g shelled mussels
sugar, freshly squeezed lime juice and fish sauce or salt to taste
1 tablespoon finely shredded basil leaves

In a medium-sized saucepan heat half the coconut cream with the curry paste and simmer for 3–4 minutes. Add peas or beans, the ginger, chillies, spring onions and tomatoes, and bring barely to the boil. Reduce heat and simmer for about 4 minutes, until peas or beans are almost done.

Add mussels to pan and season to taste with sugar, lime juice and fish sauce or salt. Simmer for about 1 minute, stir in the basil and then serve.

SERVES 3–4

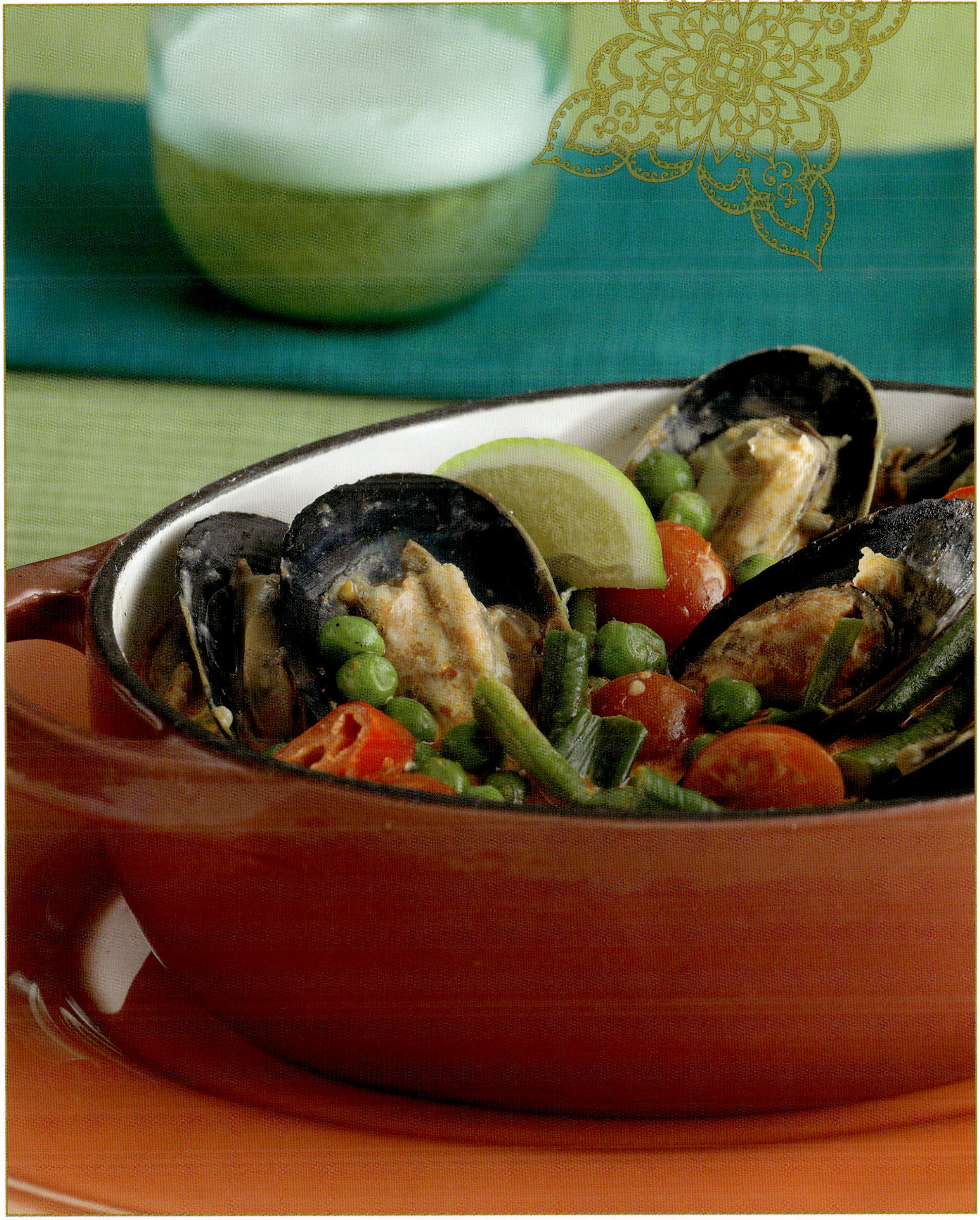

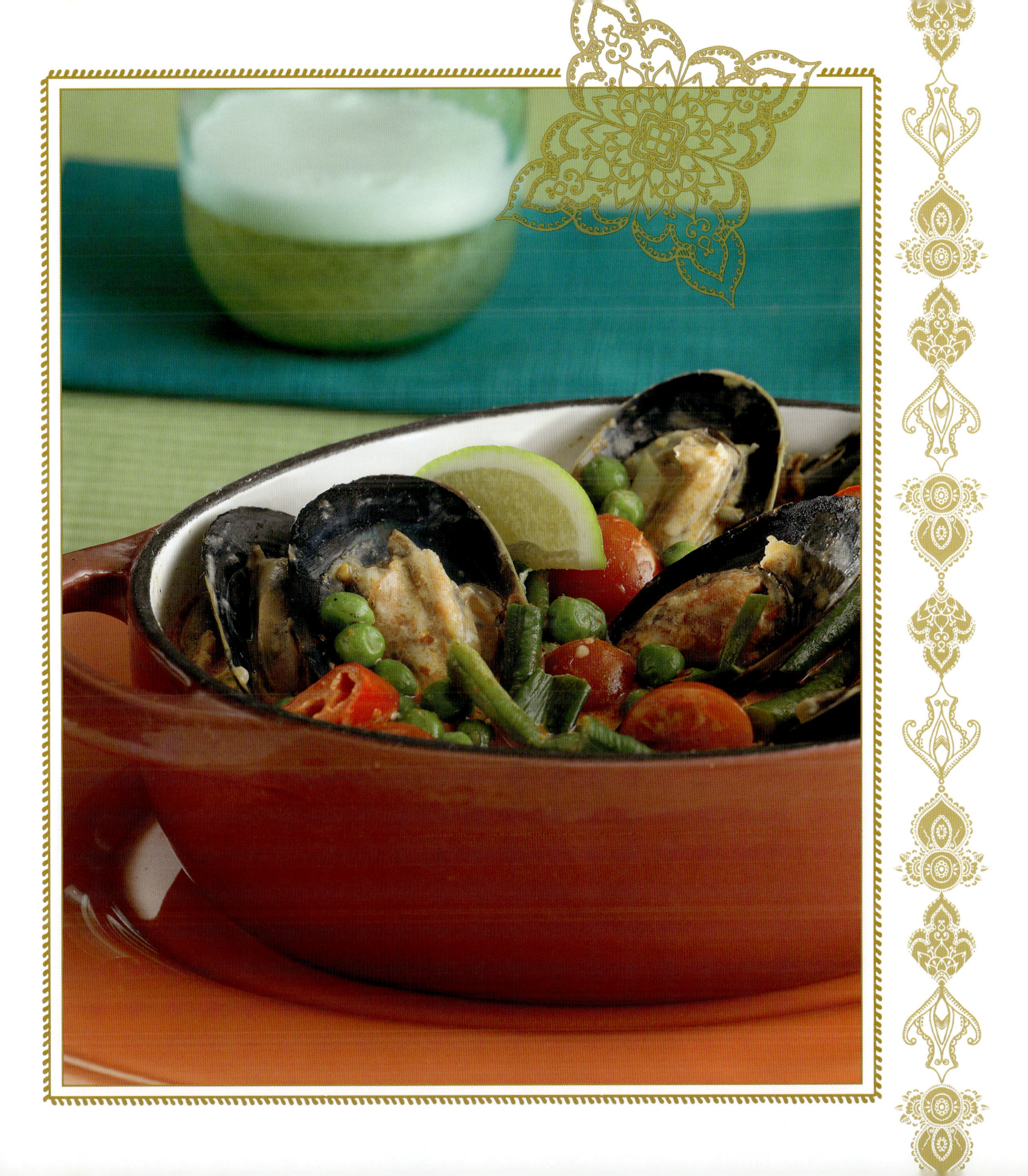

Yellow Thai curry of stuffed mussels

4 shallots, peeled
2 cloves garlic, peeled
3–4 sprigs fresh coriander
2 tablespoons fish sauce
2 tablespoons Thai yellow curry paste (page 20)
100 g pork or chicken mince
1 egg white
20 mussels on the half shell
1 × 400-ml can coconut milk
3 kaffir lime leaves
6–8 small fresh hot red or green chillies, deseeded
1½ teaspoons grated palm sugar
freshly squeezed lime juice to taste

Place shallots, garlic and coriander in a blender or food processor and grind to a smooth paste. Add 2 teaspoons of the fish sauce, 1 teaspoon of the curry paste, the mince and the egg white, and process to a smooth paste. Cover each mussel with a portion of this filling and smooth the tops.

In a wok heat ½ cup of the coconut milk with the remaining curry paste and simmer for 2–3 minutes, stirring. Add lime leaves, chillies, palm sugar, remaining coconut milk and about ½ cup water, and bring to the boil, stirring. Reduce heat, add the stuffed mussels and simmer for about 10 minutes.

Stir in remaining fish sauce and finish with a big squeeze of lime juice just before serving.

SERVES 4

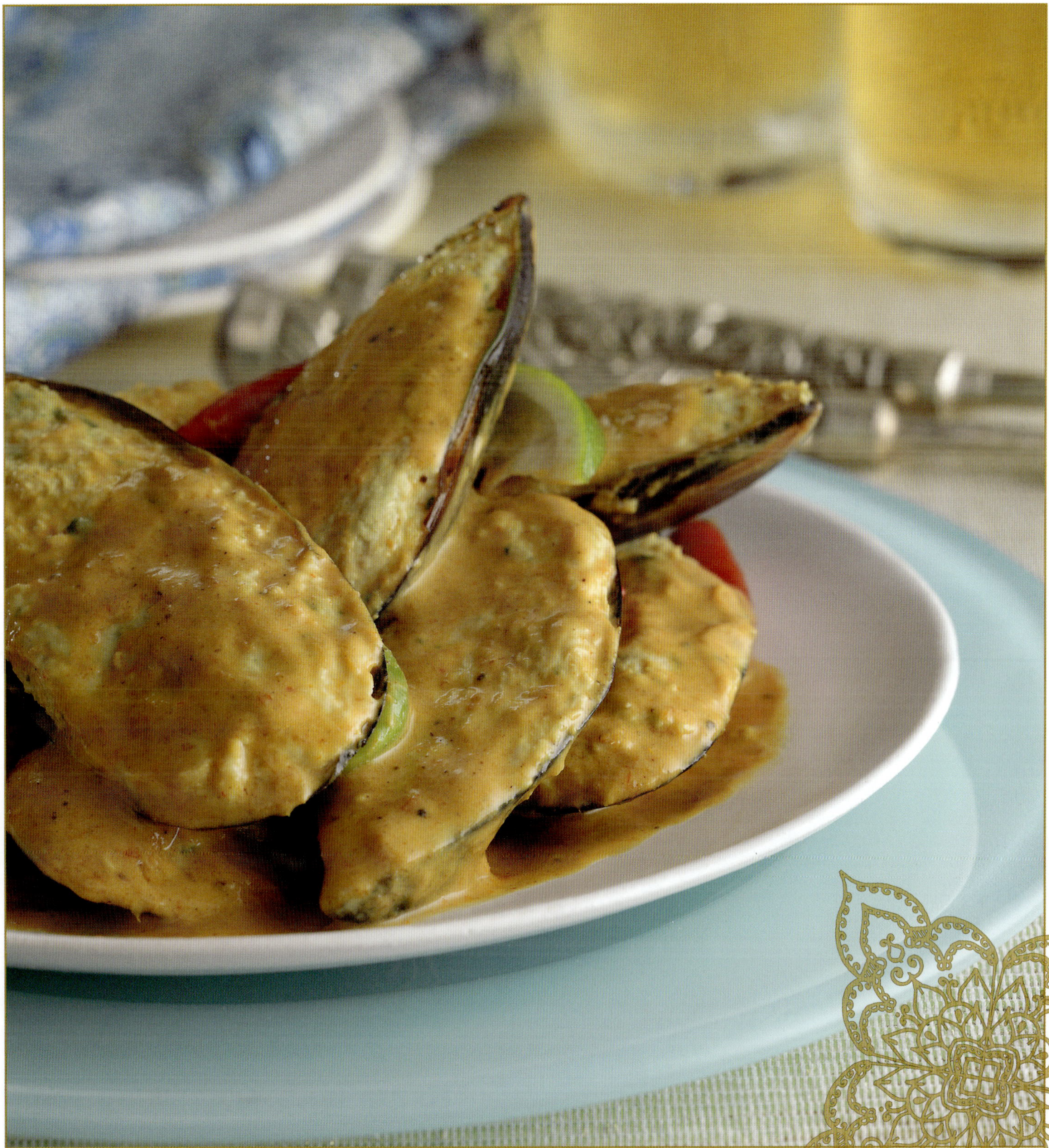

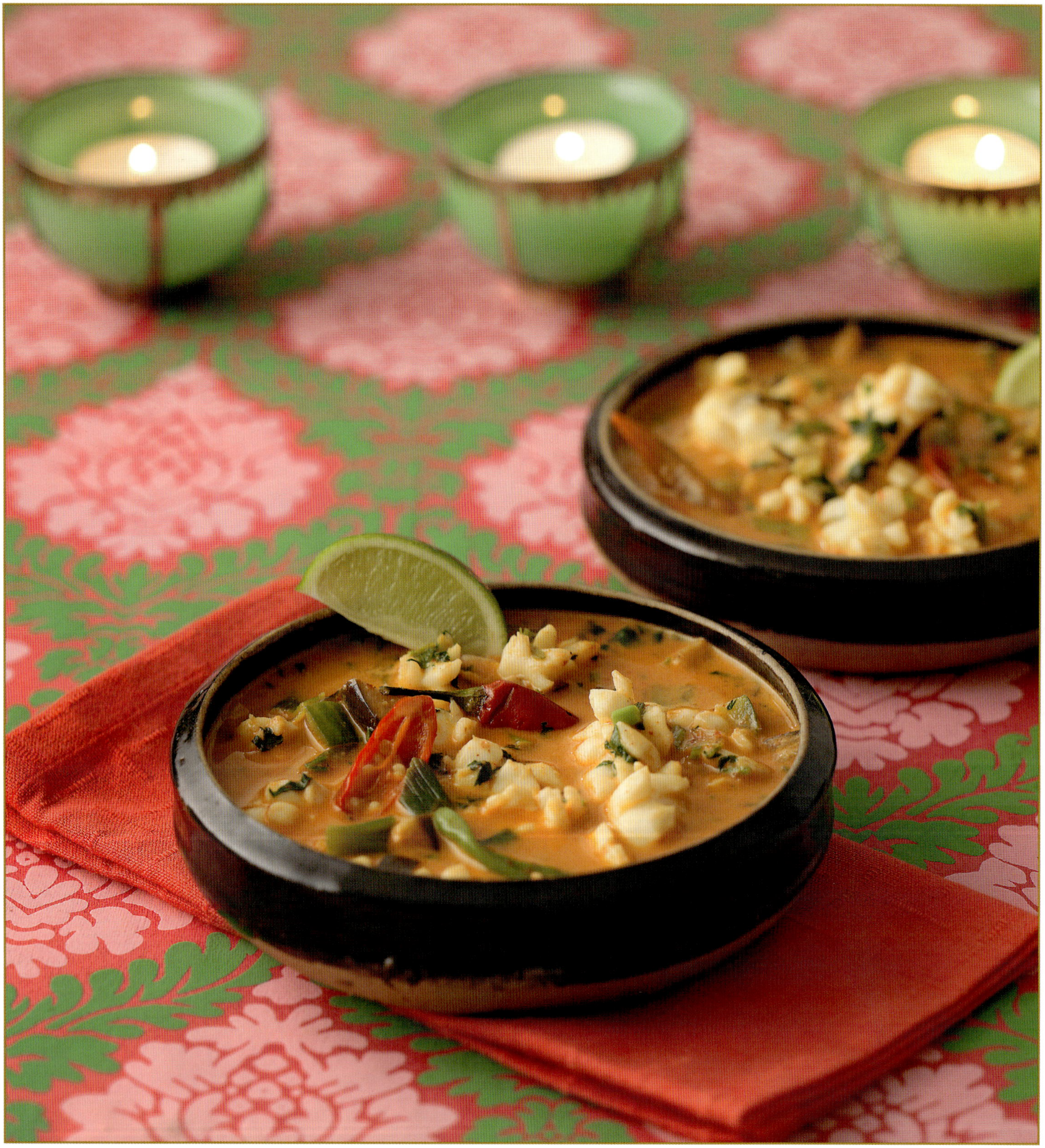

Thai red curry squid

This fiery red curry combines fresh chillies, pea-sized eggplants, tender squid and crunchy cucumber in an explosion of flavour, colour and texture.

2 large squid tubes (about 250g in total)
1½ tablespoons oil
1 tablespoon Thai red curry paste (page 17)
1½ teaspoons ground sweet paprika
¾ cup coconut cream
3–8 fresh bird's-eye chillies, deseeded if preferred
2 sprigs pea eggplants, or ¼ cup diced eggplant
2 spring onions, cut into 2-cm pieces
1 teaspoon palm sugar or soft brown sugar
2 tablespoons fish sauce
1¼ cups coconut milk
1 Lebanese cucumber, peeled, deseeded and diced
salt
chopped fresh coriander or whole basil leaves
1 lime, for squeezing

Cut open squid tubes and flatten out. With a sharp knife held at an angle, score the flesh closely, cutting about halfway through. Turn and score in the other direction to give a cross-hatch effect, then cut into pieces 5 cm × 4 cm.

Heat the oil in a saucepan and fry the curry paste for 1 minute. Add paprika and coconut cream, and simmer for 1½ minutes, stirring. Add chillies, eggplants, spring onions, sugar, fish sauce and coconut milk, and simmer for about 5 minutes.

Stir cucumber into curry mixture. Add salt to taste and simmer gently for 3 minutes. Add the squid pieces and cook just long enough for them to curl up and turn white (about 2 minutes). Stir in the coriander or basil, add a squeeze of lime juice, and reheat briefly before serving.

SERVES 4

Curried cuttlefish

You can use squid instead of cuttlefish. It would require only the very briefest cooking (1–2 minutes) in the hot sauce, or could be cooked slowly and gently in the same way as the cuttlefish.

350 g cleaned cuttlefish (or 3 large squid tubes)
1 medium-sized onion, coarsely chopped
a 2-cm piece fresh ginger, peeled
a 7-cm stem lemongrass, chopped
2–3 fresh hot red chillies, deseeded and chopped
2 cloves garlic, peeled
1 tablespoon ground almonds, raw cashews or macadamias
1 teaspoon ground black pepper
2 tablespoons mild curry powder
3 tablespoons oil
1 × 400-ml can coconut milk
1 sprig curry leaves
1 teaspoon fennel seeds, lightly crushed
salt

Cut the cuttlefish into thin strips and soak in cold water to remove any traces of ink.

In a food processor or blender grind the onion, ginger, lemongrass, chillies and garlic to a reasonably smooth paste. Add the ground nuts, the pepper, curry powder and oil, and continue to grind until quite smooth.

Transfer paste to a wok or saucepan and fry over medium heat, stirring almost continually, until very fragrant (about 4 minutes). Add the coconut milk, curry leaves and fennel seeds, with ¾ cup water and salt to taste, and bring to the boil. Reduce heat and simmer for 3 minutes, then add the cuttlefish and cook over low heat for 15–20 minutes, until tender and the sauce well reduced.

SERVES 4

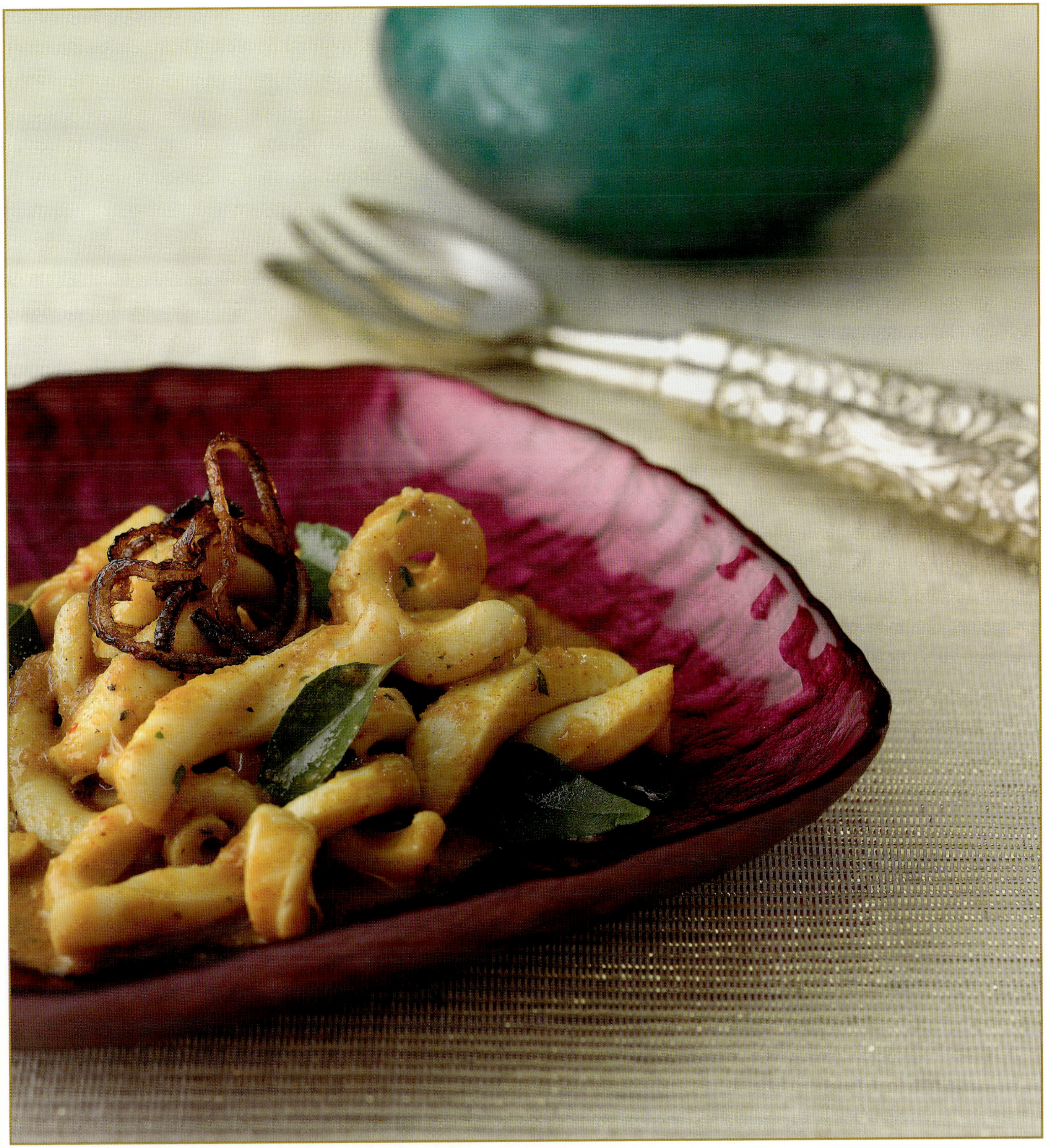

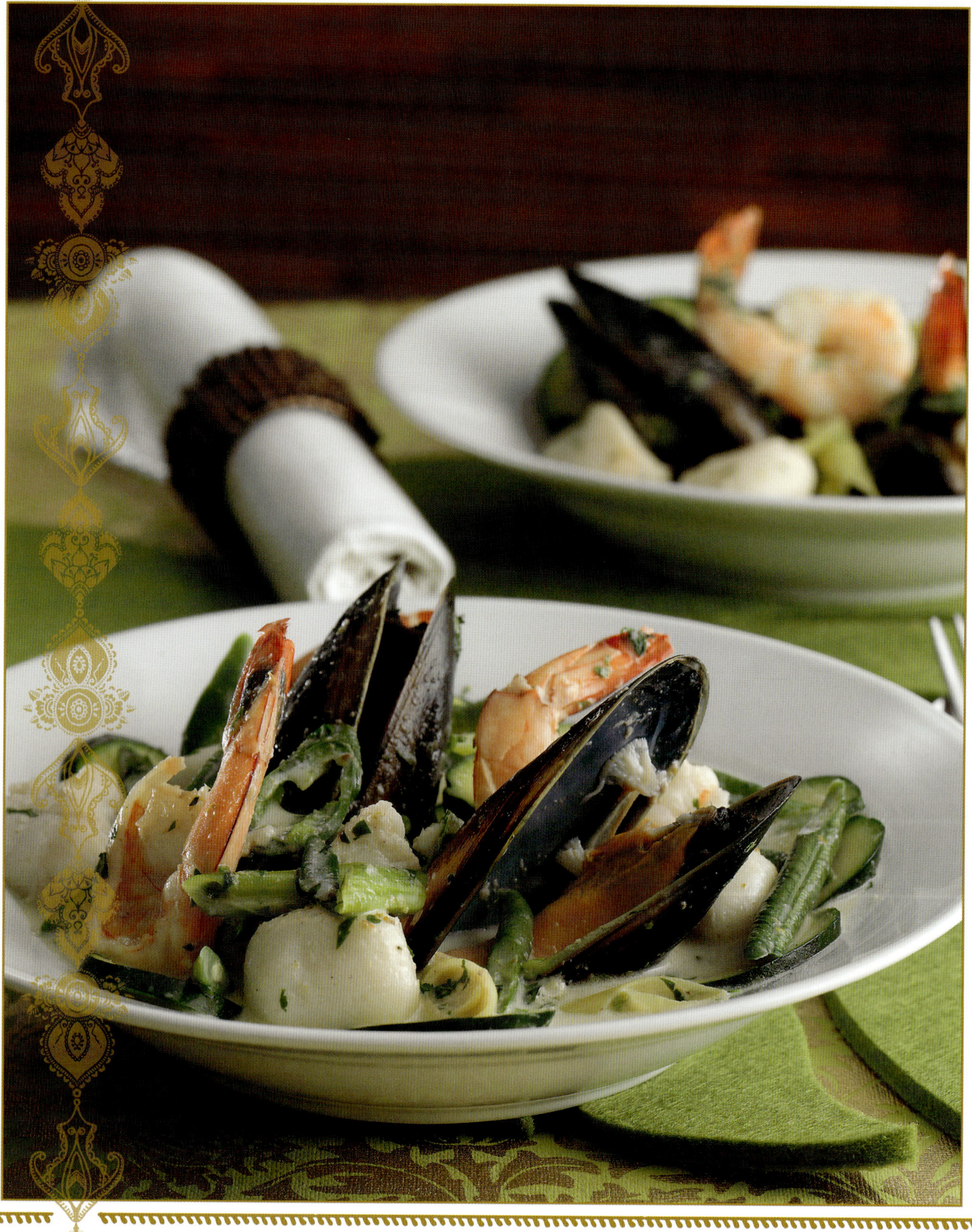

Thai chu-chi seafood curry

1 small zucchini, sliced
4–6 green beans, sliced diagonally
½ cup coconut cream
1–2 teaspoons Thai green curry paste (page 18)
1 stem lemongrass, cut into 3-cm lengths
2 kaffir lime leaves (optional)
1 small fresh hot green chilli, deseeded and roughly chopped
8 green (raw) peeled prawns, butterflied
4 frozen fish balls thawed
150 g firm white or pink fish, cubed
8 mussels on the half shell
50 g sliced bamboo shoots
2 spring onions, sliced at an angle
2–3 small sprigs green peppercorns in brine, drained
fish sauce, salt and sugar to taste
chopped fresh basil or coriander leaves

Parboil zucchini and beans in lightly salted water, then tip into a colander to drain.

In the same pan heat the coconut cream and cook for 2 minutes, then add the curry paste, lemongrass, lime leaves and chilli, and simmer for 2 minutes.

Add 1½ cups water to the pan and bring to the boil. Put in the zucchini, beans and seafood (except the mussels), bamboo shoots, spring onions, green peppercorns and 2–3 teaspoons fish sauce. Simmer gently for about 5 minutes, stirring occasionally, then add the mussels and cook for 2–3 minutes more, until seafood is tender.

Season to taste with salt, sugar and fish sauce, and stir in fresh herbs before serving.

SERVES 2–3

Singapore curry of seafood & okra

Fish and squid balls are convenient freezer items. They can be sliced into soups and curries, grilled to present on toothpicks as party finger food, and are indispensable to a lush curry laksa (page 154).

12 medium-sized green (raw) prawns, shelled (but tails left on) and deveined
1½ tablespoons ghee or oil
1 medium-sized onion, cut into slim wedges and layers separated
½ red capsicum, cut into strips
a 5-cm piece fresh lemongrass, finely sliced
2 cloves garlic, finely chopped
1½ teaspoons grated fresh ginger
1½–2 tablespoons Singapore curry powder
⅓ teaspoon ground turmeric
⅓ cup coconut cream
1 cup water or fish stock
150 g small okra, sliced thickly or halved lengthways (or use green beans, sliced)
200 g frozen fish balls, thawed
salt and pepper

Cut deeply along the centre back of each prawn, and butterfly.

Heat ghee or oil in a wok or saucepan and sauté onion and capsicum until onions are lightly browned (about 2½ minutes). Add lemongrass, garlic and ginger, and fry briefly, then add curry powder, turmeric and coconut cream, and simmer for 4–5 minutes to produce a rich sauce base.

Pour water or fish stock into pan and bring to the boil. Add the okra or beans and cook for 3–4 minutes, then add the fish balls and prawns, season to taste with salt and pepper, and simmer gently until the prawns are cooked. Serve at once.

SERVES 4

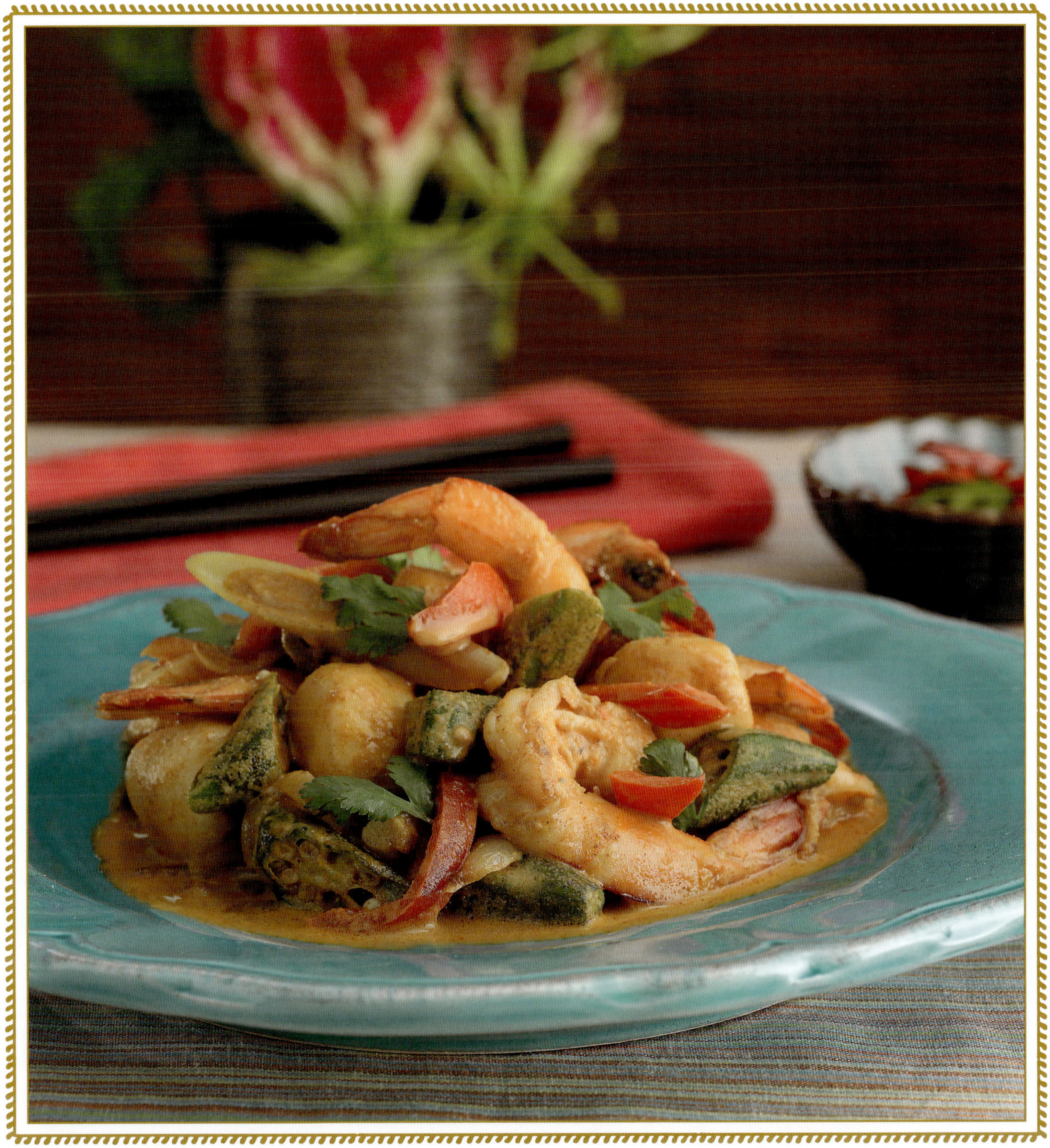

Curry laksa of seafood

A good-quality fresh marinara mix could replace the listed seafood. Fresh hokkien noodles can be added to this laksa, as well as or instead of the rice noodles.

200 g fine rice vermicelli or rice stick noodles
1 small onion, chopped
2 teaspoons oil
2 cups coconut milk
2 tablespoons laksa paste or 2–3 teaspoons Thai yellow curry paste (page 20)
1½ teaspoons fish stock powder or ¾ teaspoon dashi stock powder
1–2 fresh hot red chillies, slit lengthways and deseeded
4 very small bok choy, halved lengthways
150 g frozen fish or squid balls, thawed and cut in half
12 medium-sized green (raw) shelled prawns
1 cleaned squid tube, cut into rings
8 mussels
fish sauce, salt and pepper to taste
chopped spring-onion greens or fresh coriander, for garnish
lime wedges, to serve

Soften the noodles in a bowl of boiling water for a few minutes, then drain.

In a saucepan or wok, sauté the onion in the oil for 2 minutes, until lightly cooked. Add the coconut milk and laksa or curry paste, bring to the boil, stirring, then simmer for 2 minutes. Add 3 cups water, the stock powder, chillies and bok choy, and simmer for about 3 minutes. Last, stir in all the seafood, add fish sauce, salt and pepper to taste, and simmer gently until the seafood is tender.

Divide drained noodles between four big bowls. Ladle in the curry sauce, stirring to distribute the seafood and vegetables evenly. Sprinkle with the onion greens or chopped herbs, and add a lime wedge on a skewer to each bowl.

SERVES 4

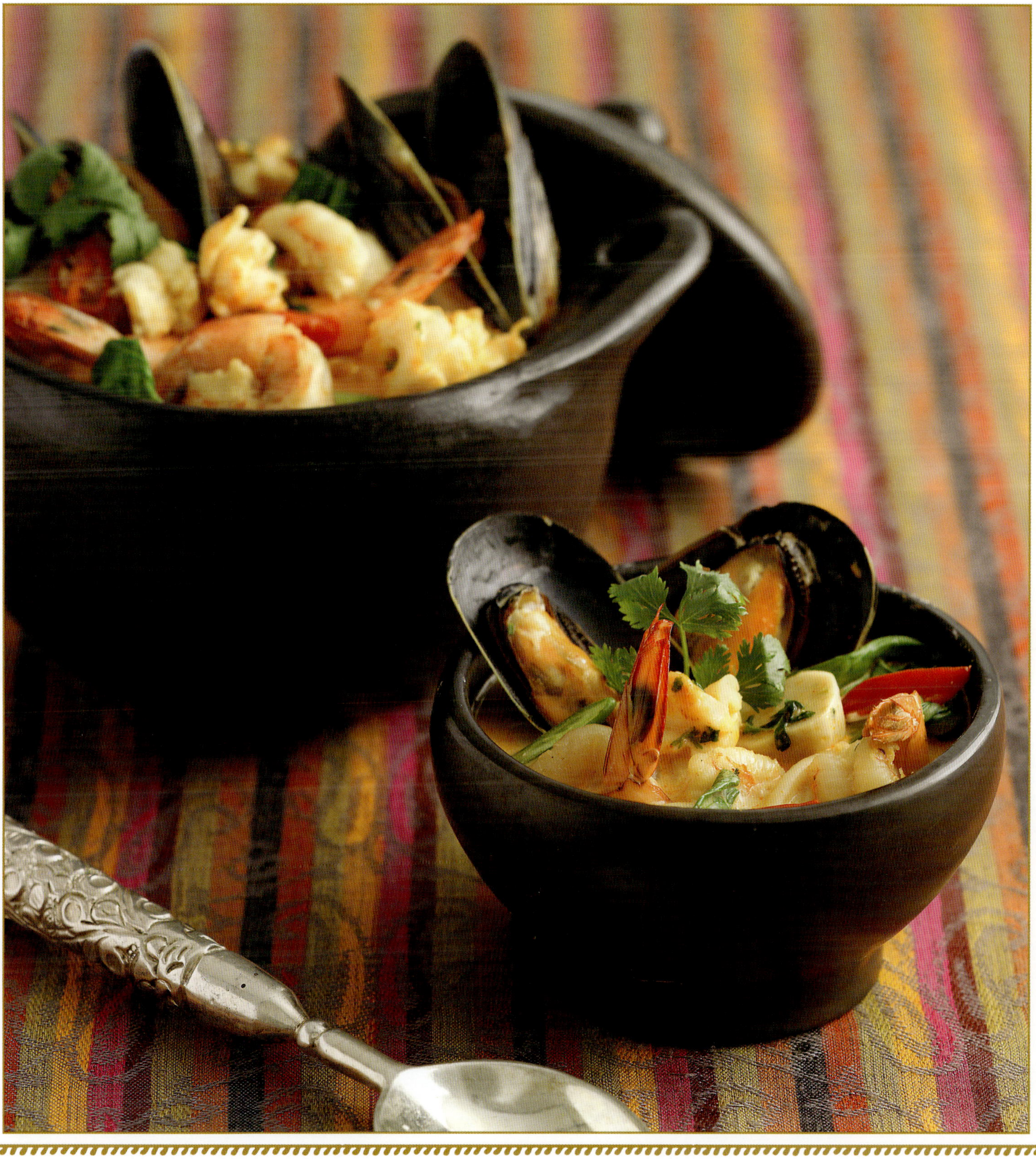

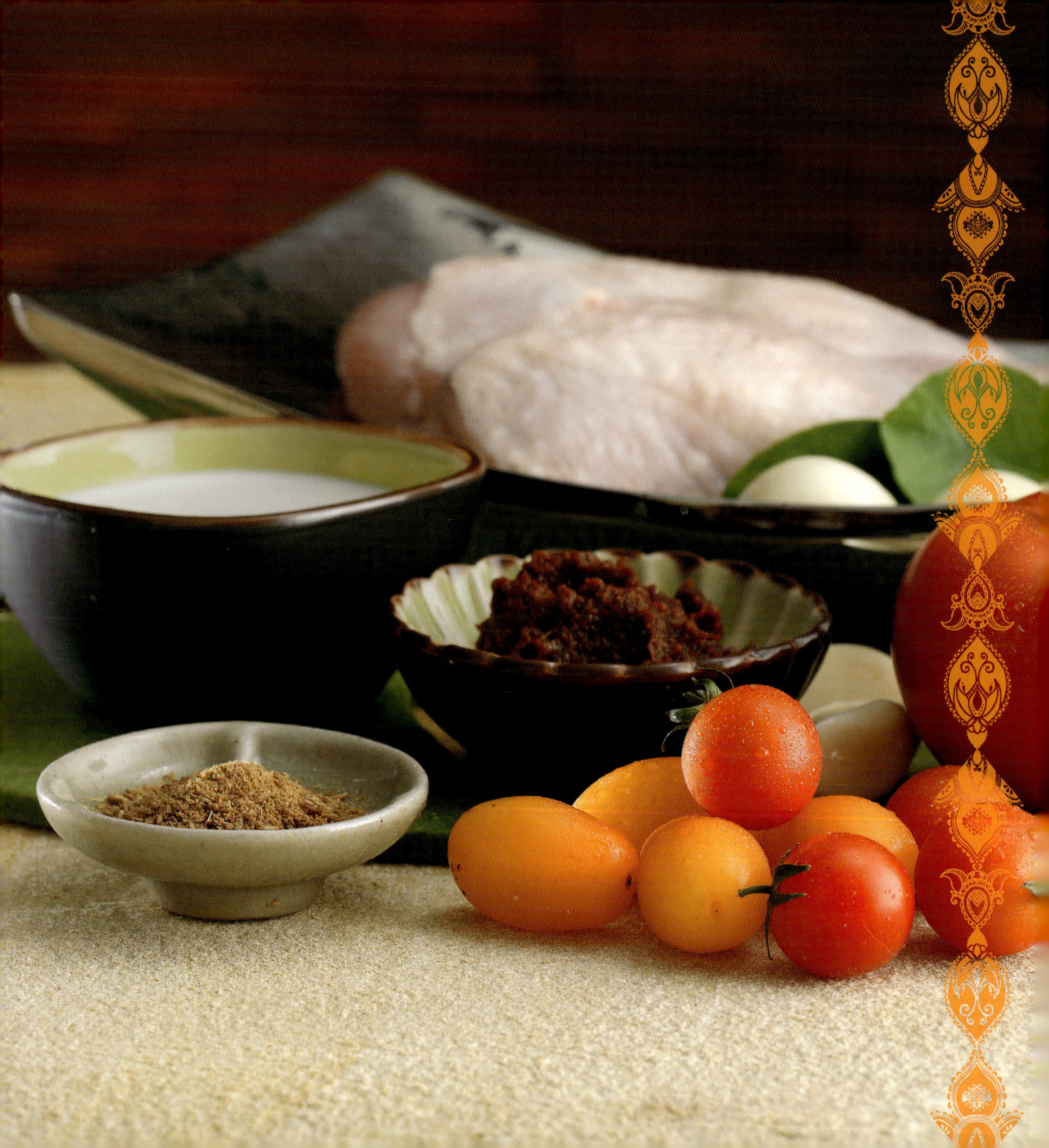

Chicken & duck curries

Its tenderness and delicate flavour make chicken a popular choice for curry cooks. It's perfect in zinging-hot green Thai curries and sumptuous Indian kormas; in curry sauces scarlet with chillies and tomatoes, tangy with tamarind and lime juice; and in velvety, emerald sauces of spinach or coriander. Tandoori-cooked chicken brings a special smoky flavour to Indian classics like butter chicken and tikka masala. The richness of duck is a perfect foil for boldly seasoned vindaloo and red curries.

Here there are quick-cook curries to get you in and out of the kitchen in less than 20 minutes, and curries featuring chicken on the bone lovingly cooked to its succulent best in rich and creamy yoghurt or coconut sauces with whole spices, fragrant spices or potent pastes. There's even a flamboyant Thai jungle curry of quail featuring fresh-from-the-vine green peppercorns.

Thai green chicken curry

Tiny pea eggplants can replace the peas.

4 green beans, sliced
¼ cup peas
1 × 400-ml can coconut milk
2 teaspoons Thai green curry paste (page 18)
4 cherry tomatoes, halved
1 fresh hot green chilli, slit lengthways and deseeded
8 small button or oyster mushrooms
¼ cup sliced bamboo shoots, well drained
220 g chicken breast, finely sliced
salt or fish sauce
sugar
fresh basil leaves

Boil the peas and beans in lightly salted water until barely tender (about 3 minutes).

In another saucepan bring coconut milk to the boil and add the curry paste. Simmer for 3 minutes, stirring frequently.

Add tomatoes, chilli, mushrooms and bamboo shoots, and simmer for 2 minutes. Stir in chicken and simmer gently for 2–3 minutes. Add drained beans and peas, season to taste with salt or fish sauce and add a little sugar to balance the chilli heat. Fold in basil leaves and serve.

SERVES 2–3

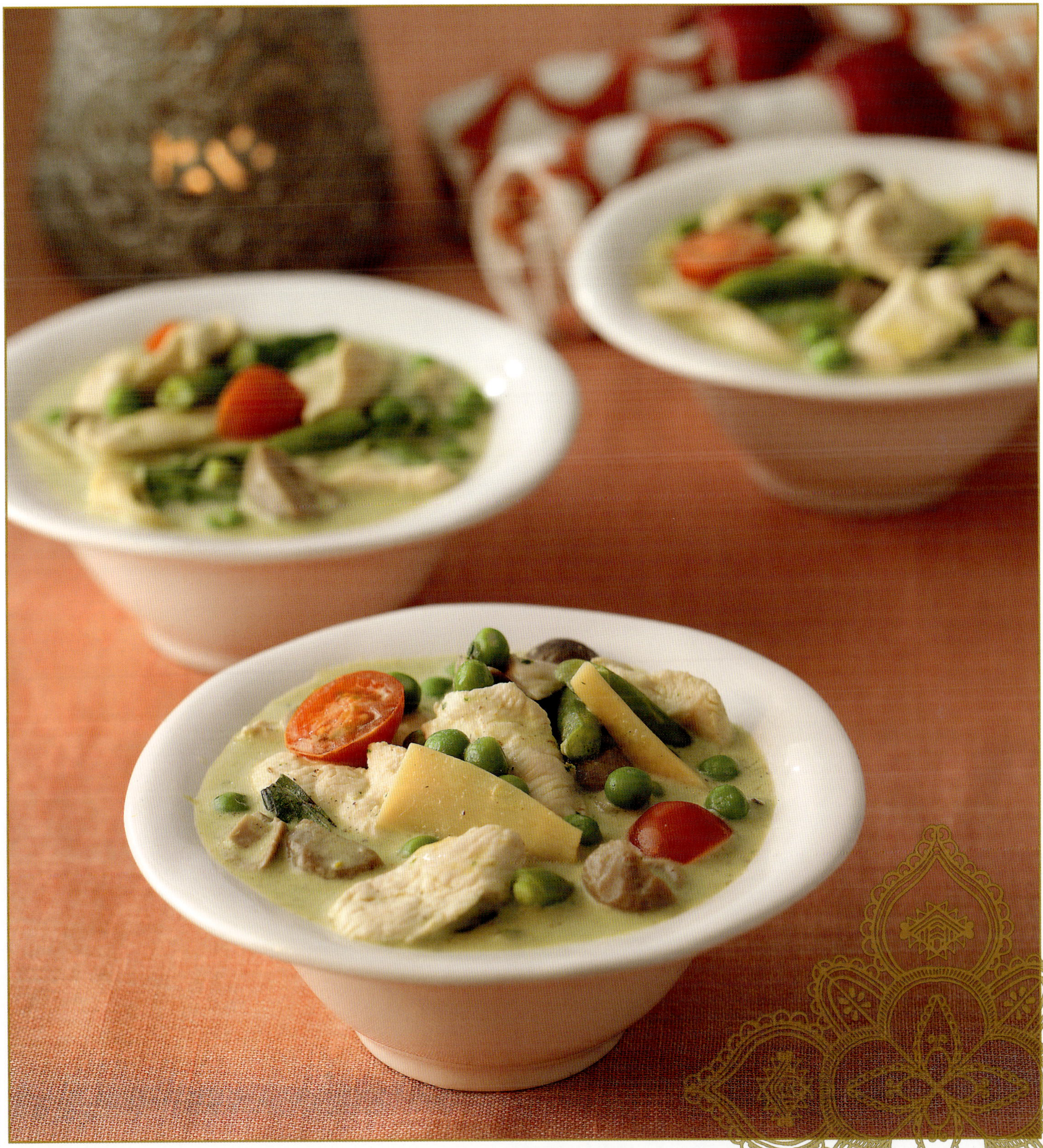

Red Thai curry of chicken & bamboo shoots

Baby bamboo shoots are now sold in most Asian food stores. They are delicious in salads and add elegance, crunch and delicate taste to a simple Thai chicken curry. Baby corn could be used instead.

1 × 400-ml can coconut cream
2–4 teaspoons Thai red curry paste (page 17)
½ cup peas
¼ red capsicum, cut into fine strips
6–8 baby bamboo shoots, drained and sliced on the diagonal
250 g chicken breast, thinly sliced
3 kaffir lime leaves
1 large fresh mild red chilli, deseeded and sliced
2 tablespoons fish sauce
1–2 teaspoons palm sugar or soft brown sugar
salt
freshly squeezed lime juice

In a saucepan simmer ½ cup of the coconut cream with the curry paste for about 4 minutes, stirring occasionally, until red oil separates and floats to the surface.

Add peas, capsicum and bamboo shoots, and stir briefly. Pour in remaining coconut cream and ½ cup water and bring barely to the boil. Reduce heat and simmer for 2–3 minutes.

Add the chicken, lime leaves and chilli, and simmer for 3–4 minutes, stirring.

Season with fish sauce and sugar, adding salt to taste. Add a squeeze of lime juice, and serve.

SERVES 2–3

Thai red chicken curry with straw mushrooms

Straw mushrooms are unique. Cut open one of these slippery little ball-shaped fungi to discover a perfect umbrella-shaped mushroom cap inside. They're grown on damp straw mats, hence the name, and what they lack in flavour they make up for with their pleasing crunchy texture. They keep for a few days in water, in the refrigerator, once the can is opened.

1 tablespoon oil
2 cloves garlic, finely chopped
4 thin slices fresh ginger, finely shredded
an 8-cm stem lemongrass, very finely shaved
3–4 teaspoons Thai red curry paste (page 17)
2 small fresh hot red chillies, slit lengthways and deseeded
1 × 400-ml can coconut cream
400 g chicken breast, thinly sliced
2 roma or vine-ripened tomatoes, cut into wedges and deseeded
2 spring onions, sliced into 4-cm pieces (finely chop some of the green tops for garnish)
¾ cup drained, sliced straw mushrooms
⅓ cup sliced bamboo shoots
1 tablespoon fish sauce
2 teaspoons palm sugar or soft brown sugar
freshly squeezed lime or lemon juice

Heat the oil in a medium-sized saucepan and fry the garlic, ginger and lemongrass briefly. Add the curry paste and chillies, and fry for about 40 seconds, stirring constantly.

Stir in ½ cup of the coconut cream and simmer for about 5 minutes, stirring often. Add the remaining coconut cream and about ⅓ cup water and bring to the boil.

Stir in chicken, tomatoes, spring onions, mushrooms and bamboo shoots, and heat very gently until the chicken becomes white and firm (about 5 minutes). Season to taste with fish sauce and sugar, and add a squeeze of lime or lemon juice.

Garnish with spring-onion greens.

SERVES 4–5

CHICKEN & DUCK CURRIES

Chicken & crunchy peanut Thai curry

600 g chicken thigh fillets, cut into 3-cm cubes
1½ tablespoons Thai red curry paste (page 17)
3 cloves garlic, crushed
2 teaspoons grated fresh ginger
1 medium-sized carrot, sliced
1 medium-sized zucchini, sliced
2 tablespoons peanut oil
1 medium-sized onion, cut into narrow wedges
1 × 400-ml can coconut milk
2 tablespoons fish sauce
2 teaspoons palm sugar
⅓ cup roasted peanuts, chopped

Place chicken in a shallow bowl, add curry paste, garlic and ginger, and massage into the chicken. Leave to marinate for ½–1 hour.

Bring a small saucepan of lightly salted water to the boil and parboil carrot and zucchini, then drain and set aside.

Heat the oil in a wok or saucepan and fry the onion until lightly coloured. Remove to a plate using a slotted spoon. In the same oil brown the chicken in several batches.

Return the onion to the pan with the chicken and add the coconut milk, fish sauce and palm sugar. Cover and simmer for about 8 minutes, or until the chicken is tender, adding a little extra coconut milk or water if needed. Stir in vegetables and peanuts, check for seasoning and simmer for a few more minutes.

SERVES 4–6

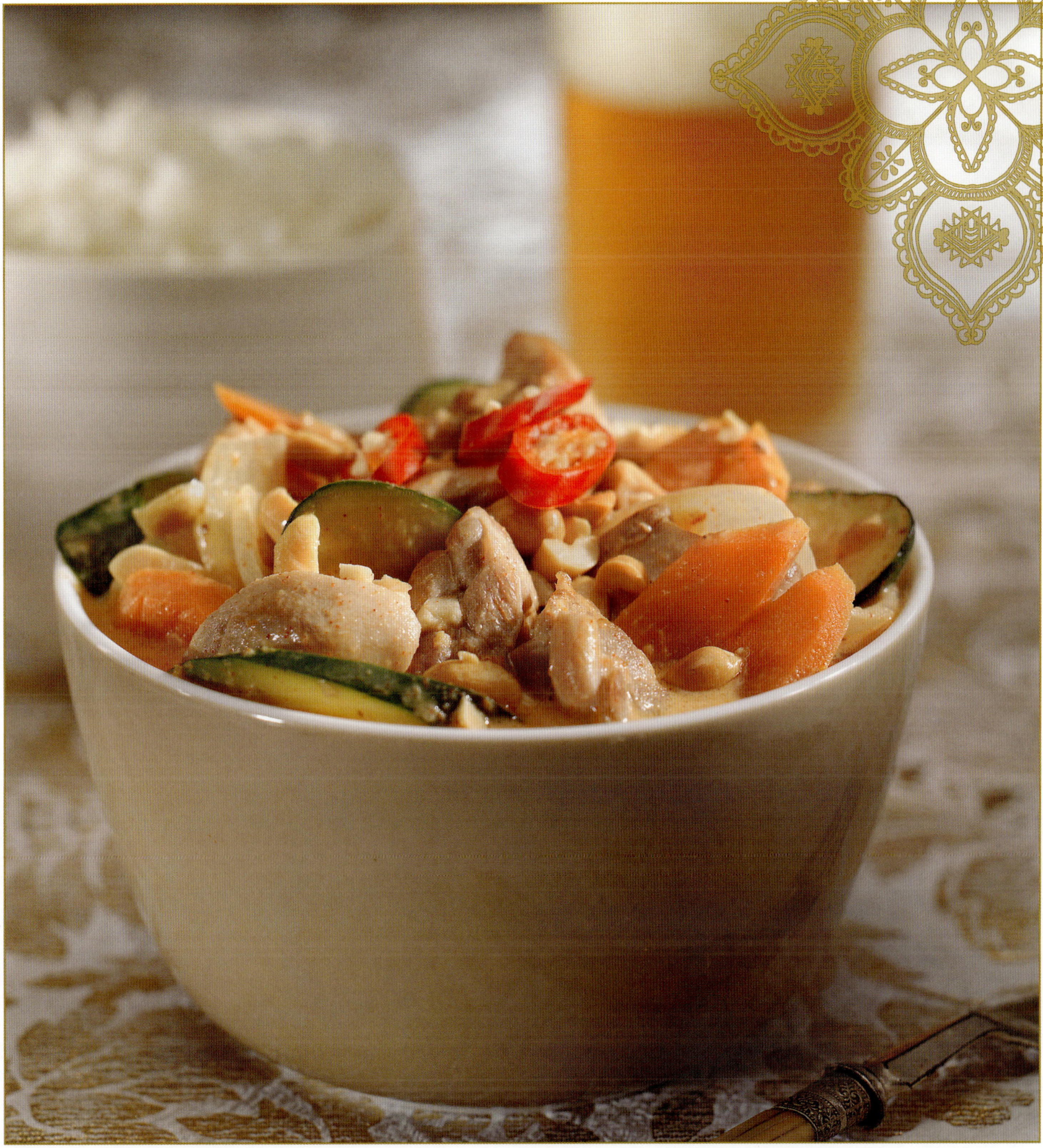

Grilled chicken & tomatoes in red curry sauce

A garnish of finely shredded kaffir lime leaves provides vibrant flavour and colour.

350 g chicken breast fillets
salt and freshly ground pepper
1 clove garlic, crushed
½ teaspoon ground cumin
oil
1½–3 teaspoons Thai red curry paste (page 17)
1 cup coconut cream
2 roma tomatoes, cut into wedges and deseeded
6 small yellow teardrop tomatoes, halved
2 kaffir lime leaves, finely shredded

For each chicken breast, press your fingers firmly on top and slide a sharp knife horizontally through the centre to make two thin flat escalopes. Season with salt and pepper and rub in the garlic and cumin. Set aside.

Heat 1 tablespoon oil in a non-stick pan or wok and fry the curry paste for 30 seconds. Add coconut cream and bring to the boil, stirring. Reduce heat, add the tomatoes and simmer gently while you cook the chicken.

Heat a grill, ribbed pan or hotplate. Brush the chicken with oil and cook for about 2 minutes on each side.

Serve chicken on warmed plates and cover with the sauce. Garnish with shredded lime leaves and serve.

SERVES 2–3

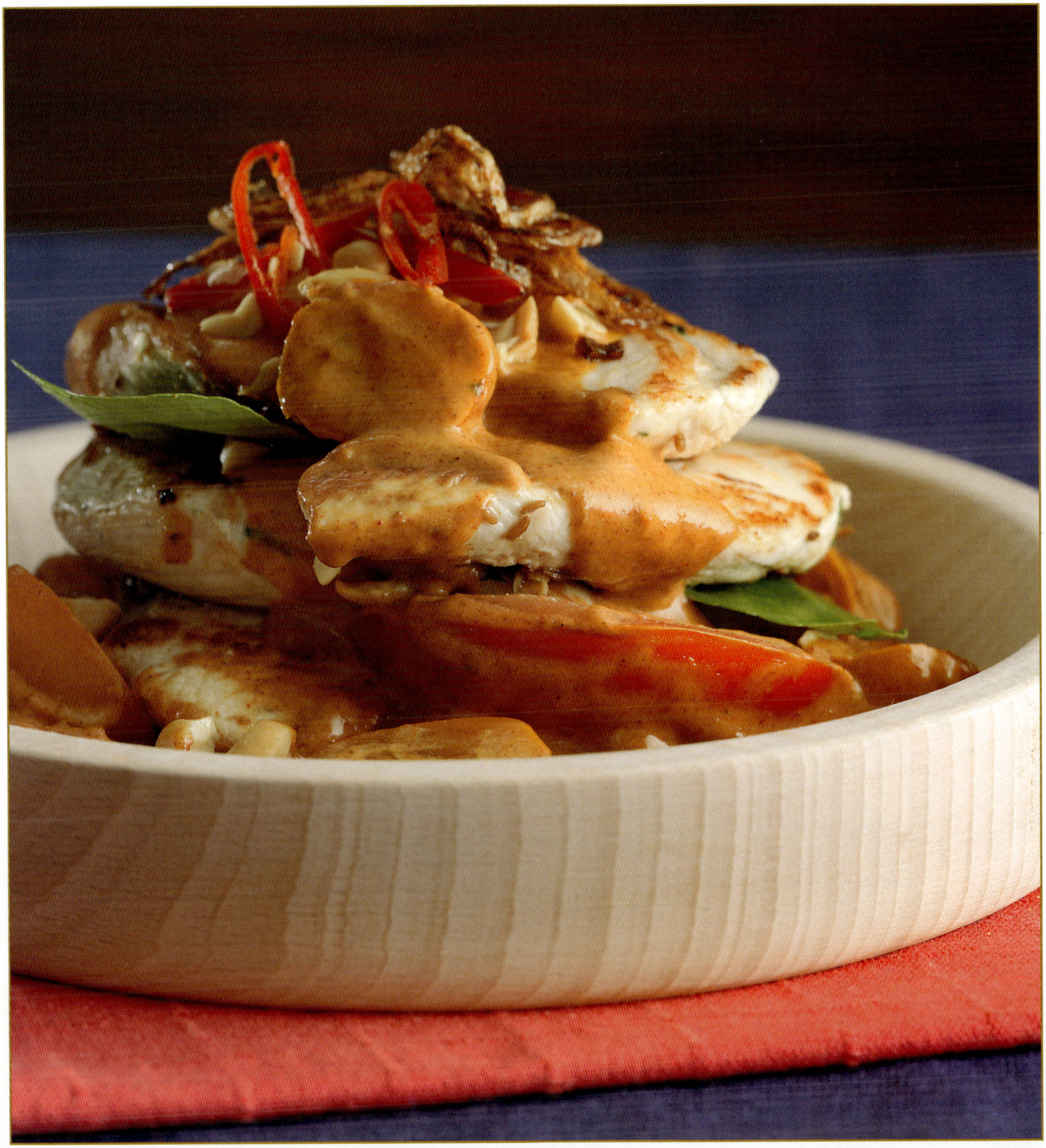

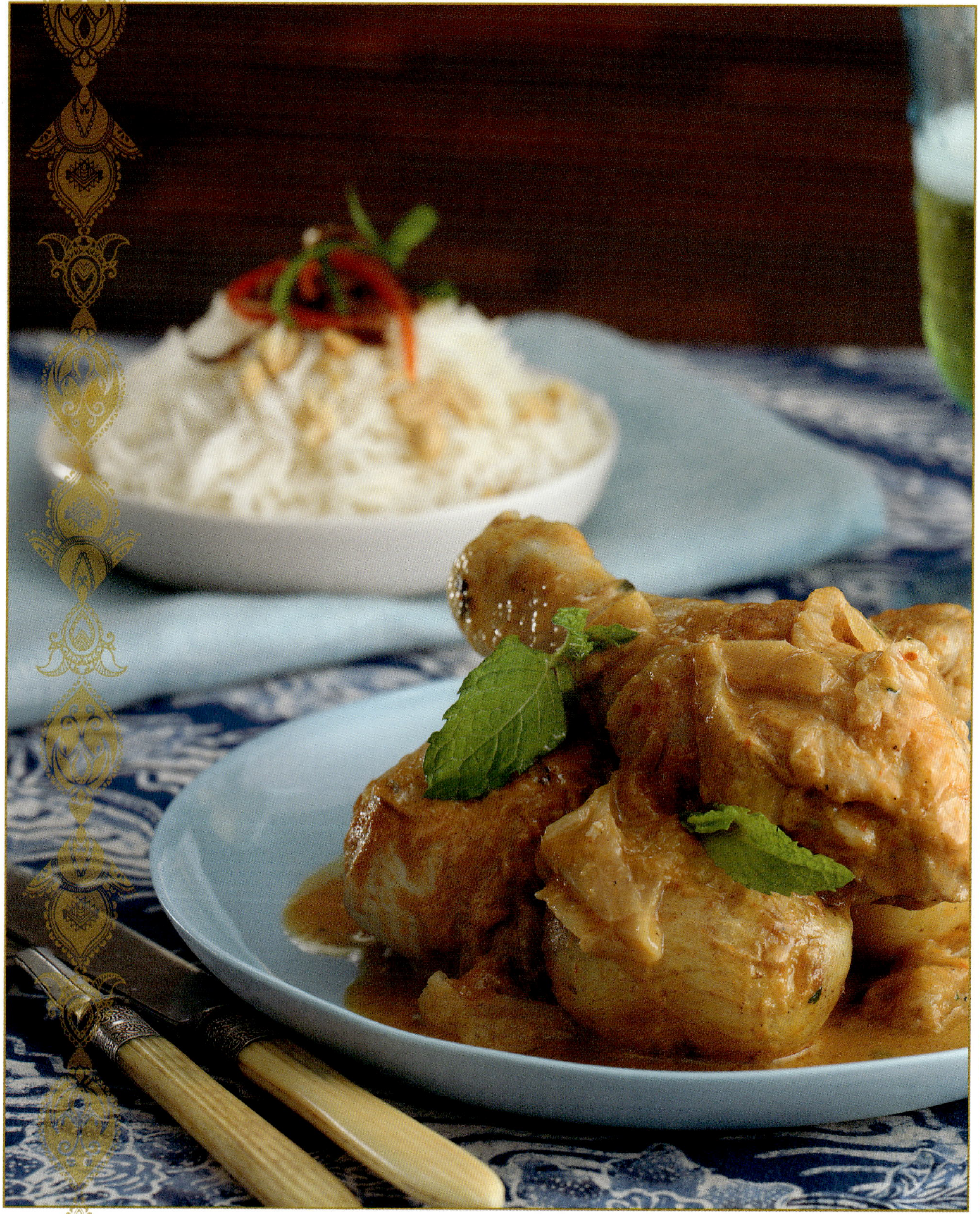

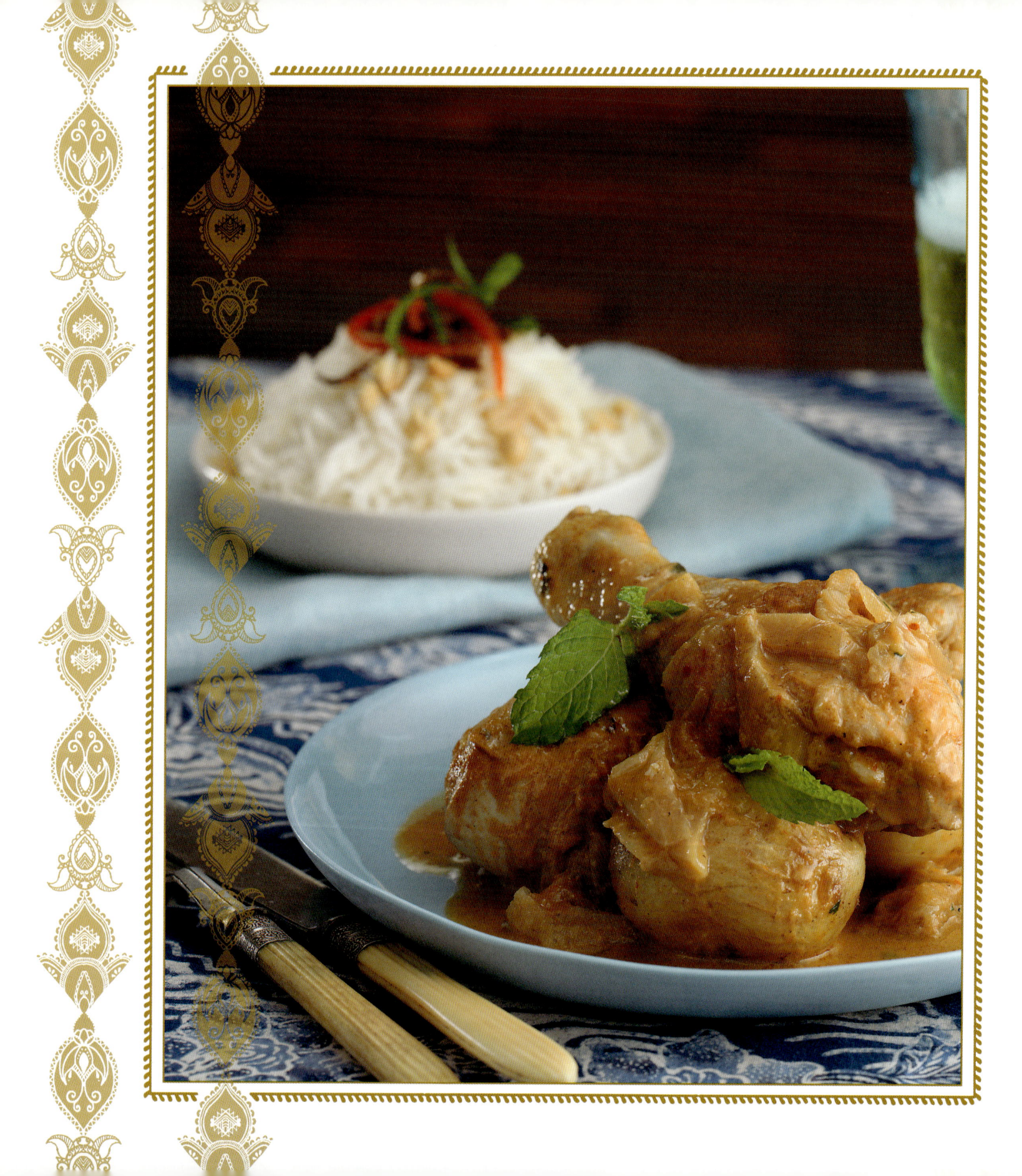

Penang curry of chicken drumsticks & potatoes

Penang curries are reasonably mild on the Thai curry heat spectrum.

12 small chicken legs
12 small new potatoes
3 tablespoons oil
1 large onion, sliced
1 × 400-ml can coconut cream
1–1½ tablespoons Penang or Mussaman curry paste (page 19)
2 cups chicken stock or water
salt and freshly ground pepper
1–2 teaspoons fish sauce
1–2 tablespoons chopped fresh basil, mint or coriander

In a large non-stick pan brown the chicken and potatoes in the oil, in batches, cooking until lightly browned. Remove to a bowl.

In the same oil fry the onion until golden-brown, stirring frequently (about 5 minutes).

Add half the coconut cream and the curry paste and simmer until very fragrant and the coconut cream is reduced by half (about 4 minutes). Add remaining coconut cream, the stock or water, chicken and potatoes, seasoning with salt and pepper to taste. Bring to the boil, partially cover, reduce heat and simmer for about 30 minutes, stirring and turning the chicken and potatoes from time to time.

When potatoes are tender, add fish sauce and chopped herbs, and serve.

SERVES 6

CHICKEN & DUCK CURRIES

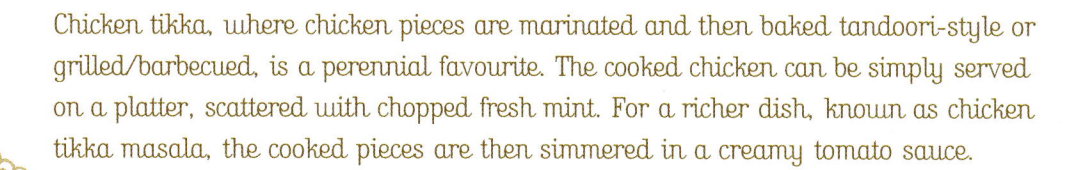

Chicken tikka masala

Chicken tikka, where chicken pieces are marinated and then baked tandoori-style or grilled/barbecued, is a perennial favourite. The cooked chicken can be simply served on a platter, scattered with chopped fresh mint. For a richer dish, known as chicken tikka masala, the cooked pieces are then simmered in a creamy tomato sauce.

Chicken tikka

¾ cup creamy yoghurt
1 tablespoon tandoori paste (page 13)
1½ teaspoons ground sweet paprika
6 chicken thigh fillets, cut into 5-cm cubes
oil or melted ghee
1½ teaspoons cumin seeds, lightly crushed
½ teaspoon ground black pepper
¾ teaspoon salt

Masala

1 large onion, roughly chopped
4 cloves garlic, peeled
a 2-cm piece fresh ginger, peeled
1 large fresh hot red chilli, deseeded
2 tablespoons ghee
1–1½ tablespoons tikka paste or hot Indian curry paste (page 13)
¾ cup canned crushed tomatoes
¾ cup cream
salt and pepper
chopped fresh coriander, mint, or slivered almonds for garnish

To make chicken tikka, first combine yoghurt, tandoori paste and paprika in a bowl, mixing well. Add the chicken and stir until evenly coated. Cover and leave to marinate for at least 20 minutes, or up to 24 hours.

Heat a grill or barbecue to medium–hot. Cover grill tray with aluminium foil and set a rack over it. Brush rack with oil or ghee. Arrange chicken pieces on the rack, allowing space between. Sprinkle with cumin, pepper and salt. Cook for about 10 minutes, turning several times, until the chicken is cooked through and the edges crisped and slightly charred.

If you are going to make chicken tikka masala, cook the chicken tikka in advance and let it cool.

To make the masala sauce, place onion, garlic, ginger and chilli in a food processor or blender and blitz to a purée. Heat ghee in a saucepan or frying pan and fry the onion paste for about 2½ minutes, stirring almost constantly. Add curry paste and cook for a few minutes, then pour in 1 cup water and bring to the boil. Reduce heat and simmer for about 6 minutes, then add tomatoes and simmer for a further 10 minutes until sauce is thick and rich.

Pour cream into pan and season to taste. Add the cooked chicken tikka and simmer for another 10 minutes, adding a little water if the sauce is too thick. Serve in a bowl, garnished with herbs, or almonds.

SERVES 4–6

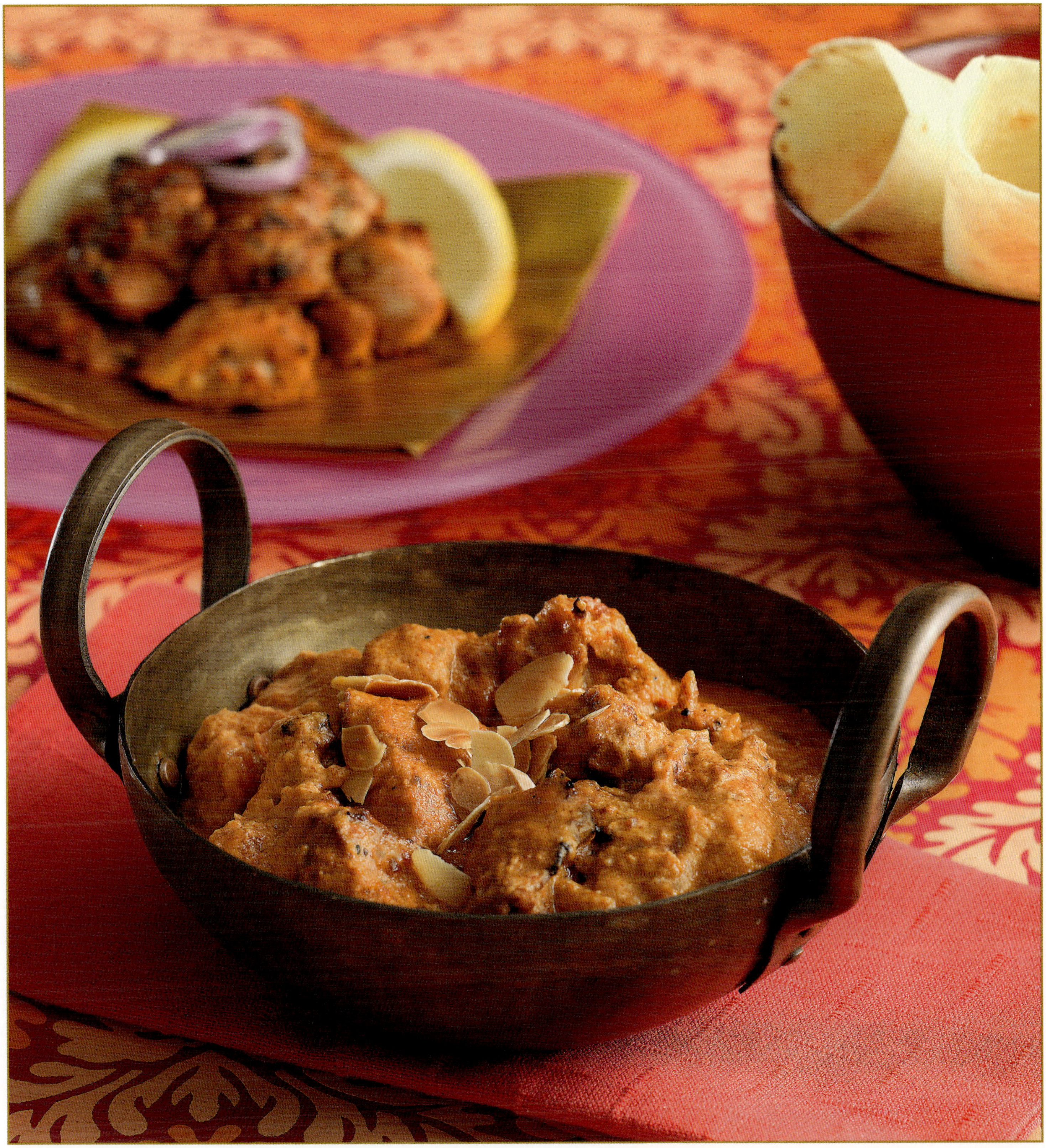

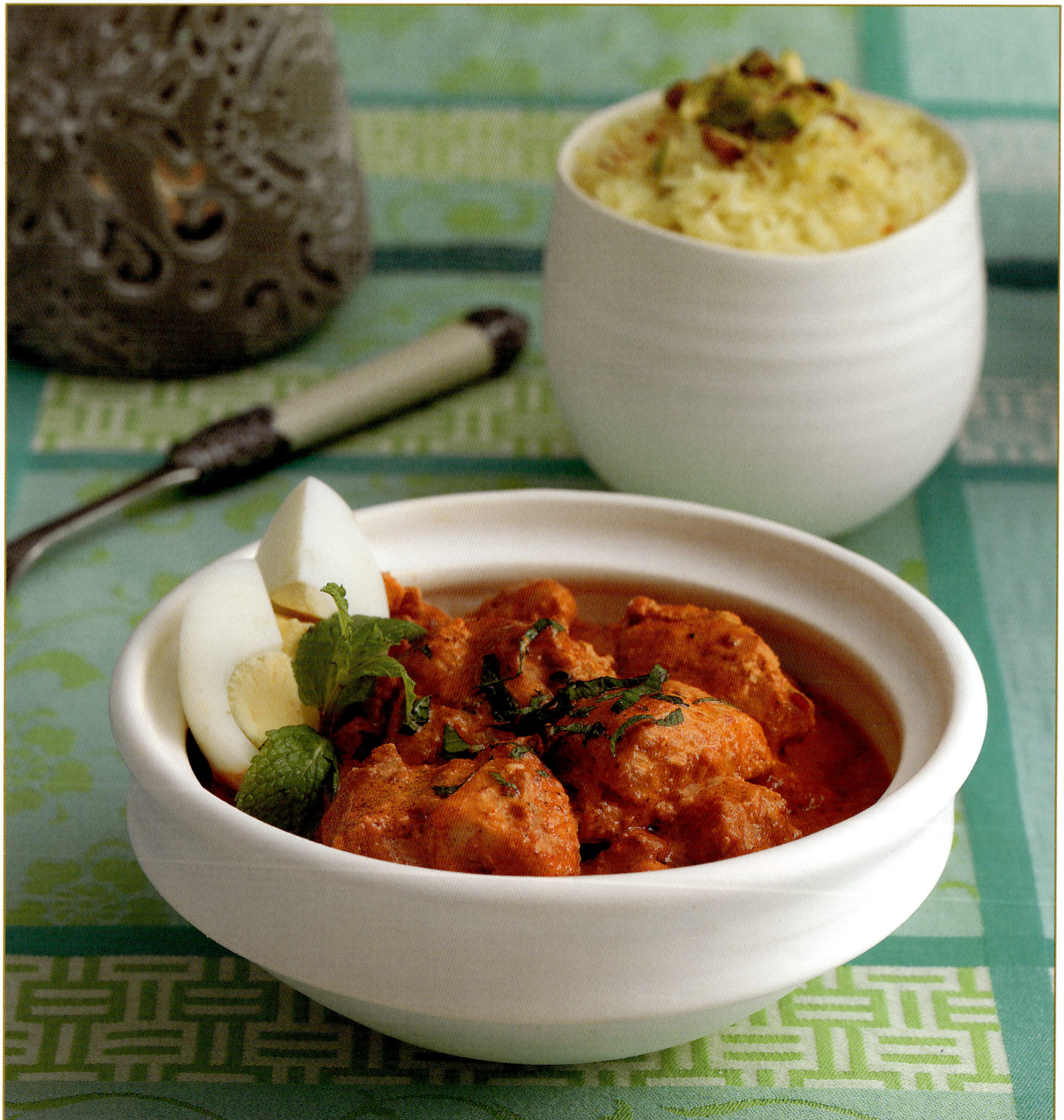

Chicken in a buttery tomato curry with dried fruit & nuts

This dish, murghi baghdadi, is an indulgent curry for special occasions. Like so many dishes integrated into Indian cuisine during the opulent Moghul era, this dish — an extravagant version of the popular Butter Chicken — has Middle Eastern origins.

1½ tablespoons blanched almonds, toasted
2 tablespoons sultanas, raisins or currants
2 tablespoons sliced dried apricots
4 tablespoons butter or ghee
600 g chicken thigh fillets, trimmed and cut into 3-cm cubes
¾ cup canned crushed tomatoes
¼ teaspoon fenugreek seeds, ground to a powder
½ teaspoon hot ground chilli
1 teaspoon sweet paprika
1⅓ teaspoons sugar
salt and freshly squeezed lemon juice, to taste
¼ cup thick cream
2 tablespoons chopped fresh mint or coriander
2 hard-boiled eggs, sliced

Fry the nuts and fruit in 3 tablespoons of the butter or ghee until nuts are golden and fruit plump and soft (about 1½ minutes). Transfer to a bowl and set aside.

Heat remaining butter or ghee in a heavy saucepan and cook the chicken gently until almost cooked (about 8 minutes), stirring frequently. Remove to a bowl using a slotted spoon.

Add tomatoes, spices and sugar to the pan and cook for about 5 minutes. Add 1 cup water, bring to the boil, then reduce heat and simmer for about 10 minutes. Season to taste with salt and add a little lemon juice. Purée in a blender, or in the pan using a stick mixer. Strain, if preferred. Return sauce and chicken to the pan, stir in the cream and simmer for about 4 minutes.

Stir in the herbs, eggs, fruit and nuts, heat gently and serve.

SERVES 4–6

Chicken in creamy spinach sauce (saag murghi)

This dish is typical of north Indian (Punjabi) cuisine – rich but not too hot.

300–400 g chopped spinach
½ cup chicken stock
4 skinless chicken breasts, cut into 3-cm cubes
salt and freshly ground pepper
⅓ teaspoon ground turmeric
3 tablespoons ghee or butter
1 small onion, finely chopped
1 clove garlic, crushed
½ teaspoon grated nutmeg
2 teaspoons garam masala (page 16)
½ cup sour cream

Pack spinach into a small saucepan and add chicken stock. Cover and simmer gently until the spinach is very tender, then tip into a food processor or blender and purée. Set aside.

Season the chicken with salt, pepper and turmeric. Heat the ghee or butter in a non-stick pan and fry the chicken in several batches until lightly coloured and almost cooked through (about 4 minutes for each batch). Remove to a plate.

In the same pan, fry the onion and garlic until soft and lightly coloured, then pour in the spinach mixture and add nutmeg and garam masala, with salt and pepper to taste. Return the chicken and any juices to the pan, stir in the sour cream and heat gently for 2–3 minutes.

SERVES 4–5

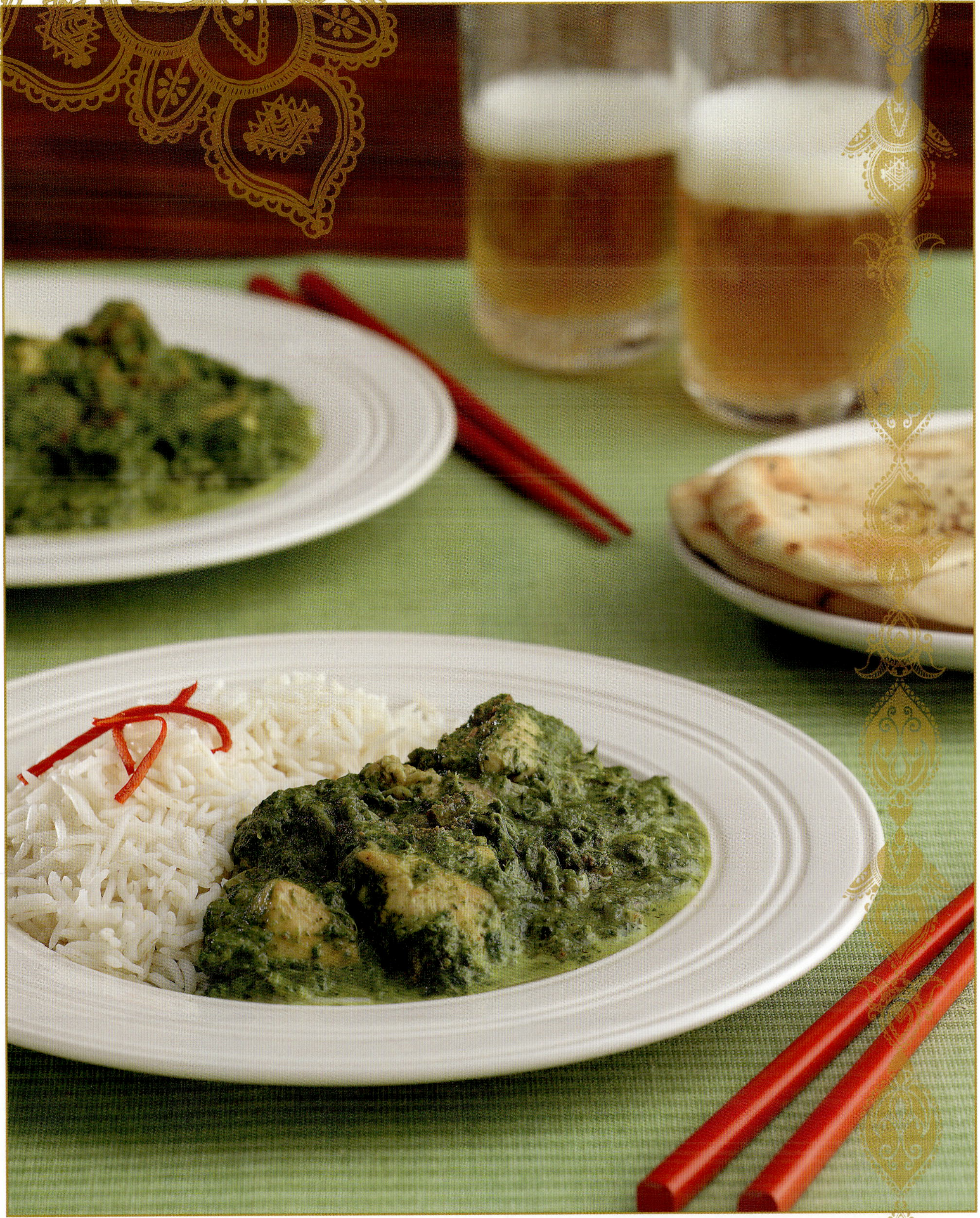

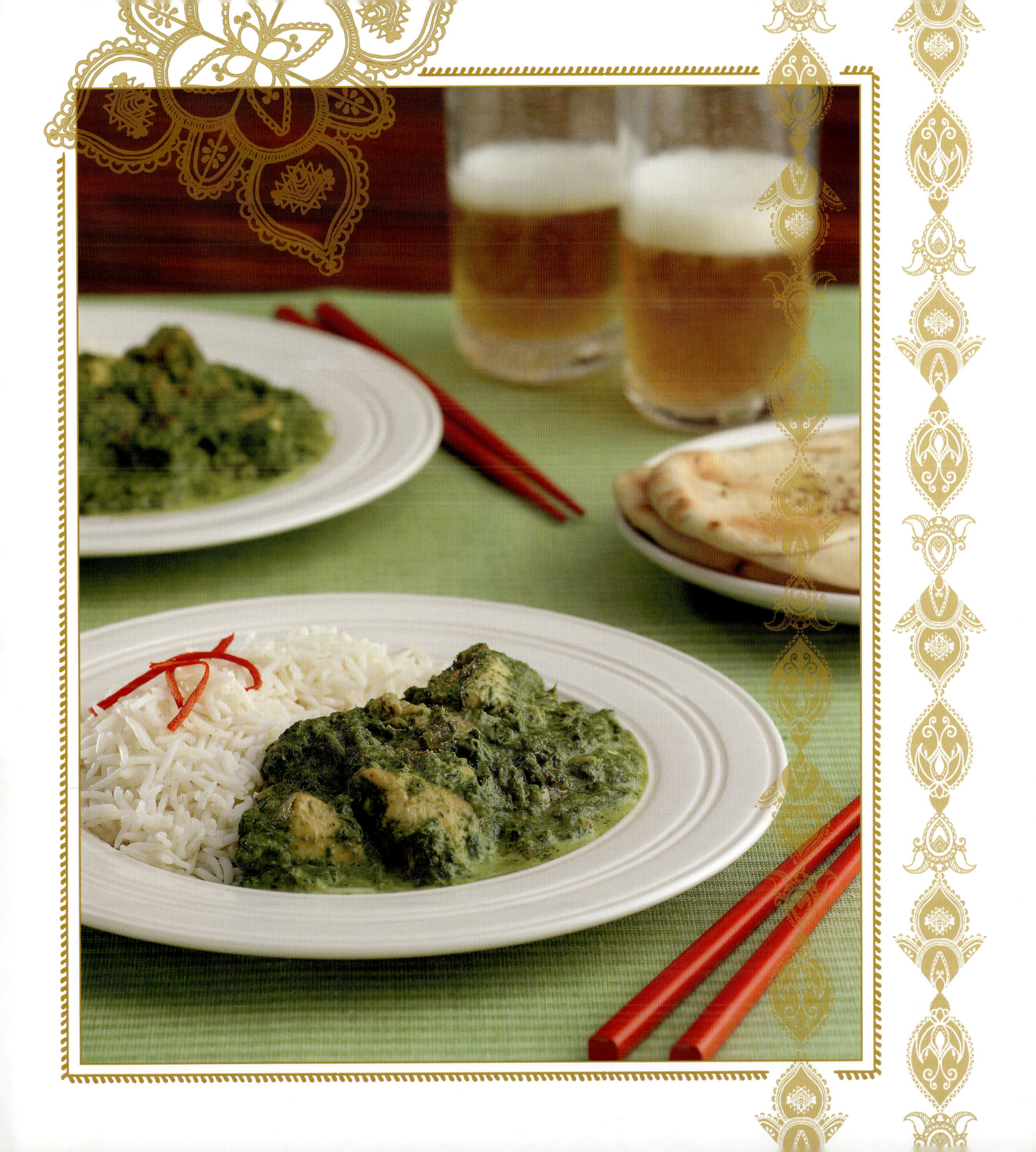

Chicken koh-i-noor

2 tablespoons ghee or oil
1 large onion, finely chopped
6–8 chicken thigh fillets, skin on
2 teaspoons grated fresh ginger
2 cloves garlic, crushed
2–4 teaspoons hot Indian curry paste (page 14)
salt and pepper
1 cup sour cream or creamy yoghurt
¾ cup canned crushed tomatoes
1 tablespoon garam masala (page 16)
⅓ cup roasted slivered almonds, coarsely ground
chopped fresh mint or coriander, for garnish

Preheat the oven to 180°C. Lightly grease an oven dish large enough to fit the chicken pieces side by side.

Heat the ghee or oil in a frying pan and fry the onion over medium–high heat until lightly golden (about 3 minutes). Spread onion evenly in prepared oven dish. With a sharp knife, slash deeply through the skin side of each chicken piece, then place in the oven dish over the onions, skin-side upwards.

Mix the ginger, garlic, curry paste and 1 teaspoon salt with the sour cream or yoghurt. Spread mixture over the chicken.

Mix the crushed tomatoes with ¾ cup water and pour carefully into the pan, taking care not to wash the yoghurt mix off the chicken. Sprinkle on half the garam masala. Cover with aluminium foil and bake in a preheated oven for about 35 minutes.

Remove the foil, stir up chicken and sauce, and season to taste with salt and pepper. Scatter the ground almonds evenly over the chicken, along with the remaining garam masala. Return it to the oven, uncovered, and bake for a further 10–15 minutes, until the nuts are golden-brown. Scatter with fresh herbs to serve.

SERVES 4–6

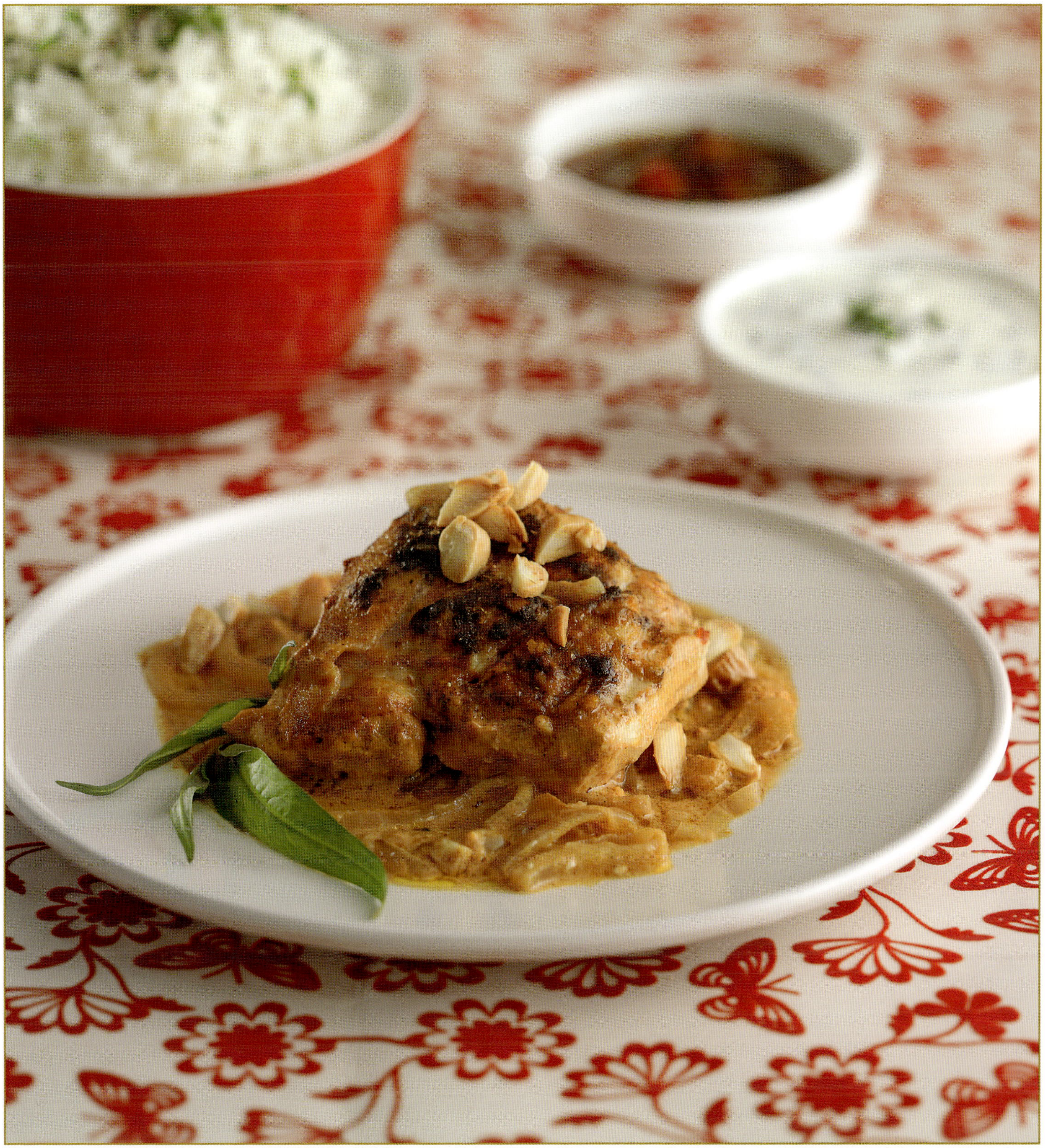

Singapore chicken in coconut curry

Now readily available from Asian stores, farmers' markets and even supermarkets, fresh galangal, turmeric root and kaffir lime leaves bring authentic flavours to Asian curries.

- 1 large onion or 8 shallots, roughly chopped
- 6 cloves garlic, peeled
- 1–3 fresh hot red chillies, deseeded
- a 2-cm piece fresh ginger, peeled
- a 3-cm piece fresh turmeric root, peeled (or use 1 teaspoon ground turmeric)
- 2 tablespoons oil
- 1 stem lemongrass, cut in half and bruised
- 3 thick slices fresh galangal
- 1 tablespoon ground coriander
- 3–4 kaffir lime leaves
- 4 chicken maryland pieces (legs and thighs), chopped into 5-cm chunks
- 1 × 400-ml can coconut cream
- salt

In a food processor or blender grind the onion, garlic, chillies, ginger and turmeric to a paste with the oil. Transfer to a saucepan and fry over medium heat with the lemongrass and galangal for about 3 minutes, stirring almost continually.

Add coriander, lime leaves and chicken pieces to pan and stir until chicken is lightly coloured and evenly coated with the seasonings. Pour in the coconut cream and 2 cups water and bring to the boil. Reduce heat, add salt and pepper to taste and simmer, uncovered, for about 35 minutes, until the chicken is very tender. Check seasonings and serve.

SERVES 4–6

Indian chicken on the bone

Many traditional curries feature meat cooked on the bone, which adds flavour to the dish. The cooked meat should be so tender that it slides readily from the bones.

2 large onions
6 cloves garlic, peeled
a 2-cm piece fresh ginger, peeled
2–3 tablespoons ghee or oil
3 teaspoons garam masala (page 16)
½–1 teaspoon ground chilli
1 teaspoon ground turmeric
2 large tomatoes, deseeded and roughly chopped
1.2 kg chicken pieces, chopped into 5-cm pieces
2–3 cups chicken stock or water
salt
2 spring onions, finely chopped
2–3 tablespoons chopped fresh coriander

Roughly chop 1 onion and slice the other. Place chopped onion in a food processor with the garlic and ginger and grind to a coarse paste.

Heat the ghee or oil in a heavy saucepan and fry the sliced onion until well browned (about 5 minutes).

Add the onion paste and stir over medium–high heat until lightly coloured (about 4 minutes). Stir in spices and tomatoes, and cook to a paste, then add the chicken and cook, turning in the sauce, for 2–3 minutes. Pour in enough stock or water to not quite cover, and add salt to taste. Cover and simmer gently until the chicken is very tender (25–30 minutes). Check seasoning, add spring onions and coriander, and simmer briefly.

SERVES 4–6

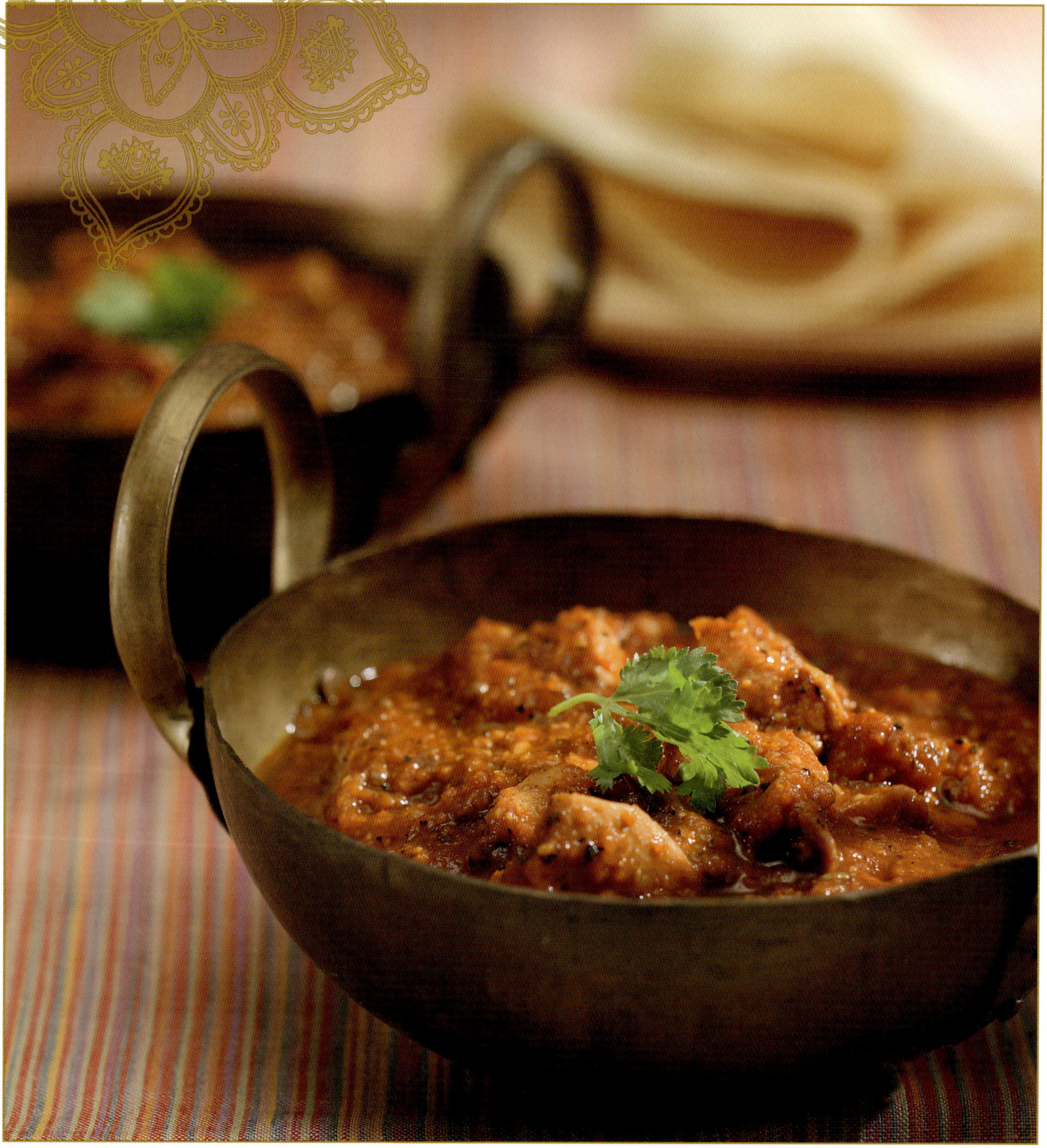

Black pepper chicken (kozhi melagu)

Black pepper lends pungent heat and unique fragrance to this dish from the Chettinad region of southern India.

2 medium-sized onions, roughly chopped
2 cloves garlic, peeled
a 2-cm piece fresh ginger, peeled
3 tablespoons ghee or oil
1½ teaspoons fennel seeds
1 teaspoon cumin seeds
1–1½ tablespoons black peppercorns, cracked
1½ tablespoons coriander seeds
2 teaspoons sweet paprika
1¼ teaspoons ground turmeric
3 teaspoons garam masala (page 16)
600 g skinless chicken thigh fillets, cut into 3-cm cubes
2 soft ripe tomatoes, deseeded and chopped
salt
4–5 tablespoons chopped fresh coriander leaves

Place onions, garlic and ginger in a food processor and grind to a purée.

In a wok or heavy saucepan heat the ghee or oil and fry the fennel seeds, cumin seeds and peppercorns for about 1½ minutes, until they begin to crackle and sputter. Add onion purée and stir over medium heat for about 4 minutes, until golden-brown. Stir in paprika, turmeric and half the garam masala, and stir for 30 seconds.

Add the chicken to pan and stir to coat with the spices, cooking for 1–2 minutes. Add tomatoes and 1½ cups water, cover the pan tightly and cook gently until the chicken is tender (10–15 minutes), and season to taste with salt.

When ready to serve, stir in chopped coriander.

SERVES 4–5

Daljit's mild chicken curry with yoghurt

- 1 kg chicken pieces, with or without skin
- 1 fresh hot green chilli, deseeded
- a 2.5-cm piece fresh ginger, peeled
- 6 cloves garlic, peeled
- 1 cup creamy yoghurt
- 1 teaspoon salt
- 2 tablespoons ghee
- 2 tablespoons chopped fresh coriander
- 2 tablespoons thick cream

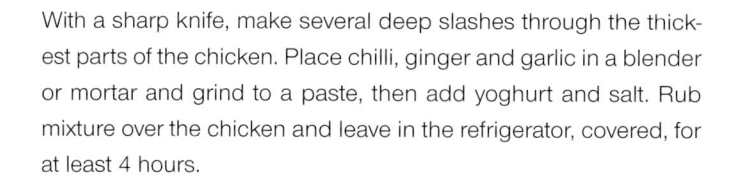

With a sharp knife, make several deep slashes through the thickest parts of the chicken. Place chilli, ginger and garlic in a blender or mortar and grind to a paste, then add yoghurt and salt. Rub mixture over the chicken and leave in the refrigerator, covered, for at least 4 hours.

When ready to cook, scrape marinade from the chicken into a bowl and reserve. Heat the ghee in a frying pan and fry the chicken pieces until evenly coloured. Add the reserved marinade and 1 cup water and cover tightly. Cook gently until the chicken is tender (about 25 minutes), turning occasionally. Stir in the coriander and cream. Check seasoning and add more salt if needed.

SERVES 4–6

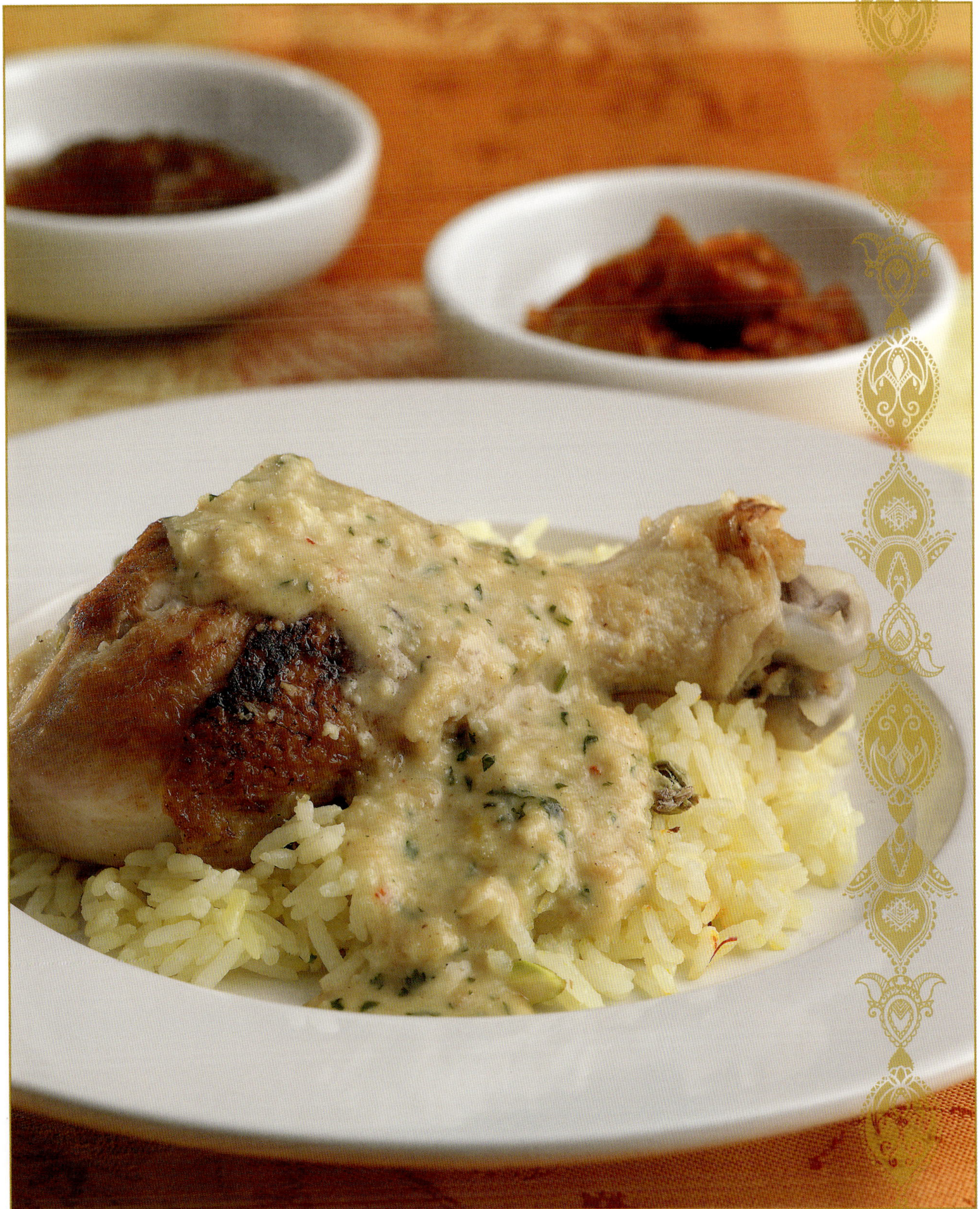

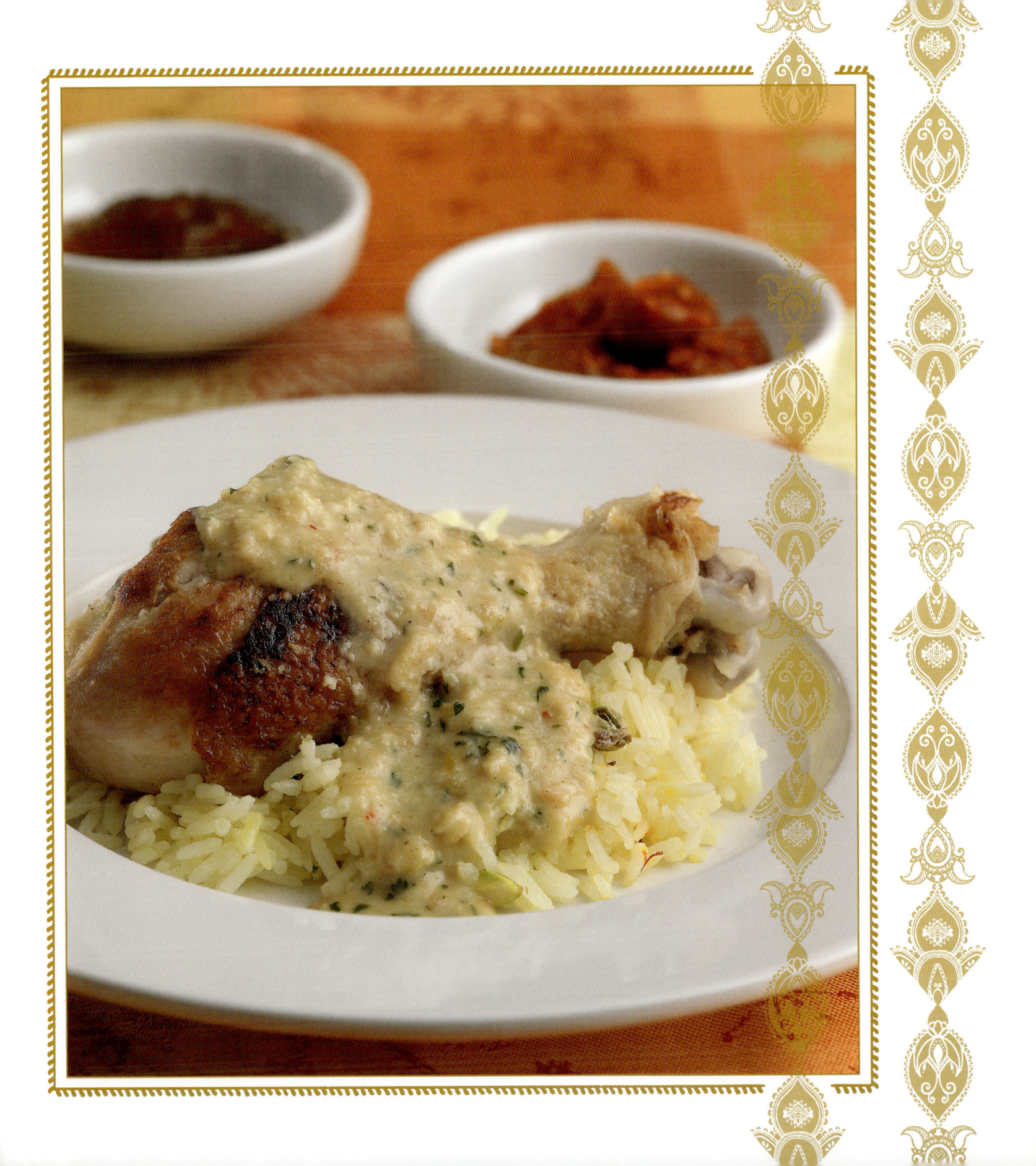

Hot Sri Lankan chicken with spinach & cashews

In Sri Lankan curries, colour and rich smoky flavour are achieved by dry-roasting the spices. In this recipe, the spices are roasted to a medium-brown, while for some recipes the spices are so darkly roasted the resultant curry is almost black.

2 medium-sized onions
3 tablespoons oil
½ cup raw cashew nuts
650 g chicken thigh fillets, cut into 3-cm cubes
4 cloves garlic, peeled
6 dried red chillies, deseeded
2 teaspoons black peppercorns
1½ tablespoons coriander seeds
1½ teaspoons cumin seeds
¾ teaspoon brown mustard seeds
1 cinnamon stick or a piece of cassia bark
1 cup coconut cream
1½ teaspoons tamarind concentrate
100 g baby spinach or water spinach leaves
salt

Slice 1 onion and roughly chop the other. Heat the oil in a heavy saucepan and fry the cashews until golden. Remove to a plate and set aside.

In the same oil, fry the sliced onion until very well browned and set aside with the cashews. Still in the same pan, brown the chicken pieces over medium–high heat. Set aside.

In a blender or mortar grind the chopped onion and the garlic to a paste.

Dry-roast the chillies, peppercorns, seeds and cinnamon or cassia until browned but not too dark. Grind to a powder in a mortar.

Reheat the pan used for the chicken and fry the onion paste for a few minutes. Add the ground spices and cook well, then stir in the coconut cream and simmer for 5 minutes. Mix the tamarind into 1 cup water and pour into the curry sauce, then simmer for 5 minutes. Return the chicken and sliced onions and cashews to the pan and simmer for about 25 minutes, until the chicken is tender, adding more water if the sauce becomes too thick.

Stir in spinach, add salt to taste and cook just long enough for the spinach to wilt.

SERVES 4–5

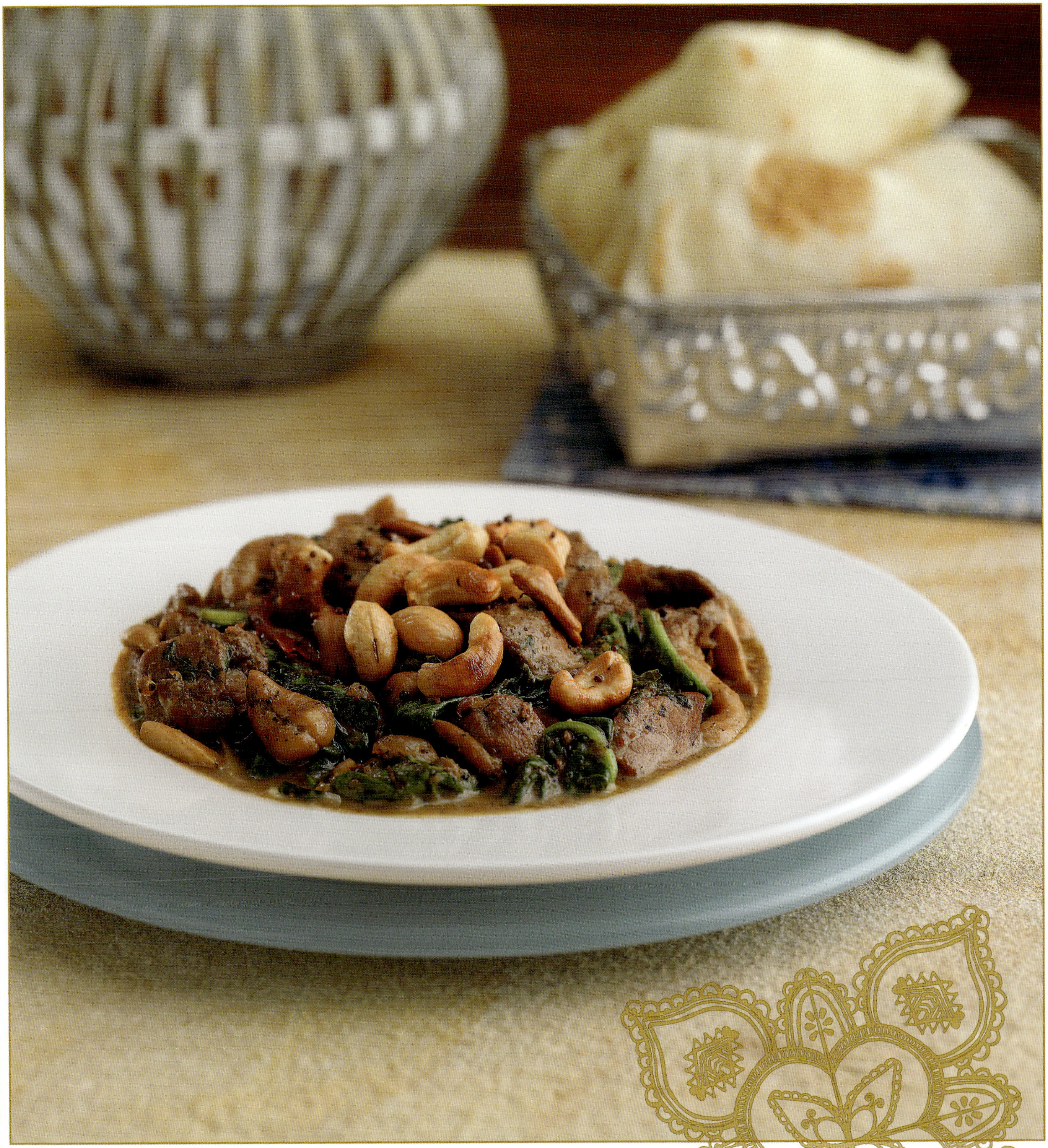

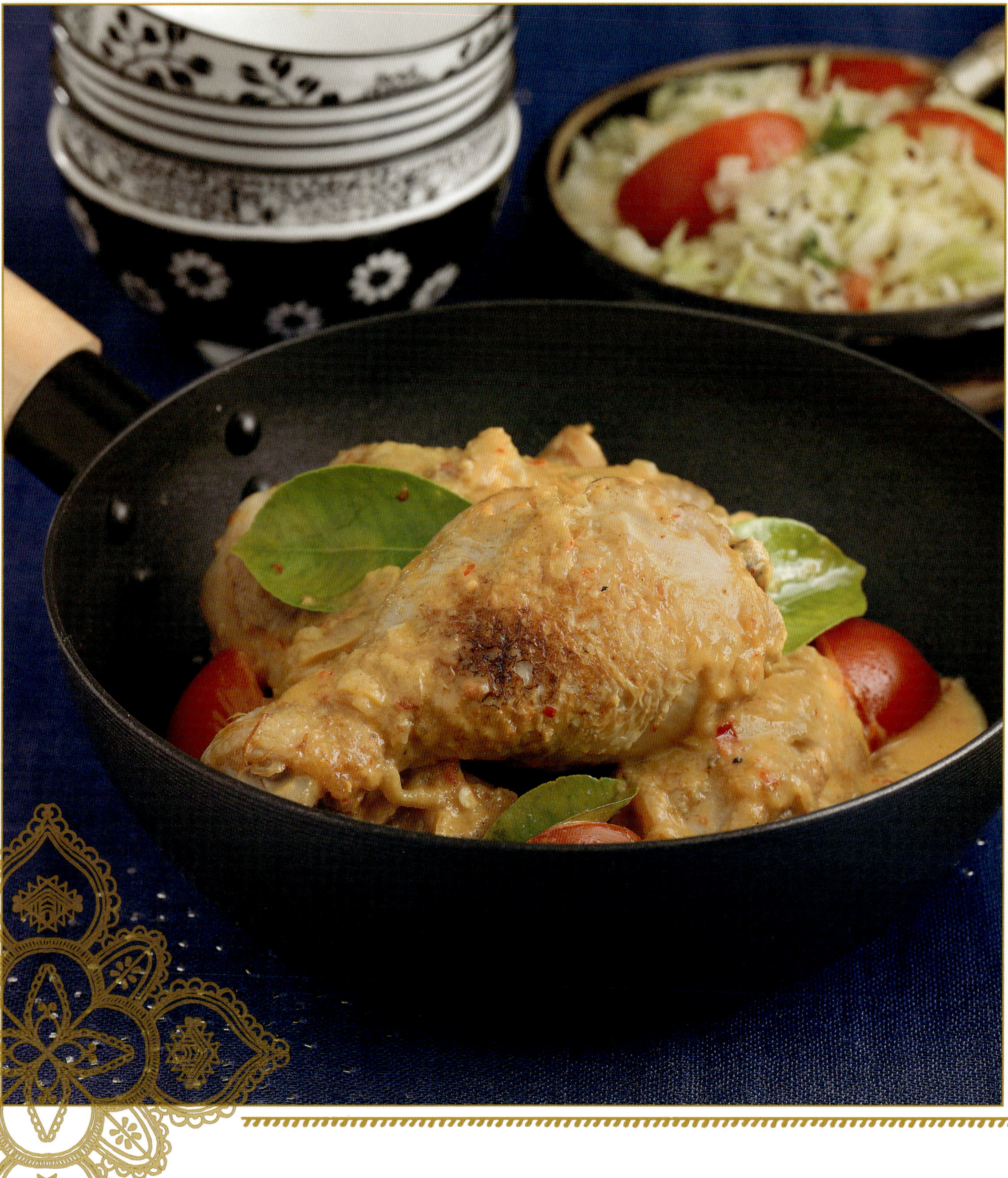

Chicken with lime leaves (ayam limau purut)

This is a Nonya dish. 'Nonya' refers to the integration of Chinese and Malay through intermarriage: as a cuisine it is a fusion of Malaccan, Portuguese, Malay and Indian.

2 medium-sized onions
2–4 fresh hot red chillies, deseeded and roughly chopped
4 cloves garlic, peeled
¾ teaspoon ground turmeric
2–3 tablespoons oil
3 slices fresh galangal, bruised
1 stem lemongrass, bruised
750 g chicken pieces, cut into 5-cm chunks
1 × 400-ml can light coconut milk
3–5 kaffir lime leaves
salt
4–5 large cherry tomatoes, halved

Roughly chop 1 onion and finely slice the other. Make a seasoning paste by grinding the chopped onion with the chillies, garlic, turmeric and 1 tablespoon of the oil in a food processor or blender.

Fry sliced onion in remaining oil for about 2 minutes, until softened and lightly coloured. Add the galangal, lemongrass and prepared seasoning paste, and fry over medium heat for about 3 minutes, stirring constantly to prevent sticking and burning. Add chicken pieces and stir to coat with the seasonings. Cook for 2–3 minutes, constantly moving and turning the chicken.

Rinse out the blender or processor with 1½ cups water and pour over the chicken. Add coconut milk, lime leaves and about 1½ teaspoons salt and bring to the boil. Reduce heat and simmer gently for 25–30 minutes, turning the chicken and stirring the sauce from time to time.

Check seasonings. Add cherry tomatoes and cook briefly until softened. Transfer to a serving dish.

SERVES 4–5

Chicken curry with coconut & cashews

1 medium-sized onion, roughly chopped
3 cloves garlic, peeled
a 1.5-cm piece fresh ginger, peeled
½ teaspoon peppercorns
1½ teaspoons cumin seeds
⅓ cup desiccated coconut
2–3 tablespoons ghee or oil
650 g chicken thigh fillets, cut into 3-cm cubes
1 large tomato, deseeded and diced
½ cup roasted unsalted cashews
⅓ teaspoon ground ginger
1½ teaspoons garam masala (page 16)
½ teaspoon ground turmeric
1 teaspoon ground coriander
½ teaspoon hot ground chilli
1 × 400-ml can coconut cream
salt
freshly squeezed lemon juice

Place onion in a food processor with the garlic and ginger and grind to a paste.

In a spice grinder or mortar grind peppercorns, cumin and coconut to a fine powder. Mix with the onion paste.

Heat ghee or oil in a heavy saucepan and brown the chicken pieces in several batches. Remove to a plate using a slotted spoon. Add the onion and spice paste to the same pan and stir over medium heat for about 4 minutes, then add the tomato, cashews and ground spices and cook for a further 4–5 minutes, adding a little water if it begins to catch on the bottom of the pan. Stir in the coconut cream and return the chicken to the pan, adding ¾ cup water and 1½ teaspoons salt.

Simmer over low heat for 20–25 minutes, adding extra water if needed, until chicken is tender and the sauce thick and creamy.

SERVES 4–5

Chicken curry laksa

120 g fine rice vermicelli

1 bundle egg or hokkien noodles

1 × 400-ml can coconut cream

2 tablespoons laksa paste or Thai yellow curry paste (page 20)

3 chicken thigh fillets, cut into 2-cm pieces

6 cups chicken stock

3–4 button mushrooms, thinly sliced

1 small zucchini, thinly sliced

4–8 small fresh hot red chillies, split and deseeded

2–3 tablespoons fish sauce

salt and freshly ground pepper

3 spring onions, chopped

1½ cups bean sprouts

2–3 tablespoons chopped fresh coriander

lime wedges, to serve

Soften the vermicelli in boiling water. Cook the noodles in a separate pot of lightly salted water, according to the directions on the pack. Drain all the noodles and set aside.

In a medium–large saucepan heat ½ cup of the coconut cream until boiling. Add curry paste and simmer for 2 minutes. Add chicken and stir to coat it with the seasoning paste. Cook for about 2 minutes, then pour in the chicken stock and bring to the boil. Add the mushrooms, zucchini and chillies and the remaining coconut cream, and cook for 5—10 minutes. Season to taste with fish sauce, salt and pepper.

Divide noodles and vermicelli between four large bowls and add some of the spring onions, bean sprouts and coriander. Ladle the soup over, distributing the chicken and vegetables evenly. Serve with lime wedges and extra fish sauce.

SERVES 5–6 (OR UP TO 8–12 AS A FIRST COURSE)

CHICKEN & DUCK CURRIES

Sri Lankan molee of chicken & vegetables

The name molee usually describes a mildly seasoned coconut curry of finely diced, sliced or grated ingredients, often served as a side dish.

2 tablespoons oil
1 large fresh green chilli, deseeded and sliced
¾ teaspoon brown mustard seeds
½ teaspoon cumin seeds
1 small onion, chopped
4–5 curry leaves
½ teaspoon ground turmeric
1½ teaspoons ground coriander
1 × 400-ml can coconut milk
salt
1 zucchini, sliced
350 g skinless chicken breast fillets, cut into bite-sized strips
200 g baby spinach or water spinach leaves
freshly squeezed lemon juice

In a medium-sized saucepan heat the oil and fry the chilli, mustard and cumin seeds over medium–high heat for about 1 minute. Add onion and fry, stirring almost continually, for 2–3 minutes, then stir in the curry leaves and ground spices. Pour in coconut milk, add a large pinch of salt and bring to the boil. Reduce heat and simmer for 2 minutes.

Add zucchini and chicken to pan and simmer for 5 or so minutes, then stir in the spinach and cook until vegetables are tender (about 3 minutes). Check for salt and finish with a squeeze of lemon juice.

SERVES 2–3

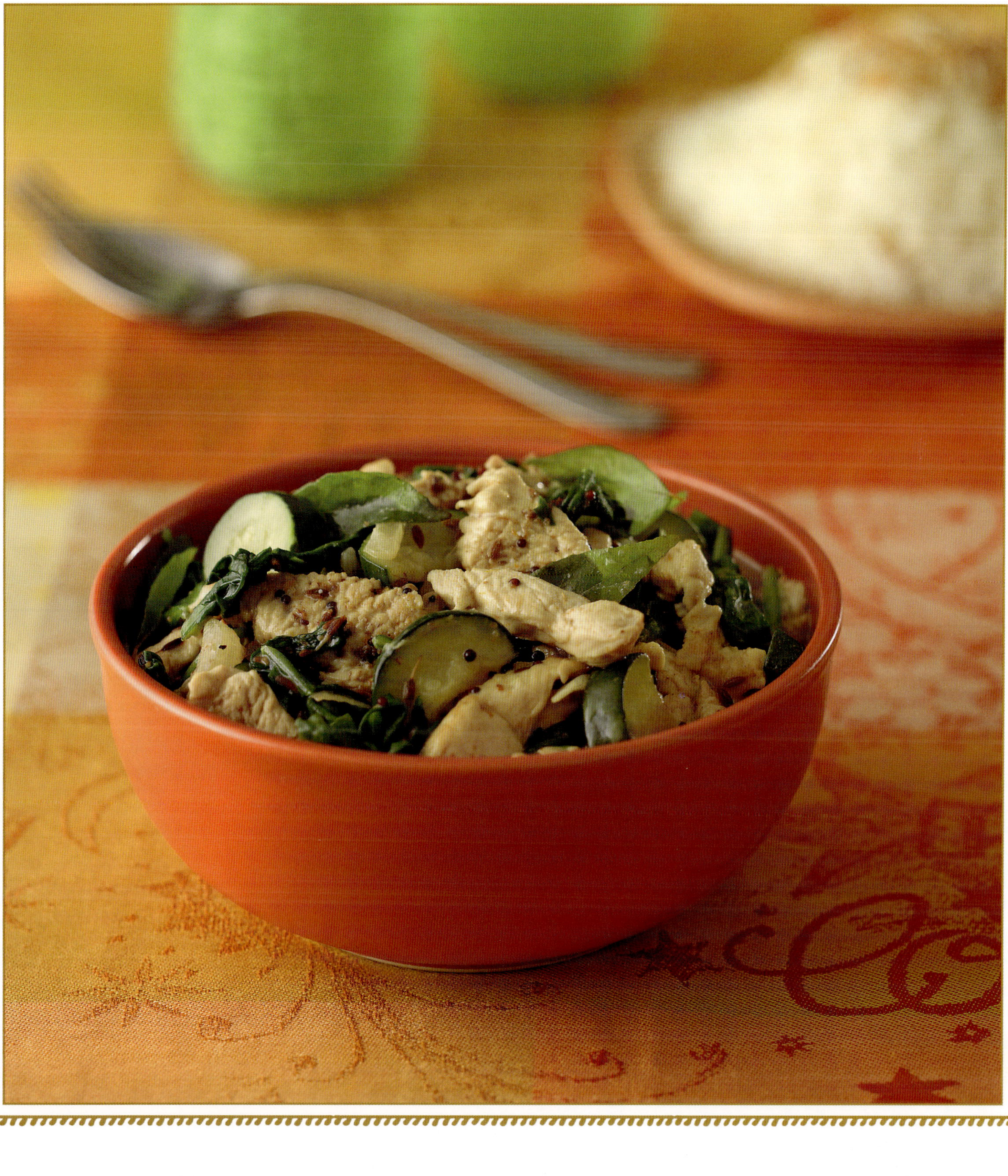

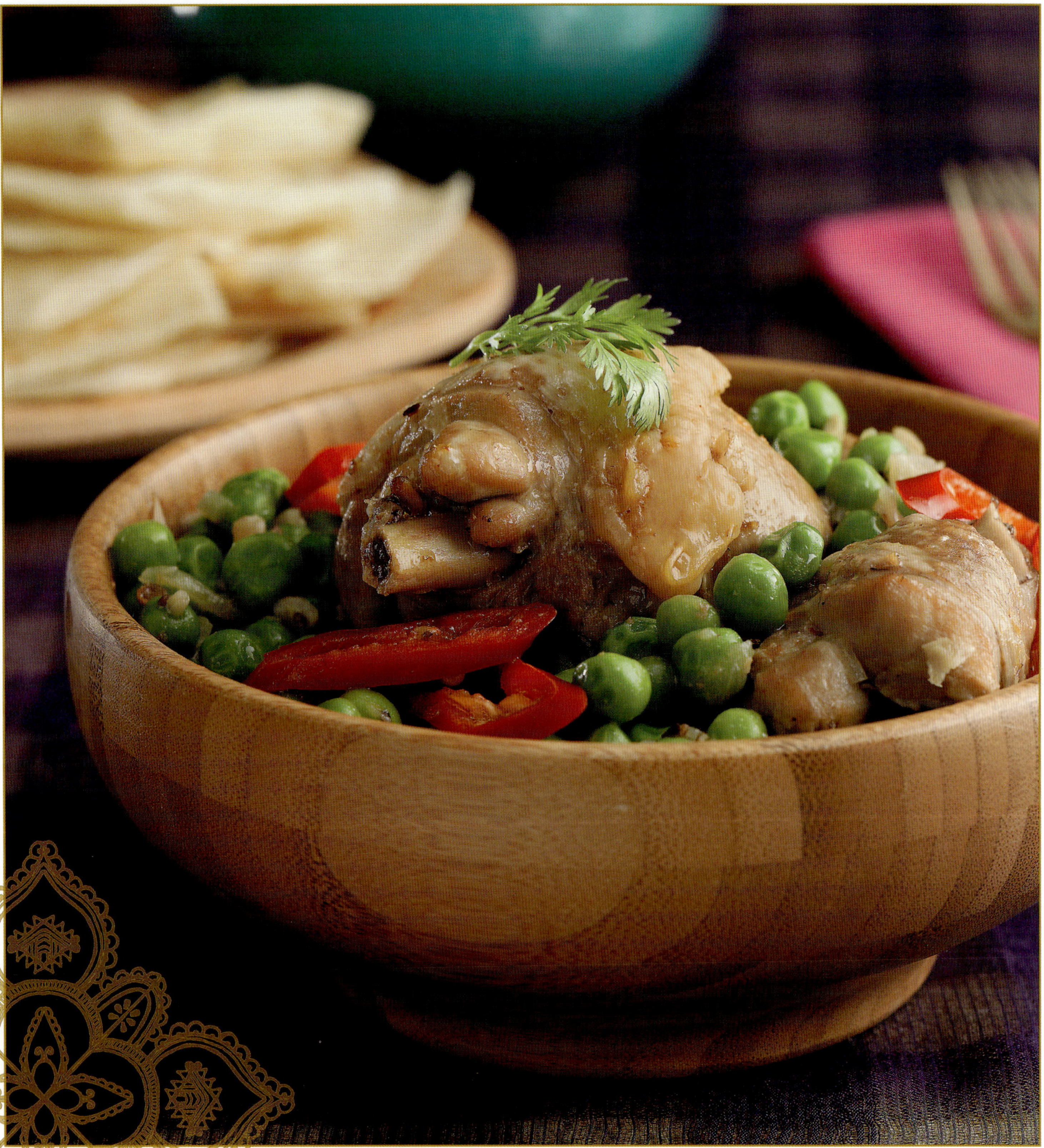

Malay chicken curry with red chillies & peas

- 6 small chicken legs, chopped in half
- 3 chicken thighs on the bone, each cut into 4 pieces
- 4 thin slices fresh ginger, finely shredded
- 4 whole cloves
- 1 cinnamon stick
- 3 cardamom pods, cracked
- 3–6 dried red chillies, deseeded
- 1½ tablespoons coriander seeds
- 1 teaspoon cumin seeds
- 2–3 tablespoons ghee or oil
- 8 shallots, finely sliced
- 2–3 cloves garlic, chopped
- ¼ teaspoon fennel seeds, crushed
- ¼ teaspoon fenugreek seeds, crushed
- ½ teaspoon black peppercorns, crushed
- ¾ cup coconut cream
- 1 cup peas

Place chicken in a saucepan with enough water to barely cover and add the ginger, cloves, cinnamon and cardamom pods. Bring to the boil, reduce heat and simmer for about 15 minutes.

In another saucepan dry-roast the chillies, coriander and cumin seeds for about 1½ minutes over medium–high heat, until very aromatic. Transfer to a spice grinder and grind finely.

Heat the ghee or oil in the same pan and fry the shallots and garlic for about 1½ minutes, then add the crushed and ground spices and fry, stirring constantly, until very fragrant (about 1½ minutes). Add the coconut cream and simmer for 5 minutes.

Transfer chicken pieces to the pan, and add enough of the poaching water to half cover. Simmer until the chicken is completely tender (10–15 minutes). Add the peas, check seasonings and cook until peas are done.

SERVES 6–8

Chicken curry with green peppercorns

Dinner for two and a quiet night of television? This smooth and spicy curry takes only two commercial breaks to prepare!

350 g chicken breast fillet, cut into 1-cm strips
1 ½ tablespoons oil
2 spring onions, chopped
1 clove garlic, crushed
½ teaspoon grated fresh ginger
3 teaspoons mild Indian curry paste or powder (page 14)
¾ cup chicken stock
¼ cup cream or sour cream
salt
2 teaspoons green peppercorns in brine, drained

In a wok or pan stir-fry the chicken in the oil until lightly browned and partially cooked (about 2 ½ minutes). Remove to a plate.

Sauté the spring onions, garlic and ginger in the same pan until lightly coloured. Add the curry paste or powder and cook briefly, stirring, then add the chicken stock and cream or sour cream and heat gently for 2 minutes.

Return the chicken to the pan and add salt and the peppercorns and simmer gently until chicken is tender (about 5 minutes).

SERVES 2

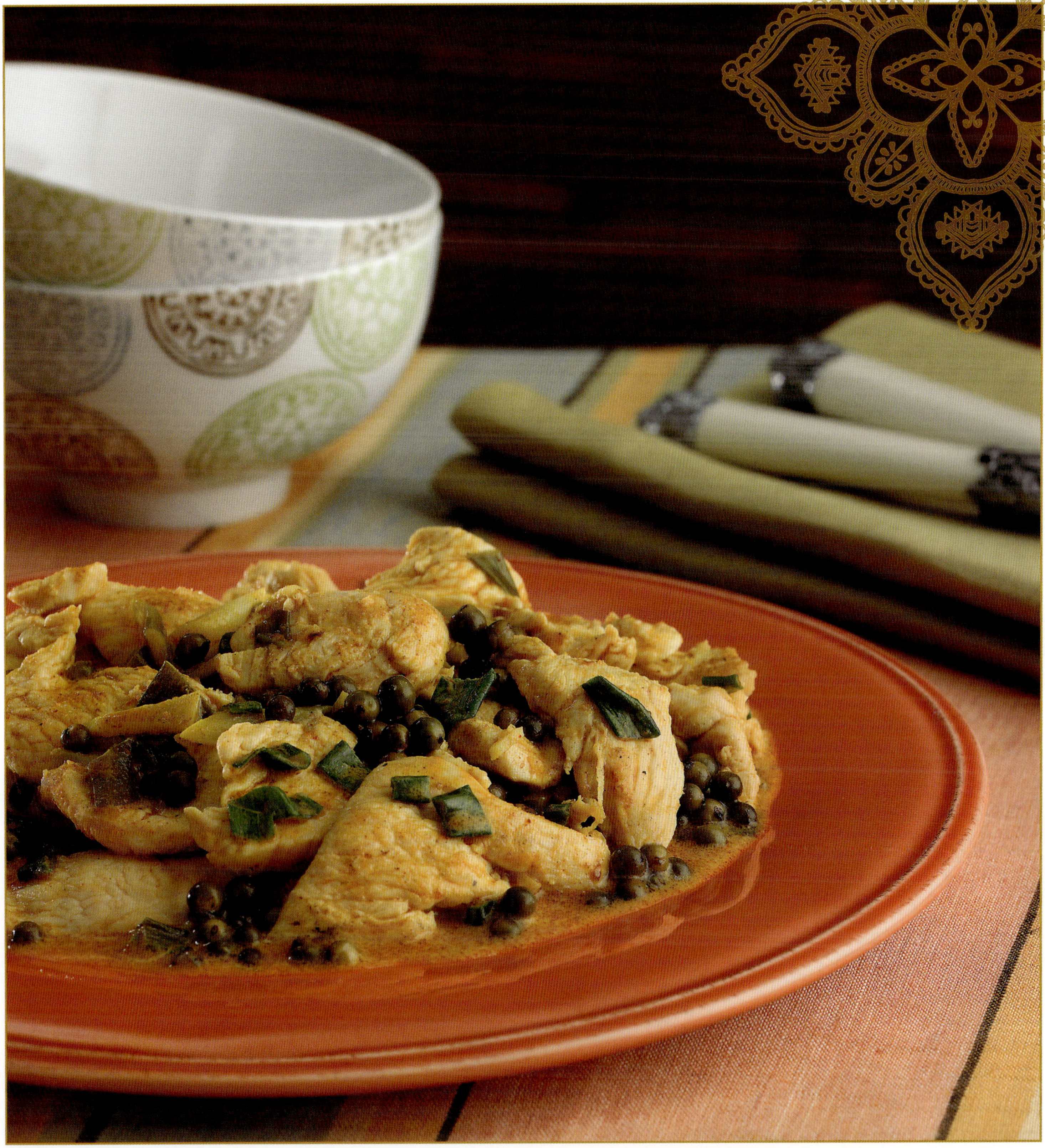

Roast chicken & mango curry

What to do with leftover roast chicken? Simple! Turn it into a curry.

½ roast chicken (or use turkey)
2 spring onions, chopped
3–4 button mushrooms, sliced
2 tablespoons oil or butter
2 teaspoons mild curry powder or paste
½ teaspoon grated fresh ginger
¾ cup chicken stock
1 mango cheek (fresh, canned or frozen), diced
chopped fresh coriander, dill or mint
¼ cup cream, coconut cream or sour cream

Strip chicken (or turkey) meat from the bones and cut into bite-sized chunks. Set aside.

In a small pan sauté the spring onions and mushrooms in the oil or butter until softened (about 2 minutes). Add the curry powder or paste and the ginger, and cook briefly.

Pour in chicken stock and bring to the boil. Reduce heat and simmer for 2–3 minutes. Add the chicken, mango, herbs and cream and simmer very gently until heated through (about 6 minutes).

SERVES 3–4

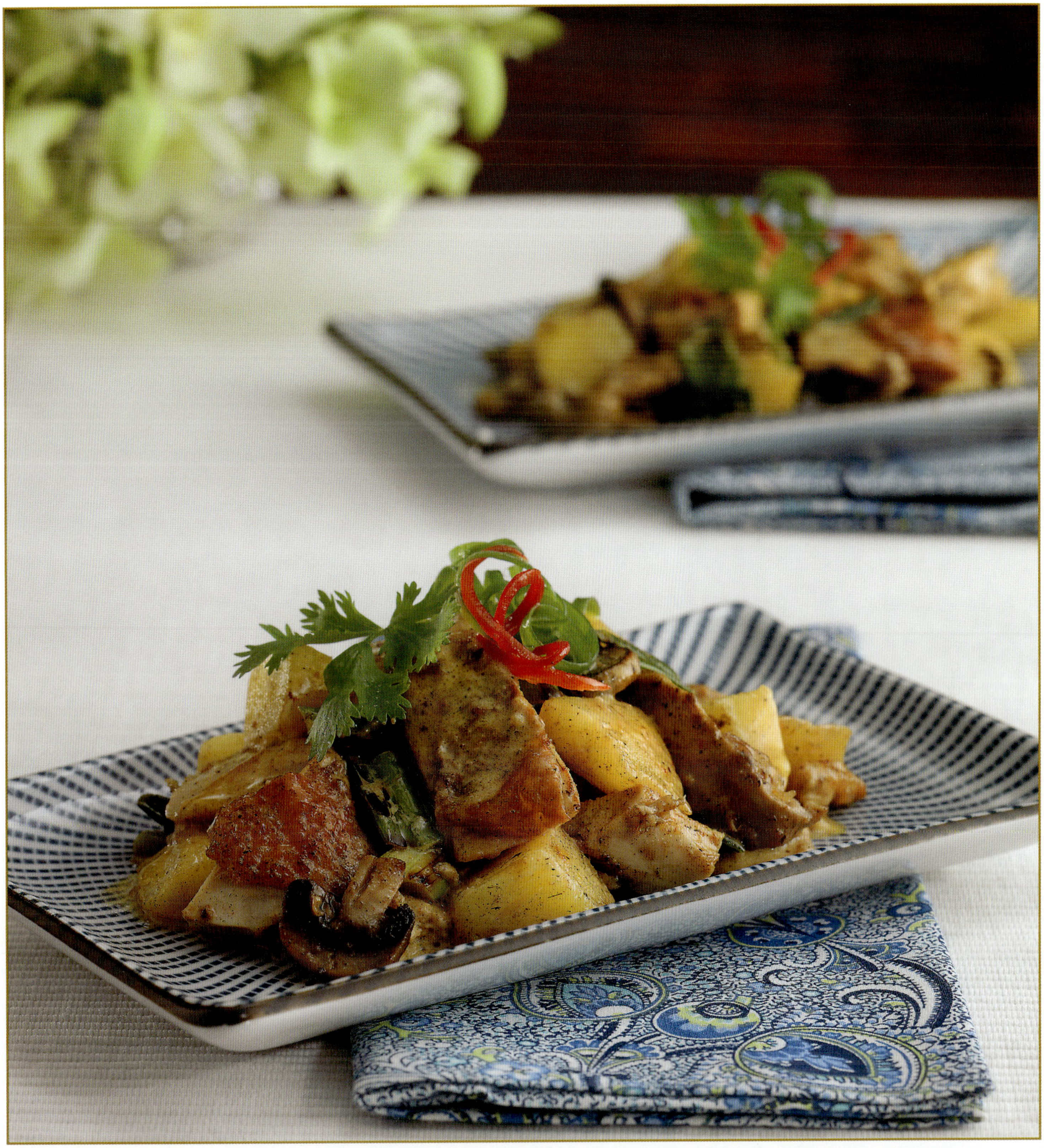

Chicken & tomatoes in hot curry

This is a south Indian dish.

4 chicken thigh fillets, preferably with skin on, cut into 2-cm slices
2–3 tablespoons ghee or oil
1 medium-sized onion, finely chopped
3 large ripe tomatoes, deseeded and diced
3 tablespoons coconut milk powder
1 tablespoon hot Indian curry paste (page 14)
1 teaspoon hot red chilli paste
2 teaspoons grated fresh ginger
1½ cups chicken stock or water
salt
freshly squeezed lime juice
chopped fresh coriander

Brown the chicken in the ghee or oil until half cooked (about 5 minutes). Remove to a plate.

Cook onion in the same pan until lightly coloured (about 3 minutes), then add the tomatoes, coconut powder, curry paste, chilli paste, and ginger, and cook for 5 minutes, stirring constantly over medium–high heat.

Return the chicken to the pan and cook for a few minutes, stirring, before adding the stock or water and salt. Partially cover and simmer gently until the chicken is tender and the sauce quite thick (about 15 minutes). Squeeze in lime juice to taste, add fresh coriander and serve.

SERVES 4

Malaysian chicken liver curry (kari kering hati ayam)

The richness of curried chicken livers tends to see this dish served alongside another curry or as a side dish for a spicy grill.

1½ tablespoons oil or ghee
3 shallots or 1 small onion, finely chopped
2 cloves garlic, chopped
2 teaspoons grated fresh ginger
400 g chicken livers, trimmed and halved
a 4-cm piece cinnamon stick
2 whole cloves
1 cardamom pod, cracked
2 teaspoons ground cumin
½ teaspoon fennel seeds, crushed
salt and pepper
1 cup coconut milk
2 hard-boiled eggs, cut into wedges (optional)
3 large cherry tomatoes, halved (optional)
chopped fresh Vietnamese mint, basil and coriander

Heat oil or ghee in a medium-sized saucepan or sauté pan and sauté onion, garlic and ginger over medium heat, until softened and lightly coloured (about 2 minutes). Add the livers and brown lightly, turning carefully. Stir in the spices, seasonings and coconut milk and simmer gently until livers have changed colour and are firm (5–6 minutes). Add egg wedges and tomatoes (if using) and heat gently for 1–2 minutes.

Transfer to a serving dish and garnish with chopped herbs.

SERVES 4–6

Jungle curry of quail with bamboo shoots & choko

Thailand's tropical rainforest regions yield a bounty of exotic funghi, tangled vines bearing several kinds of pepper and edible peppery leaves, edible rhizomes, and game meats. From this native habitat come intensely flavoured 'jungle' curries. Small Thai eggplants precooked in brine are available at Asian food stores and can replace the fresh variety if you can't find any.

- 4 quails
- a 1-cm piece fresh ginger, roughly chopped
- 2 tablespoons oil
- 1½ tablespoons Thai jungle curry paste (page 21)
- 2 tablespoons fish sauce
- 3 kaffir lime leaves
- ½ choko or zucchini, cut into chunks
- ¼ cup sliced bamboo shoots
- 4 small Thai apple eggplants, quartered
- ¼ cup straw mushrooms, halved
- 3 cherry tomatoes, halved
- 1 fresh hot green chilli, split lengthways and deseeded
- 2 sprigs green peppercorns in brine

Trim off the necks and cut quails in half along the centre back and breastbone. With a small knife trim around the rib cage and along the backbone to debone, leaving bones in legs. Cut off wings at the second joint, leaving just the shoulder bone intact.

Place the quail trimmings in a small saucepan with 3 cups water and the ginger and bring to the boil, then reduce heat and simmer for 20 minutes. Strain, discarding bones and reserving the stock.

Cut each quail half in two, cutting neatly between breast and thigh. Heat the oil in a frying pan or saucepan and cook the quails in batches, until well browned and almost cooked (about 4 minutes). Remove to a plate.

Add the curry paste to the pan and fry for about 1½ minutes, until very fragrant. Add the fish sauce and fry briefly, then add the prepared stock, choko or zucchini, bamboo shoots, eggplants and mushrooms and simmer for 6–7 minutes. Add the quail, tomatoes, chilli and peppercorns and continue to simmer until the quail and vegetables are tender (about 5 minutes).

SERVES 6

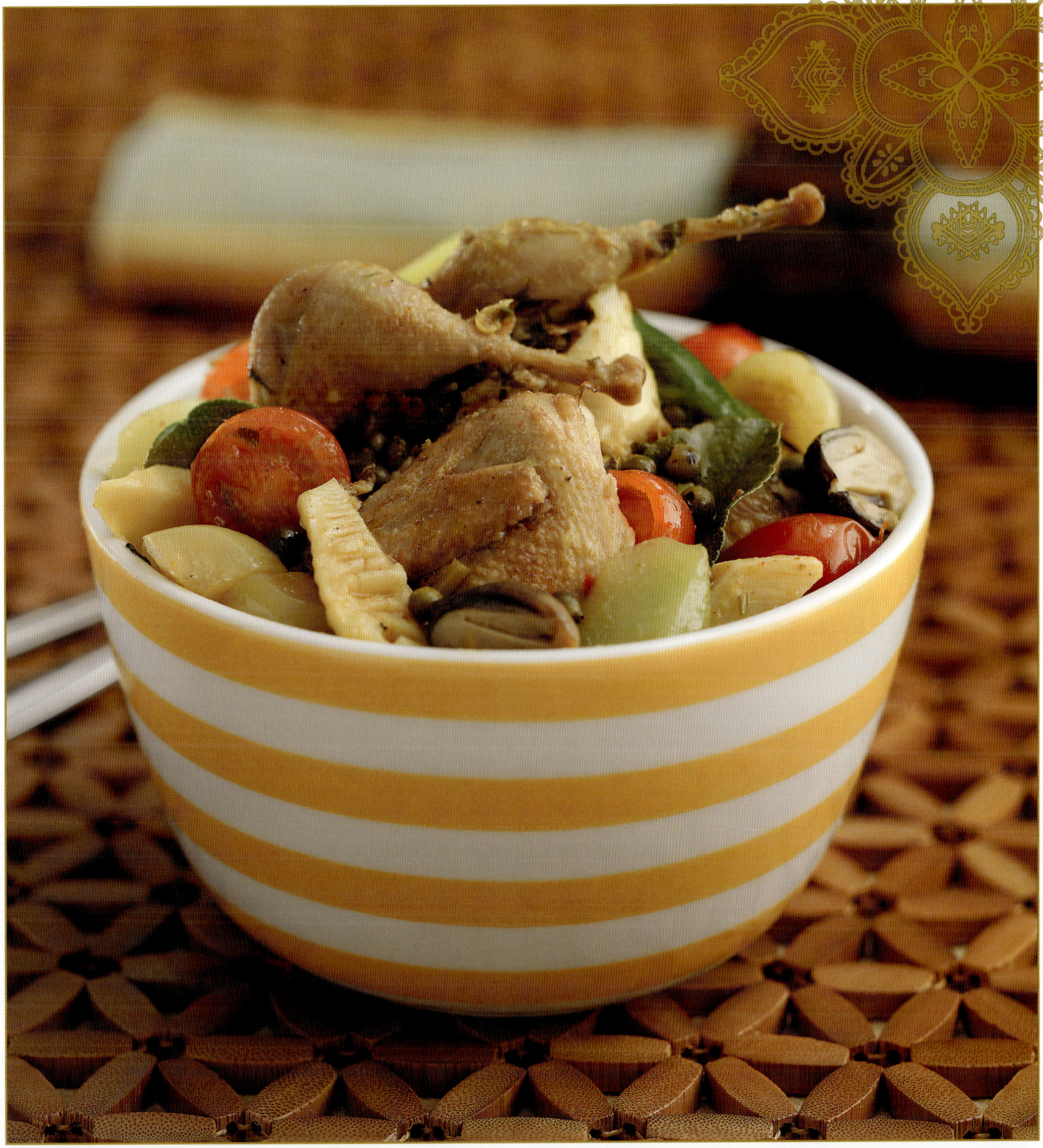

Breast of duck in fiery vindaloo sauce

Creamy raita with cucumber and fresh mint is a perfect side dish to balance the intense heat of vindaloo. Poaching the duck breasts in oil makes them superbly moist and tender. If you prefer, you can brown them by shallow-frying in a pan and finish in a hot oven.

- 2 medium-sized onions, finely chopped
- 2–3 tablespoons ghee or oil
- 2 large tomatoes, deseeded and chopped
- 3 cloves garlic, crushed
- ½ teaspoon red chilli paste (optional)
- 2 tablespoons vindaloo paste (page 11)
- 1½ teaspoons sugar
- 1 tablespoon freshly squeezed lemon juice or 2 teaspoons tamarind concentrate
- 3 fresh or frozen duck breasts (if frozen, thaw in refrigerator overnight)
- 4 cups oil, for deep-frying

Fry the onions in the ghee or oil until well browned (about 8 minutes). Add tomatoes, garlic, chilli paste and 1½ tablespoons of the vindaloo paste and cook, stirring frequently, for about 5 minutes. Add sugar, lemon juice or tamarind and 2 cups water, and simmer for 15–20 minutes until the sauce is well reduced. Taste, and stir in remaining vindaloo paste if needed.

Meanwhile gently poach the duck breasts in the oil until tender and light-brown (about 15 minutes). Carefully remove with a slotted spoon and drain well. Slice duck thickly and warm gently in the hot sauce.

SERVES 4

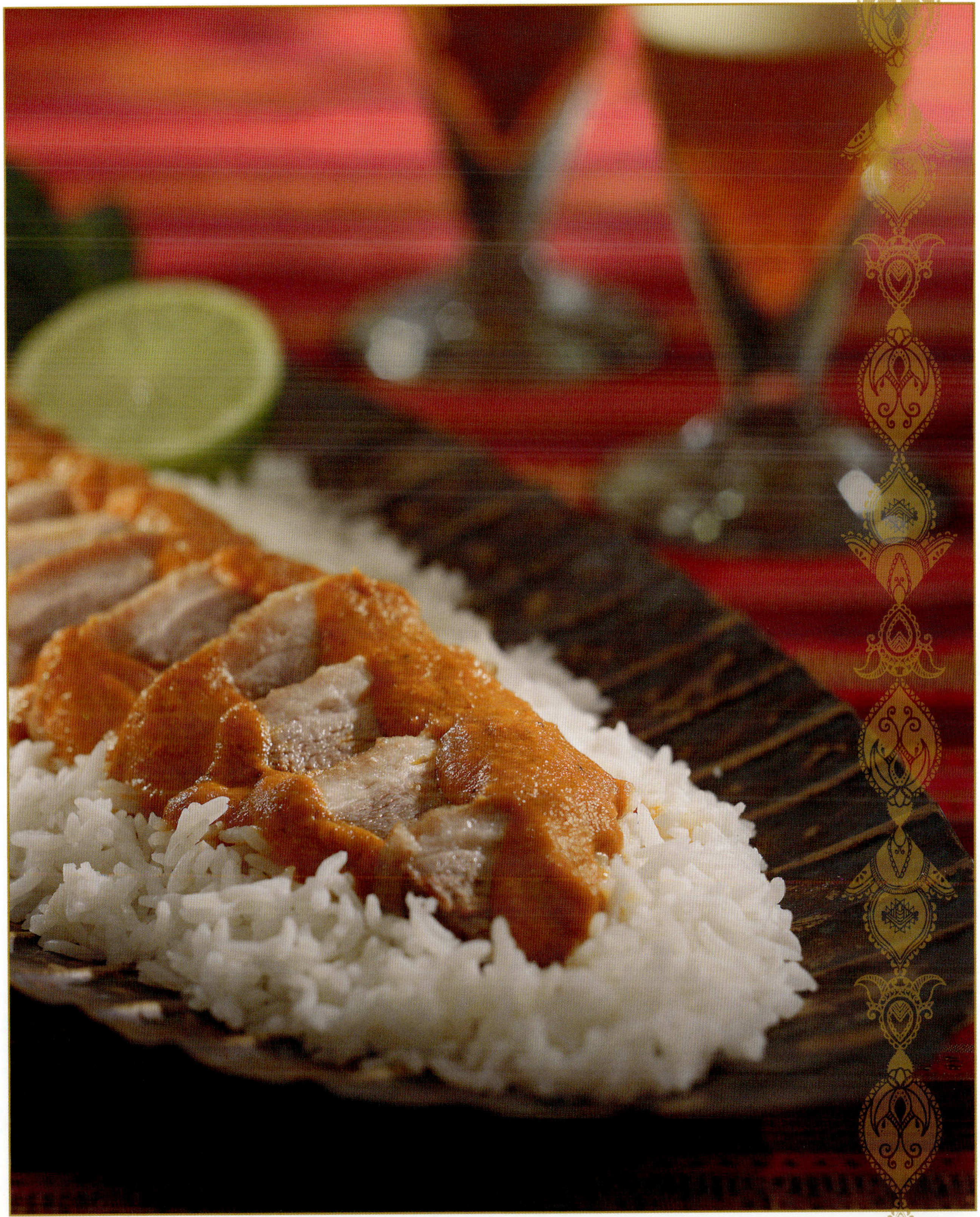

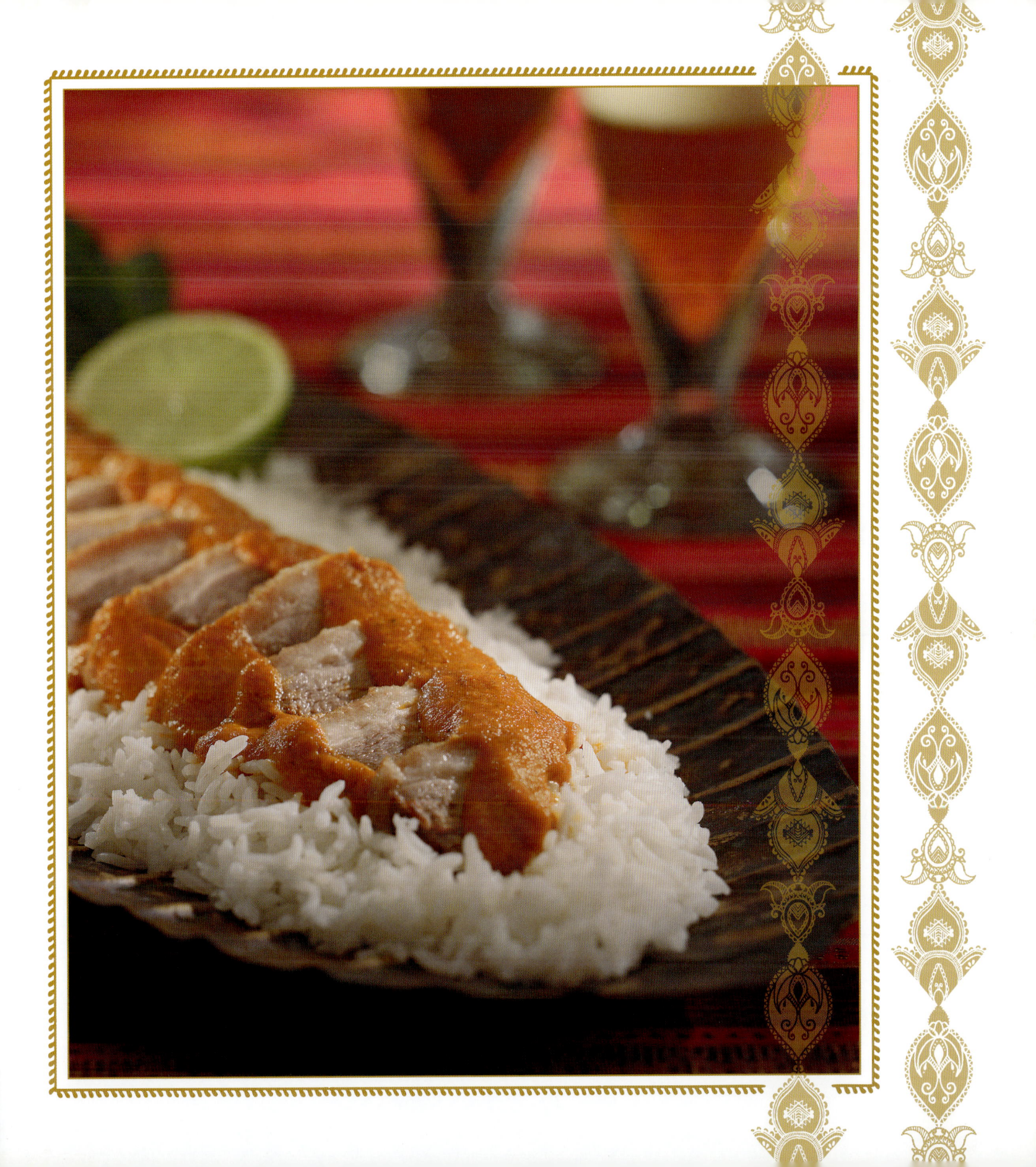

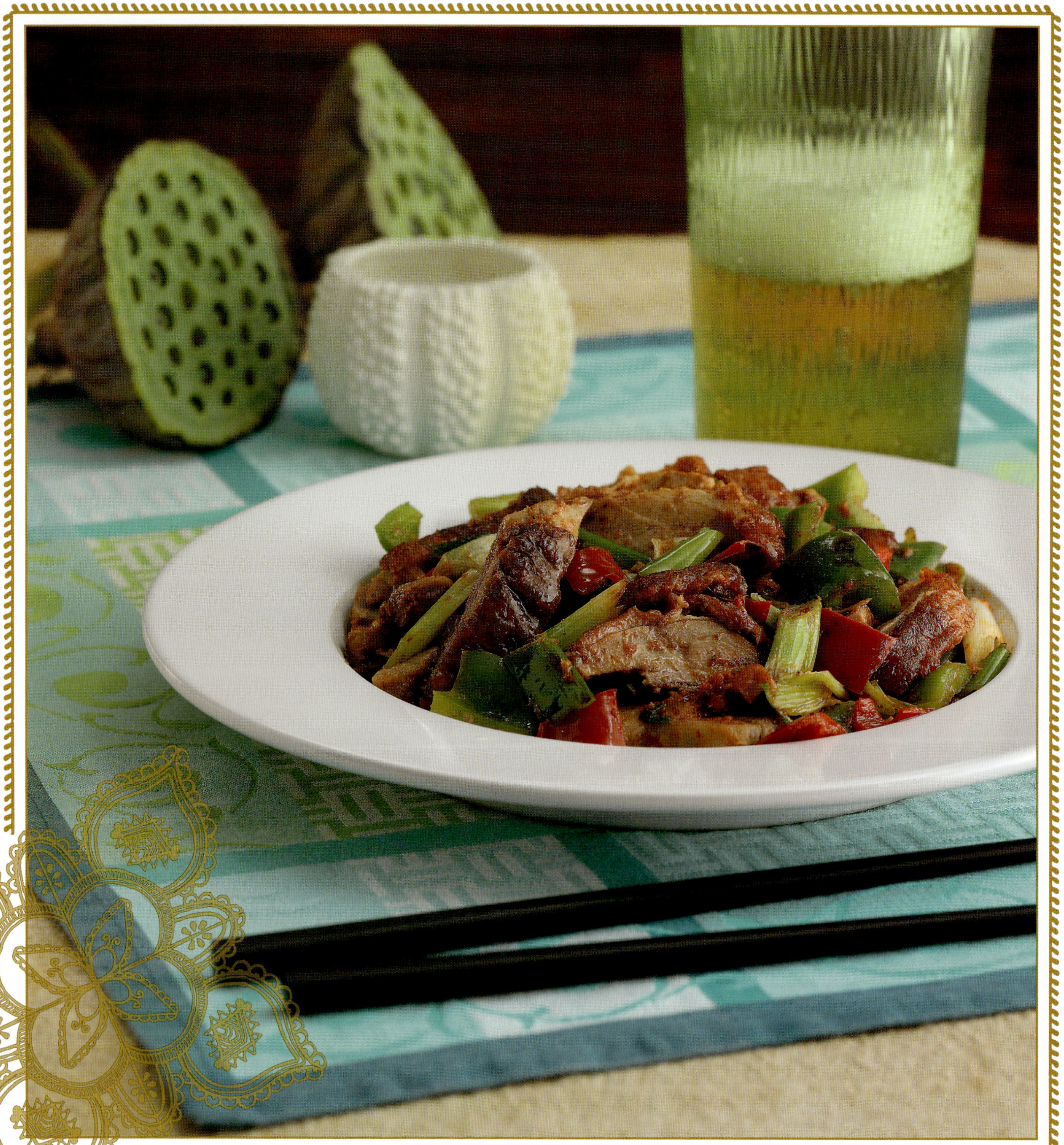

Roast duck red curry stir-fry with spring onions

Not quite a curry, but with all the punch and flavour you'd expect from one, and ready in minutes.

½ Chinese roast duck
2–3 teaspoons Thai red curry paste (page 17)
2 tablespoons oil
4 spring onions, cut into 4-cm pieces
½ red or green capsicum, cut into fine strips
fish sauce

Remove the duck meat from the bones and cut into 1-cm slices.

In a wok or frying pan fry the curry paste in the oil for about 40 seconds, until very fragrant. Add the spring onions and capsicum, and stir-fry until they soften, adding a small amount of water if needed to prevent the spices catching on the base of the pan. Put in the duck meat and add a generous splash of fish sauce. Stir-fry just long enough to warm the duck.

SERVES 2–3

Javanese padang curry of duck & red chillies

Use a cleaver to chop the duck (still on the bone). Alternatively, if you have an obliging supplier ask them to do it for you.

2 medium-sized onions
6 cloves garlic, peeled
a 3-cm piece fresh ginger, peeled
3 fresh hot green chillies, deseeded and roughly chopped
2 stems lemongrass, trimmed
3 tablespoons oil
1 large duck (about 2 kg), chopped into 5-cm pieces
a 4-cm piece fresh galangal, peeled and cut in half
1 × 400-ml can coconut cream
2 teaspoons tamarind concentrate
2 teaspoons green peppercorns
salt

Roughly chop 1 onion and finely slice the other. Place the chopped onion in a food processor or blender with the garlic, ginger, chillies and one of the lemongrass stems (chopped). Grind to a reasonably smooth paste.

Heat the oil in a wok or saucepan and fry the sliced onion until well browned (about 5 minutes). Add the onion-garlic paste and fry for 2–3 minutes. Mix in the duck pieces and stir over medium-high heat for 1–2 minutes, taking care the onions do not catch and burn. Add remaining lemongrass stem, the galangal and coconut cream, and cover the pan. Reduce heat and simmer gently for 10 minutes, stirring once or twice.

Mix tamarind with 1½ cups water and pour into the pan, adding peppercorns with salt to taste. Mix well. Increase heat until the sauce begins to bubble, then reduce heat again and simmer until duck is tender (about 30 minutes), stirring from time to time and adding extra water if needed.

SERVES 6–8

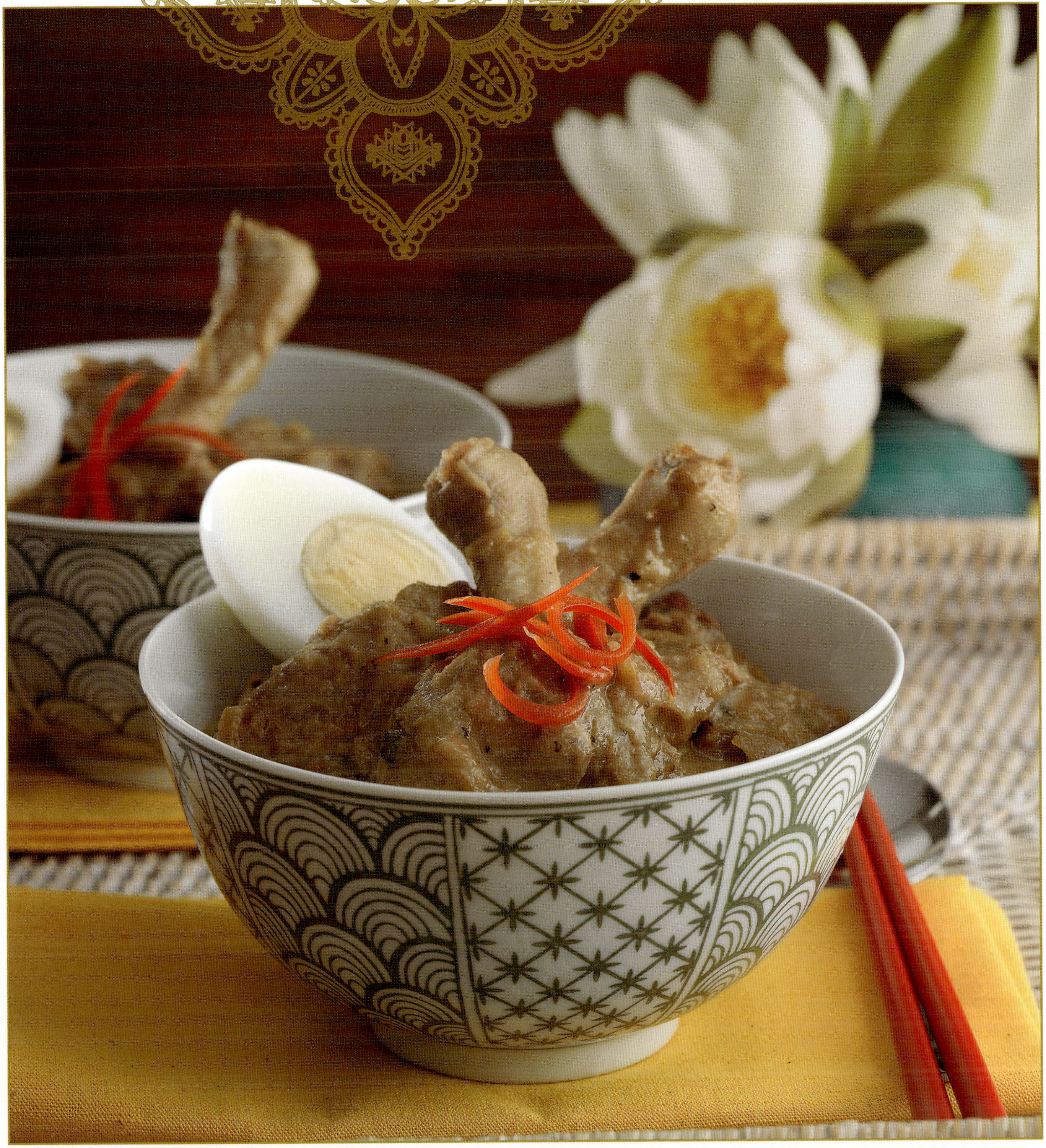

Balinese duck baked in banana leaves

Bebek betutu is a special-occasion dish in Bali. A whole plump duck is seasoned with aromatic herbs and spices, wrapped in banana bark and leaves, and cooked in a pit of smouldering coconut husks, which impart a tantalising smokiness to the meat. A kettle barbecue and hot charcoal gives a comparable result, but the easiest method is to cook it in a slow oven.

1 teaspoon shrimp paste
1 large onion, roughly chopped
3 cloves garlic, peeled
a 10-cm stem lemongrass, roughly chopped
a 2-cm piece fresh ginger, peeled
a 3-cm piece fresh turmeric, peeled (or ¾ teaspoon ground turmeric)
1–2 fresh hot red chillies, deseeded
2–3 teaspoons grated palm sugar
6 macadamias or candlenuts
2 teaspoons salt
1 teaspoon cracked black pepper
4 kaffir lime leaves
banana leaves
1 large duck (about 2.5 kg), cut into serving portions (boned or not, as you prefer)
tomato and onion sambal (page 290)

Preheat the oven to 160ºC.

Wrap the shrimp paste in foil and roast in a small pan without oil for a few minutes, turning frequently. Unwrap and set aside.

In a food processor, grind the onion, garlic, lemongrass, ginger, turmeric, chillies, shrimp paste, sugar and nuts to a paste. Add salt, pepper and lime leaves, and pulse to partially break up the leaves.

Line an oven dish with a banana leaf large enough to completely wrap the duck. Place a piece of baking paper of the same size on top. Spread half the seasoning paste in the centre of the paper and cover with the duck pieces. Spread remaining paste over the duck, wrap up the paper and then fold over banana leaves, tucking in ends securely. Cover the top of the oven dish with foil. Bake for about 2½ hours, until the duck is meltingly tender.

Remove from the oven and let rest for 10 minutes before unwrapping. Slice, and serve with a sambal.

SERVES 8–10

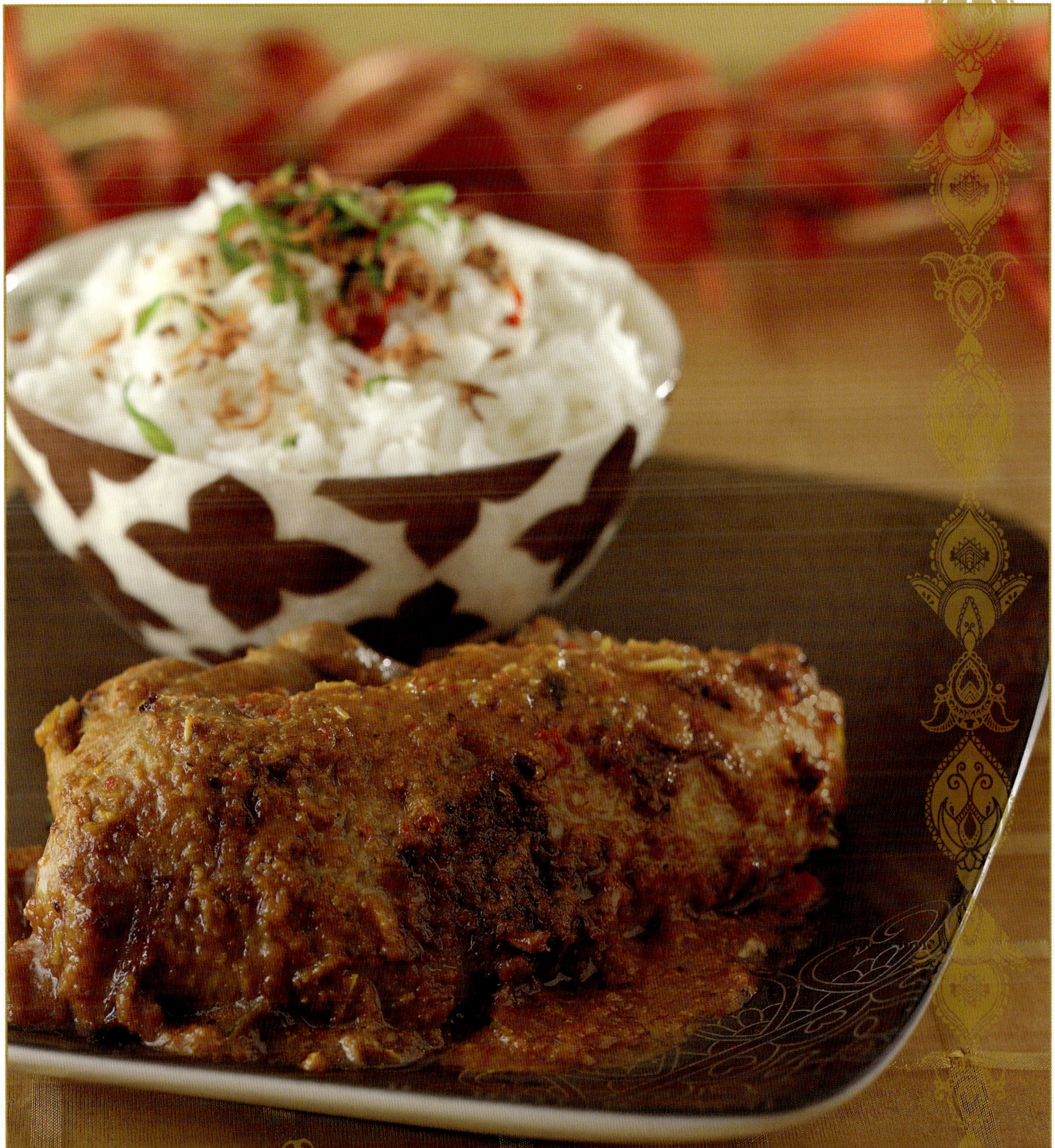

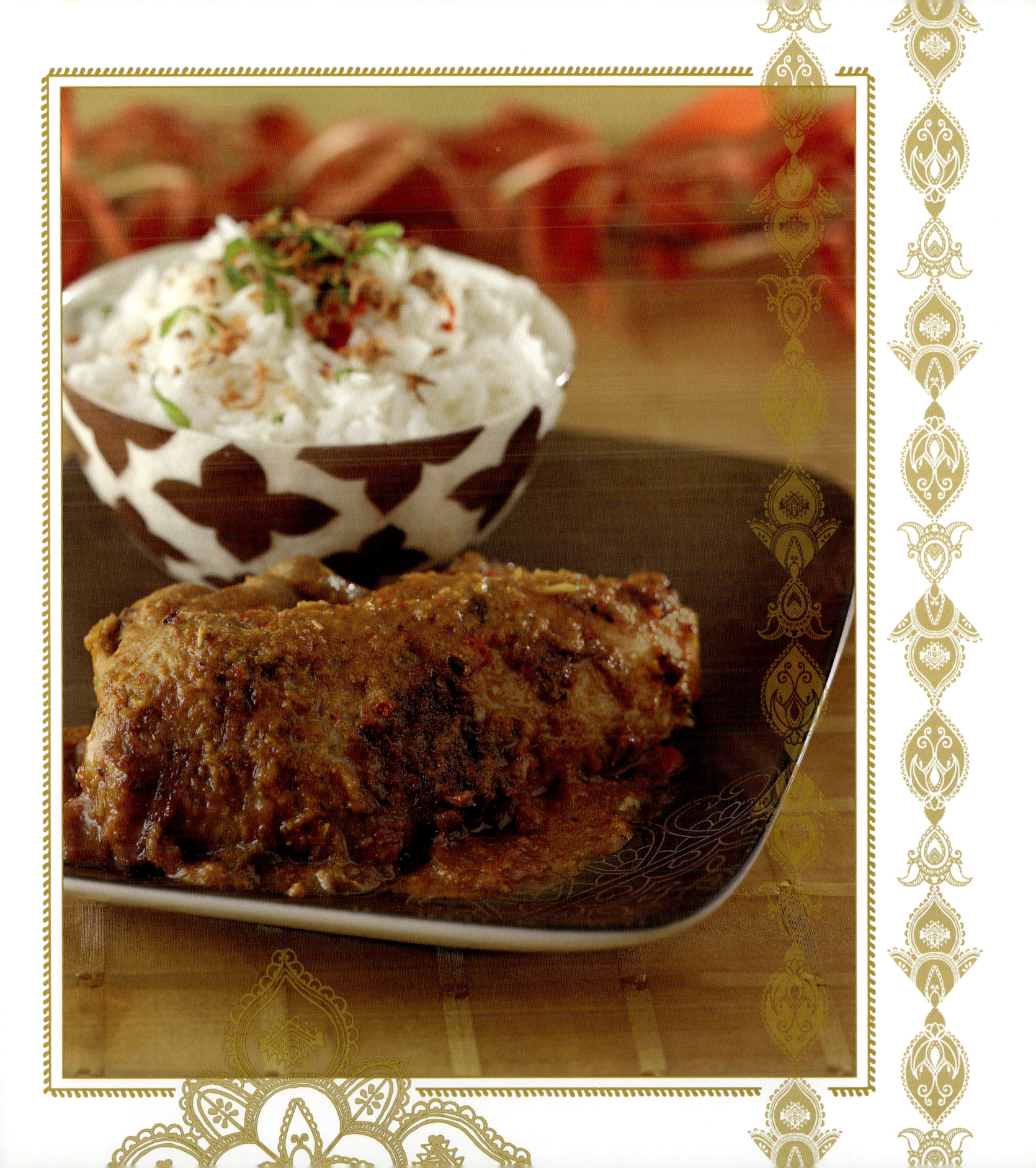

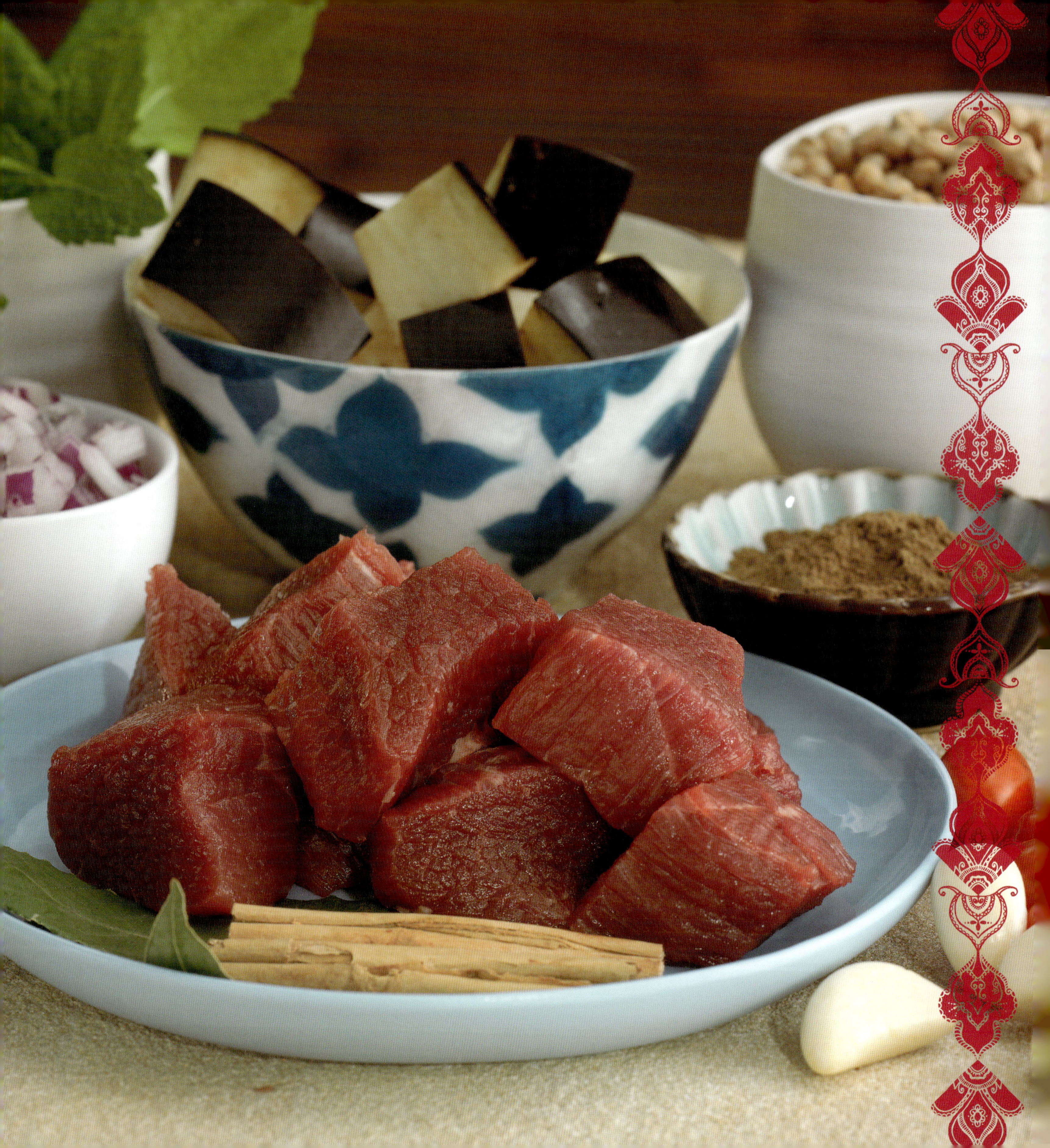

Meat curries

Beef curries are popular in the west, but religious taboos and land scarcity limit the amount of beef on the Indian menu. Lamb (interchangeable with goat and mutton) is the first choice for Indian meat curries, while game makes cameo appearances in the hunting season in the mountainous north. Pork and beef, including offal, come into their own in the Southeast Asian cuisines. Even the hard-working water buffalo is a popular meat for the curry pot.

Braising cuts are preferred for Indian, Malaysian and Indonesian curries, cooked long and slow to succulent tenderness with masses of spices, yoghurt and cream for smoothness, and tamarind for sweet tartness. In contrast, Thai cooks use thinly sliced prime cuts, which cook in minutes in their fiery, coconut-based sauces vibrantly coloured with herbs and chillies – making Thai curries a perfect choice for quick meals.

Mild & creamy lamb korma

2 medium-sized onions
3–4 tablespoons ghee or oil
2 cloves garlic, peeled
a 2-cm piece fresh ginger, peeled
700 g boned lamb shoulder, cut into 3-cm pieces
1¼ cups creamy yoghurt
3 tablespoons finely ground cashews, almonds or pistachios
½ teaspoon ground mild chilli
3 teaspoons ground coriander
1 cinnamon stick
5 cardamom pods, cracked
5 whole cloves
salt
1½–2 teaspoons garam masala (page 16)

Finely chop one onion and fry in the ghee or oil over medium heat until soft and lightly coloured (about 5 minutes). Roughly chop remaining onion, place in a food processor with the garlic and ginger, and grind to a paste.

Stir the onion paste into the cooked onions and cook gently for 2–3 minutes. Add the lamb, increase heat slightly and cook for another 2 minutes, stirring. Stir in yoghurt, nuts, chilli, coriander and whole spices with ¾ teaspoon salt and 1 cup water.

Cover and simmer gently for about 35 minutes, stirring occasionally until meat is tender. Check seasoning, adding salt to taste. Transfer to a serving dish, sprinkle garam masala over, and serve.

SERVES 4–5

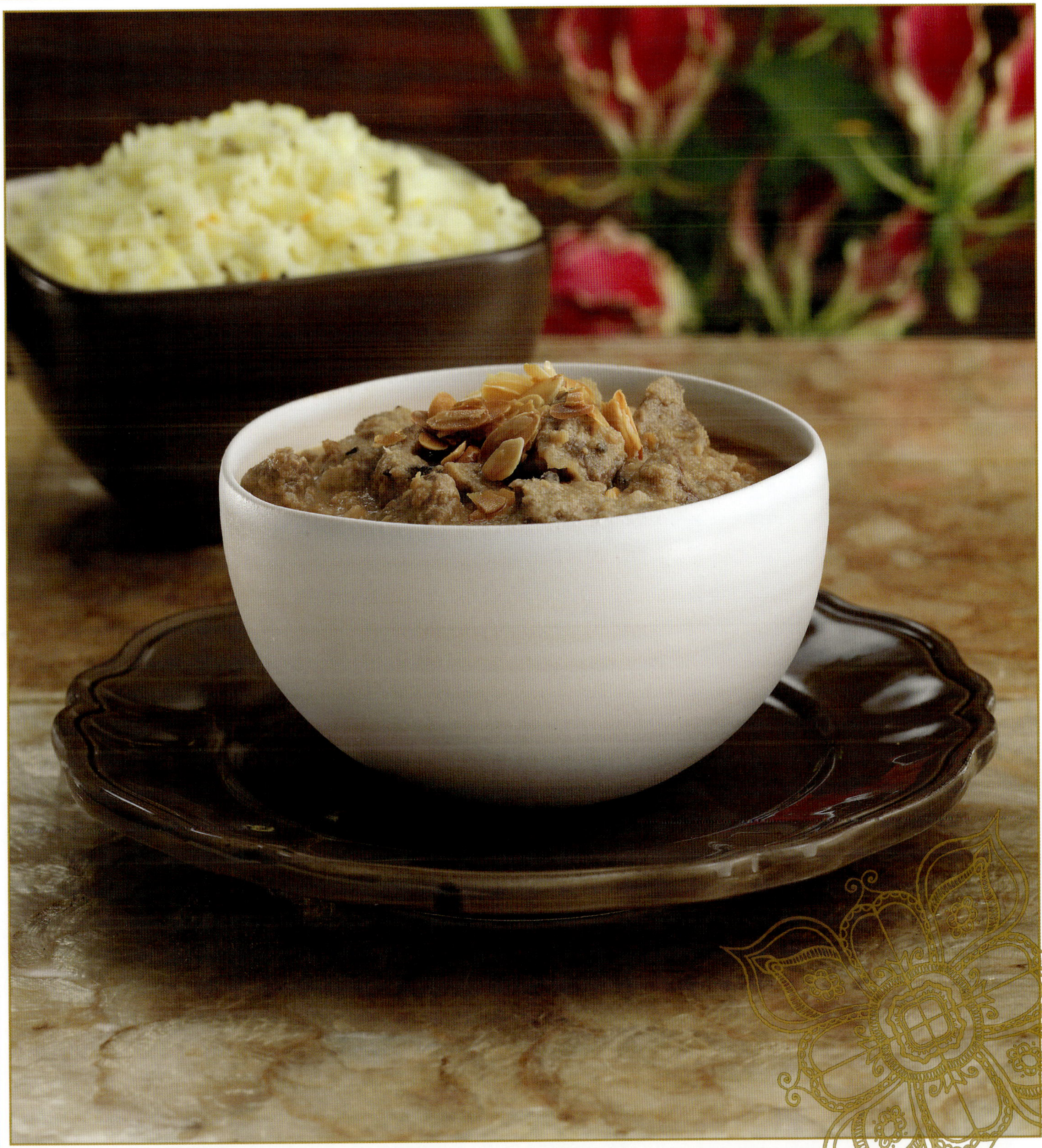

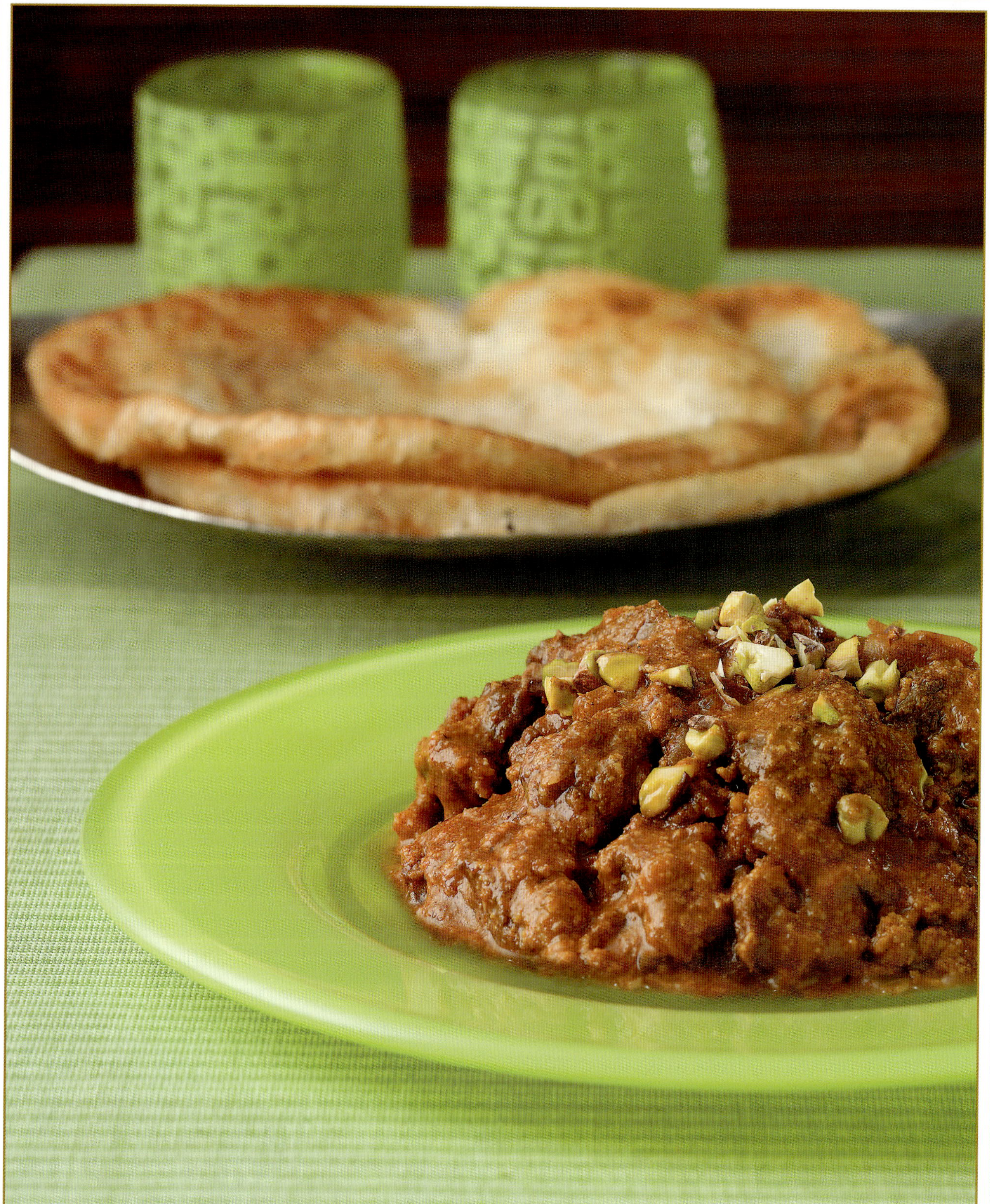

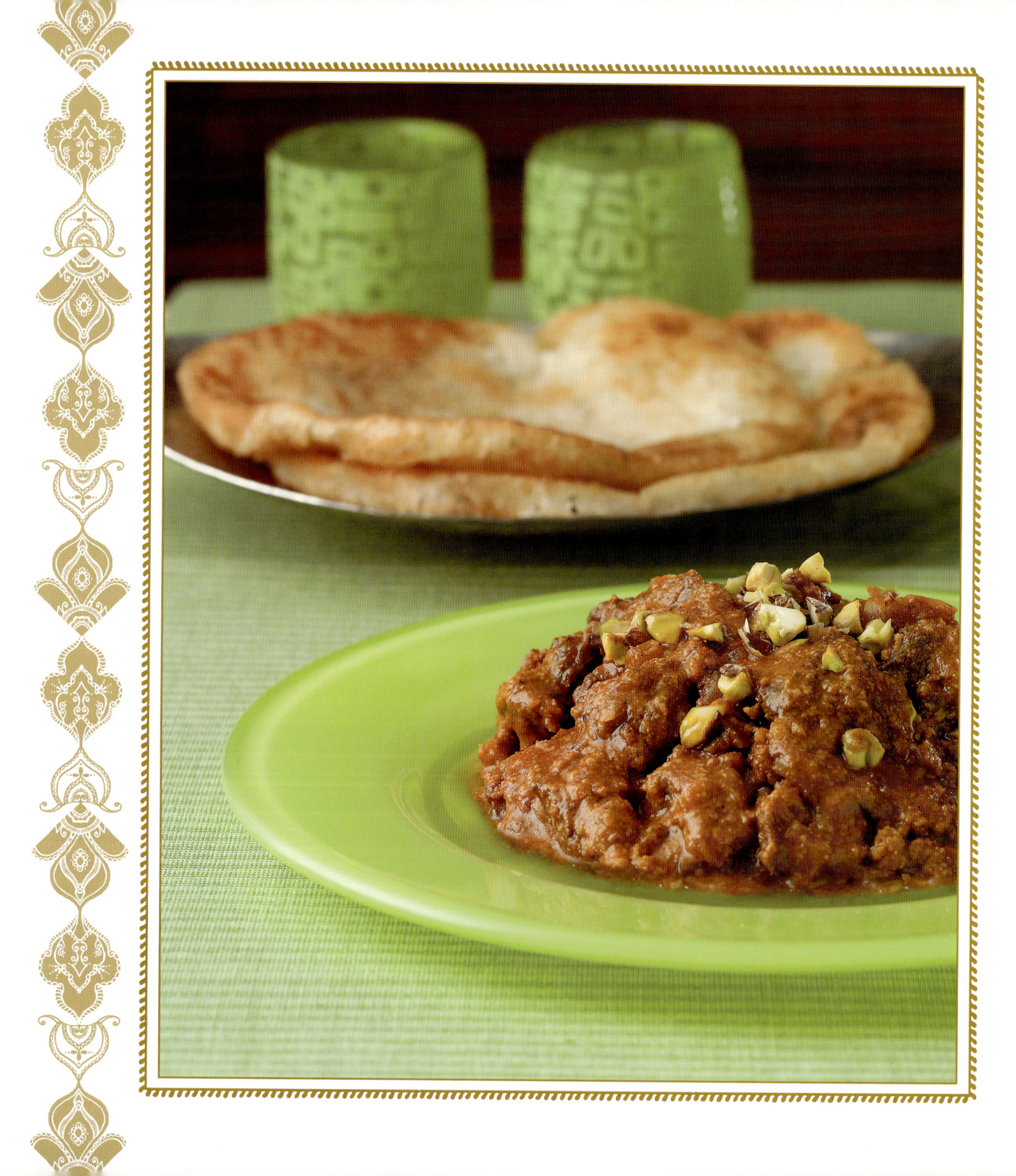

Kashmiri rogan josh

There are so many versions it is difficult to select the best representative of this popular curry, which originates in Kashmir. The lamb can be boneless or on the bone, onion and garlic do not feature in recipes from Hindu households, and different ingredients are used to produce the traditional red colour — mild Kashmiri chilli and sweet paprika, tomato paste and even the coral-like cock's-comb flower which flourishes in the Himalayan foothills.

5 tablespoons ghee or oil
1 medium-sized onion, finely chopped
3 cloves garlic, finely chopped
5 whole cloves
1 cinnamon stick, broken
8 cardamom pods, cracked
1 teaspoon black peppercorns
2 bay leaves
1 kg lamb loin chops, halved (or 650 g lean lamb, cut into 2.5-cm cubes)
1 teaspoon ground ginger
2 teaspoons ground coriander
1 teaspoon fennel seeds, ground to a powder (optional)
3 teaspoons ground sweet paprika
1 teaspoon tomato paste
1 teaspoon ground hot chilli
¾ cup creamy yoghurt
salt

Heat the ghee or oil in a large saucepan and fry the onion, garlic, cloves, cinnamon, cardamom, peppercorns and bay leaves until the onions are soft and lightly browned and the spices very fragrant. Add the meat and stir over medium–high heat until lightly coloured.

Stir in the ground spices and tomato paste, and add the yoghurt a couple of tablespoons at a time, stirring over medium heat for 40 seconds between each addition, until all the yoghurt is used up.

Pour in 2 cups water and add about 1⅓ teaspoons salt. Stir to scrape any browned bits from the bottom of the saucepan, and bring to the boil. Reduce heat and simmer for about 1 hour, tightly covered. (It can also be cooked in a preheated oven at 180°C.) Stir every 20 minutes. When the meat is tender, the sauce should be thick and quite red. If the sauce is too thin, simmer uncovered for a few minutes to reduce. Check seasoning, and serve.

SERVES 6

Lamb with spinach

Saag and *palak* are the Indian names attached to curries with a spinach-based sauce. They can be seductively creamy, delicately spiced or quite fiery, and in some recipes the sauce is jade-green, consisting practically of spinach only. This fast-track variation is a tasty solution for busy cooks. As it's ready in minutes, microwaved rice or purchased Indian bread are perfect accompaniments.

½ cup creamy yoghurt
½ teaspoon crushed garlic
2 teaspoons freshly squeezed lemon juice
salt and pepper
½ teaspoon ground chilli (optional)
3 teaspoons garam masala (page 16)
2 tablespoons butter or ghee
250 g lamb backstrap or fillet, thinly sliced
120–200 g baby spinach leaves
2–3 tablespoons cream or sour cream

In a bowl mix the yoghurt with the garlic, lemon juice, a large pinch each of salt and pepper, the chilli powder (if using) and half the garam masala. Mix well and set aside.

In a non-stick pan heat the butter or ghee and sauté the sliced lamb until it changes colour (about 2 minutes). Add the yoghurt mixture, stir well and simmer gently for 2–3 minutes.

In a small saucepan steam-cook the spinach with 3 tablespoons water until it wilts. Blitz with a stick mixer or purée in a blender, then stir into the curry.

Simmer gently for a few more minutes, add the cream or sour cream and remaining garam masala, and check seasonings before serving.

SERVES 2

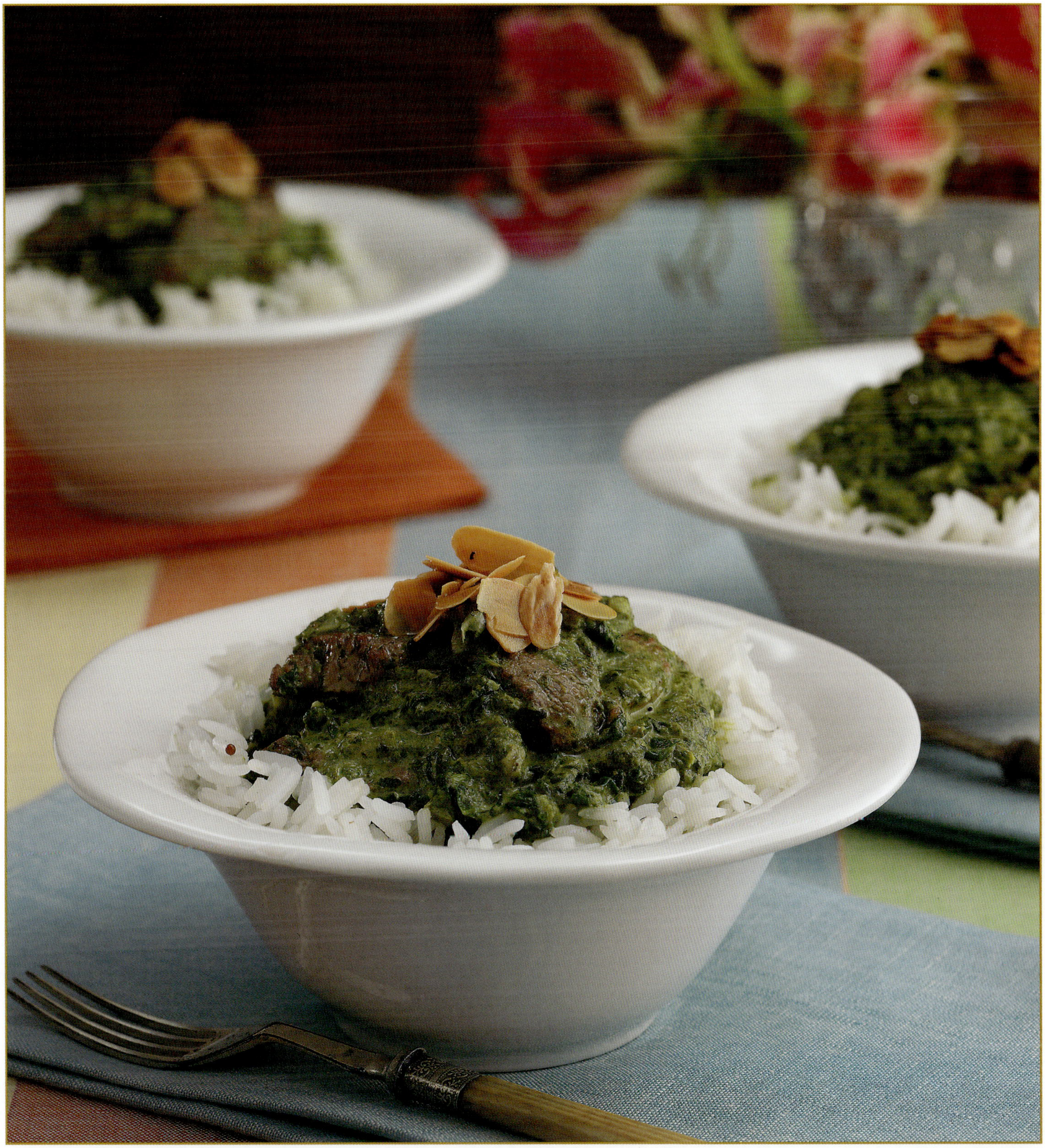

Lamb in saffron almond cream (shahi korma)

- 2 medium-sized onions
- 4 cloves garlic, peeled
- a 1.5-cm piece fresh ginger, peeled
- 1–2 dried red chillies, deseeded and soaked in hot water for 20 minutes
- 2 tablespoons coriander seeds
- 1½ tablespoons poppy seeds (or almond meal)
- 3 tablespoons ghee
- 650 g lean lamb, cut into 3-cm cubes
- 2 bay leaves
- 1 cinnamon stick
- 4 whole cloves
- 5 cardamom pods, cracked
- 1 cup creamy yoghurt
- ¾ teaspoon sugar
- 1½ teaspoons salt
- ¾ cup thick cream
- ¼ cup slivered almonds
- ¼ cup sultanas
- 10 saffron threads
- rose water (optional)

Roughly chop one onion and finely slice the other. Place chopped onion in a food processor or blender with the garlic, ginger and drained chillies, and grind to a paste. Set aside.

In a small pan dry-roast the coriander and poppy seeds until fragrant (about 1½ minutes). If using almond meal, add after dry-roasting seeds and cook it to golden-brown. Transfer pan contents to a spice grinder and grind to a fine powder.

Heat the ghee in a heavy pan and brown the meat in batches. Remove and set aside. Add the sliced onions to the pan and cook gently for about 7 minutes, until soft and translucent (do not brown). Add the onion paste and cook for 3–4 minutes, stirring.

Return lamb to the pan and add the ground spices, whole spices and yoghurt. Cook, stirring, over medium heat for about 10 minutes, until the liquid is well reduced and clinging to the meat. Pour in water not quite to cover, add sugar and salt, cover pan and simmer for about 25 minutes, stirring occasionally. Finally, stir in the cream, almonds and sultanas and simmer gently for 5–6 minutes.

Infuse the saffron threads in 1–2 tablespoons hot milk or water and pour over the korma. Check seasonings, sprinkle with a few drops of rose water (if using), and serve.

SERVES 4–6

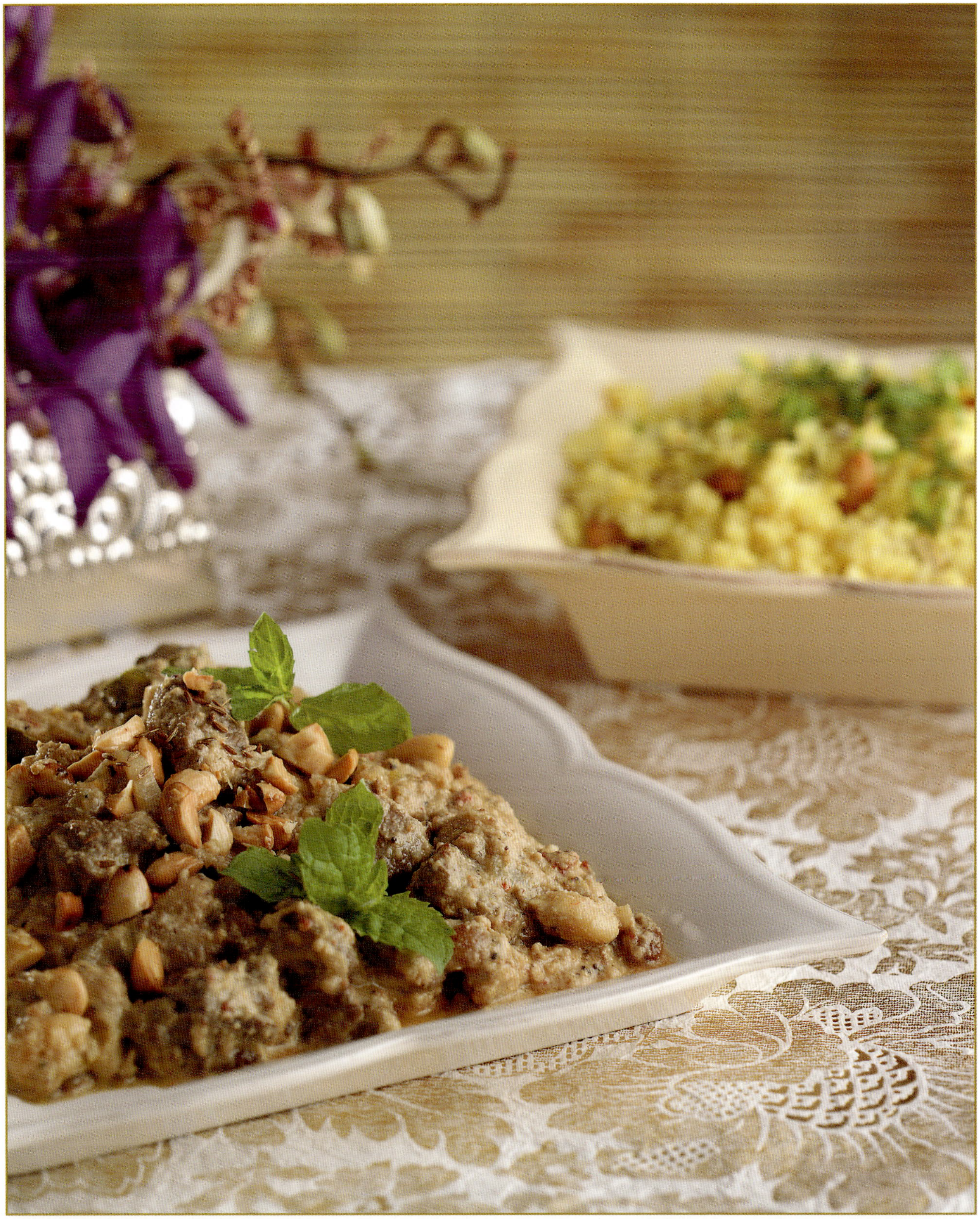

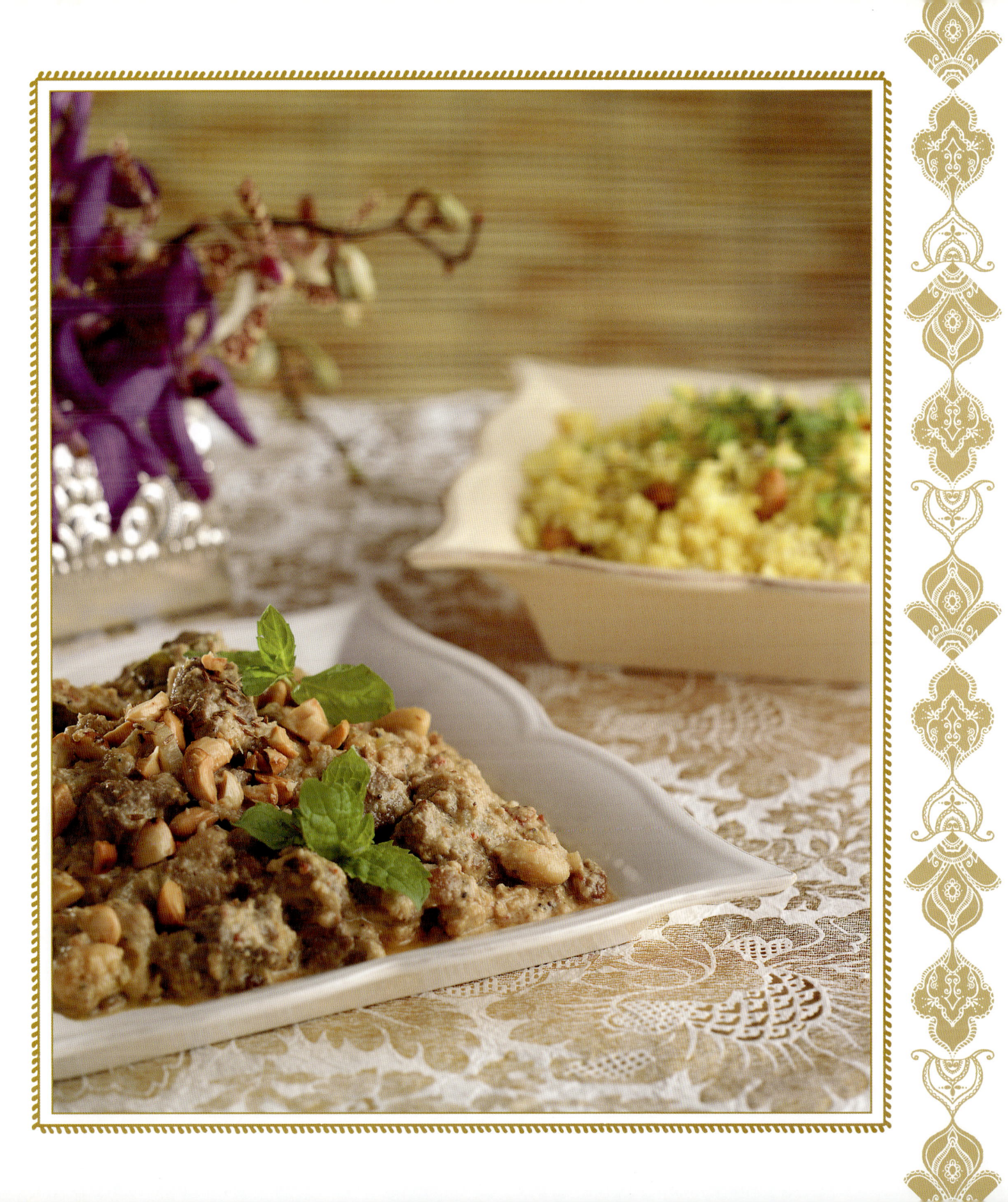

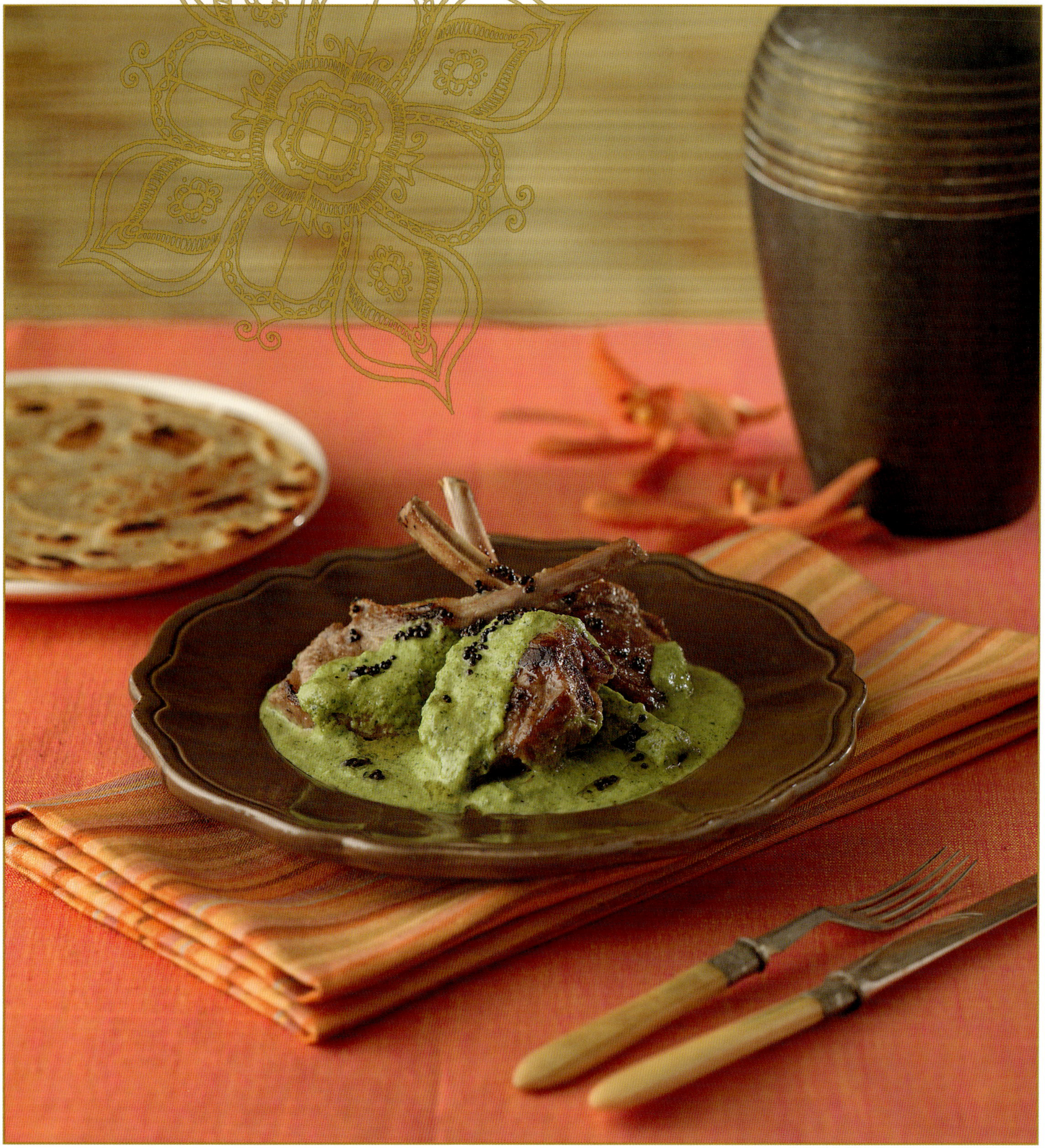

Lamb cutlets with green coriander sauce

- 1 small onion, peeled and quartered
- 2 large cloves garlic, peeled
- a 2-cm piece fresh ginger, peeled
- 2 fresh hot green chillies, deseeded and chopped
- 1 bunch (about 150 g) fresh coriander, roughly chopped
- 2 tablespoons ghee or oil
- 12 'Frenched' lamb cutlets
- 1 tablespoon ground almonds or poppy seeds
- 2 teaspoons garam masala (page 16)
- 1 teaspoon ground turmeric
- 1½ teaspoons salt
- ¾ cup light cream, coconut milk or water
- extra ghee or oil and ½ teaspoon brown mustard seeds (optional)

Place onion, garlic, ginger, chillies and coriander in a blender or food processor and grind to a paste. Set aside.

Heat the ghee or oil in a large frying pan and fry the cutlets in two batches until browned on the surface and cooked to pink inside (about 3 minutes each side). Remove to a plate and keep warm. Add the seasoning paste to the pan and fry over medium–high heat, stirring almost continually, for about 2 minutes.

Mix ground almonds or poppy seeds, garam masala, turmeric and salt into pan. Add cream, coconut milk or water and simmer for about 4 minutes, stirring often. Return the cutlets to the pan and simmer in the sauce just long enough to warm them.

Transfer cutlets and sauce to a serving dish.

For a sizzling, fragrant garnish, in a small clean pan melt a little ghee or oil and fry the mustard seeds until they begin to pop and sputter, then pour over the cutlets and serve.

SERVES 4–6

Parsi-style lamb curry

Migrants from Persia, the Parsis settled the west coast of India more than 1000 years ago, melding their own culinary and cultural traditions with those of their new homeland.

650 g lean lamb, cut into 2-cm cubes
2½ tablespoons ghee or oil
2 medium-sized onions, finely sliced
3–4 cloves garlic, finely chopped
3 teaspoons grated fresh ginger
2 teaspoons hot ground chilli
¾ teaspoon ground turmeric
1 cinnamon stick, broken
6 whole cloves
2 cardamom pods, cracked
1 tablespoon garam masala (page 16)
2 teaspoons salt
2 medium-large potatoes, peeled and cubed
3–4 silverbeet leaves, finely shredded

In a heavy saucepan brown the lamb in batches in the ghee or oil. Remove from the pan and set aside.

Using the same pan brown the onions for about 6 minutes, stirring often. Add garlic and ginger, fry briefly and add the ground and whole spices. Return the lamb and stir to coat each piece with the seasonings. Pour in 2 cups water, add the salt, cover, and simmer for about 20 minutes. Add potatoes and continue to simmer, partially covered, until both lamb and potatoes are tender (about 20 minutes), stirring occasionally.

Stir silverbeet into the curry and cook gently for 2–3 minutes, until tender. Check seasoning, and serve.

SERVES 4–6

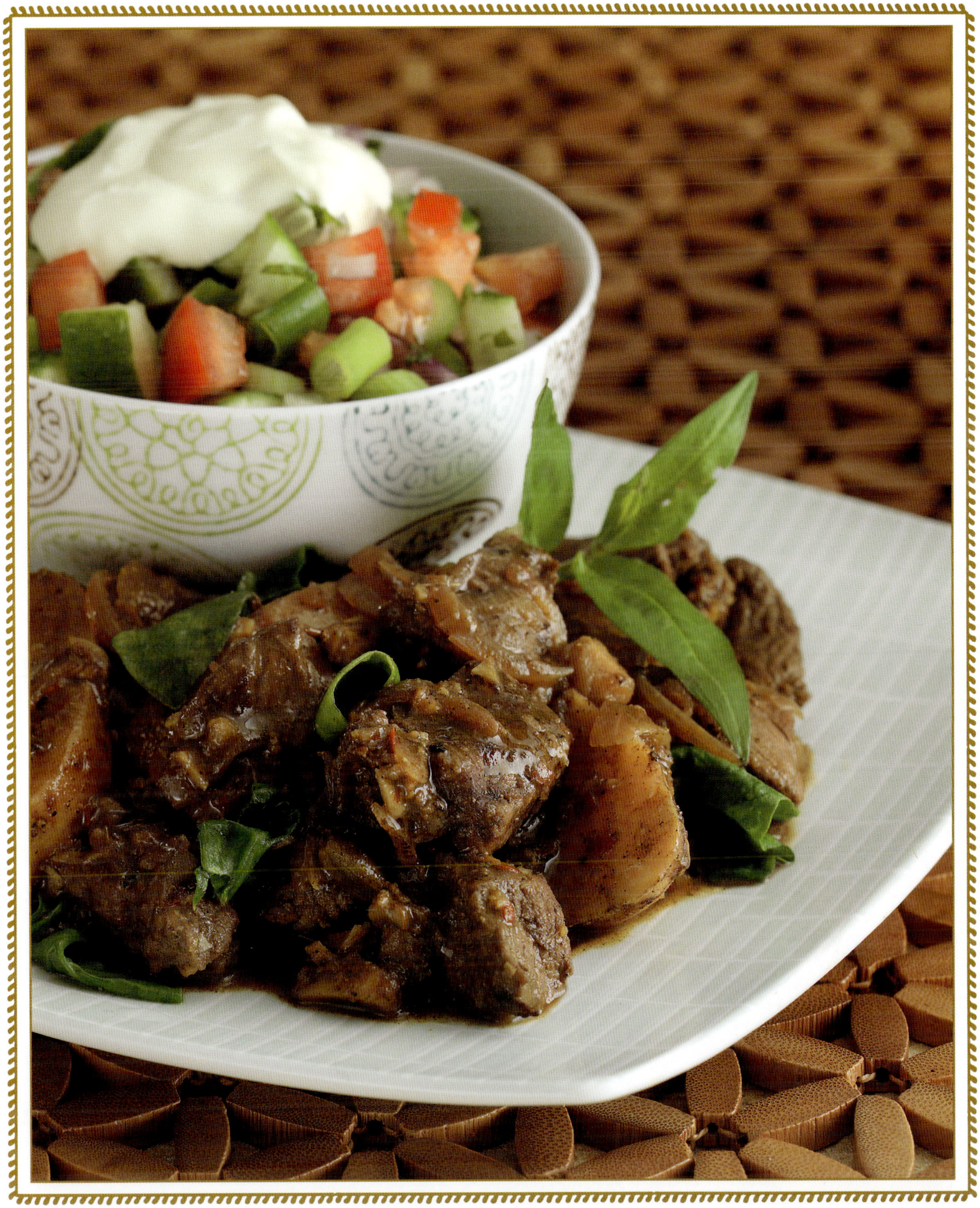

Indonesian gulai of lamb

A curry style popular in Nonya cuisine and also in Indonesia, gulais are coconut milk curries infused with local herbs and spices to give flavours which range from sour and hot to sweet and tangy, or very very spicy.

700 g lean lamb, cubed
salt and pepper
3–4 tablespoons oil
2 medium-sized onions, peeled and quartered
6 cloves garlic, peeled
a 2-cm piece fresh ginger, peeled
a 3-cm piece fresh turmeric, peeled (or use ¾ teaspoon ground turmeric)
1 teaspoon shrimp paste
2 thick slices fresh galangal
1½ tablespoons ground coriander
2 fresh hot red chillies, slit lengthways and deseeded
1 × 400-ml can coconut cream
2 teaspoons palm sugar or soft brown sugar
1½ teaspoons salt
a few fresh basil or Vietnamese mint leaves

Season lamb lightly with salt and pepper. Heat a wok or saucepan with 2 tablespoons of the oil and brown the lamb pieces in several batches, until evenly coloured. Remove to a plate.

Place onions, garlic, ginger and fresh turmeric (if using) in a blender or food processor and grind to a coarse purée.

Reheat the pan, add the remaining oil and the shrimp paste, galangal, ground turmeric (if using), coriander and chillies, and fry for 1 minute. Add the onion purée and fry over medium–high heat for about 5 minutes, stirring frequently. Add the sugar.

Return meat to pan and stir to coat evenly with the seasonings. Pour in the coconut cream and add 2 cups water and the sugar and salt. Bring slowly to the boil, reduce heat and simmer for about 35 minutes,stirring occasionally, until the lamb is very tender. Add extra water if needed: the sauce should be quite generous. Fold in basil or Vietnamese mint, check for salt, then serve.

SERVES 4–6

Curried minced lamb with peas (keema mattar)

Serve this simple curry with chapatis for scooping, or cook puffy puris (page 293), slit them open and stuff with the curry as a hand-held snack. Any leftovers make a delicious filling for toasted sandwiches or topping for breakfast toast.

- 1 medium-sized onion, finely chopped
- 1 large tomato, deseeded and diced
- 2 tablespoons ghee or butter
- 600 g lean lamb or beef mince
- 1 clove garlic, crushed
- 2 teaspoons garam masala (page 16)
- 2–3 teaspoons mild curry powder
- salt and pepper
- ¾ cup peas
- ¼ cup chopped fresh coriander or mint (or 60 g baby spinach leaves)
- 1–2 tablespoons thick or sour cream (optional)

In a medium-sized saucepan brown the onion and tomato in ghee or butter. Add minced meat and garlic, increase heat slightly, stirring and chopping the meat to break up lumps, and cook for 8–10 minutes, until well browned.

Stir the garam masala and curry powder through the meat, add 1 cup water, with salt and pepper to taste, and simmer for about 7 minutes, stirring often. Add peas and herbs or spinach and cook until tender (about 5 minutes).

Stir in cream or sour cream (if using) just before serving.

SERVES 4–6

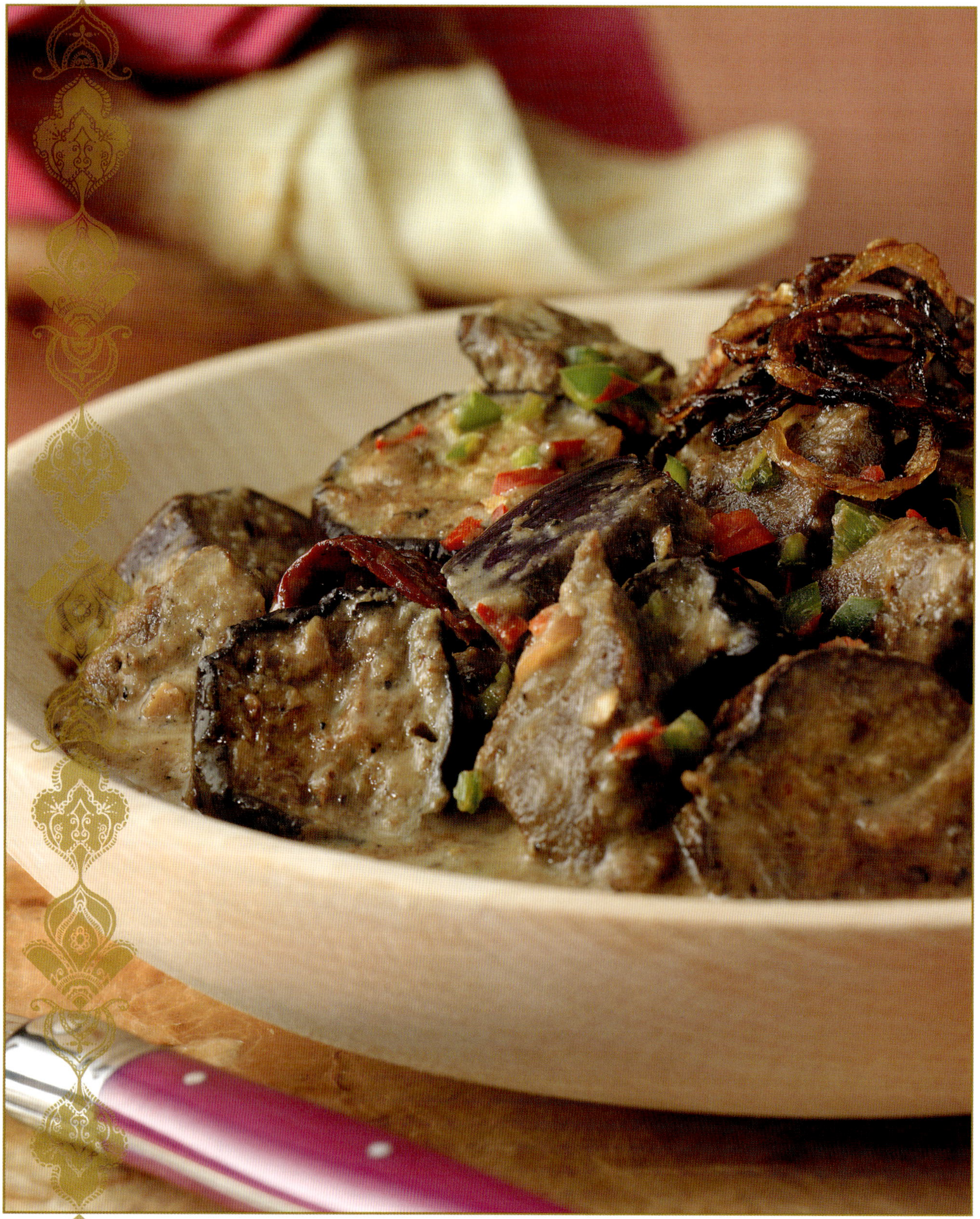

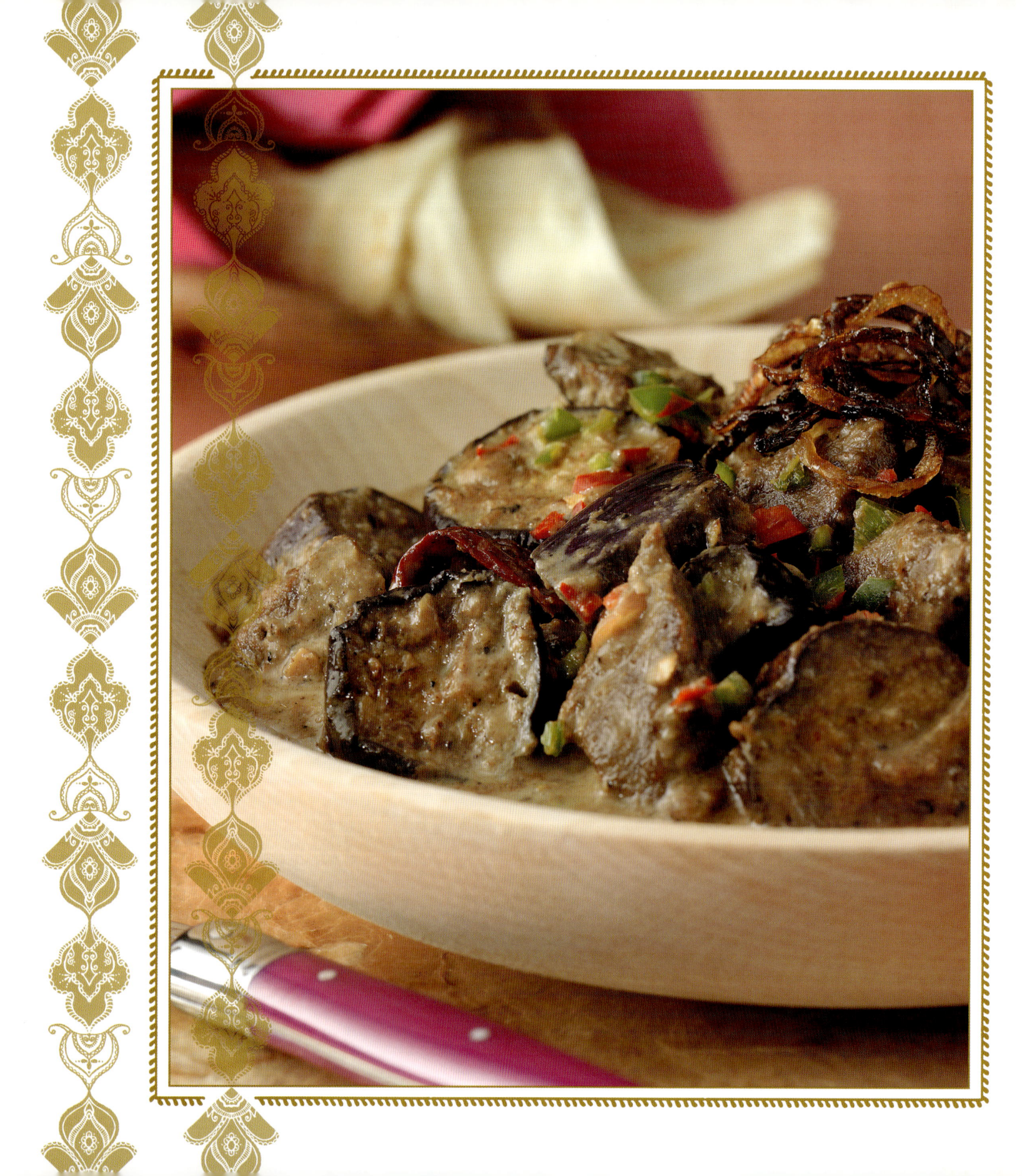

Malaysian lamb & eggplant curry

1½ tablespoons coriander seeds
2½ teaspoons cumin seeds
1⅓ teaspoons black peppercorns
¾ teaspoon fennel seeds
½ teaspoon brown mustard seeds
1½ tablespoons poppy seeds or slivered almonds
2 large onions
6 cloves garlic, peeled
a 2-cm piece fresh ginger, peeled
2 fresh hot red chillies, deseeded
a 3-cm piece fresh turmeric, peeled (or use 1 teaspoon ground turmeric)
2–3 tablespoons ghee or oil
600 g lean lamb, mutton or goat, cut into 3-cm cubes
3–4 slender Asian eggplants or 1 large eggplant, cut into 3-cm chunks
1 × 400-ml can coconut cream
8 curry leaves
4 whole cloves
1 cinnamon stick
5 cardamom pods, cracked
salt
freshly squeezed lime juice

In a small pan dry-roast the coriander, cumin, peppercorns, fennel, mustard and poppy seeds or almonds for about 2 minutes until lightly browned and very fragrant. Tip into a spice grinder and grind to a fine powder.

Chop one of the onions roughly, place in a blender or food processor with the garlic, ginger, chillies and fresh turmeric, and grind to a paste. Slice remaining onion finely.

Heat the ghee or oil in a heavy pan and brown the meat in two or three batches. Remove to a plate and set aside. In the same pan fry the sliced onion until well browned (about 4 minutes), then add the onion paste and stir over medium–high heat for a minute or two, until aromatic.

Return meat to pan, add the eggplant and stir to coat with the seasonings, then add the ground spices (including the turmeric, if using ground) and mix well. Cook for 2–3 minutes over medium heat. Pour in the coconut cream and 1¼ cups water, add the curry leaves, whole spices, and salt to taste, and bring to the boil. Reduce heat and simmer covered for 25–30 minutes, until the meat is tender. Squeeze lime juice over, discard cinnamon stick, and serve.

SERVES 4–6

Balti lamb & zucchini curry

Lamb fillet is supremely tender and cooks in minutes. If another cut is used, it may require longer cooking.

360 g lamb fillet or backstrap
3–4 teaspoons Balti curry paste (page 13)
3 teaspoons chopped fresh mint
salt and pepper
1½ tablespoons oil
1 zucchini, sliced
2 spring onions, chopped
¼ cup creamy yoghurt

Trim away any silvery skin on the lamb and place meat in a bowl with the curry paste, 1 teaspoon of the mint and ½ teaspoon each of salt and pepper. Mix well and leave for 20 minutes.

When ready to cook, scrape off and reserve the seasoning paste and slice the lamb. Heat a wok or non-stick pan, add the oil and stir-fry the lamb until it changes colour (about 2 minutes). Remove to a plate.

Add the reserved marinating paste to the pan with the zucchini and onion, and stir-fry for 30 seconds. Stir in ⅔ cup water and simmer for 4–5 minutes until zucchini is almost tender. Return the meat to pan, add the yoghurt and remaining mint and check seasonings, adding more salt or pepper if required. Heat through gently.

SERVES 2

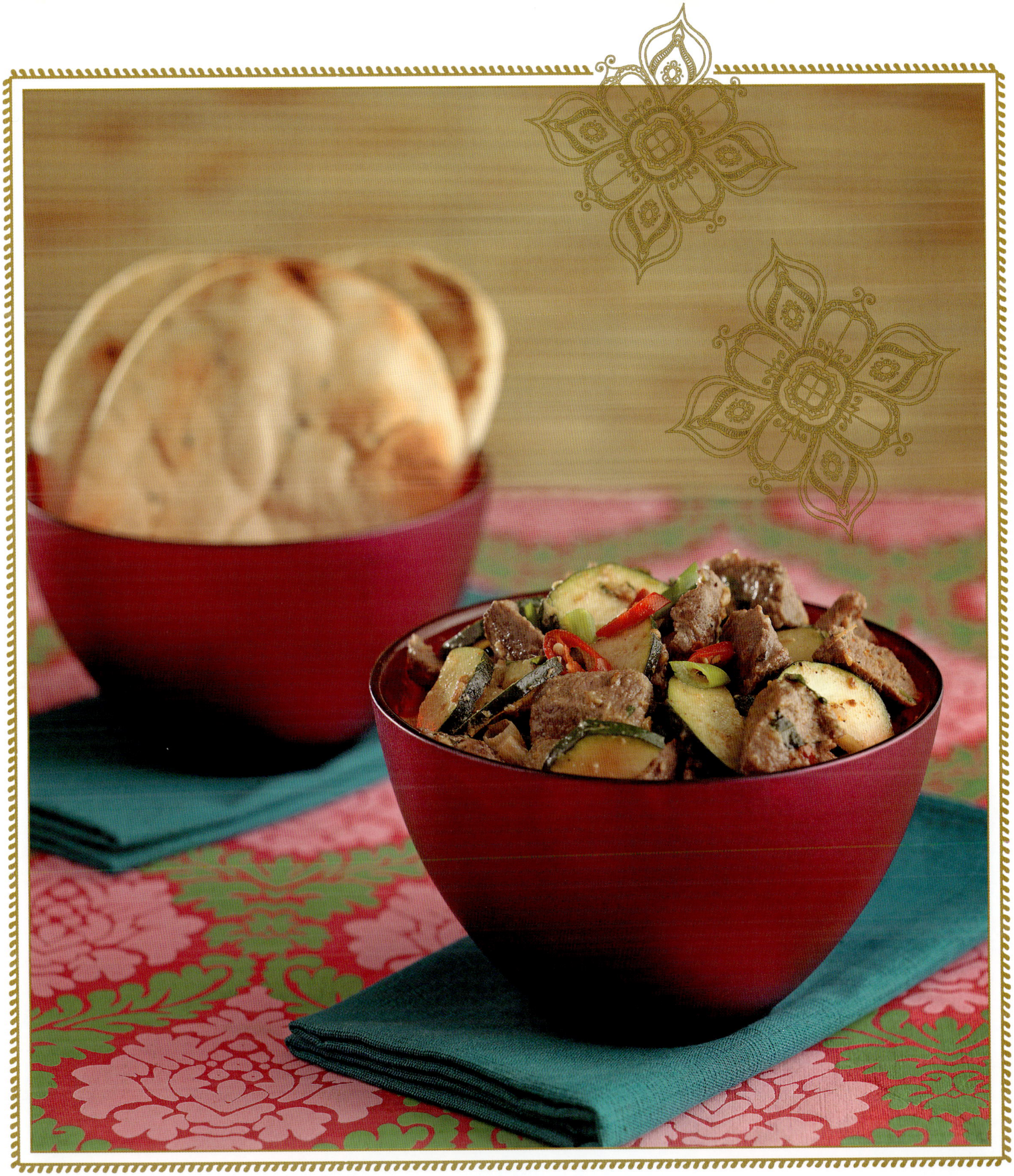

Fifteen-minute meat curry with tomatoes & peas

1 tablespoon vindaloo or other hot Indian curry paste (page 13)
2 cloves garlic, crushed
1½ teaspoons grated fresh ginger
3 tablespoons oil
500 g lamb backstrap or beef rump, cut into bite-sized strips
1 large onion, finely chopped
1 × 425-g can crushed tomatoes
½–1 teaspoon hot red chilli paste
1 teaspoon sugar
¾ cup frozen peas
salt
2 tablespoons chopped fresh mint or coriander

In a bowl mix the vindaloo or curry paste, garlic and ginger with 1 tablespoon of the oil. Add the meat, mix well, cover with plastic wrap and refrigerate for 3–4 hours, stirring occasionally.

When ready to cook, heat the remaining oil in a medium-sized saucepan or wok and sauté the onion until well browned (about 5 minutes). Add the meat and sauté for about 2 minutes, until lightly and evenly coloured. Remove to a bowl.

Pour tomatoes into the pan and add about ¾ cup water, the chilli paste and sugar. Bring to the boil and simmer for about 5 minutes, then add the peas and cook for about 4 minutes. Check for salt, return the meat and onions to the pan and simmer gently for 5 or so minutes. Garnish with chopped herbs.

SERVES 4

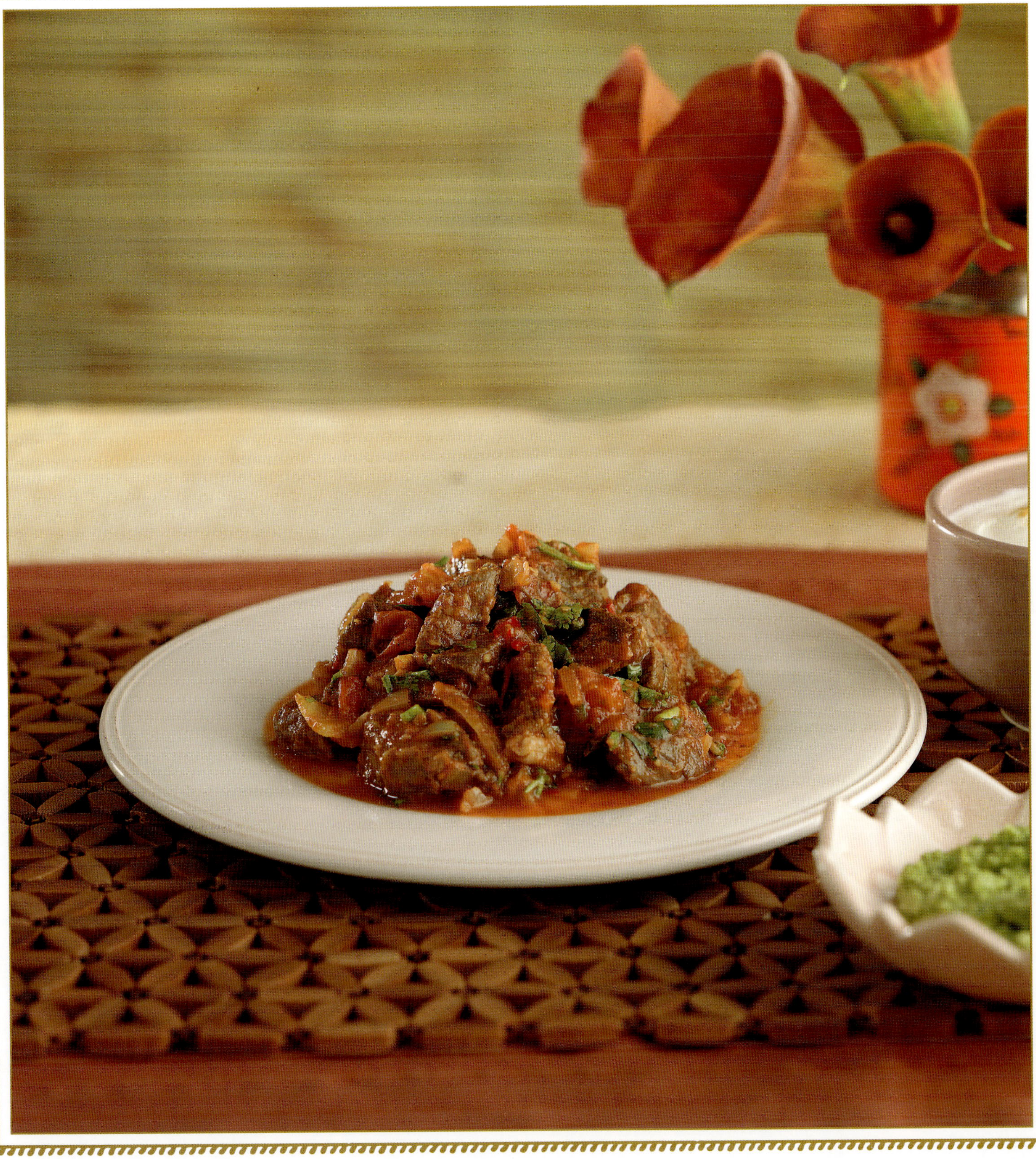

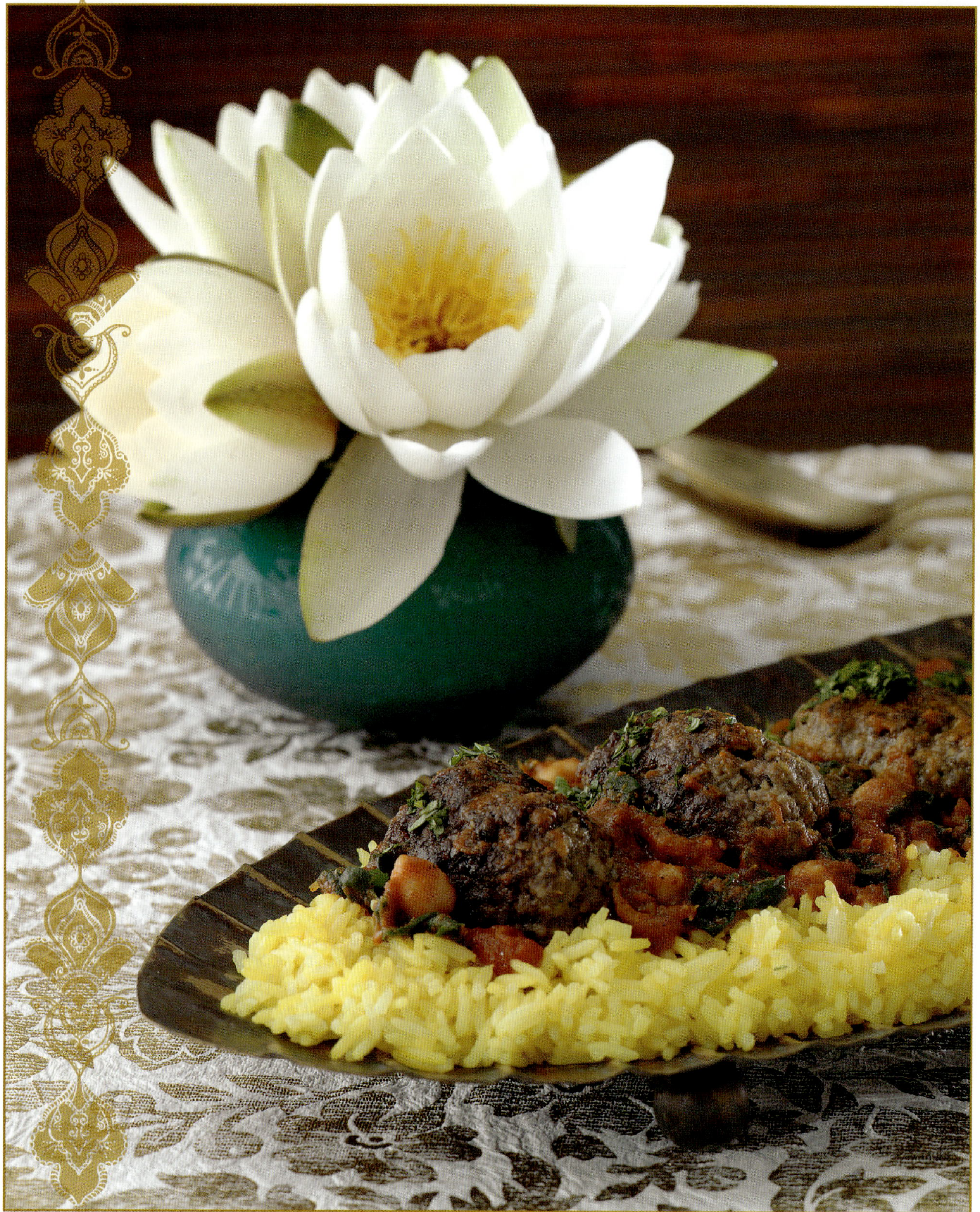

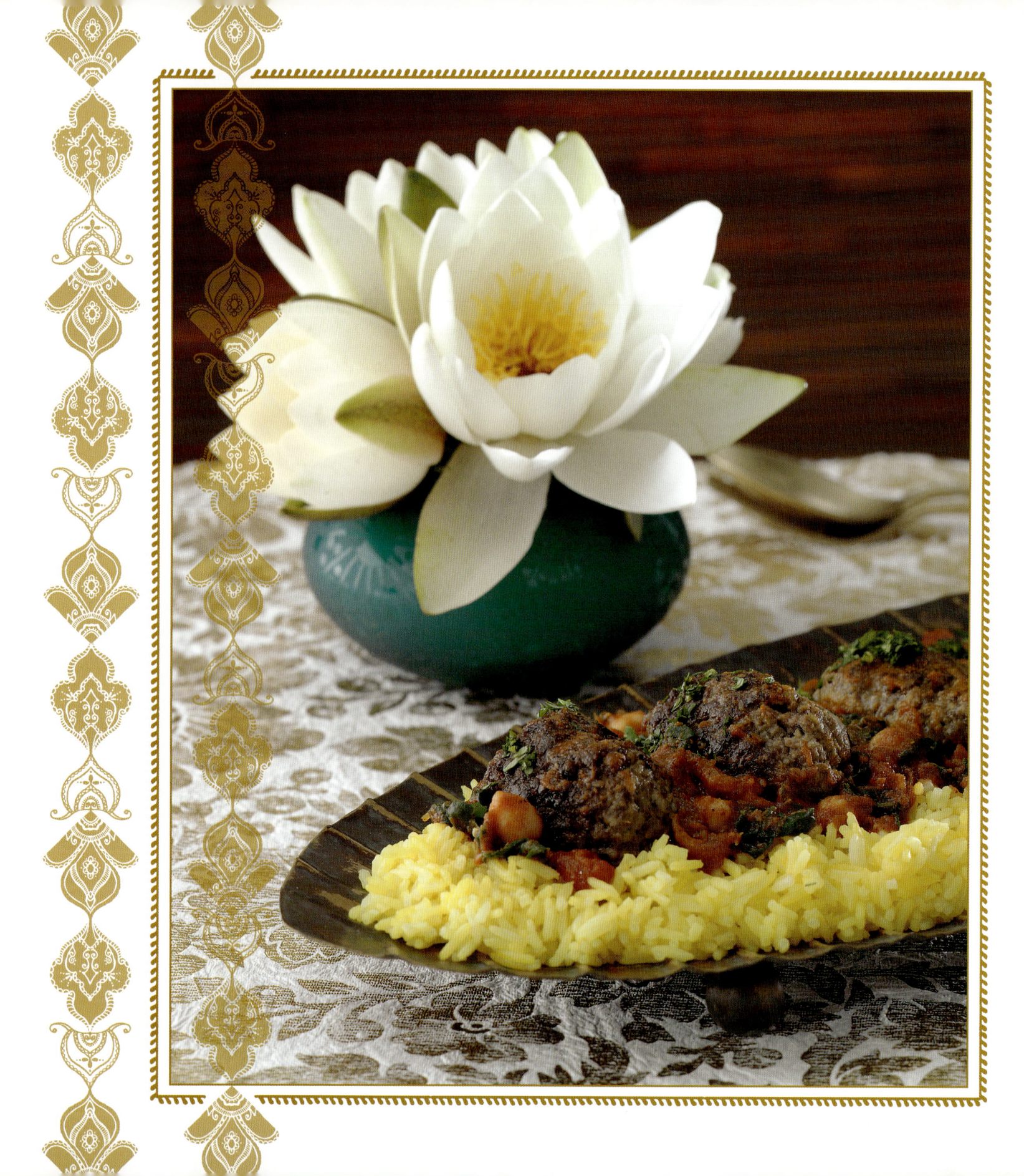

Kofta curry with chickpeas & tomatoes

Koftas
2 slices day-old white bread, crusts removed
1 medium-sized onion, roughly chopped
2 cloves garlic, peeled
a 1-cm piece fresh ginger, peeled
4–5 sprigs fresh coriander
2 teaspoons ground coriander
1 teaspoon salt
600 g lamb or beef mince
2 cups oil

Curry sauce
2 tablespoons ghee or oil
1 large onion, sliced
1 tablespoon ground coriander
2 teaspoons ground cumin
¾ teaspoon ground turmeric
1 × 425-g can crushed tomatoes
1 × 425-g can chickpeas, drained
1–2 leaves silverbeet, shredded
salt and pepper

To make koftas, place bread, onion, garlic, ginger, fresh and ground coriander, and salt in a food processor and grind to a paste. Add about one-third of the meat and grind until well mixed. Tip into a bowl and mix thoroughly with the remaining mince. With wet or oiled hands, form into sausage shapes about 5 cm long.

Heat the oil and deep-fry koftas until lightly browned (about 3 minutes). Remove and set aside to drain.

For the curry sauce, heat the ghee or oil over medium–high heat and fry onion until well browned (about 4 minutes). Add spices, cook briefly and then stir in the tomatoes with 2 cups water. Bring to the boil, reduce heat and simmer for 8–10 minutes.

Add chickpeas, silverbeet and koftas to the pan, with salt and pepper to taste, and simmer gently for 10 minutes, adding a little more water if the sauce is too thick.

SERVES 6

Lamb & lentil hotpot

Known as dhansak, this is a traditional Sunday meal in many households in the central Indian states. Lamb cooked with lentils and vegetables is accompanied by rice gleaming brown with caramelised onions and spices, a tomato and onion kachumbar (salad), and little kebabs or meatballs.

3 cloves garlic, peeled

a 2-cm piece fresh ginger, peeled

4–6 dried red chillies, deseeded and soaked in hot water for 20 minutes

1 tablespoon coriander seeds

2 teaspoons cumin seeds

⅓ teaspoon black peppercorns

3 cardamom pods, cracked

3–4 tablespoons ghee or oil

1 large onion, finely sliced

600 g lean lamb, diced

½ cinnamon stick

1 teaspoon ground turmeric

1 large tomato, diced (or 1 cup canned tomatoes)

½ cup each of lentils and split peas

2 cups diced mixed vegetables (e.g. eggplant, pumpkin, carrot, turnip)

2 teaspoons tamarind concentrate

2 teaspoons palm sugar or soft brown sugar

salt

In a spice grinder or blender grind the garlic, ginger and drained chillies to a paste.

Dry-roast the coriander, cumin, peppercorns and cardamom in a small pan for about 2 minutes, until fragrant. Transfer to a spice grinder or mortar, and grind to a fine powder.

Heat the ghee or oil in a saucepan and fry the onion over medium heat until well browned and beginning to caramelise (about 5 minutes). Set some of the onion aside for garnish, then add the garlic paste and the meat to the pan and brown for 5 minutes, stirring often. Add the cinnamon stick, turmeric and the tomato and cook for 2–3 minutes, stirring often.

Pour in 4 cups water and bring to the boil. Reduce heat and simmer for about 15 minutes. Stir in the lentils, split peas and vegetables, and continue to cook until they are tender (lentils may take up to 40 minutes), adding extra boiling water as needed.

Stir in tamarind, sugar and salt to taste. Transfer to a serving dish and garnish with the reserved caramelised onions.

SERVES 6

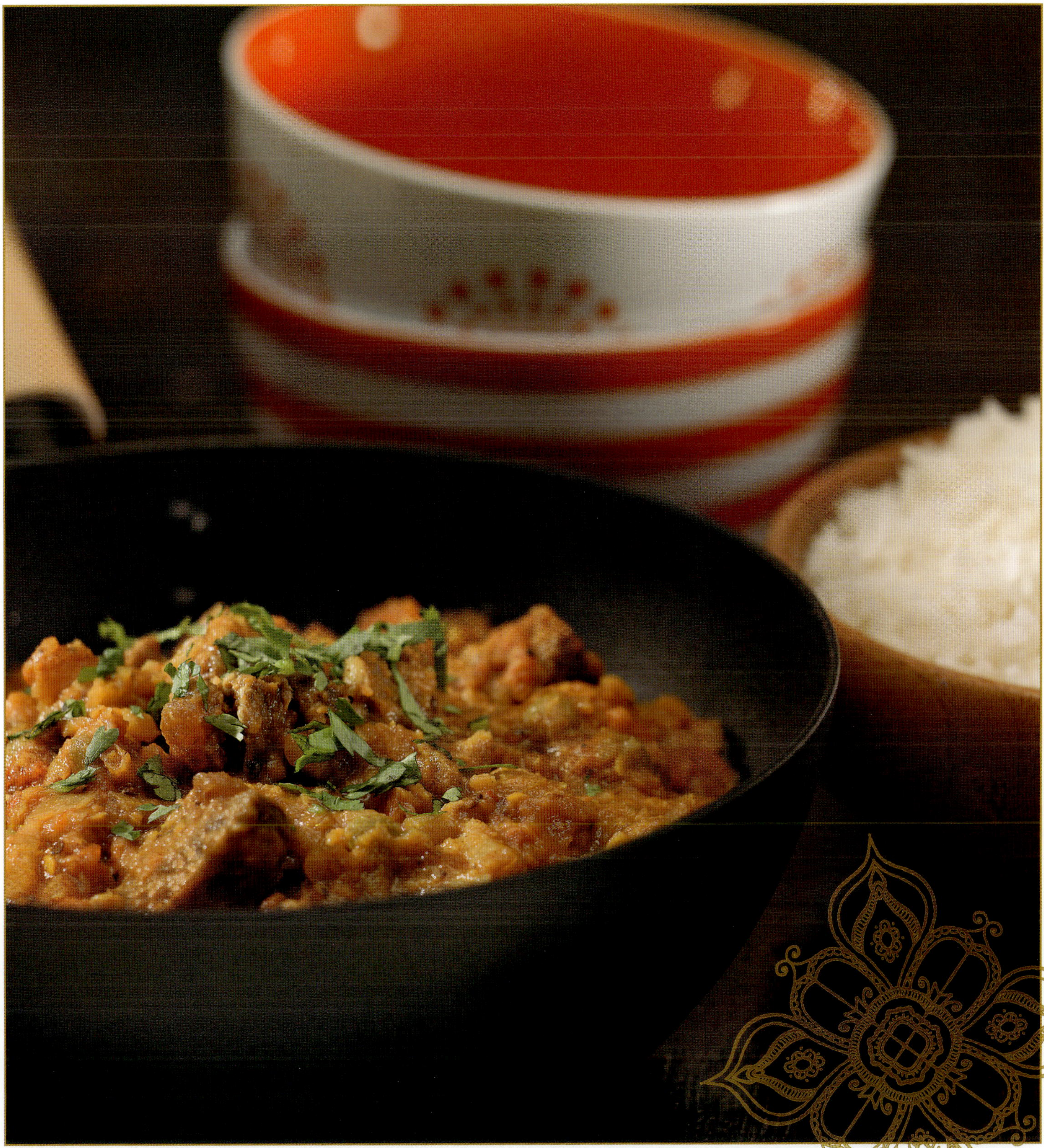

Lamb-shank curry

- 2 large lamb shanks
- salt and pepper
- plain flour
- 2–3 tablespoons oil or ghee
- 1 large onion, finely chopped
- 4 cloves garlic, chopped
- 1½ teaspoons chopped fresh ginger
- 1½ tablespoons ground coriander
- 2 teaspoons ground cumin
- 1 tablespoon garam masala (page 16)
- ¾ cup creamy yoghurt
- 1 dried red chilli, halved and deseeded
- 4 whole cloves
- 4 cardamom pods, cracked
- 1 star anise
- 1 cinnamon stick, broken in half
- 2 large potatoes, cubed
- 2 tablespoons blanched almonds
- 2 tablespoons sultanas
- 2 tablespoons cream
- ½ teaspoon sugar (optional)

Rinse and dry the shanks, season with salt and pepper, and coat with flour. In a largeish saucepan heat the oil or ghee and brown shanks all over. Remove to a plate and set aside.

In the same pan brown the onion for about 5 minutes. Add garlic, ginger and ground spices and cook for 1 minute, stirring. Add yoghurt and ½ cup water, return the shanks and cook, uncovered, until the liquid has evaporated.

Add whole spices to pan with another 2½–3 cups water, cover, and simmer for 40–45 minutes. Add potatoes and cook for a further 15 minutes, then stir in the almonds, sultanas, cream and sugar (if using), and salt to taste. Simmer for another 10–15 minutes, until lamb and potatoes are tender. If cooking for four people, strip meat from the bones before serving.

SERVES 2–4

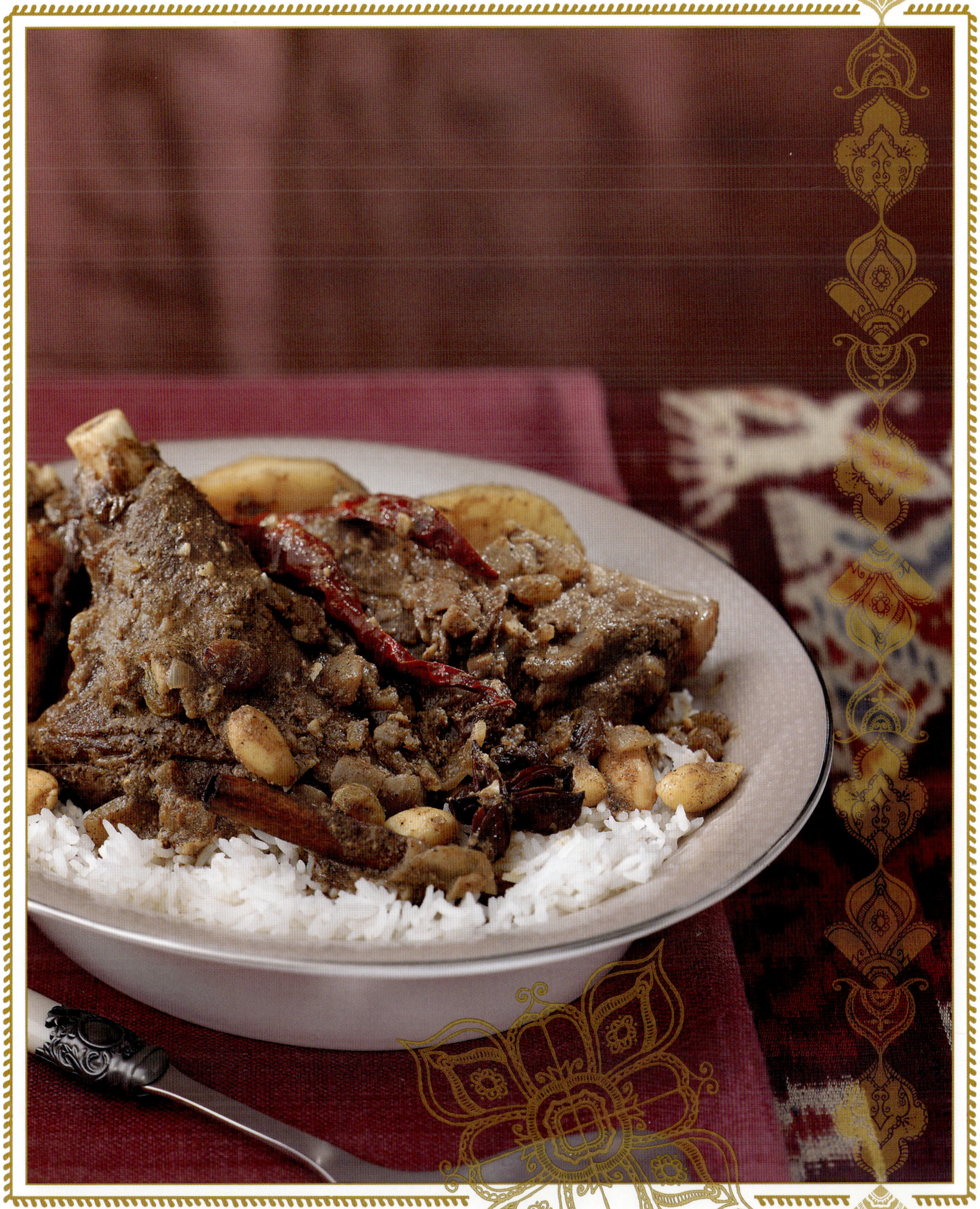

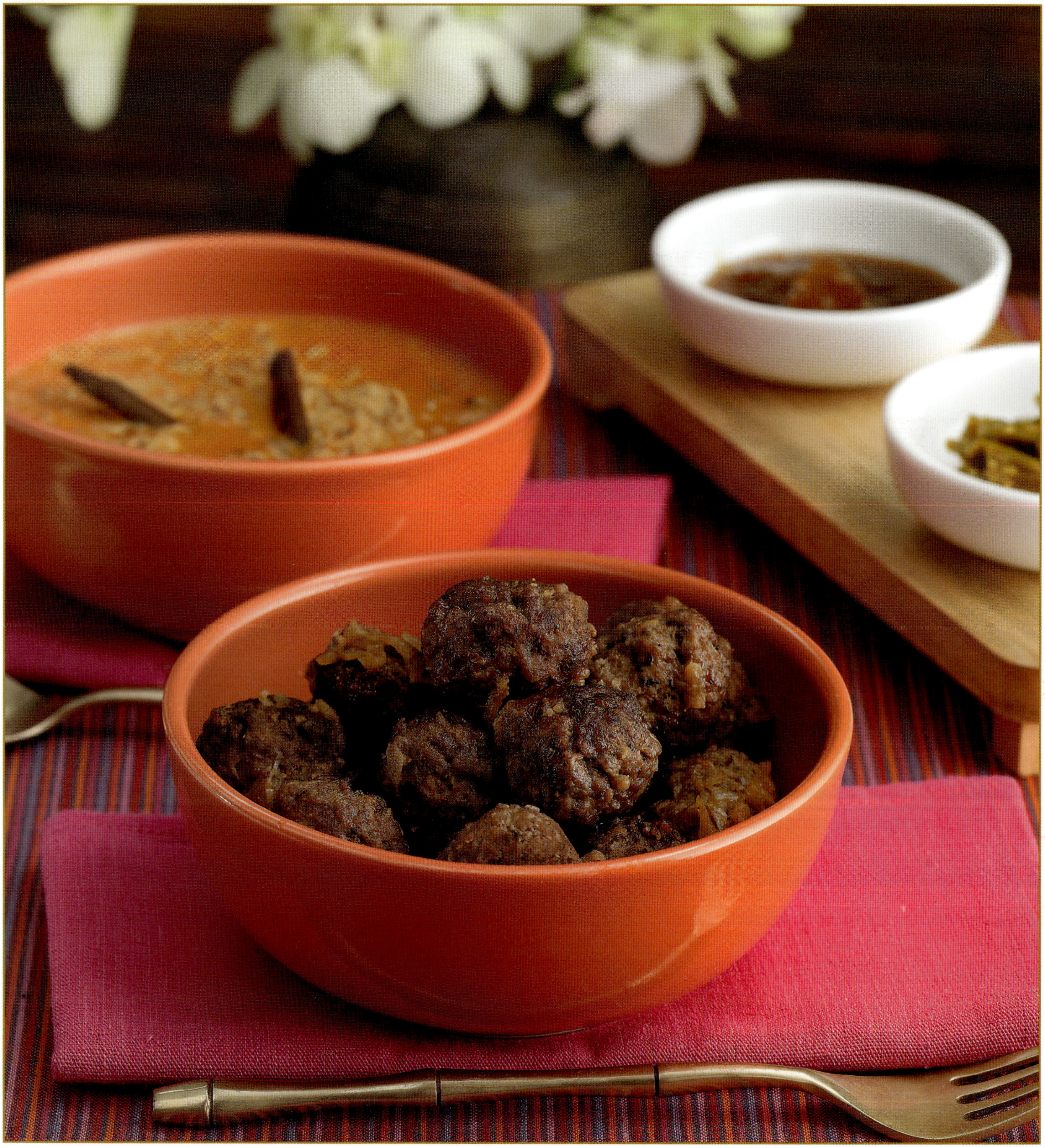

Meatballs in mild & creamy curry sauce

These quantities make about 24 meatballs.

Meatballs

700 g lamb, pork or beef mince
2 slices sourdough bread, crusts removed
1 medium-sized onion, quartered
2 cloves garlic, peeled
salt and pepper
oil for frying

Curry sauce

1 large onion, finely chopped
2 cloves garlic, crushed
a 2-cm piece fresh ginger
2–3 tablespoons ghee, butter or oil
1½ tablespoons ground coriander
2 teaspoons garam masala (page 16)
½ teaspoon ground sweet paprika
1 green apple, peeled and grated
3 cups stock or water
2 whole cloves
1 cinnamon stick
1 teaspoon sugar
¾ cup cream
salt and pepper

To make meatballs, break up the mince in a bowl. Chop the bread to crumbs in a food processor and add to the meat. Blend or process the onion and garlic to a paste. Add a handful of the meat and breadcrumb mixture to the processor, with a large pinch each of salt and pepper, process again and then mix with the remaining meat and breadcrumbs. Knead to a smooth paste and use wet hands to form mixture into about 24 meatballs, flattening them slightly. Set aside.

To make the sauce, sauté the onion, garlic and ginger in the ghee, butter or oil until soft and lightly browned (about 5 minutes), stirring frequently. Add coriander, garam masala, paprika and grated apple, and sauté for 1 minute, stirring. Pour in the stock or water, add the cloves, cinnamon and sugar, and simmer for about 15 minutes, until onion and apple are soft and reduced.

While the sauce is simmering, heat 4 cm of oil in a large non-stick frying pan and fry the meatballs on both sides until well browned (about 3 minutes). Transfer to the curry sauce, add cream and simmer for 20 minutes. Check for salt and pepper, and serve.

SERVES 4–6

Beef & pumpkin red curry

400 g pumpkin, peeled and thinly sliced

salt

2 tablespoons Thai red curry paste (page 17)

1 × 400-ml can coconut milk

3 kaffir lime leaves

4–8 small fresh hot chillies, left whole

2 tablespoons fish sauce

3 teaspoons palm sugar

400 g beef rump steak or oyster blade, thinly sliced

chopped spring-onion greens, to serve

basil leaves, to serve (optional)

Bring a pan of lightly salted water to the boil and simmer pumpkin for 6–8 minutes, until just tender. Drain and set aside.

In a wok combine the curry paste and ½ cup of the coconut milk and simmer, stirring, until oil separates and sauce is very fragrant (about 3 minutes).

Add the remaining coconut milk, the lime leaves, chillies, fish sauce and palm sugar, and bring to the boil, then reduce heat and simmer for 1–2 minutes.

Add beef and pumpkin to pan and cook gently for about 5 minutes or until the pumpkin is quite tender, adding a little water or extra coconut milk if needed.

Stir in the spring-onion greens and basil (if using), and serve.

SERVES 4–6

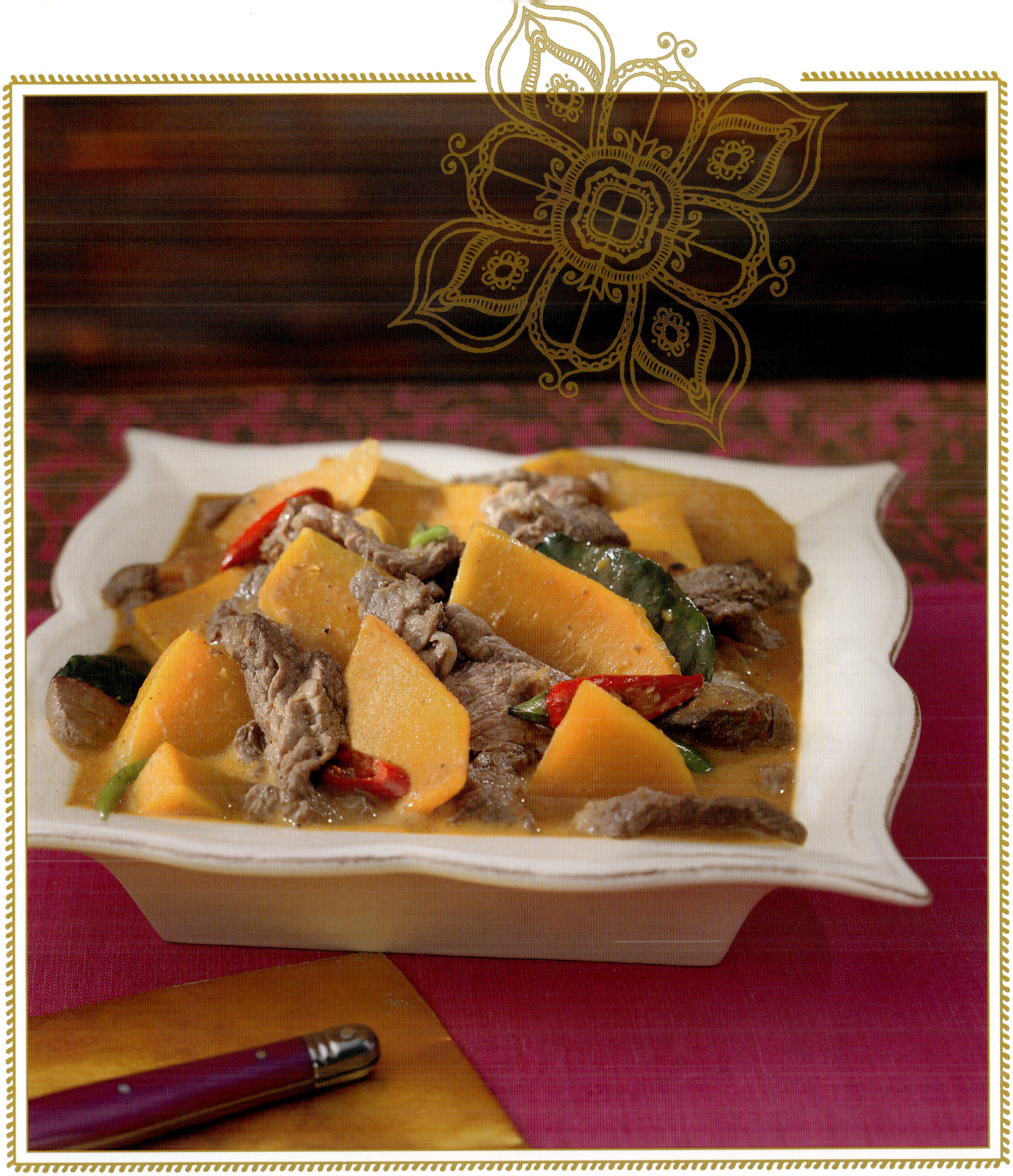

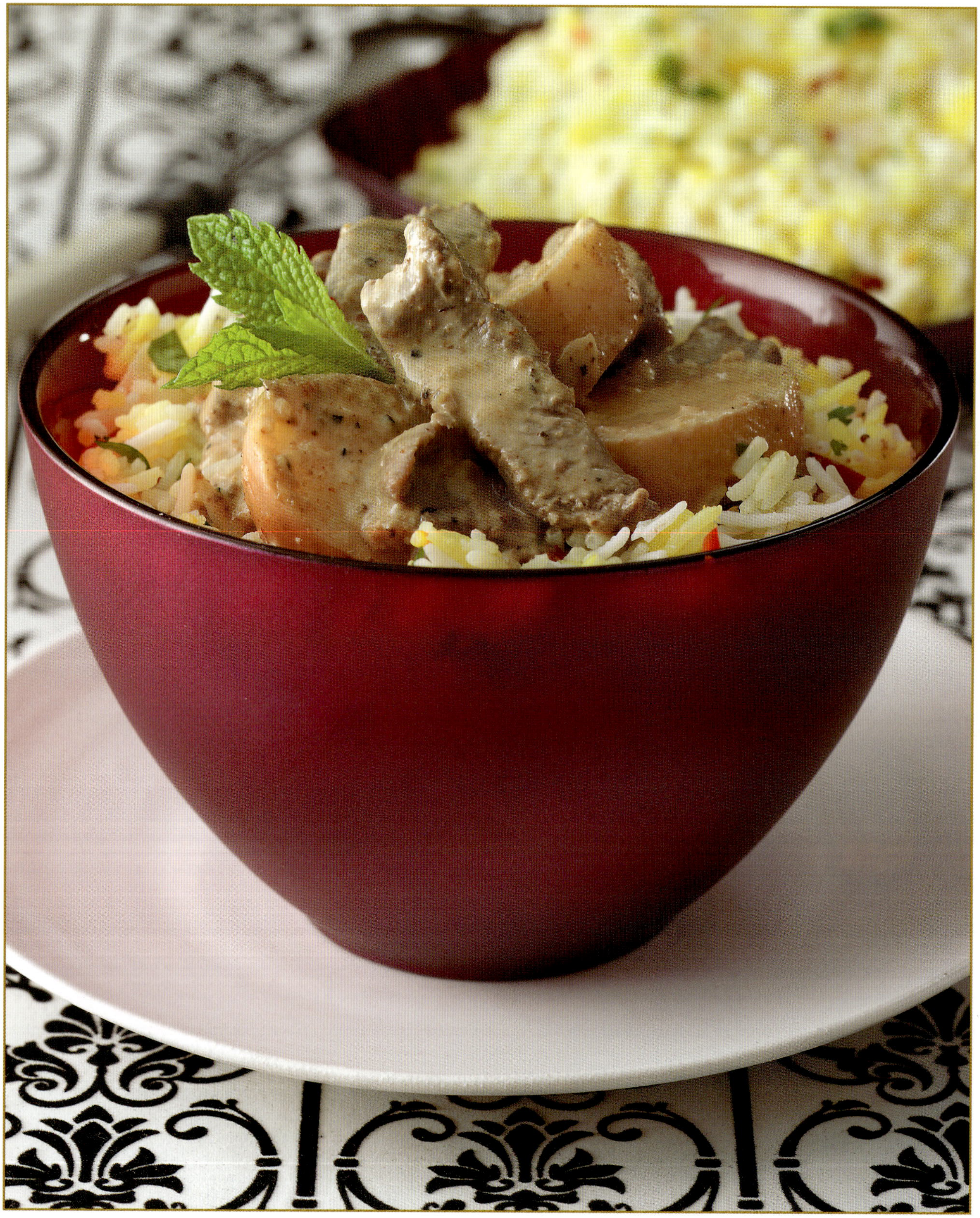

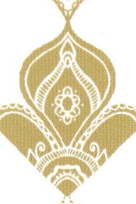

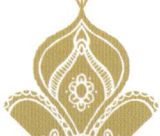

Fast-cook Mussaman beef curry

Tender steak sliced thinly, and a microwave boost to the potatoes, cut the preparation and cooking time of this classic to less than 15 minutes.

1 large potato, cut into 2-cm cubes
500 g beef rump steak, thinly sliced
salt and pepper
2 tablespoons oil
2 cloves garlic, grated
1 teaspoon finely grated fresh ginger
1 teaspoon bottled chopped lemongrass
1 cinnamon stick or 1 piece cassia bark
1½ tablespoons Thai Mussaman curry paste (page 19)
1 × 400-ml can coconut cream
1 teaspoon ground cumin
1½ tablespoons crunchy peanut (or macadamia) butter
salt and/or fish sauce, to taste
freshly squeezed lime juice (optional)
chopped fresh coriander, basil, or mint for garnish

Rinse potatoes, place in a microwave dish, cover, and microwave on high for 3 minutes.

Season beef lightly with salt and pepper. Heat the oil in a non-stick pan or wok and stir-fry slices until lightly coloured. Remove to a plate and set aside.

Add garlic, ginger, lemongrass, cinnamon or cassia, and curry paste to the pan and stir-fry for 30 seconds. Add ½ cup of the coconut cream and boil for 2–3 minutes, until reduced and very aromatic. Add the remaining coconut cream and 1 cup water, the potatoes and the cumin, and bring to the boil. Simmer until the potatoes are tender (about 5 minutes).

In a small bowl stir some of the hot curry sauce into the nut butter and pour back into the pan, adding salt or fish sauce to taste, and a squeeze of lime juice if you like. Return meat to pan and warm through gently. Serve garnished with chopped herbs.

SERVES 4–5

Thai beef & bamboo shoots in red curry

Stir-frying with curry paste and coconut cream makes for a speedy, spicy main dish.

4–5 green beans or 2 snake beans, cut into 2-cm pieces
2 tablespoons oil
250 g beef rump steak, cut into thin strips
1 small onion, cut into thin wedges and layers separated
½ red capsicum, cut into thin strips
2–4 teaspoons Thai red curry paste (page 17)
¾ cup coconut cream
½ cup sliced bamboo shoots, drained
3–4 button or oyster mushrooms, sliced
salt, fish sauce and pepper, to taste
freshly squeezed lime juice
fresh basil or coriander leaves, to serve

Bring 1 cup water to the boil in a wok or large non-stick pan and boil the beans for 2 minutes. Drain, refresh in cold water, then set aside.

Heat the oil in the same pan and stir-fry the beef for about 1½ minutes, until evenly coloured. Remove to a plate. Add sliced onion and capsicum to the pan and stir-fry for 2 minutes, until partially softened. Stir in curry paste and fry for about 20 seconds, then add the coconut cream and mix well.

Bring curry sauce to the boil and simmer for 1–2 minutes. Add bamboo shoots, mushrooms and prepared beans, and season to taste with salt and fish sauce, black or white pepper, and lime juice. Stir in about ¼ cup water, and return the meat to the pan with any liquid from the plate.

Heat gently for 2–3 minutes, fold in the herbs, and serve.

SERVES 2–3

Indonesian beef curry

In the Sumatran kitchen, this curry is often made with buffalo meat. You can substitute the juice of one lemon for the tamarind.

3 tablespoons oil
1 kg beef shin or brisket, cut into 3-cm cubes
2 medium-sized onions, finely chopped
2 teaspoons grated fresh ginger
2–3 teaspoons grated fresh turmeric (or 1 teaspoon ground turmeric)
2 cloves garlic, chopped
1½ teaspoons shrimp paste
1–2 teaspoons sambal ulek or hot chilli paste
2 teaspoons palm sugar or soft brown sugar
1 stem lemongrass, cut into four pieces
2 fresh hot green chillies, slit lengthways and deseeded
10 curry leaves
1 × 400-ml can coconut cream
salt
¼ cup ground macadamias, almonds or candlenuts (optional)
2–3 teaspoons tamarind concentrate
3 tomatoes, cut into wedges
6 snake beans or 10 green beans, cut into 4-cm pieces

Heat the oil in a frying pan or saucepan and brown the beef in batches. Set aside. In the same oil brown the onions for about 4 minutes, until well coloured. Add the ginger, turmeric, garlic and shrimp paste, and fry until well mixed with the onions. Add sambal ulek or chilli paste, the sugar, lemongrass, chillies and curry leaves, and again stir until lightly cooked (about 1 minute).

Return the meat to the pan, add the coconut cream and 3 cups water, and bring to the boil, stirring occasionally. Reduce heat and simmer for 1¼ hours. Add salt to taste, the ground nuts (if using), tamarind or lemon juice, tomatoes and beans, and simmer for about 25 minutes, or until the meat is very tender.

SERVES 6

Penang beef curry with peanuts

If you can't find Penang curry paste, you can use Thai red or Mussaman curry paste instead. The heat of this curry is tempered by the palm sugar.

1 × 400-ml can coconut cream
2–2½ tablespoons Penang or Mussaman curry paste (page 19)
500 g beef rump or other grilling cut, sliced into thin strips
½ cup roasted peanuts, macadamias or cashews
3 kaffir lime leaves
3 tablespoons fish sauce
3 tablespoons grated or crumbled palm sugar
fresh basil leaves, to serve
1 fresh hot red chilli, deseeded and finely shredded, to serve

Heat half the coconut cream in a saucepan and add the curry paste. Bring to the boil, stirring, and simmer for 2 minutes. Add the beef and cook for about 5 minutes only.

Grind the nuts to a fine powder and stir into the curry with the lime leaves, fish sauce, sugar, remaining coconut milk and about ¾ cup water. Bring barely to the boil and simmer for about 15 minutes, stirring occasionally. Stir in the basil leaves and chilli just before serving.

SERVES 4

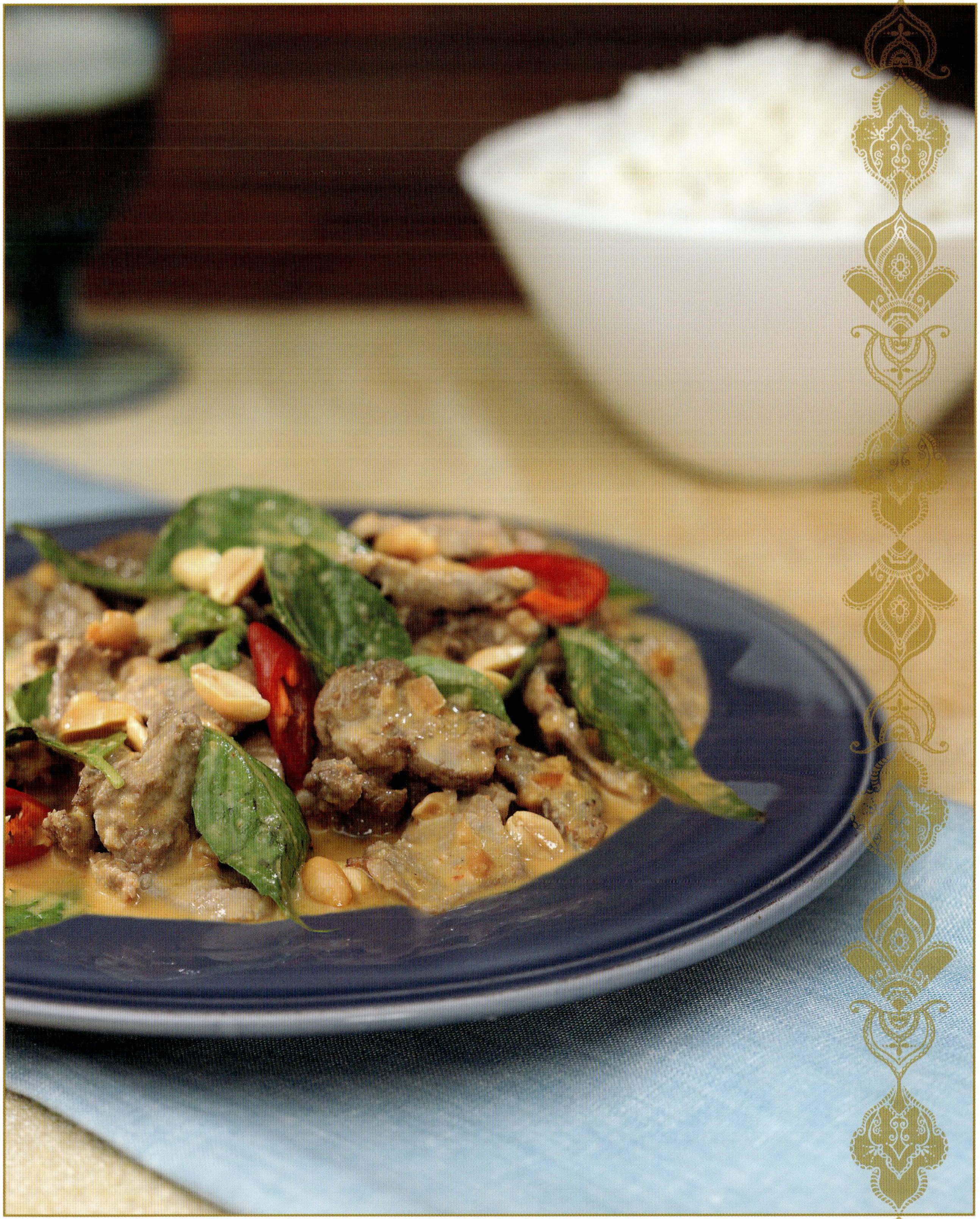

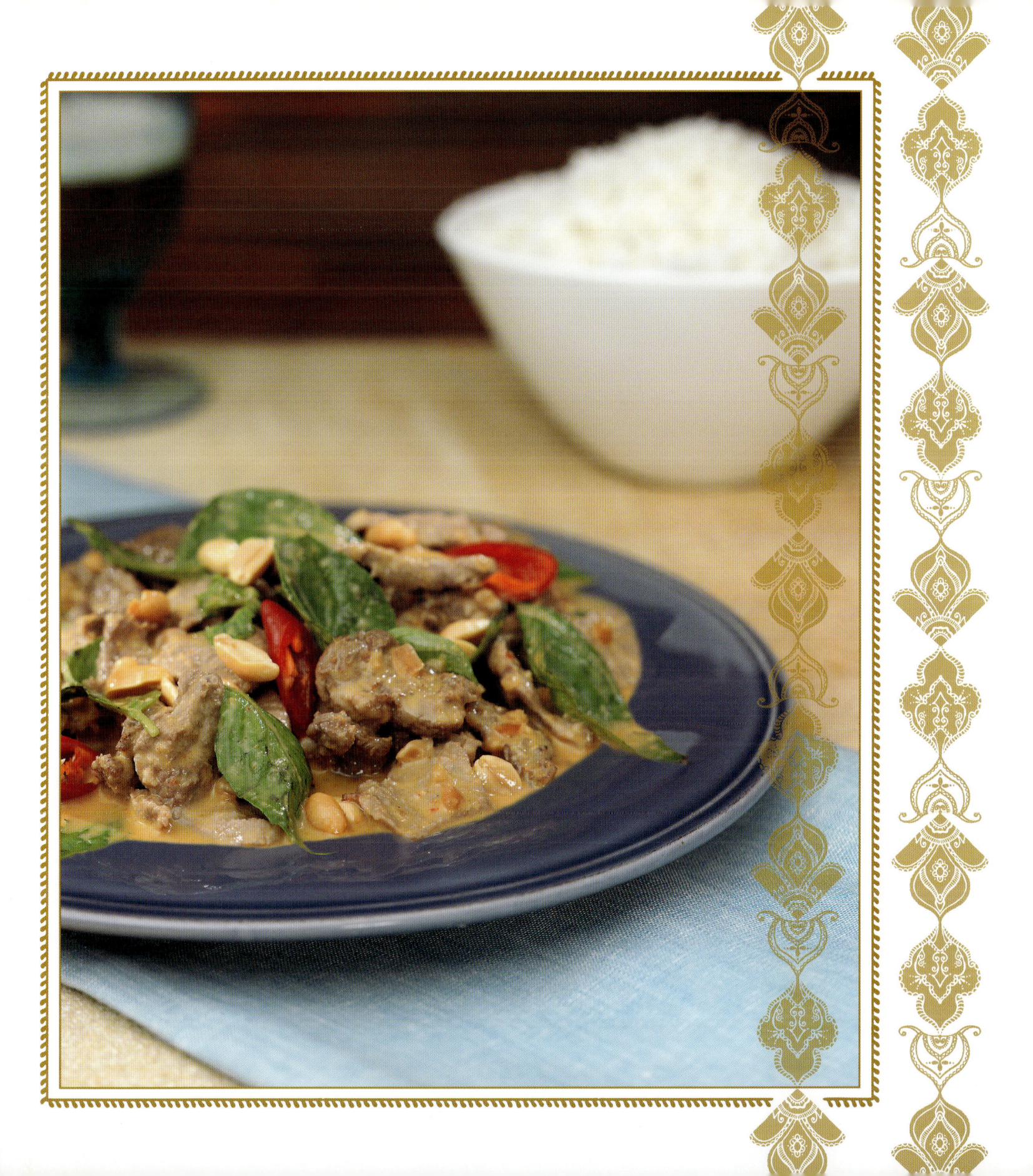

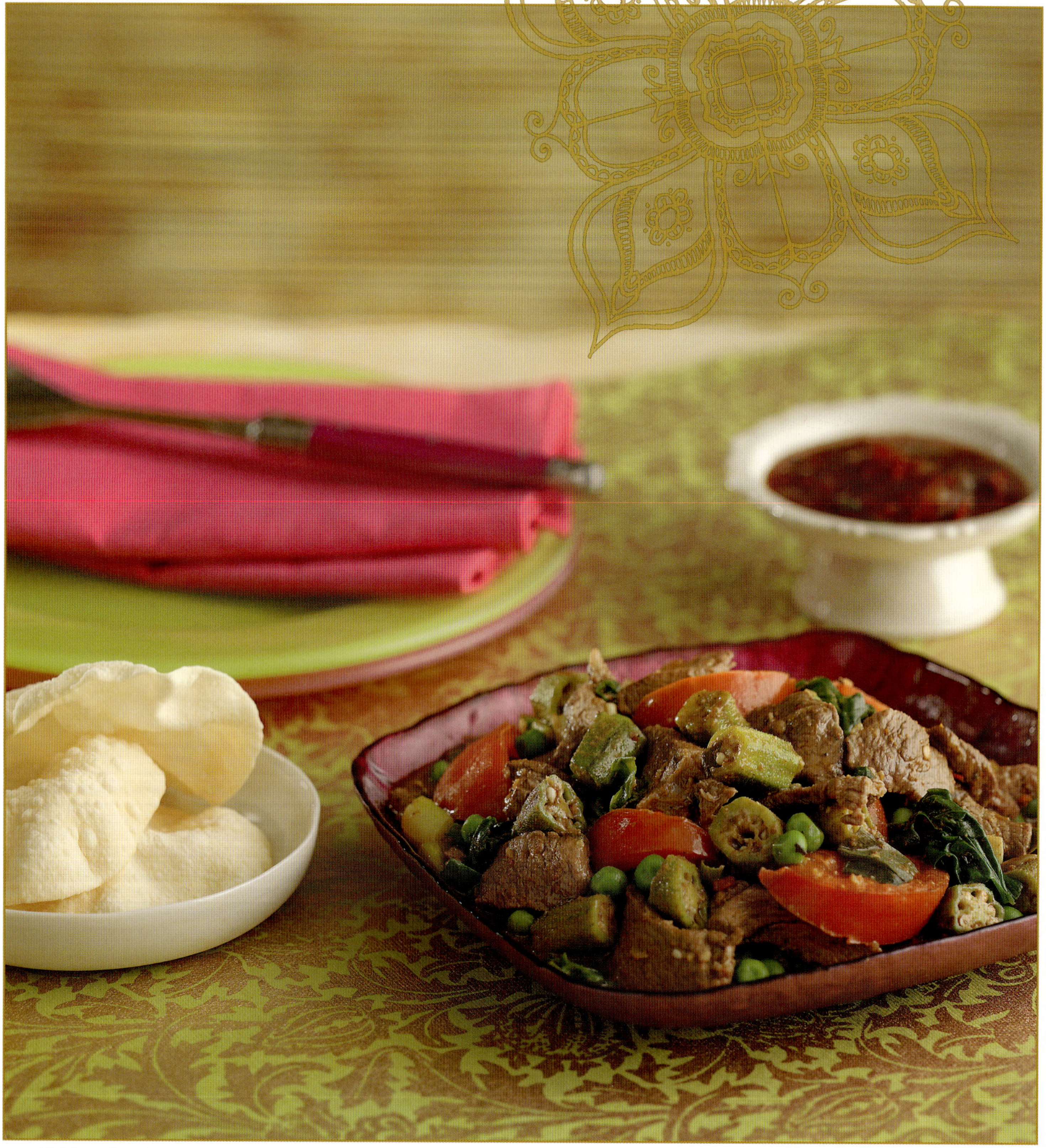

Fast & fiery Madras beef curry

Serve with oven-warmed naan bread or chapatis, a sweet fruit chutney and a tangy little salad of tomato and onion, or a raita with cucumber or banana.

3 tablespoons oil
650 g beef rump steak, thinly sliced
3 spring onions, chopped
3 cloves garlic, crushed
2 teaspoons grated fresh ginger
2 tablespoons hot Indian curry paste (page 14)
1 large tomato, cut into wedges
150 g frozen sliced okra, spinach or peas
salt and pepper
chopped fresh coriander or mint, to serve

Heat the oil in a large pan and fry meat in batches until lightly browned. Remove to a plate and set aside.

In the same pan sauté the spring onions, garlic, ginger and most of the curry paste for 2 minutes, stirring, then add the tomato and vegetables and 1¾ cups water. Bring to the boil and simmer for about 6 minutes, adding remaining curry paste if needed.

Return meat to the pan, season to taste and stir in the chopped herbs. Cook briefly, serve.

SERVES 3–4

Beef vindaloo

Vindaloo is best cooked a day or two in advance so that the intense flavours can meld and mellow. Gently reheat to serve.

3 tablespoons coriander seeds
1 tablespoon cumin seeds
1½ teaspoons black peppercorns
6 dried chillies, deseeded and soaked in hot water for 20 minutes
1 tablespoon white vinegar
1 tablespoon tamarind concentrate
8 cloves garlic, peeled
1 large onion, roughly chopped
a 3-cm piece fresh ginger, peeled
1 kg stewing beef (e.g. shin), cut into 4-cm cubes
3 tablespoons ghee or oil
6 whole cloves
1 cinnamon stick
2 teaspoons fenugreek seeds
1 teaspoon fennel seeds
2 bay leaves
3 cups beef stock or water
salt

In a small pan, dry-roast the coriander, cumin and peppercorns over medium heat for about 2 minutes, stirring. Transfer to a spice grinder and grind to a powder.

In a food processor or blender grind the chillies, vinegar, tamarind, garlic, onion and ginger until smooth and pasty. Add the ground spices and combine well. Spread over the meat and mix in well, massaging with the hands. Cover dish, and leave for 2 hours (or overnight in the refrigerator) to marinate.

Heat the ghee or oil and sauté the meat until lightly browned. Add the whole spices, bay leaves and beef stock or water, and bring to the boil.

Cover the pan, reduce heat and simmer for about 1¾ hours until the meat is tender, adding salt to taste in the last half hour of cooking.

SERVES 6

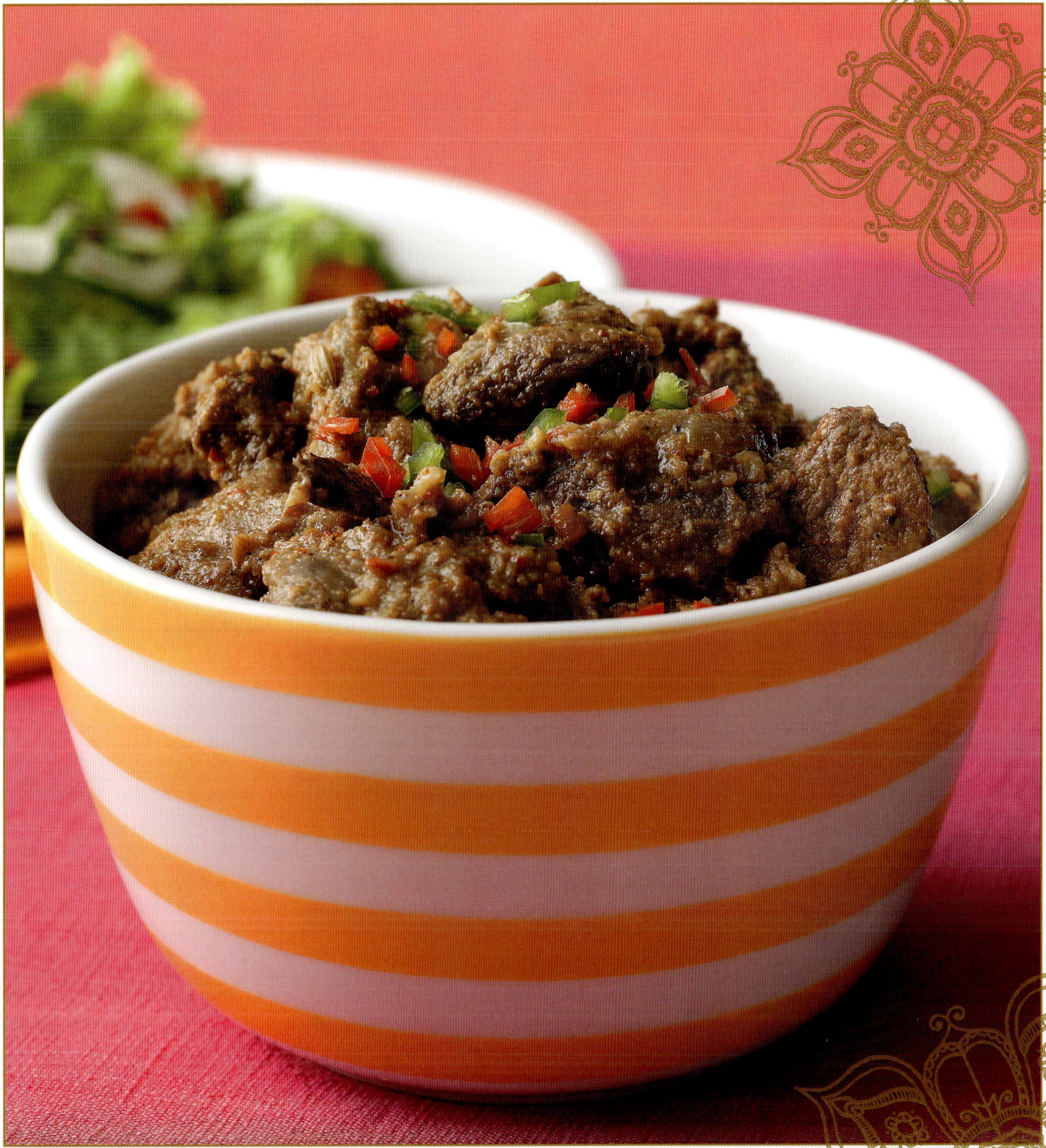

Sumatran beef rendang

Arguably one of the most popular of all curries, rendang is an Indonesian curry in which meat or other main ingredients are slow-simmered in spiced coconut milk until the liquid is reduced to an aromatic, caramelised glaze.

- 1.2 kg stewing beef (e.g. shin), cut into 4-cm cubes
- 1 stem lemongrass, bruised and cut in half
- 8 curry leaves
- 1–2 fresh hot red chillies, slit lengthways and deseeded
- a 2-cm piece fresh galangal, cut in half
- a 6-cm piece cassia bark, or 1 cinnamon stick
- 1½ × 400-ml cans coconut milk
- 3 medium-sized onions
- 4 cloves garlic, peeled
- a 2-cm piece fresh ginger, peeled
- 1½ teaspoons salt
- 2–3 tablespoons oil
- 2 tablespoons coriander seeds
- 2 teaspoons cumin seeds
- ¾ teaspoon black peppercorns
- ½ cup desiccated coconut
- 2 teaspoons tamarind concentrate
- 1½–2 teaspoons palm sugar or soft brown sugar

Place beef, lemongrass, curry leaves, chillies, galangal and cassia or cinnamon in a saucepan and add the coconut milk and enough water to barely cover. Bring to the boil, reduce heat and leave to simmer.

Cut 1½ of the onions into chunks and place in a blender or food processor with the garlic and ginger. Grind to a smooth paste, adding a little water if needed. Stir into the curry, adding the salt.

Finely slice remaining onions and fry in the oil until very well browned and almost dry (but take care they do not burn, or they will become bitter). Stir into the curry.

Wipe out the frying pan and reheat. Add coriander, cumin and peppercorns and the desiccated coconut and dry-roast until the spices are fragrant and the coconut a rich golden-brown. Pour into a spice grinder, grind to a powder and then stir into the curry. Continue to cook, uncovered, until the meat is tender and the liquid almost dried up (about 1¼ hours).

Mix tamarind and sugar with ½ cup water and pour into the curry. Check seasonings, adding more salt if needed. Continue to cook, stirring often, until the sauce has reduced to a thick glaze on the meat.

SERVES 6

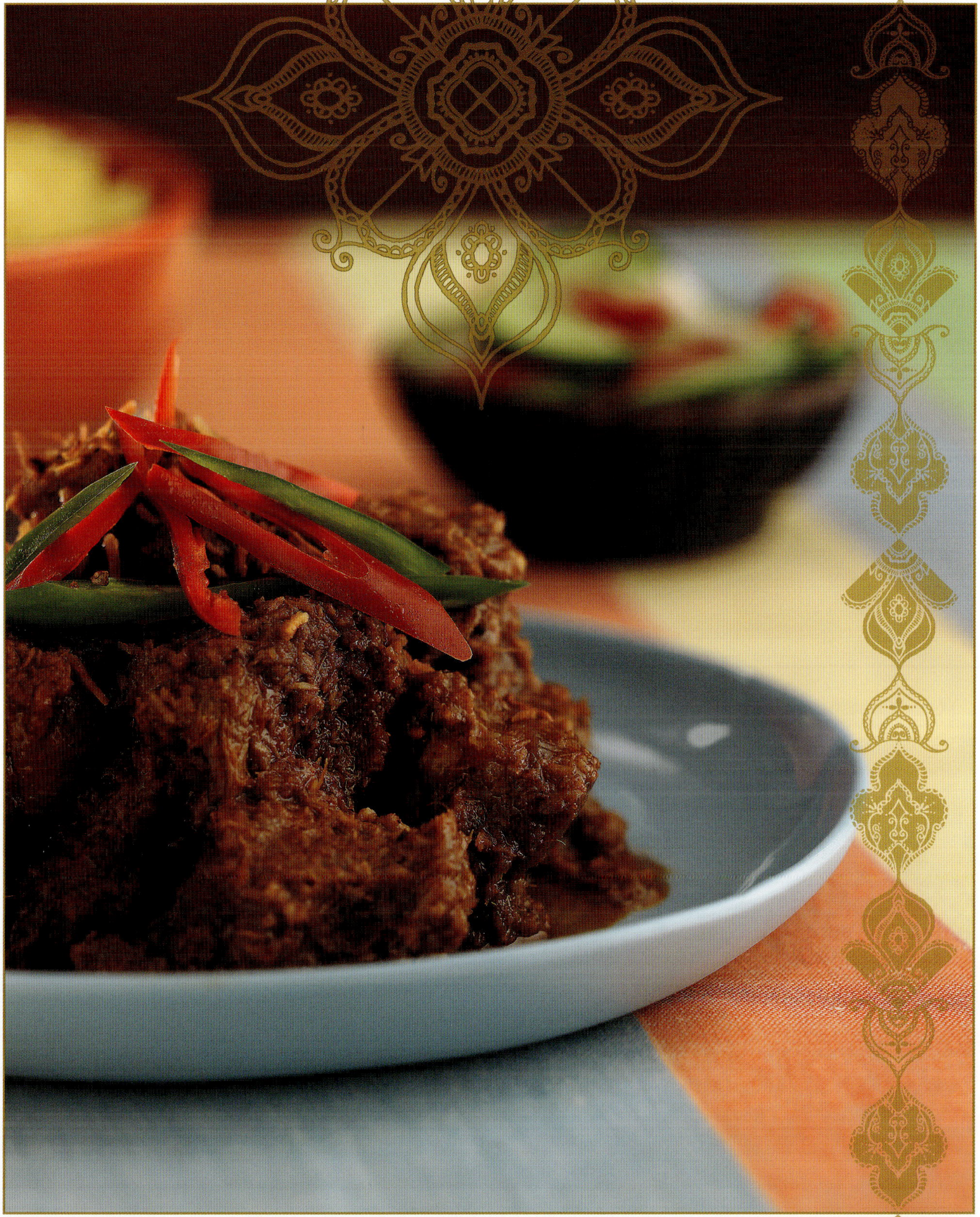

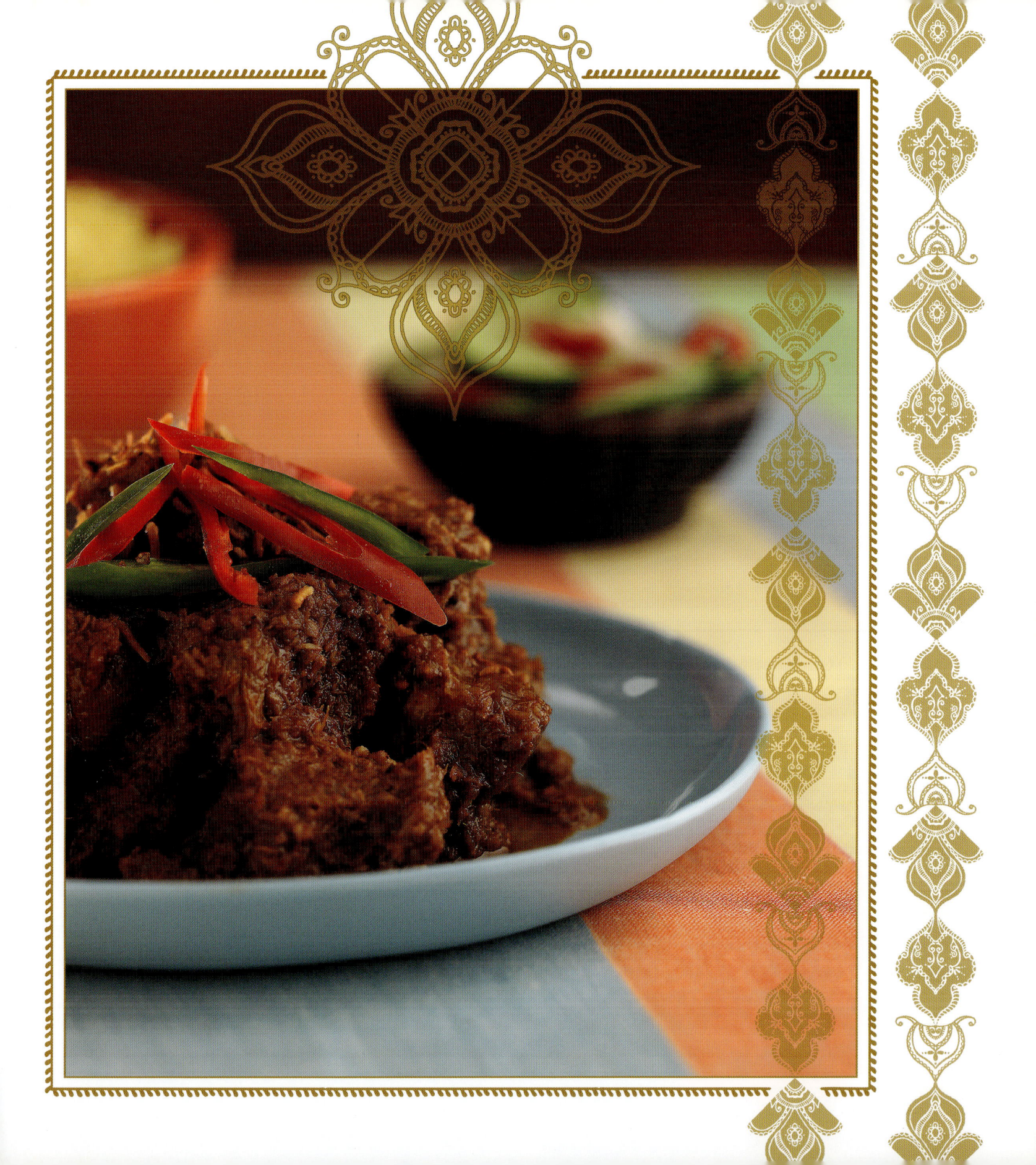

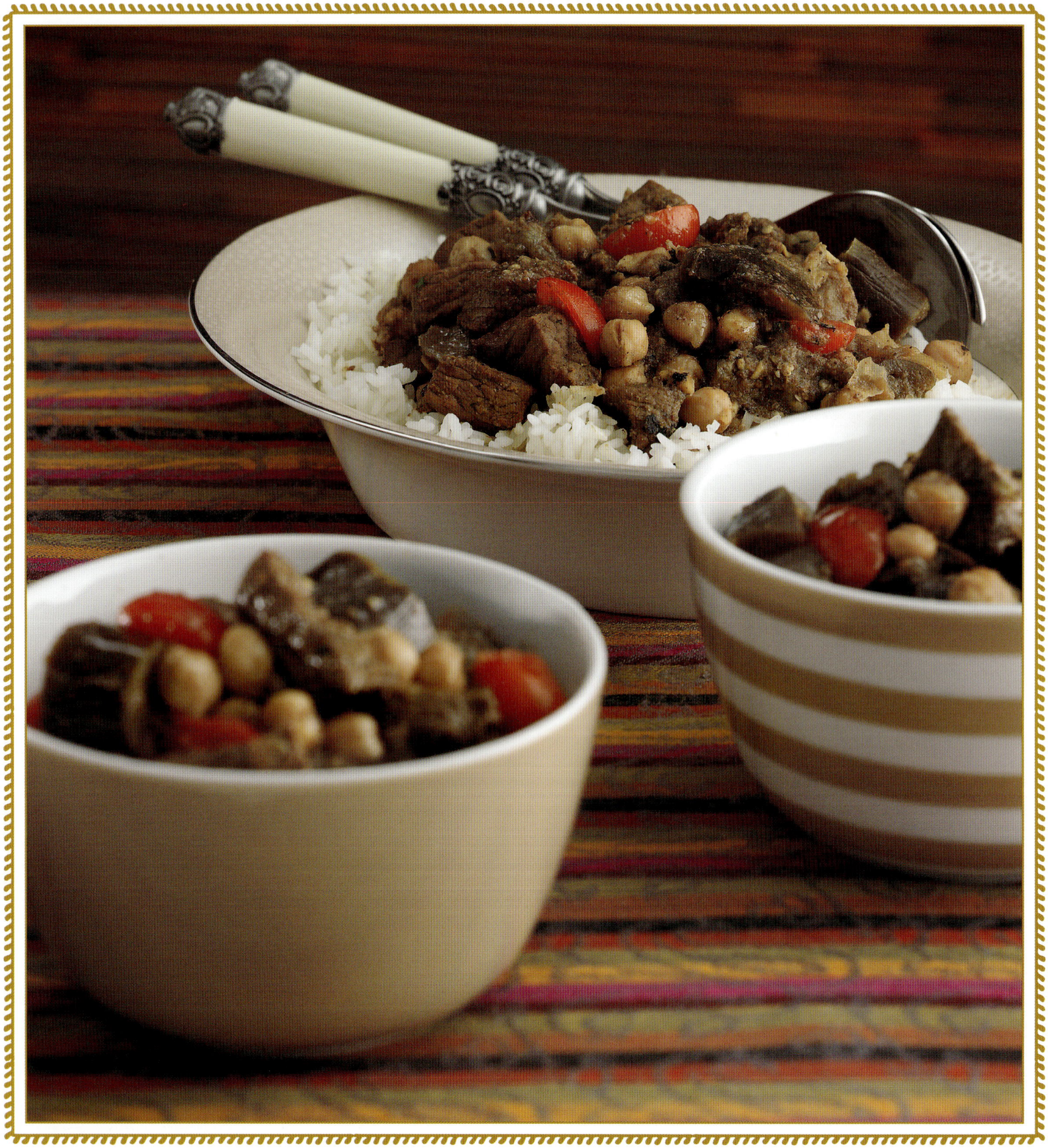

Beef curry with eggplant & chickpeas

1 large onion, roughly chopped
3 cloves garlic, peeled
a 2-cm piece fresh ginger, peeled
3 tablespoons ghee or oil
3 slender Asian eggplants (or 1 medium-sized eggplant), cut into 3-cm cubes
600 g beef shin or other stewing beef, cut into 3-cm cubes
1 tablespoon ground coriander
1½ tablespoons garam masala (page 16)
½ teaspoon ground turmeric
1½ teaspoons salt
3 bay leaves
1 cinnamon stick
4 cups water or beef stock
1 × 400-g can chickpeas, drained
8–10 cherry tomatoes
chopped fresh coriander or mint (optional)

Place onion, garlic and ginger in a food processor or blender and grind to a purée. Heat oil or in a medium–large saucepan and brown eggplant and onion purée for about 5 minutes, stirring almost continually. Add the cubed meat and stir over high heat until lightly browned (about 3 minutes).

Sprinkle the ground coriander and 1 tablespoon of the garam masala into the pan with the turmeric and salt, and mix in well. Add bay leaves, cinnamon and water or stock, and bring to the boil.

Reduce heat and simmer for about 50 minutes, stirring occasionally. Add chickpeas and tomatoes and cook for a further 10–15 minutes.

Stir in remaining garam masala, chopped coriander or mint (if using), and serve.

SERVES 6

Balti meat & mushroom curry

Balti is a quick-cook curry cuisine, essentially a stir-fry using curry spices. Balti curry paste can be replaced by any Indian curry paste from mild to vindaloo, depending on your heat preference.

2½ tablespoons oil
250 g beef, venison or kangaroo rump, cut into thin strips
1 clove garlic, crushed
1 medium-sized onion, sliced
3 large button or portobello mushrooms, sliced
3–4 teaspoons Balti curry paste (page 13)
½ teaspoon cumin seeds
¼ cup cream or creamy yoghurt
salt and pepper

Heat the oil and fry the meat with the garlic until barely cooked (about 2 minutes), then remove to a plate.

Add onion to the pan and stir-fry for 2 minutes, then add the mushrooms and continue to stir-fry for about 2 minutes more until onion is tender and mushrooms have softened and begun to give off liquid. Return meat to pan, add the curry paste and cumin seeds, and stir everything together over medium–high heat for 1 minute.

Pour in about ¼ cup water (or beef stock if you prefer) and the cream or yoghurt, and season with salt and pepper. Simmer just long enough for the sauce to coat the meat and vegetables. Serve as is with rice, or wrap in a warmed roti or chapati.

SERVES 2–3

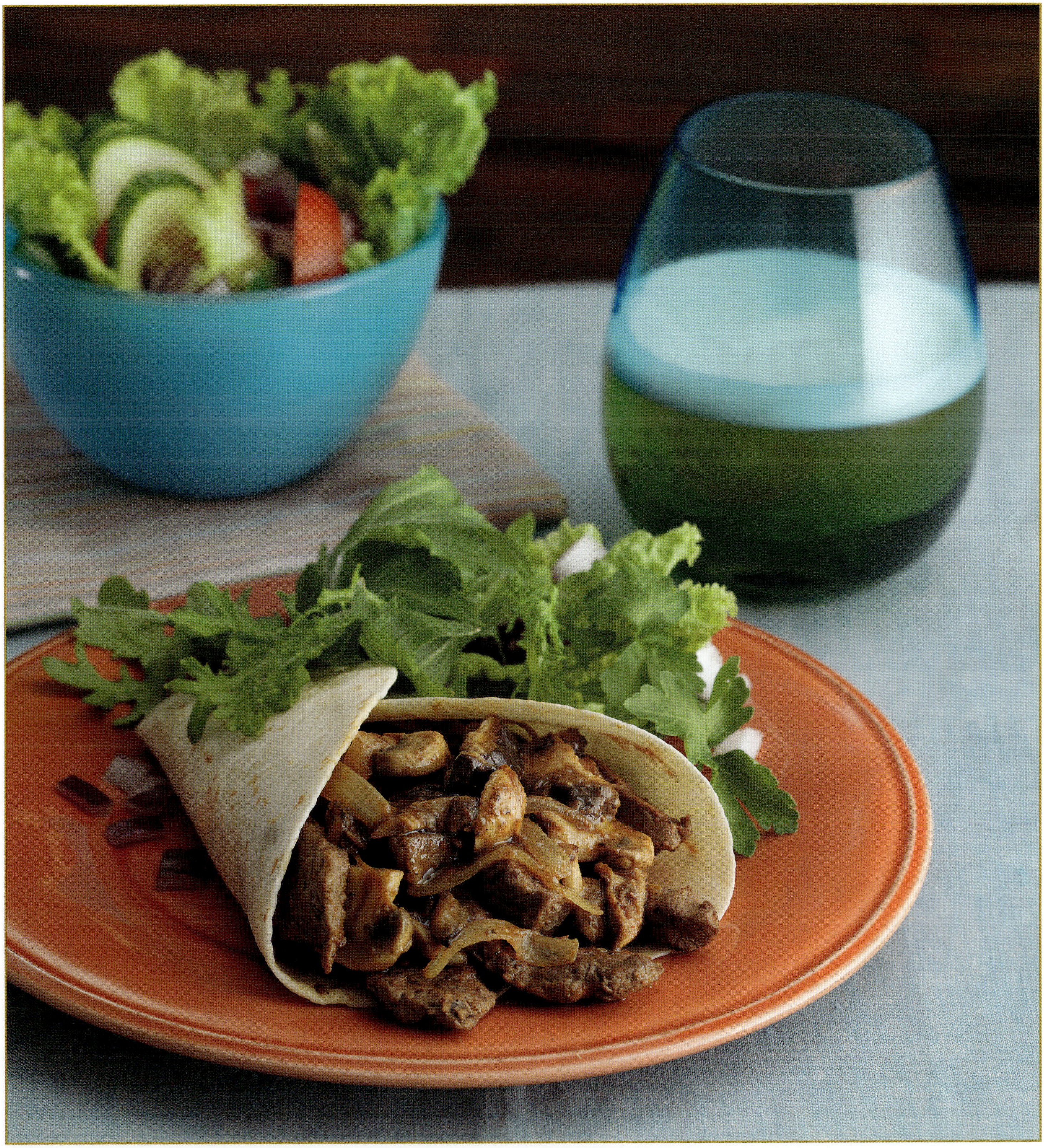

Pork diablo

European colonisers of the small Malaysian state of Malacca from the sixteenth century infused the local cuisine with some of their own culinary traditions. This fiery Portuguese 'devil' (diablo) curry is one such evolution and remains a favourite today. It is usually served with sliced hard-boiled egg, cucumber and a fruity chutney.

1 kg lean pork, cubed
1 tablespoon kecap manis (sweet soy sauce)
1 tablespoon grated palm sugar or soft brown sugar
2 tablespoons white vinegar or rice vinegar
6 cloves garlic, mashed with 1 teaspoon salt
6 dried red chillies, deseeded and soaked in hot water for 20 minutes
a 10-cm stem lemongrass, thinly sliced
1 teaspoon shrimp paste
6 candlenuts or macadamias
1 tablespoon coriander seeds
1 teaspoon cumin seeds
½ teaspoon black peppercorns
1 teaspoon ground turmeric
3 tablespoons ghee or oil
8 shallots, thinly sliced
5 thin slices fresh young ginger, finely shredded
extra 1 stem lemongrass, bruised
salt

In a bowl mix the pork with the kecap manis, sugar, vinegar and garlic, and leave to marinate for ½–1 hours stirring occasionally.

Drain chillies and grind to a paste in a spice grinder or blender with the sliced lemongrass, shrimp paste and nuts.

In a small pan, dry-roast the coriander, cumin and peppercorns, then grind to a fine powder, adding the turmeric.

Heat the ghee or oil and fry the chilli and nut paste for 1 minute, stirring, then add the shallots and the ground spice mix and stir well. Add the pork and its marinade, the ginger and extra lemongrass. Mix everything together well, add 2 cups water and simmer for about 1¼ hours, tightly covered.

After this time remove the lid and stir the pork, adding salt to taste. Continue to simmer over low heat, stirring occasionally, until pork is quite tender and has absorbed much of the liquid.

SERVES 6

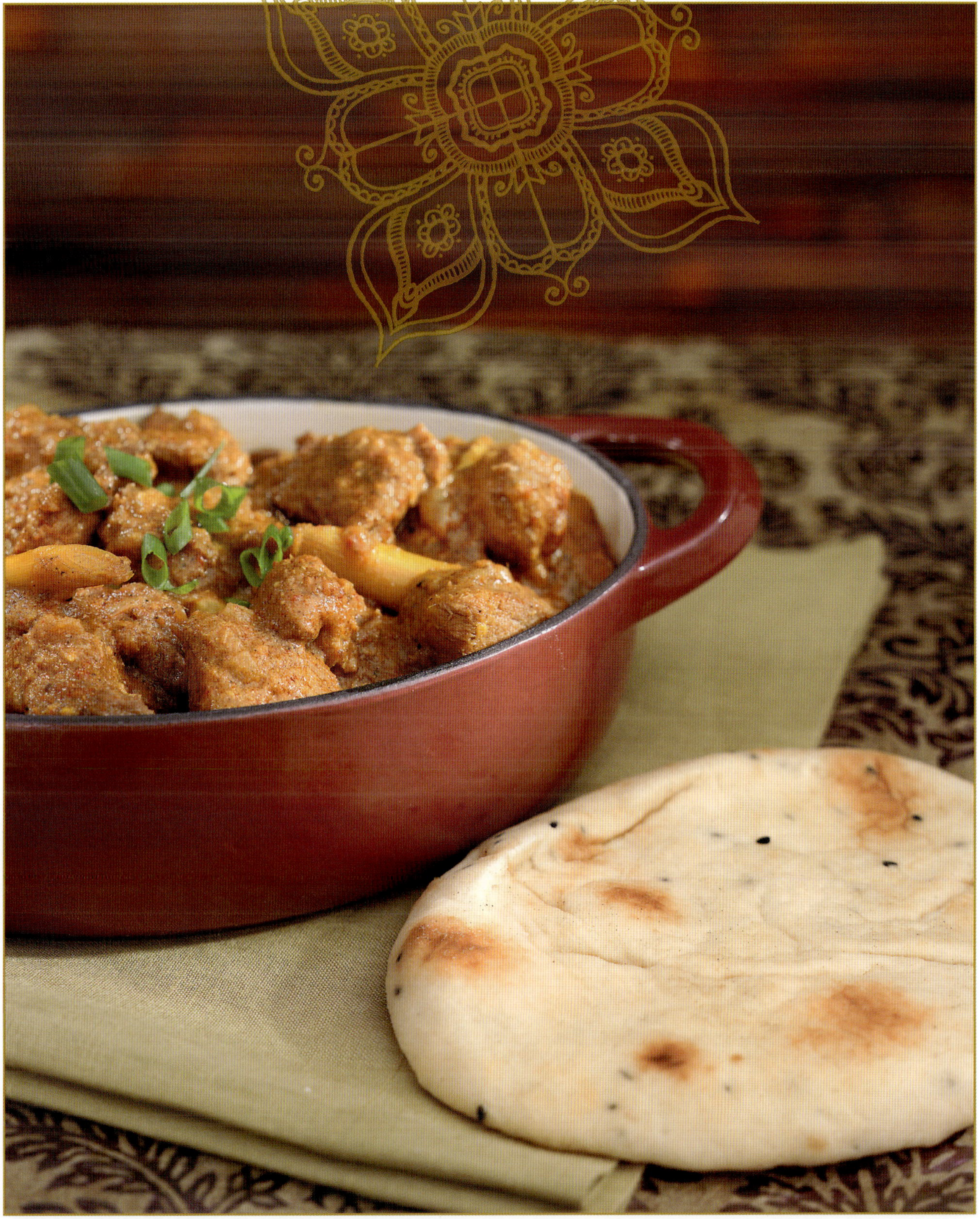

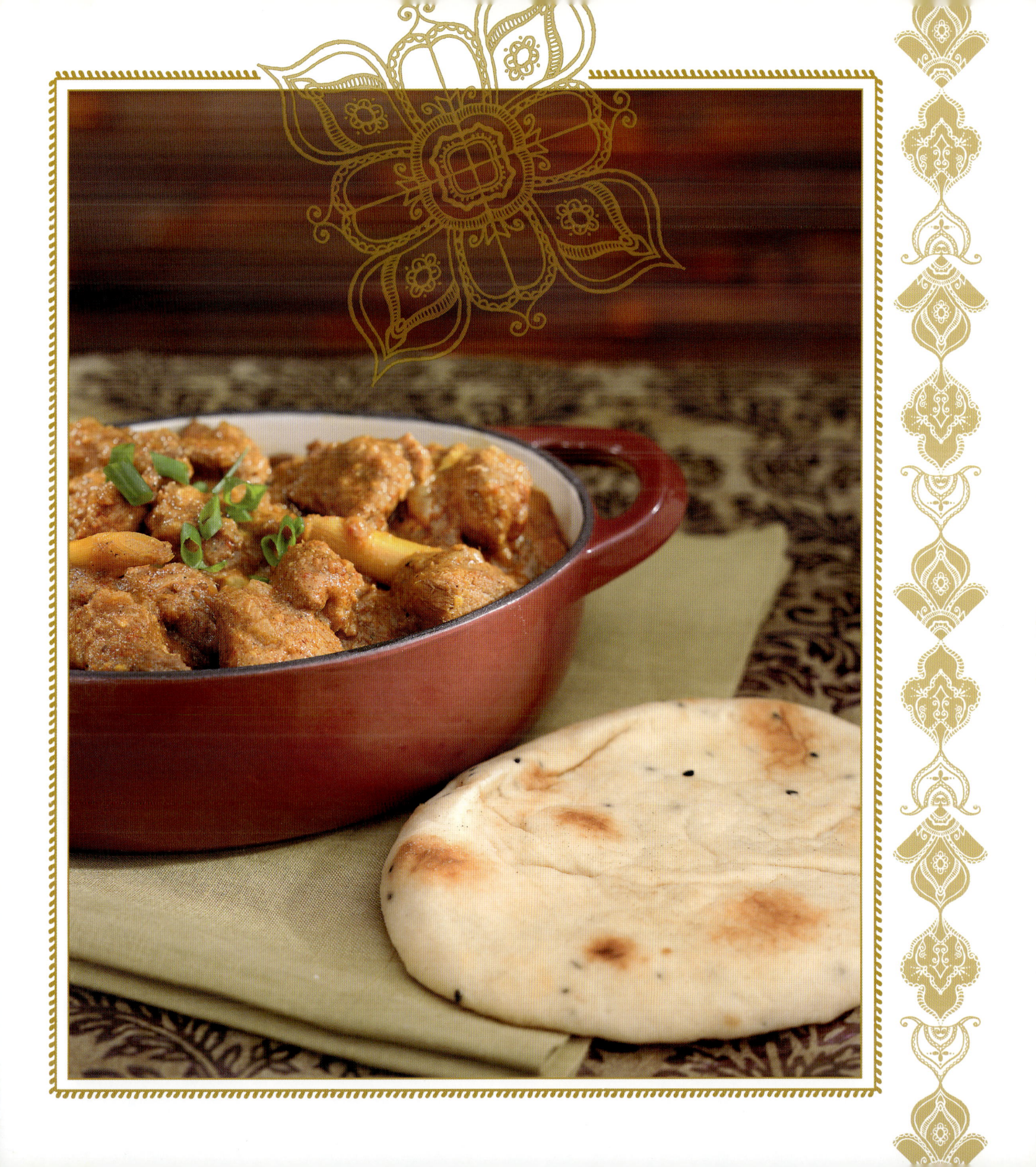

Goan pork vindaloo

- 10 dried red chillies, deseeded and soaked in hot water for 20 minutes
- 8 cloves garlic, peeled
- a 4-cm piece fresh ginger, diced
- 2 teaspoons tamarind concentrate
- 1 tablespoon white vinegar
- 1 kg boneless pork shoulder, cut into 3-cm cubes
- 1½ teaspoons cumin seeds
- ½ teaspoon black peppercorns
- 2 teaspoons ground sweet paprika
- 3 tablespoons ghee or oil
- 3 medium-sized onions, finely chopped
- 10 curry leaves
- 4 whole cloves
- ½ cinnamon stick
- 1 star anise, broken into pieces
- 1½ teaspoons salt

Drain chillies and place in a blender or food processor with the garlic and ginger. Grind to a smooth paste, add tamarind and vinegar, and grind again briefly. Spread mixture over the pork, massaging in well.

In a small pan dry-roast the cumin and peppercorns until fragrant (about 1½ minutes). Transfer to a spice grinder and grind to a fine powder, adding the paprika. Sprinkle evenly over the pork and stir well to coat each piece. Cover and refrigerate for 2 hours, or overnight.

When ready to cook, heat the ghee or oil in a large pan and fry the onions over medium heat for about 10 minutes, until well coloured and very soft. Add curry leaves, cloves, cinnamon and star anise, and the marinated pork. Stir over medium heat for about 5 minutes. Pour in water to barely cover the pork, and add the salt. Simmer for about 1 hour, until the pork is very tender and the sauce thick, tart and hot.

SERVES 6

Thai red curry pork with pineapple

300 g lean pork, finely sliced
2 tablespoons oil
1–1½ tablespoons Thai red curry paste (page 17)
2–3 teaspoons grated palm sugar or soft brown sugar
½ teaspoon red chilli paste or sambal ulek (optional)
1 × 400-ml can coconut cream
½–1 tablespoon fish sauce
6 kaffir lime leaves
1–2 mild fresh red chillies, slit lengthways and deseeded
1 cup chopped fresh pineapple
8–10 fresh basil leaves

Blanch the pork in gently boiling water for 30 seconds. Pour into a colander to drain.

Heat the oil in a wok or saucepan and fry the curry paste over medium heat for 1 minute. Add sugar, chilli paste (if using), ⅓ cup of the coconut cream and the fish sauce, and simmer for 2–3 minutes. Stir in the remaining coconut cream, the lime leaves and chillies, and bring to the boil. Add pork and cook gently for 1–2 minutes, then stir in the pineapple and basil leaves. Warm through, check seasonings and serve.

SERVES 3–4

Rangoon pork curry

Burmese curries reflect the country's geographical advantage of having two of the great curry nations – Thailand and India – as its neighbours. Curries served in the restaurants of Burma's capital, Rangoon, in roadside food stalls and in homes from coast to jungle-dense mountains, intermarry spices with local ingredients to interesting effect, as in this classic.

Jars and cans of pickled garlic are sold in Asian food stores. Like pickled onions, they have a sweet/sharp taste which adds interesting cameos of flavour to a hot curry.

1 kg boneless pork shoulder, cubed
a little oil
1 stem lemongrass, bruised
a 2-cm piece fresh ginger, chopped
3 cloves garlic, chopped
3 fresh hot red chillies, deseeded and sliced
1 teaspoon shrimp paste
1 teaspoon ground turmeric
1½ tablespoons dark soy sauce
2 tablespoons palm sugar or soft brown sugar
1 tablespoon tamarind concentrate
salt and pepper
fish sauce
sweet pickled garlic (optional)

Preheat the oven to 190°C.

Lightly grease an oven dish and add the pork, lemongrass, ginger, garlic and chillies. Mash together the shrimp paste, turmeric, soy sauce, sugar and tamarind with ½ cup water and pour evenly over the pork. Add another 1–1½ cups water, 1 teaspoon salt, and pepper to taste.

Cover the dish with a lid or a double layer of aluminium foil and bake for 35–40 minutes. Uncover, stir up, and check seasonings, adding fish sauce and salt to taste. Increase the heat to 200°C and continue to cook until the pork is tender and aromatic, stirring occasionally. Stir in 2–3 tablespoons sweet pickled garlic (if using) before serving, or offer it in a small dish on the side.

SERVES 6

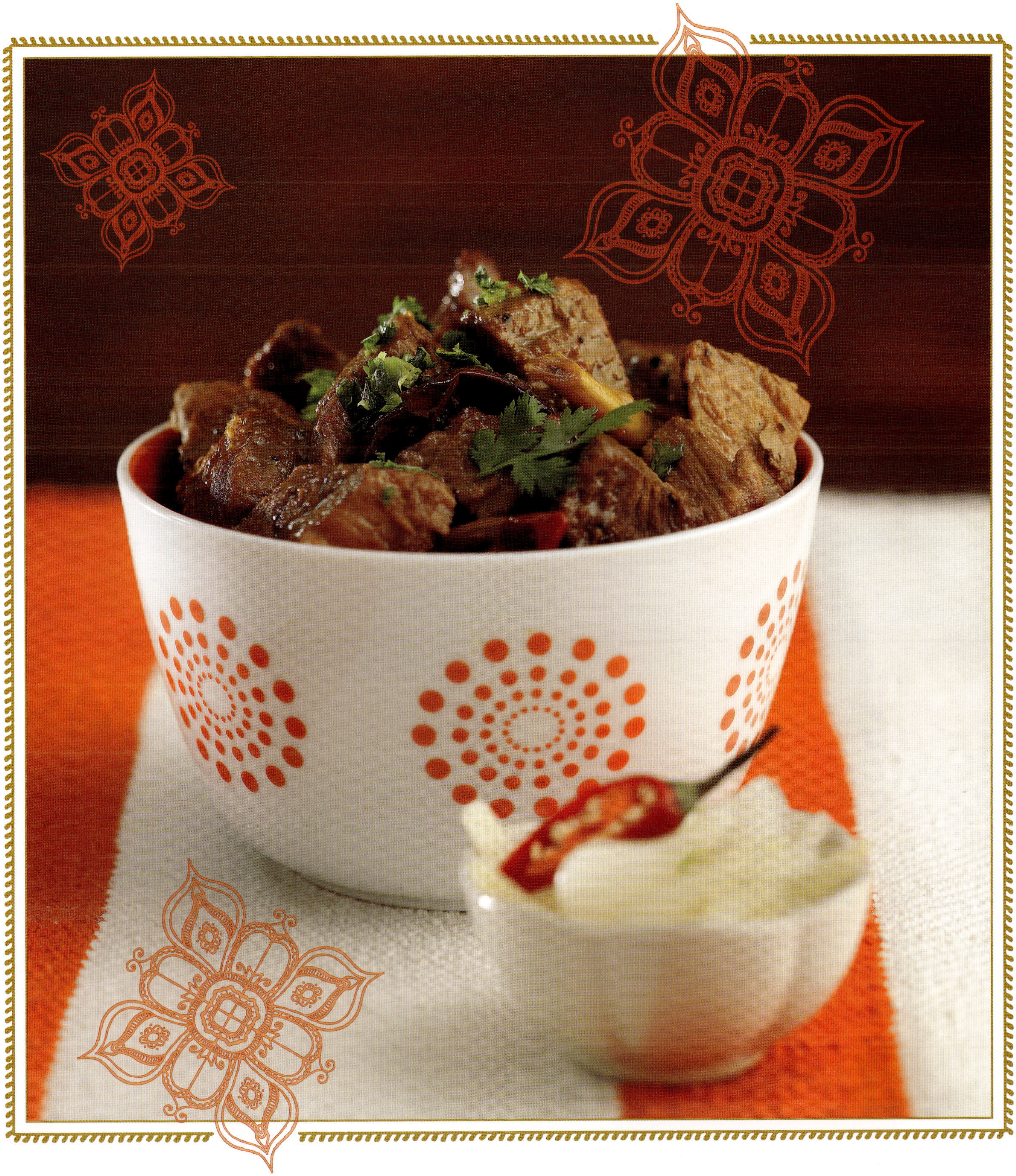

Nonya spiced pork & potato curry

For this dish you can remove the rind from the pork or leave it on, as you prefer.

- 1 small onion, peeled and halved
- 3 cloves garlic, peeled
- 2 fresh red chillies, deseeded
- 1 teaspoon ground turmeric
- 1 teaspoon ground chilli or chilli flakes
- 3–4 tablespoons oil
- 3 tablespoons ground coriander
- 1 × 400-ml can coconut cream
- 600 g pork belly, cut into 3-cm cubes
- ¾ teaspoon fennel seeds
- 1 cinnamon stick
- 2 whole cloves
- 1 star anise
- 1 teaspoon salt
- 5 kipfler potatoes, peeled and cubed

In a blender or mortar grind the onion, garlic and chillies to a paste. Heat the oil in a heavy-based pan and fry paste for about 1½ minutes, stirring. Add the ground spices and fry for 40 seconds, then add half the coconut cream and simmer for 4–5 minutes, stirring.

Add pork to pan and stir over high heat for 40 seconds or so, then add remaining coconut cream, the whole spices, salt and 1 cup water. Cover the pan, simmer for about 30 minutes, then add the potatoes and continue to simmer, turning occasionally and adding a little more water if needed, until pork is tender and potatoes cooked. Check and adjust seasoning, and serve.

SERVES 4–6

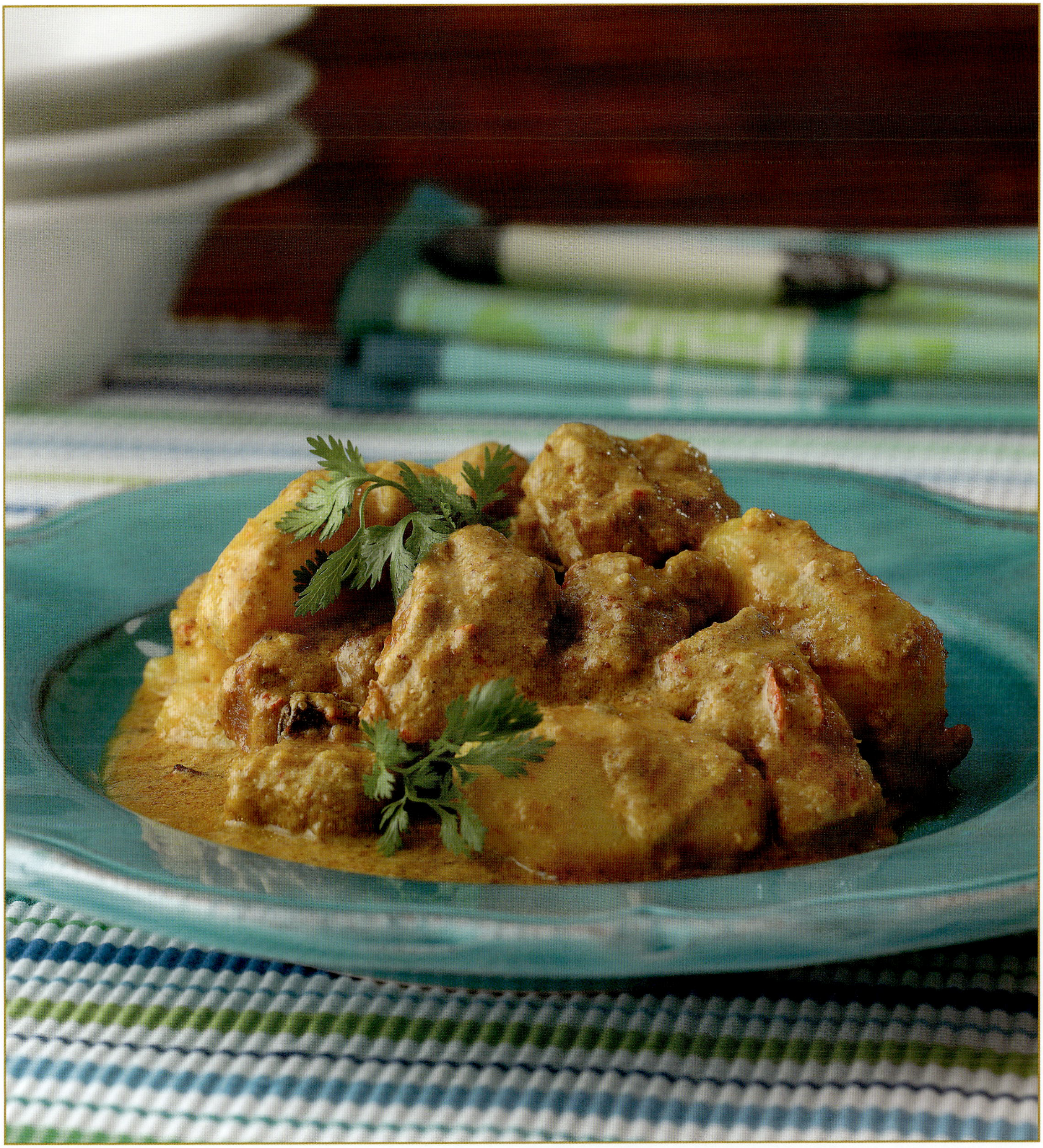

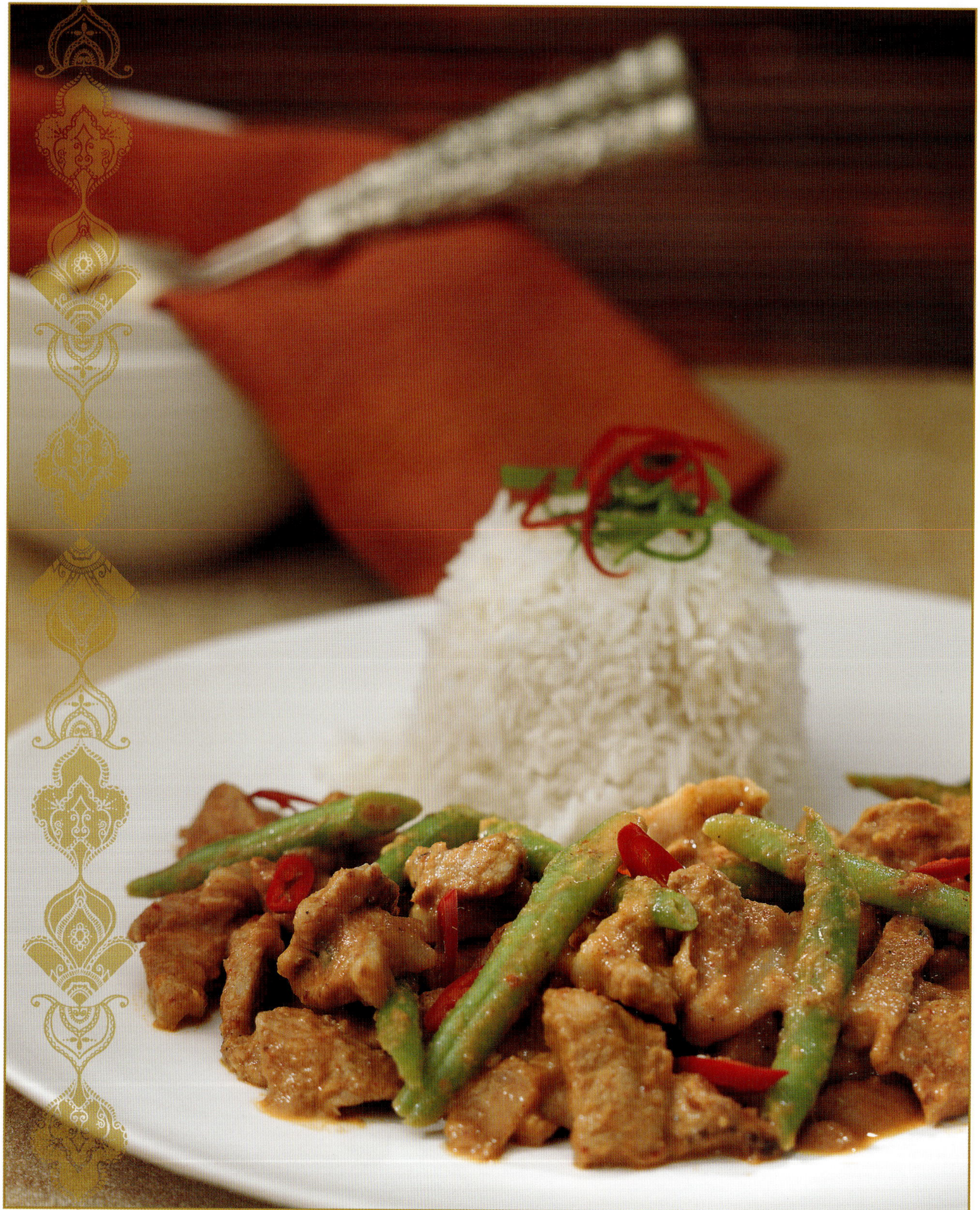

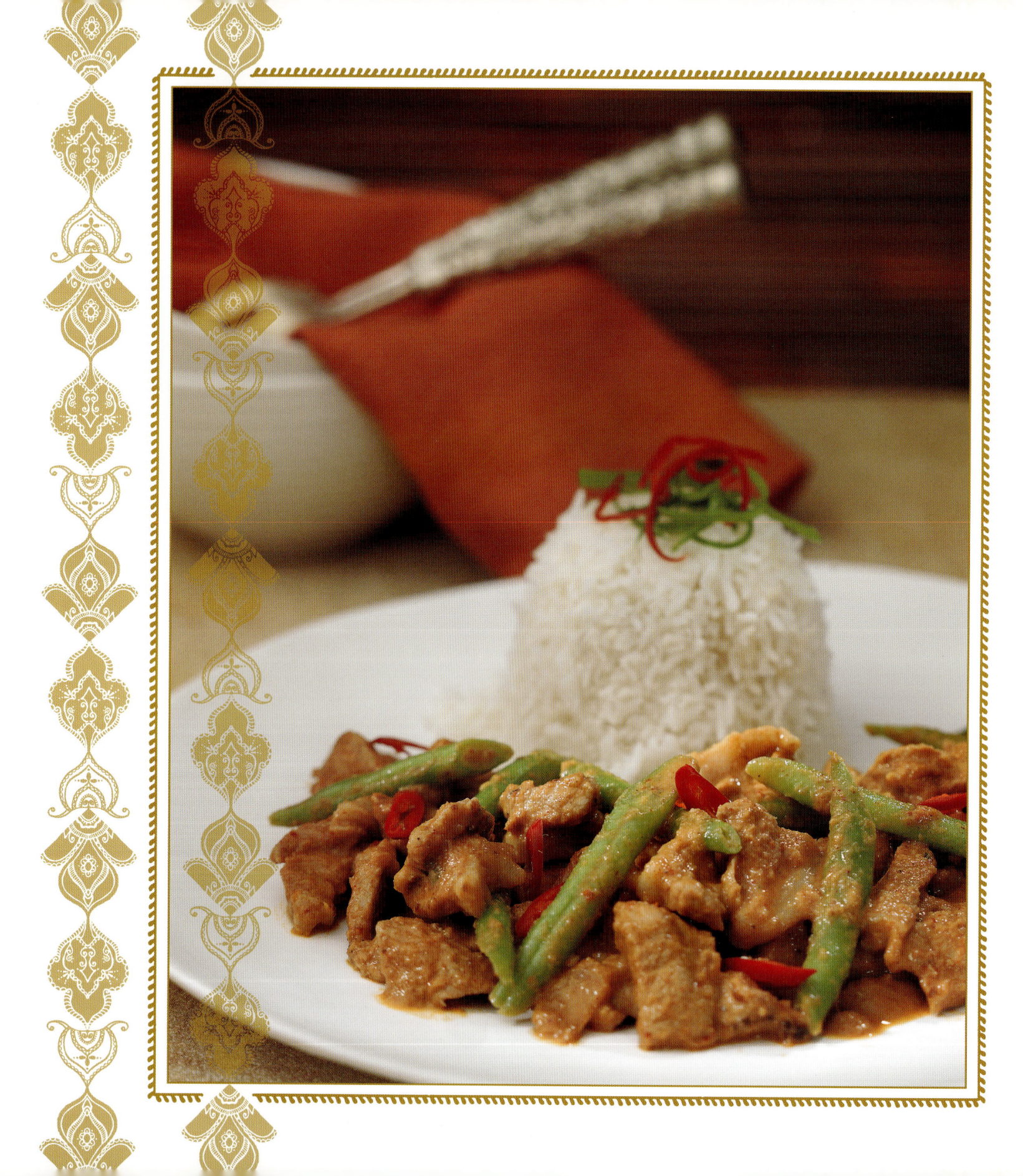

Stir-fried red curry of pork & green beans

Eating this dish in Thailand could be likened to a gastronomic form of Russian roulette, almost every mouthful being loaded with chillies of incendiary heat. Here the chilli volume is turned down to a less fiery level. It's worth seeking out the slender, dark-green snake beans, which have more flavour and a crisper texture than their paler counterparts. Asian food stores and most supermarkets stock them.

6 green beans or 2 snake beans, cut into 4-cm pieces
1 large pork chop (350–400 g) with a selvage of fat
1 small onion, peeled
a 2-cm piece fresh ginger, peeled
1 clove garlic, crushed
½ teaspoon red chilli paste or sambal ulek
2 tablespoons oil
1½–2 teaspoons Thai red curry paste (page 17)
2–3 tablespoons coconut cream
½–1 teaspoon palm sugar or soft brown sugar
fish sauce, to taste

Heat 1 cup water in a wok or non-stick frying pan and boil the beans for about 2 minutes, until crisp-tender. Drain, and refresh in cold water. Wipe out the pan.

Trim around the chop bone and skin, and discard. Cut the meat into thin slices, each with a little edge of fat. Place in a bowl and set a fine nylon strainer over the bowl. Grate onion and ginger into the strainer and press the juices through with the back of a wooden spoon (reserve the solids). Mix juices with the pork, adding the garlic and chilli paste, and leave for 10 minutes.

When the pork is ready to cook, heat the wok or pan and add the oil. Stir-fry the pork with the onion solids for about 3 minutes over medium–high heat, stirring almost continually. Add the curry paste, coconut cream and drained beans, and mix in well. Continue to cook over medium–high heat until pork and beans are coated with the seasonings, adding sugar and fish sauce to taste.

To increase the curry gravy, stir in ½–¾ cup water or coconut milk and simmer gently, seasoning to taste.

SERVES 2–3

MEAT CURRIES   265

Thai green pork curry

1 × 400-ml can coconut cream
1 × 400-ml can coconut milk
1 teaspoon salt
400 g meaty pork spare ribs, sliced
1 stem lemongrass, bruised
1 tablespoon Thai green curry paste (page 18)
2 tablespoons fish sauce
1 large fresh hot chilli, deseeded and sliced
2 teaspoons green peppercorns (fresh or in brine)
3 kaffir lime leaves
fresh basil leaves (optional)

Combine half the coconut cream with the coconut milk and the salt in a saucepan, and add the pork and lemongrass. Bring to the boil, reduce heat and simmer for about 25 minutes or until pork is tender, stirring occasionally.

Pour remaining coconut cream into another saucepan, add the curry paste and cook over medium heat, stirring continually, for about 5 minutes. Add the fish sauce and cook briefly, then add this mixture to the pork with the chilli, peppercorns and lime leaves. Simmer for 5–6 minutes, then stir in the basil leaves (if using).

SERVES 4–6

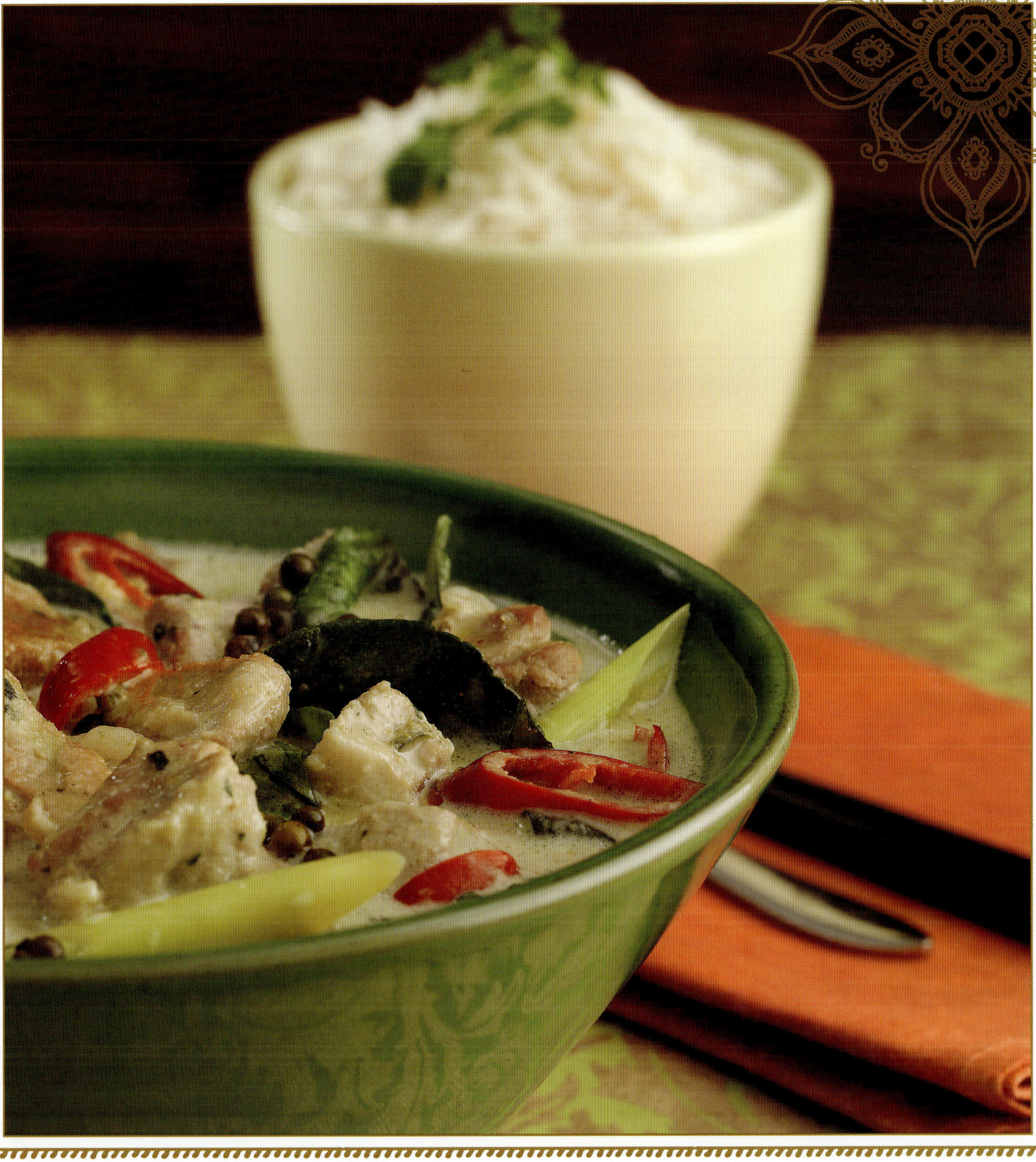

Malay pork, dried-shrimp & pineapple curry

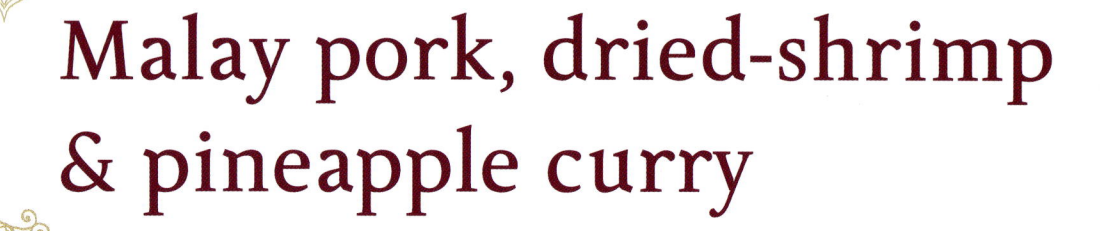

Tart and tangy flavours often feature in Malaysian curries. Tamarind, fresh lime, pineapple and the bitter local fruits belimbing (star fruit) and asam gelugor (a relative of the mangosteen) imparting sour, citrusy flavours.

750 g boneless pork leg or shoulder, cut into 3-cm cubes
1 tablespoon dark soy sauce
3 teaspoons tamarind concentrate
2 tablespoons oil
3 tablespoons dried shrimp
1½ teaspoons brown mustard seeds
3 cloves garlic, crushed
8 curry leaves
8 shallots, finely sliced
1 stem lemongrass, bruised and cut into 3–4 pieces
2–4 fresh hot red chillies, slit lengthways and deseeded
a 4-cm piece fresh galangal, cut into chunks
1 teaspoon ground turmeric
salt and pepper
2 tablespoons ground candlenuts or macadamias
1⅓ cups diced fresh pineapple

Place pork in a bowl, add soy sauce and tamarind, mix well and leave for 1 hour, stirring twice.

In a heavy saucepan heat the oil and fry the dried shrimp, mustard seeds, garlic and curry leaves for 1 minute, stirring. Add shallots, lemongrass, chillies and galangal, and fry for 1 minute, stirring continually.

Add the pork and its marinade to the pan and stir until coated with the seasonings. Add turmeric, salt and pepper to taste, and about 1½ cups water, bring to the boil, cover and simmer for 25 minutes. Add the ground nuts and cook for a further 20 minutes or so, uncovered, until the pork is tender and the sauce thick. Stir often, and add a little extra water if the sauce is becoming too reduced.

Add the pineapple, check seasonings and cook just long enough to warm through.

SERVES 6

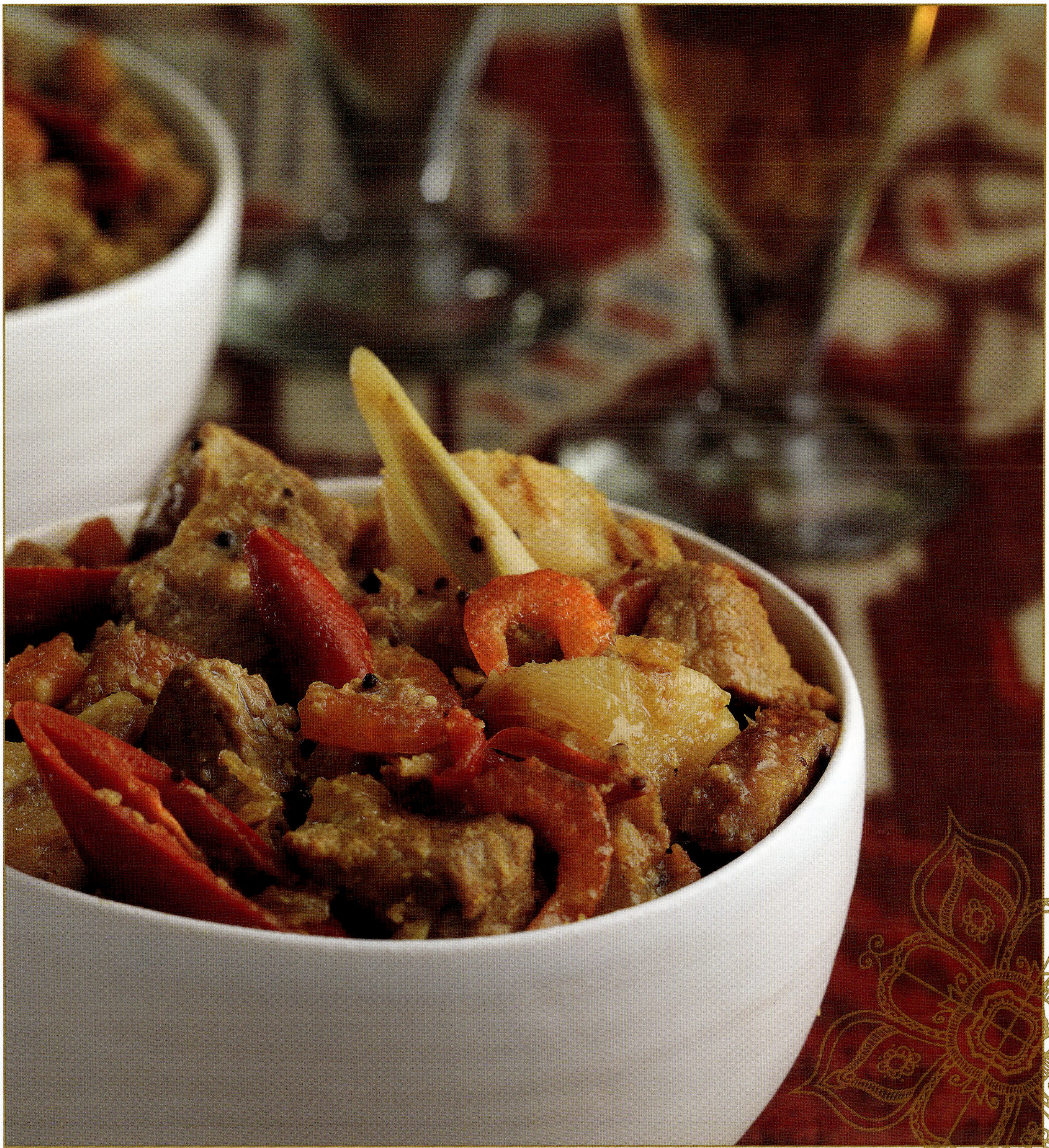

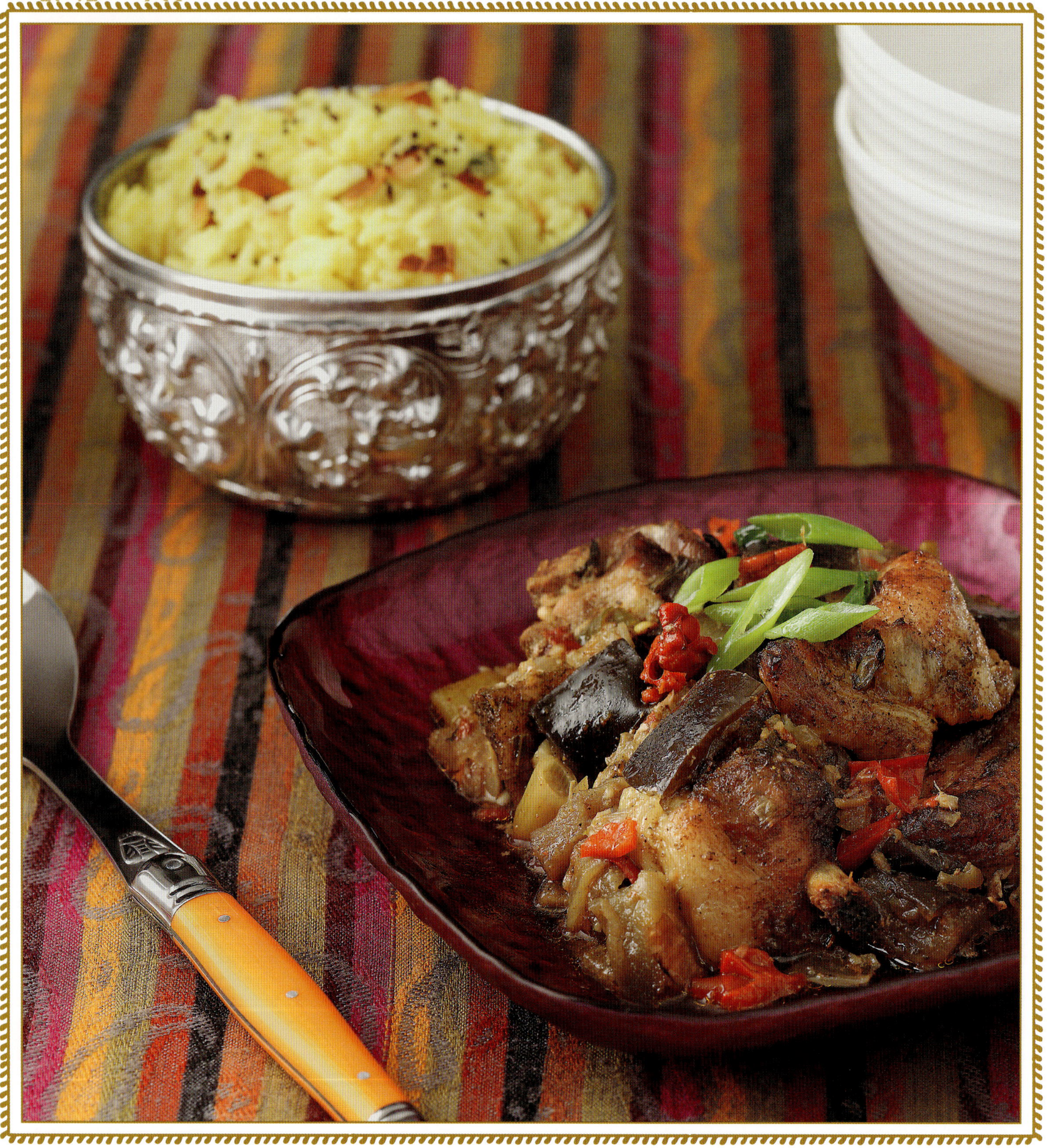

Pork ribs in hot masala

Winter party food that needs nothing more than rice to satisfy.

2 kg meaty pork ribs or pork belly, cut into 3-cm pieces
2 tablespoons vindaloo paste (page 11)
1 tablespoon garam masala (page 16)
6 cloves garlic, chopped
a 4-cm piece fresh ginger, finely chopped
2–4 hot red chillies, deseeded and chopped
2 large onions, finely chopped
1 medium-sized eggplant, cut into 3-cm cubes
5 spring onions, cut into 3-cm pieces
salt and pepper
chopped fresh coriander, or spring-onion greens for garnish

Preheat the oven to 180°C.

Mix pork with the vindaloo paste, garam masala, garlic, ginger and chillies, and stir well.

Spread onions in a large oven dish and add 2½–3 cups water. Lay the seasoned pork on top, and top with the eggplant and spring onions. Season lightly with salt and pepper, cover with foil, place in oven and cook for 1½–2 hours.

After this time, remove the foil, skim off excess fat and check seasoning. Transfer to a serving dish, or serve in the casserole, garnished with chopped coriander or spring-onions.

SERVES 8–12

Game curry with Sri Lankan roasted spices

You can use venison, kangaroo or wild duck for this potent curry.

750 g game stewing meat, cut into 3-cm cubes
3 tablespoons Sri Lankan roasted spices (page 14)
3 tablespoons oil
1 medium-sized onion, chopped
1 sprig curry leaves
salt and pepper
chopped fresh coriander

In a bowl mix the meat thoroughly with the spices, cover, and refrigerate for 3–4 hours, stirring up occasionally.

Heat the oil in a heavy saucepan and fry the onion with the curry leaves until well browned. Add the meat and stir over medium-high heat until very aromatic (4–5 minutes). Add water to barely cover, bring to the boil, then reduce heat and simmer for about 50 minutes, or until meat is very tender. Season to taste with salt and pepper and stir in the coriander before serving.

SERVES 4–6

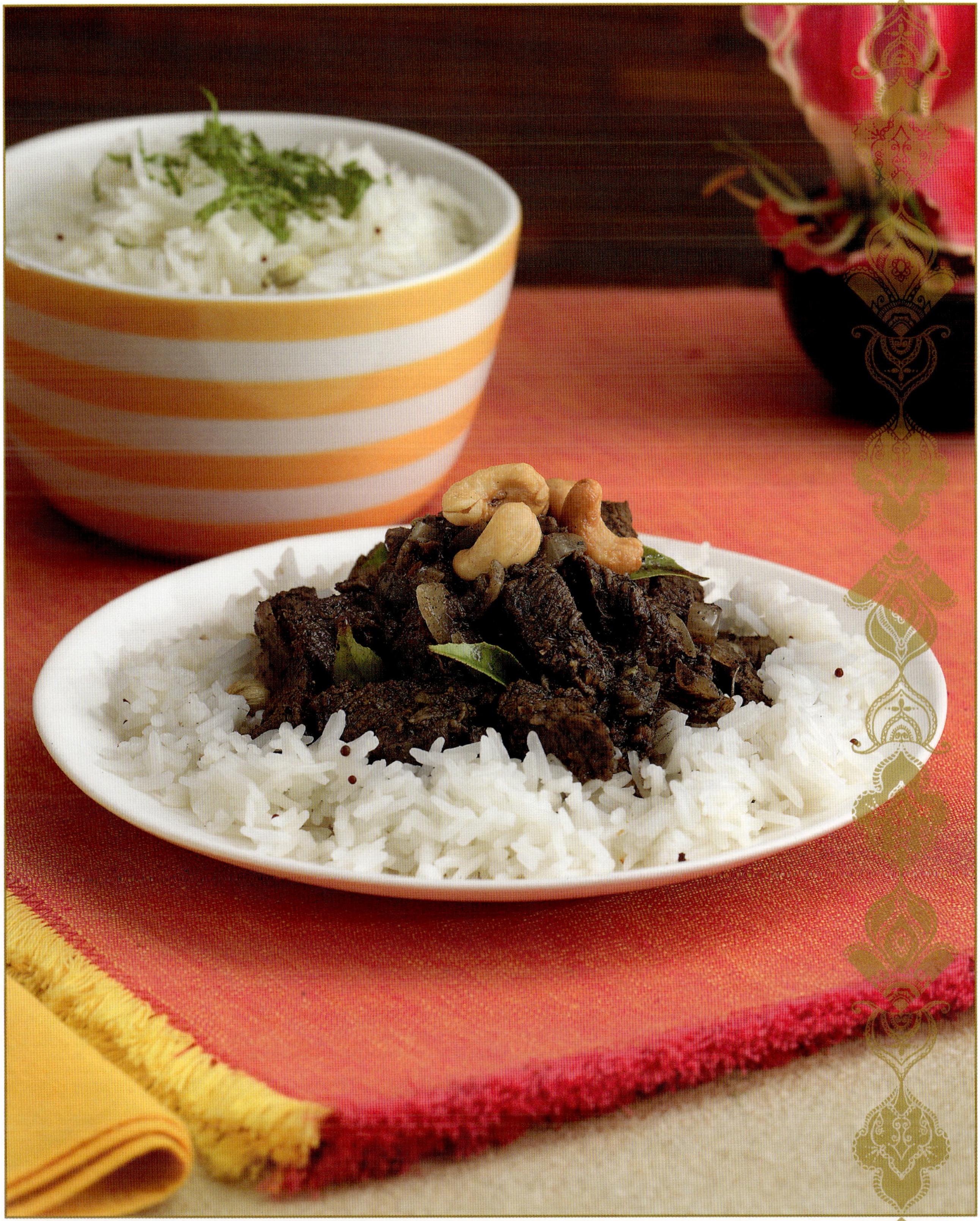

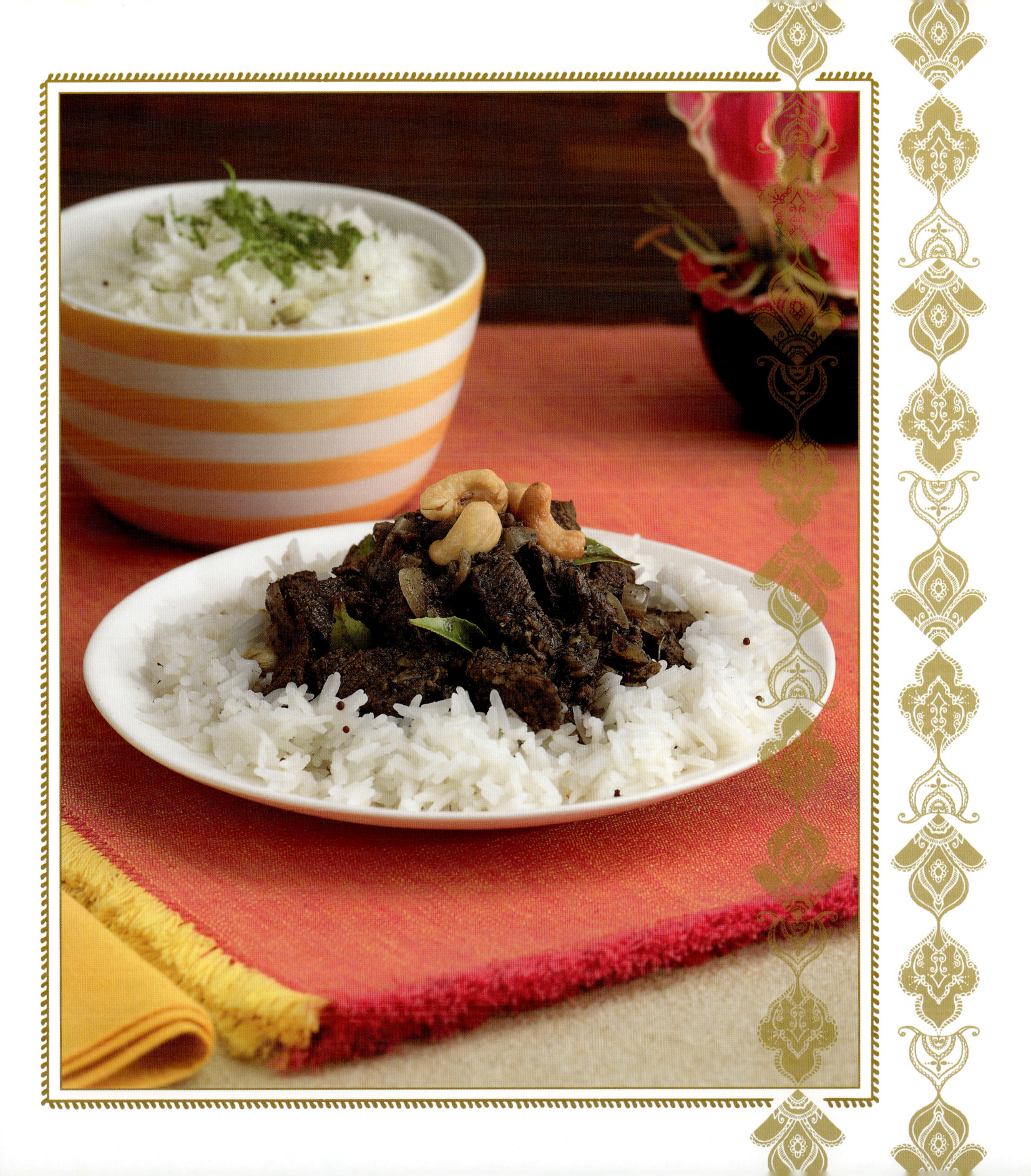

Young goat curry with potatoes

In some Kashmiri households, the potatoes are fried golden and crisp before being returned to the pot.

3 tablespoons ghee
2 medium-sized onions, finely chopped
4 cloves garlic, chopped
a 2-cm piece fresh ginger, grated
1 cinnamon stick
3 dried red chillies, deseeded
4 cardamom pods, cracked
750 g young goat (or lamb) shoulder or leg, cut into 4-cm chunks
4 medium-sized pink-skinned potatoes, scrubbed and quartered
1½ teaspoons salt
¾ cup light cream
pinch of saffron threads (optional)

Heat the ghee in a heavy saucepan and fry the onions for about 5 minutes over medium heat, stirring frequently, until lightly browned. Add garlic and ginger, cook briefly, then add the cinnamon, chillies, cardamom and meat, and stir over medium–high heat until browned.

Place potatoes on top of the meat, pour in about 2½ cups warm water and add the salt. Cover and bring to the boil, reduce heat and simmer until the potatoes are just tender (about 18 minutes). Remove potatoes and set aside to cool.

Stir cream into the curry gravy and simmer, uncovered, until the liquid is well reduced and the meat very tender. Infuse the saffron (if using) in 2 tablespoons boiling water and stir into the curry. Return potatoes to simmer in the curry until heated through. Arrange meat and sauce in a serving dish, surrounded by the potatoes.

SERVES 6

Calf's liver curry (masala kaleji)

450 g calf's or lamb's liver, skinned and cut into small cubes
¾ cup milk
1 medium-sized onion, grated
2 teaspoons grated fresh ginger
1 clove garlic, finely chopped
2 teaspoons ground coriander
½ teaspoon ground chilli
½ teaspoon ground turmeric
2 tablespoons ghee
½ teaspoon cumin seeds
½ cinnamon stick
1 large tomato, deseeded and chopped
salt and pepper

Place liver in a bowl with the milk and leave for 10 minutes to neutralise the raw smell, then drain, rinse well and drain again. Mix the onion, ginger, garlic and ground spices to a paste.

Melt the ghee in a saucepan or small non-stick frying pan and fry the cumin seeds and cinnamon stick for a few seconds. Add the onion paste and cook over medium heat, stirring frequently, for about 2½ minutes. Add ¾ cup water and the tomato, cover, and cook for 4–5 minutes.

Stir liver into pan and simmer gently for 20–25 minutes, until tender, seasoning to taste with salt and pepper.

SERVES 4

Black-pepper liver curry

- 450 g lamb's or calf's liver
- ¾ teaspoon salt
- 1 teaspoon tamarind concentrate
- 1 teaspoon crushed red chilli or sambal ulek
- ⅓ teaspoon ground turmeric
- 1 medium-sized onion, peeled
- 3 tablespoons ghee, or a mix of oil and ghee
- 1½ teaspoons crushed fresh ginger
- 2 tablespoons chopped coriander leaves
- 2–3 teaspoons cracked black pepper

Cut the liver into small cubes, pulling away any scraps of skin and membrane, and trimming away other inedible bits.

In a bowl mix the salt, tamarind, chilli and turmeric. Place a strainer over the bowl and grate the onion into it, pressing the liquid through. Add cubed liver to the bowl and mix well. Set aside for at least 20 minutes.

Heat a heavy saucepan with the ghee (or oil and ghee) and fry the grated onion with the ginger over medium heat for about 2 minutes, stirring. Add the liver and increase the heat. Stir until the liver is only just cooked, then add the pepper and coriander and cook for another minute, stirring constantly.

SERVES 4–5

Sausage curry

Sausages in a spicy curried sauce go well over smoothly whipped mashed potato.

1½ tablespoons butter or oil
12 thin sausages
3 spring onions (white parts and half of the greens), chopped
1–1½ tablespoons mild Indian or Mussaman curry paste
8 cherry tomatoes, cut in half
1 tablespoon sweet fruit chutney
salt and pepper

Heat a non-stick pan with butter or oil. Cook the sausages over medium heat, turning frequently, until well browned. Push to one side of the pan, add the spring onions (save some of the greens for garnish) and fry for 1 minute.

Add curry paste and tomatoes to the pan and fry briefly, then pour in 1½ cups water and bring to the boil. Reduce heat and simmer gently for about 10 minutes. Stir in the chutney, and season to taste with salt and pepper. Transfer to a serving dish and garnish with reserved spring-onion greens.

SERVES 4–6

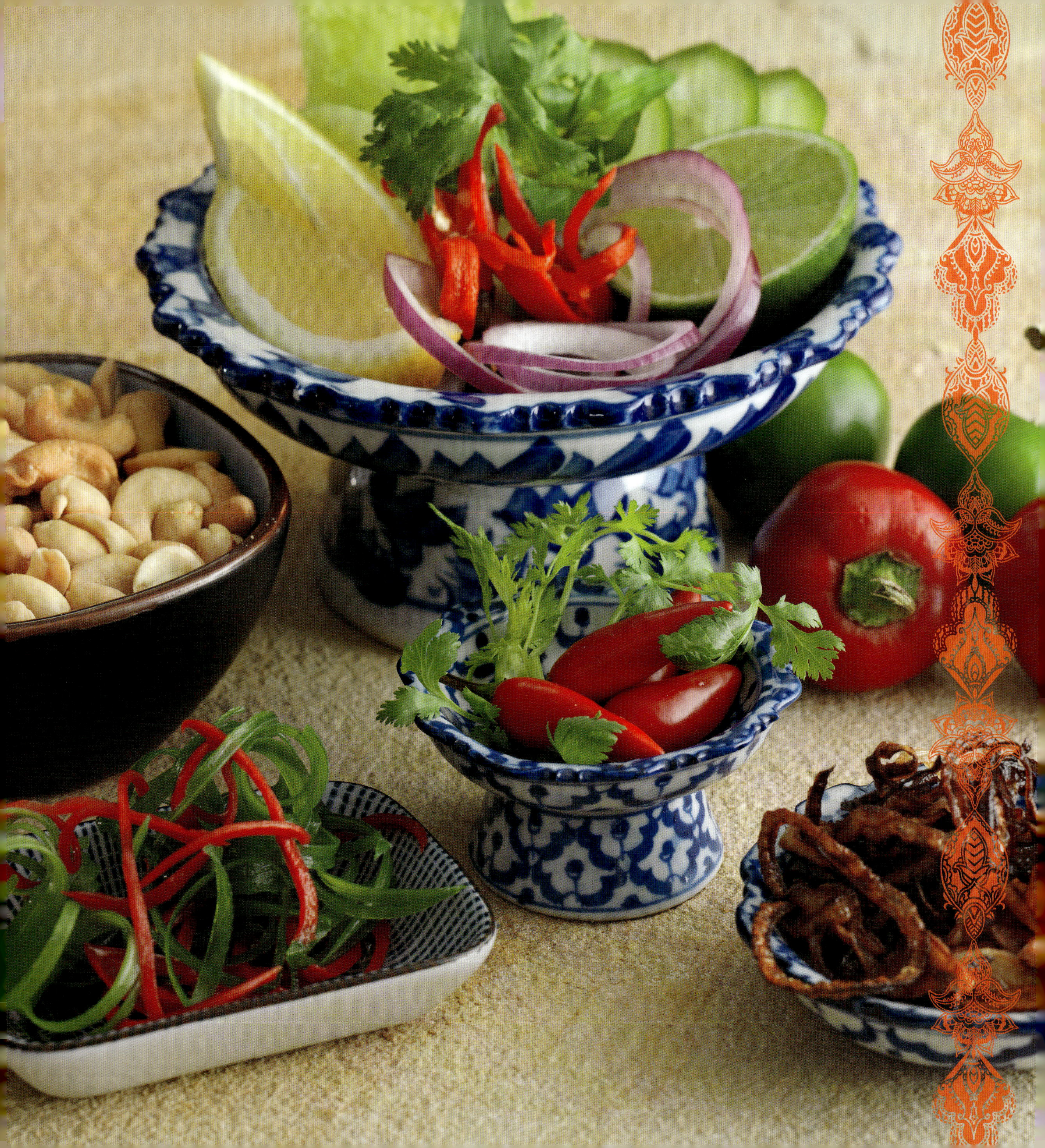

Accompaniments & side dishes

Flat breads, rice and side dishes are an essential element of the curry-eating experience. Breads and fragrant rice are perfect for soaking up every last drop of the delicious curry gravy. Sassy sambals, zingy relishes, fruity chutneys and creamy yoghurt sauces act as a counterbalance to mouth-searing heat. Fresh, tart and often crunchy salads coolly complement smoky and subtle spiciness. You'll find recipes for all these indispensable extras in the following pages.

Rice

Arguably the most important ingredient in Asian cooking, rice is served with most curries, even when bread is also an accompaniment. Two to two and a half cups of raw rice will yield 4–5 cups of cooked rice, which is enough to serve 4–6 people. Leftover rice can be frozen.

Basmati rice ›

1½ cups basmati rice
3 cups water

Rinse rice and drain. Place in a small saucepan, add water and leave to sit for 30 minutes.

Bring to the boil, stirring frequently, then reduce to a simmer and cook gently until rice is tender (do not stir the rice as it cooks, as this can make it gluggy).

After about 6 minutes the rice should have absorbed the water and the surface be pocked with steam holes. Cover tightly and continue to cook over very low heat for 5 minutes, then remove from heat and let sit another 5 minutes without opening the pan.

SERVES 4–6

Variations

Buttery ghee rice. Stir 2 tablespoons of ghee into the cooked rice and let sit, covered, for 5–6 minutes.

Saffron rice. Add ½ teaspoon powdered saffron or a pinch of saffron threads to the cooking water.

Gold and white rice. Divide cooked rice in half and fold ½ teaspoon saffron powder through one half. Let sit, covered, for 5–6 minutes, stirring twice. Mix white and yellow rice together to serve.

Fruit and nut rice. Add 1–2 tablespoons currants, sultanas or craisins and 1–2 tablespoons slivered almonds or roughly chopped cashews to the rice when almost cooked.

Lemon and spice rice. Fry ½ teaspoon each of brown mustard seeds and ground turmeric with 10 curry leaves in 2 tablespoons sesame or vegetable oil, until the mustard seeds sputter. Add 3–4 cups cooked basmati rice and the juice of 1 large lemon, and mix thoroughly.

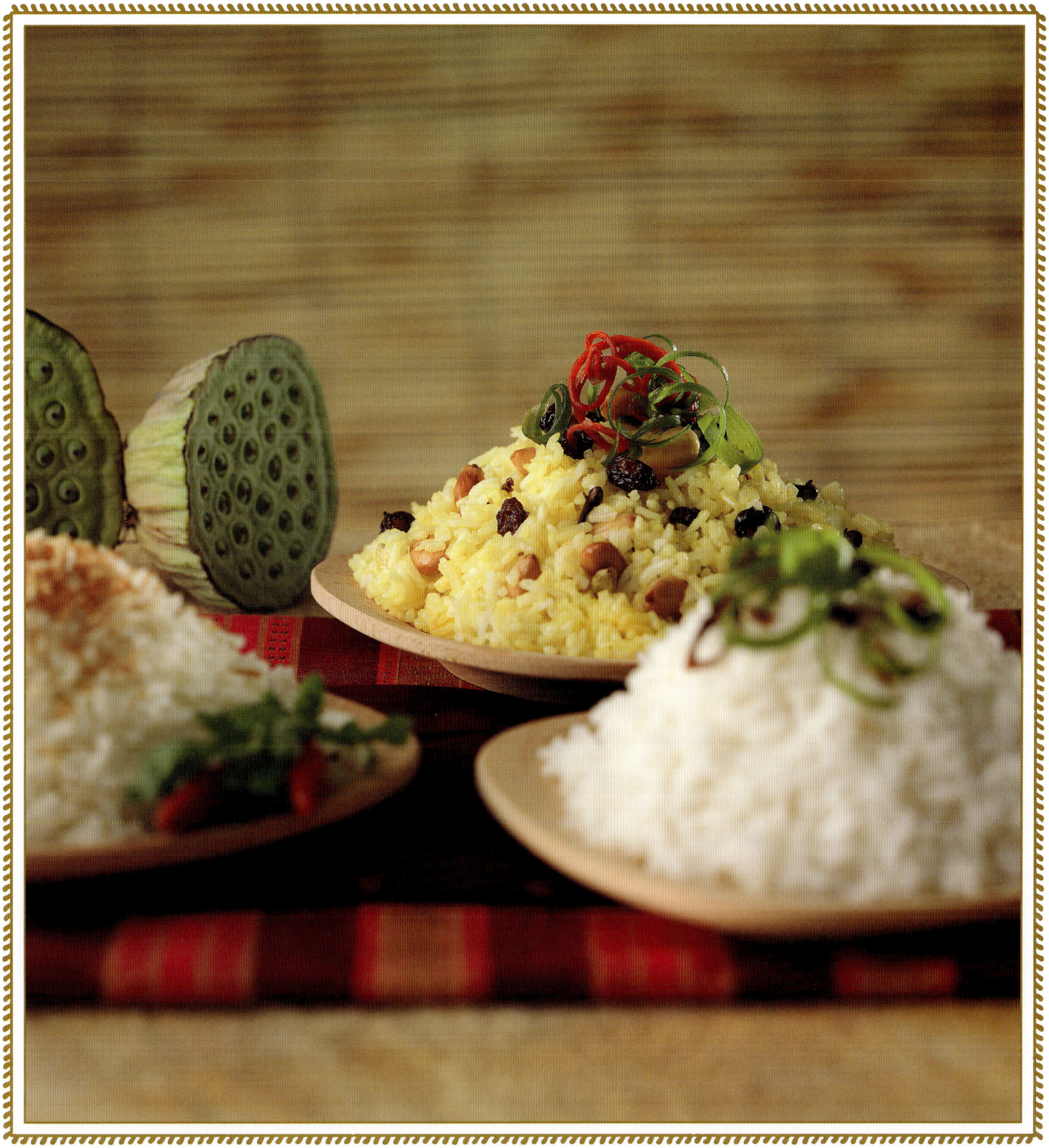

Sticky rice

Soak 2 cups of short-grain, glutinous rice overnight. The next day rinse the rice in several changes of water and drain. Place in a steamer (traditionally a cone of woven cane), cover with a damp cloth or lid, and steam for about 20 minutes, or until tender. Keep in the fridge until ready to use.

To make compressed rice cubes, cook sticky rice as instructed above and then, while hot, press it into a square mould and wait for a few minutes. Unmould the rice and cut into cubes to serve.

Quick-cook rice and vermicelli

You can now buy microwaveable pre-cooked rice, which is ready in as little as 90 seconds. Fine rice vermicelli also makes a speedy alternative to traditionally cooked rice dishes. With the quick-cook rice, simply follow the instructions on the packet; soak rice vermicelli for 3–5 minutes in boiling water to soften, then drain well and it's ready to use.

Steamed white rice

2½ cups long-grain white or jasmine rice
3½ cups water
1 teaspoon salt

Rinse and drain rice, and place in a saucepan with the water and salt. Bring to the boil, immediately reduce heat to very low and simmer gently for about 15 minutes. Remove from heat and let sit for 5–10 minutes before serving.

To flavour the rice in the traditional Thai way, push a piece of pandanus leaf into the cooked rice before leaving to rest.

SERVES 4–6

Variations

Coconut rice. Replace the water with coconut milk.

Yellow rice. Cook in water or coconut milk, adding 1 teaspoon ground turmeric.

Nasi goreng. Add sautéed diced chicken or baby prawns, egg, spring onions, bean sprouts or shredded Chinese cabbage (wombok) to the cooked rice, and flavour with shrimp paste, sambal ulek and kecap manis.

Crisp-fried onions or garlic

Crunchy fried onions, shallots or garlic give an appealing final touch to Southeast Asian curries. Fried garlic is so deliciously nutty it's hard to resist sprinkling it over everything – try it over rice and vegetable curries, especially.

20–30 shallots, 8 small red onions
   or 2 heads garlic
vegetable or peanut oil

Skin the shallots, onions or garlic and cut into thin lengthways slices.

Heat the oil in a wok over high heat, add the shallots, onions or garlic, and reduce heat a little. Fry, stirring frequently with a slotted spoon, until well browned – be very vigilant in the last few minutes, to ensure they do not burn. Retrieve slices and cool on a cake rack set over several layers of absorbent paper.

When cool, the slices should be quite crisp. Store immediately in a small airtight container (they will keep for several weeks).

Coconut chilli sambal ›

¾ cup desiccated coconut
1–2 teaspoons hot red chilli flakes
1 teaspoon ground coriander
salt and sugar to taste
1 tablespoon white vinegar
1 small tomato, deseeded
   and finely chopped
2–3 sprigs fresh coriander

Place the ingredients in a food processor or blender and process, using the pulse control, until reasonably finely chopped.

Use at once, or keep in the refrigerator in a small covered container for 3–4 days.

MAKES ABOUT 1 CUP

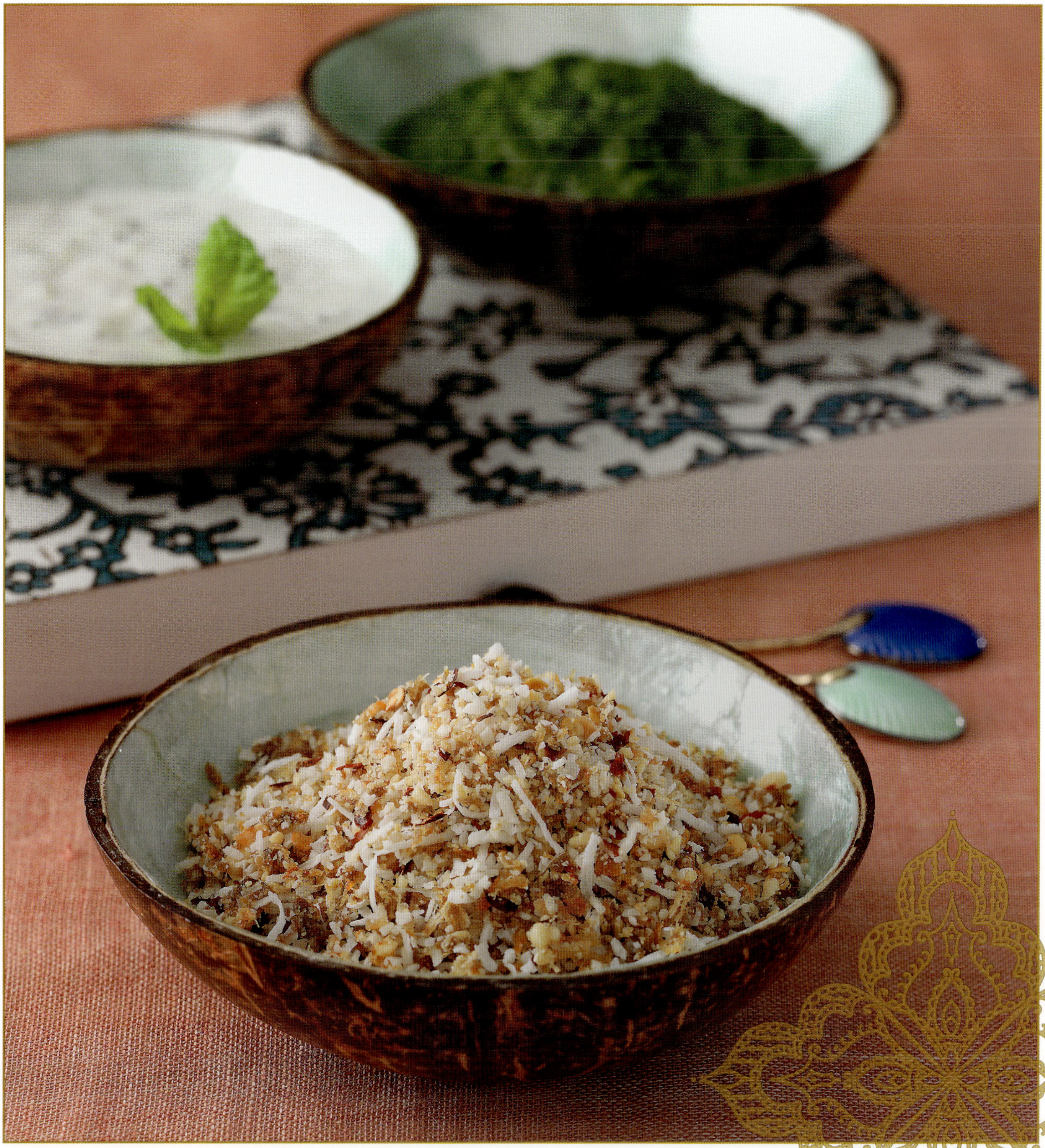

Fresh mint chutney

2 cups fresh mint leaves
2 spring onions (white parts and half of the greens)
1–2 fresh hot green chillies, deseeded
3 teaspoons sugar
1 tablespoon white vinegar
salt

Chop the mint, spring onions and chillies in a food processor or blender until well pulverised. Add sugar, vinegar and salt to taste and process again briefly.

Check the flavour, adding extra vinegar or sugar if needed. This will keep for a few days in the refrigerator.

MAKES ABOUT 1 CUP

Simple raita

Creamy blends of yoghurt and flavourings are designed to soothe stomachs and palates battle-scarred by an excess of chillies and curry spices. Add grated fresh beetroot or carrot, grated fresh or toasted desiccated coconut, mashed banana, chopped basil or mint, garam masala or toasted cumin seeds.

¾ cup creamy yoghurt
½ cup grated cucumber, well drained
1–2 tablespoons chopped fresh mint or dill
salt, pepper, sugar and ground cumin to taste

Whip together the yoghurt, cucumber and mint. Season to taste with salt, pepper, sugar and cumin.

MAKES ABOUT 1 CUP

Banana and onion raita

½ ripe banana
2 spring onions, white parts only
½ teaspoon salt
⅓ teaspoon grated fresh ginger
1 cup creamy yoghurt

Mash the banana in a bowl. Very finely chop the spring onions with the salt and ginger, then stir into the banana. Add the yoghurt and beat until smooth.

MAKES ABOUT 1½ CUPS

Kachumbar

A crunchy, tangy side dish for tandoori meals.

2 red onions, finely sliced
1 small cucumber, coarsely grated
a 10-cm piece daikon (white radish), coarsely grated
2 tomatoes, deseeded and finely sliced
1 fresh hot green chilli, deseeded and sliced
1 tablespoon chopped fresh coriander
1 tablespoon freshly squeezed lemon juice or white vinegar
¾ teaspoon chaat masala, or extra lemon juice
salt

Combine all the vegetables in a bowl, then cover with cold water and refrigerate for 1 hour. Drain well and toss in a paper towel or spin in a salad spinner.

Return vegetables to the bowl. Add the chilli, coriander, lemon juice or vinegar, chaat masala and salt to taste. Mix well and serve.

SERVES 4–6

Ginger & date chutney

3 large cloves garlic, crushed
1 small onion, grated
2½ tablespoons chopped stem ginger in syrup
1 cup chopped pitted dates
1 tablespoon crushed red chilli or sambal ulek
3 tablespoons brown sugar
3 tablespoons brown vinegar

Place all the ingredients in a small non-stick saucepan with water to not quite cover. Bring to the boil, reduce heat and simmer gently, stirring from time to time, until thick.

Check seasonings, adding a little salt and pepper. Remove from the heat and let cool.

Store in small, tightly sealed jars for up to three months.

MAKES 1½ CUPS

Pickled vegetables

2 Lebanese cucumbers
1 large carrot, peeled and finely sliced
1 large onion, finely chopped
1½ teaspoons salt
2 teaspoons sugar
½ cup white vinegar
¼ cup boiling water

Wash cucumbers and cut lengthwise in half. Scoop out seeds, then slice flesh finely.

In a bowl combine the vegetables with the salt, sugar, vinegar and water. Mix and lightly crush with fingers or a wooden spoon for 1 minute, then let marinate for at least 20 minutes. Drain before serving.

SERVES 4-6

Coconut, peanut & shrimp paste sambal

Sprinkle over curries, rice and vegetables, or serve in a small dish as a side.

½ cup desiccated coconut
½ cup roasted peanuts
2 tablespoons dried shrimp
1 teaspoon shrimp paste
1 large dried red chilli
    or 1–2 teaspoons chilli flakes
½ teaspoon salt

Place all the ingredients in a blender or spice grinder and grind to a coarse powder.

Store in an airtight container.

MAKES 1¼ CUPS

Fresh tomato and onion sambal

1 cup deseeded and diced tomatoes
½ cup chopped spring onions
½ cup deseeded and diced cucumber
1 fresh hot red chilli, finely chopped
2 tablespoons chopped fresh mint
   and/or basil
2 teaspoons sugar
1 tablespoon rice vinegar
salt and pepper

Combine all the ingredients and mix well. Chill for at least one hour before serving.

MAKES ABOUT 2 CUPS

Fresh chilli sambal

Jalapeno chillies are fiery hot! You can buy them fresh at many greengrocers and some supermarkets.

2 green jalapeno chillies, deseeded
2 fresh hot red chillies, deseeded
1 spring onion (white part and 4 cm of the green)
3 teaspoons sugar
½ teaspoon salt
1 tablespoon chopped fresh coriander or basil
2 tablespoons white vinegar

Finely chop the chillies and spring onion, and place in a mortar or spice grinder with the sugar, salt, herbs and vinegar. Grind to a paste.

Use at once, or refrigerate for up to 5 days.

MAKES ABOUT ⅔ CUP

Chapatis & rotis

These names are pretty well synonymous and refer to rounds of unleavened flat bread.

250 g finely milled Indian wholemeal flour (atta)
warm water
ghee

Sift the flour into a bowl and add ½ cup warm water. Work into a pliable dough, adding a little extra water or flour if needed (the dough should be soft enough to work, but not the least bit sticky).

Turn dough out onto a board and knead vigorously for 6 or 7 minutes. Wrap in a damp cloth or cling wrap and set aside for 1 hour.

Divide dough into 8–12 pieces and roll into balls. On a very lightly floured board, roll the balls out into thin rounds.

Heat a heavy iron plate or non-stick pan and rub with a paper towel dipped in ghee (the surface should be smooth, but not oily). Over medium–high heat cook the chapatis/rotis one at a time until dry and lightly browned on one side, then turn and cook the other side. You can encourage them to puff up by pressing a balled-up kitchen towel onto the middle of the bread.

Wrap in foil and keep warm in a low oven while you cook the remainder.

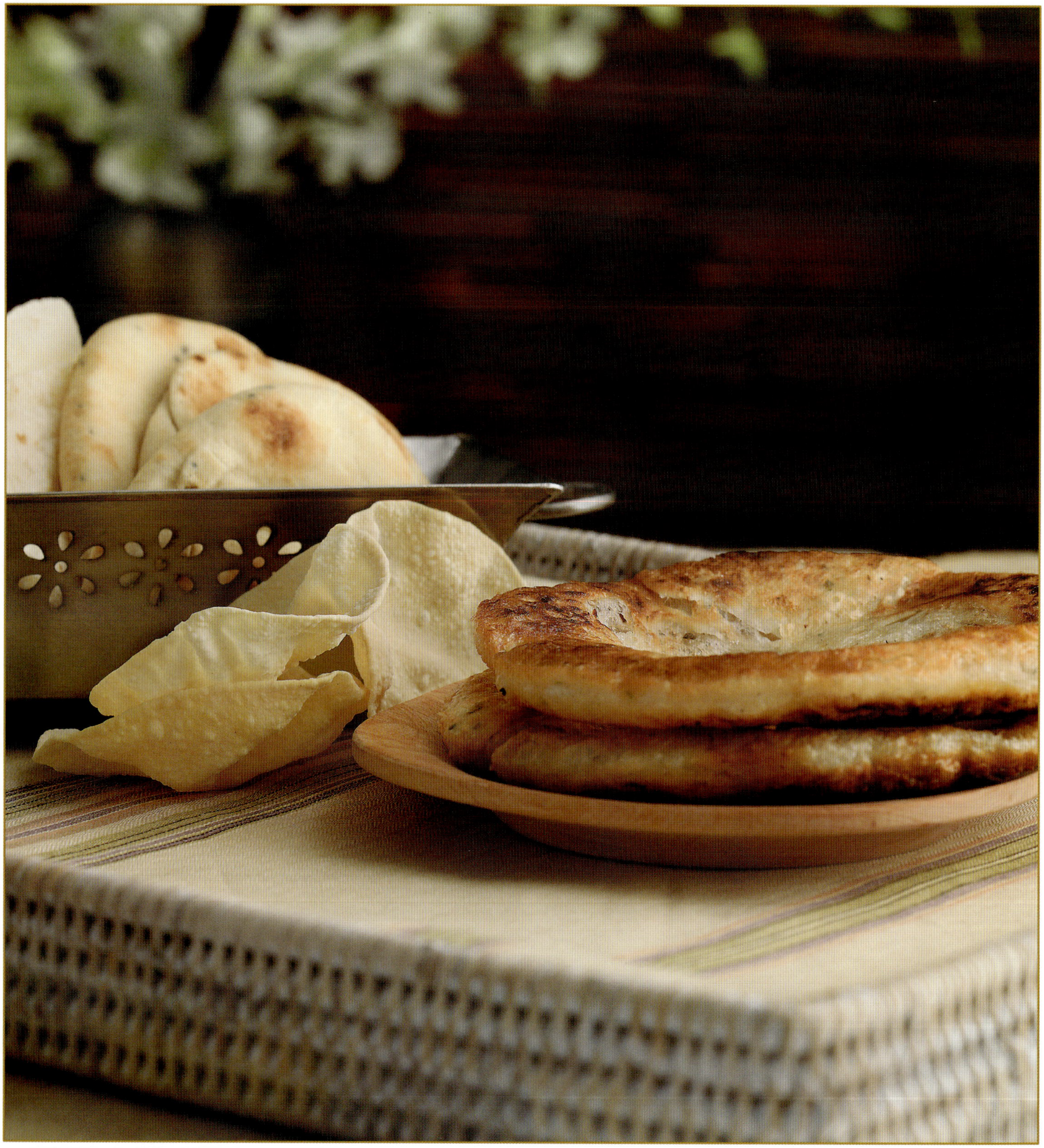

Puris

Follow the recipe for chapatis/rotis (page 291), adding ¾ teaspoon salt and rubbing 1 tablespoon ghee or butter into the flour before you begin.

The dough should be slightly stiff. Knead for 5–6 minutes, then roll into a sausage shape and cut into 12 pieces. Roll these into balls and then roll each out into a round on a very lightly floured board.

Heat oil or ghee for deep-frying and fry one or two puris at a time, until puffed and golden-brown, turning once or twice.

Drain well and serve hot.

‹ Parathas

These are another form of flat bread, often stuffed with vegetables before cooking.

Frozen parathas, both pre-cooked and uncooked, are now readily available. Thaw uncooked parathas until barely softened, then shallow-fry in oil or ghee, turning once or twice, until golden-brown, crisp and flaky. Pre-cooked frozen parathas can be shallow-fried, oven-heated, or warmed with a slick of oil or ghee in a non-stick pan or on a hotplate. Brush with melted ghee before serving.

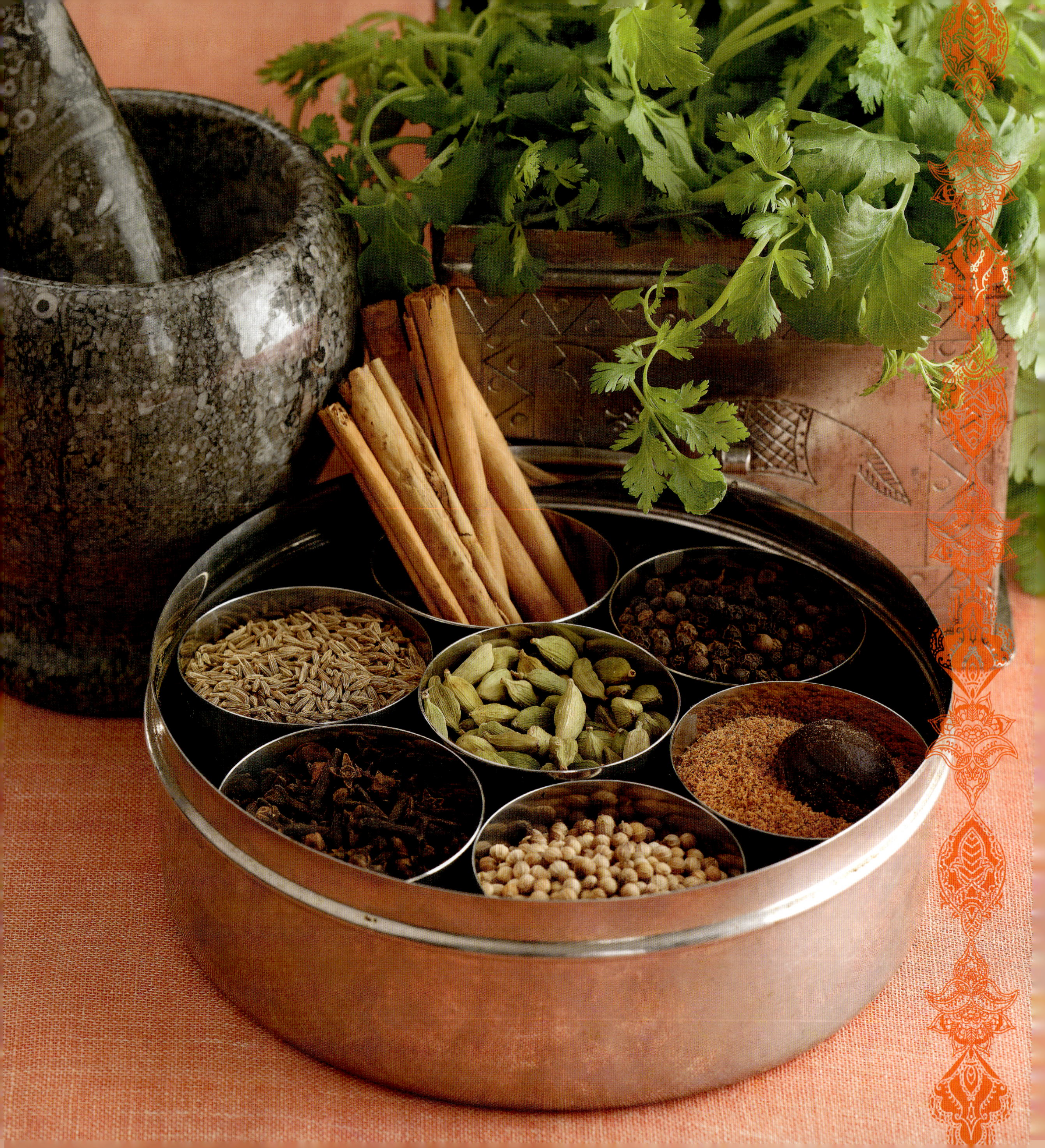

Curry spices & special ingredients

Spice is the defining element of Indian, Sri Lankan and Malay curries, though less important in Indonesia and rarely used in Thailand and Burma, where fresh ingredients impart the predominant flavours.

Nothing beats the fragrance of freshly ground spices, so buy them whole and dry-roast before grinding. When storing spices, use small glass jars with tightly fitting lids and keep them in a dry cool place.

Ajwain (also known as carom)
A small, tear-shaped seed with a fragrance similar to thyme. It is sprinkled over tandoori and rice dishes, used in pickles and chutneys, and occasionally in curries. Caraway or celery seeds may be used instead.

Asafoetida
A strong-smelling dried gum used as a seasoning and anti-flatulent, particularly in Indian vegetarian cooking. It has a resinous, garlicky flavour. Available as lumps or granules, and in powdered form, it should be used sparingly.

Bamboo shoots
They add a distinctive, earthy flavour to Thai curries, but if you don't care for them you can leave them out. Canned, sliced bamboo shoots are fine, and should be added in the last few minutes of cooking. Any unused shoots can be stored in a container in the refrigerator and will keep fresh for about 1 week, with a change of water every two days. Do not freeze.

Banana leaves
Practical as well as decorative, as wrappers for cooked food, lining for serving plates, and even as dinner plates themselves. Most Asian food stores and many florists stock banana leaves. They will keep for a week or more in the refrigerator, in a plastic bag.

Basil
A quintessential ingredient in Thai curries, usually added at the last minute. Basil is one of the easiest herbs to nurture in pots or a herb garden: plant as many varieties as possible, including Thai (or Asian) and the purple-leafed one. Also look for pineapple basil, which is great with curries of all kinds. Store harvested or purchased basil by standing stems in a jug of water, covering the top with a plastic bag and refrigerating; or enclose loosely in damp paper towel and keep in the crisper.

Bean sprouts
Should be absolutely fresh and crisp, or they will impart a peculiar, bitter flavour to a curry. Buy only as much as you require for a particular recipe. Blanch in boiling water and refresh in cold water before use. Bean sprouts will keep freshest on layers of paper towel in a plastic container, in the vegetable crisper: store for up to 4 days.

Besan
See chickpeas.

Candlenuts (also known as kemeri nuts)
Starchy nuts grown in Indonesia and used, ground to a paste, to thicken and enrich curries. (Candlenuts should not be eaten raw.) Macadamias or cashews, unroasted and unsalted, are suitable substitutes.

Caraway
Has the aroma and flavour of liquorice, and is interchangeable with fennel seeds in a recipe.

Cardamom
A delicate, fragrant spice comprising small glossy seeds within a smooth pale-green pod. Cardamom pods should be cracked or crushed before use. The seeds alone can be used instead (allow 8–10 for every pod specified). Ground cardamom, like other ground spices, rapidly loses its fragrance, but can be used at a pinch; keep it tightly capped.

Cassia bark
Similar to cinnamon, but with a coarser texture and less refined aroma and flavour. It is sold as flat, red-brown chips which are used whole or ground to a powder. Cinnamon sticks (quills) can be used instead.

Chaat masala
A tart blend of spices used particularly in vegetable dishes: it is likely to include amchur (dried mango powder), salt, cumin, coriander, fennel, chilli and black pepper. You can find it in Asian food stores.

Chickpeas and chickpea flour
Handy store-cupboard ingredients. Canned chickpeas are great for quick curries, while smooth, pale-yellow chickpea flour (besan) is used in batters and coatings for snacks, and fried foods, and as a thickener.

Chilli, ground and flakes
These easily spoil, so buy small quantities and replace often to avoid a musty taste. If ground chilli (chilli powder) clumps, throw it out. Get to know the intensity of the powder or flakes you buy (some are incendiary). Begin with less than a recipe calls for, and taste before adding more.

Chillies, fresh
So important to curry cooking that it's hard to believe they are not native to the curry-eating regions but rather are an import from South America. Chillies not only provide heat, from mild to mind-blowing, but also flamboyant decoration for curries and rice dishes when shredded, sliced, or carved into 'flowers'. The taste test is always best when buying chillies, as they have a tendency to change character, and therefore degree of heat, depending on where they grow. The largest chillies are usually the mildest; the very small Thai chillies and the plump, smooth-skinned jalapeno and squashed, orange-skinned scotch bonnets the hottest. But nothing is set in stone, so it's advisable to test before use: bite into the tip end, or press a fingernail into the flesh, and taste the juice. Milk, beer, yoghurt or ice-cream are the best defence against chilli palate burn.

Choko
A bland-flavoured gourd that is an excellent alternative for some of the harder-to-obtain melons and squashes used in Asian curry cooking.

Cinnamon
Adds delicate, sweet flavour to curries and rice dishes. Cinnamon sticks (also known as quills) are curled strips of fine cinnamon bark and are used whole or broken; the whole spice is preferable to ground cinnamon. Cassia bark has a similar flavour and fragrance.

Cloves
Fragrant flower buds with an intense flavour and a strongly numbing effect on the throat and tongue, so should be used sparingly. They are an ingredient of garam masala and other spice mixes used in Indian cuisine, and are used in both sweet and savoury cooking. Whole cloves keep for ages, but the powdered form rapidly loses its flavour.

Coconut
The various products can bring a smooth creaminess or nutty crunch to curries. The white flesh of ripe coconuts is grated to use fresh, is dried to make

desiccated (shreds or flakes) or powdered coconut, or squeezed to extract **coconut cream**. The last is in turn infused in water to produce the thinner product labelled as **coconut milk**. In any recipe coconut cream can be diluted with equal parts water to make coconut milk. **'Light' coconut milk**, with reduced fat content, is also available. **Coconut powder** is mixed into warm water to make coconut milk or cream, and desiccated coconut can also be infused to the same effect. **Creamed coconut** is a concentrated form of coconut milk: sold in blocks, it is grated or chopped and mixed with water before use. Unused coconut milk or cream can be frozen in small plastic containers. **Freshly grated** or **desiccated coconut** are added to curries of south Indian, Sri Lankan or Malaysian/Indonesian origin, to thicken and add nutty appeal, or toasted as a garnish and in some recipes used as an ingredient for flavouring and colouring a curry sauce.

Coriander

Used extensively in curry cooking, as the fresh herb and dried seed. Keep both ground and whole coriander seeds on hand. **Coriander leaves** are used in curry pastes, in sauces, and as a garnish. Wrap bunch loosely in damp paper towel and store in a plastic container in the refrigerator. Freeze unused roots and stems for use in curry pastes; the leaves can also be frozen (chop, then mix with coconut milk before freezing).

Cumin

The second most commonly used curry spice, after coriander. The slender brown seeds are used whole and ground in curry spice mixes and pastes, and fried as a fragrant garnish. As with most spices, dry-roasting before grinding enhances flavour.

Curry leaves (also known as kari leaves)

Small shiny, pointed leaves with a spicy aroma, added to most curries from southern India and Sri Lanka, and often fried in ghee or oil as a final flourish (tempering). They are available, fresh or dried, from supermarkets or Asian food stores, and can be frozen.

Dried shrimp

Whole tiny sun-dried prawns much used in Asian and Southeast Asian cooking, including curry mixes. Available in packets from Asian food stores and many supermarkets.

Eggplants

They come in several forms, from spherical to long, slender, white or purple. Thai **pea eggplants** are a tiny, pea-sized green variety with a grainy texture; they grow in clusters and are added whole or in bunches to curries. Occasionally found fresh in Asian stores, they can be frozen; green peas can be substituted in most recipes. **Apple (ball) eggplants** are the size of a golf ball and may be white, striped, green or purple; they are usually sliced or quartered. The more familiar large globe eggplant is often used in curries as well, usually being cut into chunks and fried in oil before adding.

Fennel

A fragrant, lemony, liquorice-tasting seed compatible with seafood and many vegetables. It is commonly used whole or lightly crushed in curries or fried in oil or ghee as a garnish.

Fenugreek

An unusual spice with small tan-coloured seeds and an aroma suggesting maple syrup. The seeds last for ages, which is a good thing as you probably won't use it often.

Fish balls
Sold frozen in Asian food stores, these are useful for quick curries. Keep some in the freezer.

Fish sauce
This is to Thai cooking what soy sauce is to Chinese food. It adds salty flavour to curries, but its other attribute, despite its unpleasantly pungent smell, is that it accentuates the flavours of other ingredients. Keep the bottle tightly closed when not in use.

Galangal
Resembles fresh root ginger, but its skin is a deeper tan colour and it bears small, tender pink shoots which are edible and make an attractive garnish. Fresh galangal (in Thailand known as kha) is available in Asian food stores: it is usually peeled and cut into chunks or slices for use, and is usually discarded before serving as it is too hard and woody to eat. Fresh ginger can be used instead, but as its flavour is stronger use half the quantity specified. Dried whole or ground galangal is available, but is a poor cousin to the fresh product.

Garam masala
An aromatic blend of spices used to season curries and to sprinkle over finished dishes. Its chief spices are coriander, cumin, peppercorns, cloves, cardamoms, cinnamon and nutmeg, though it can contain many others, following recipes handed down through families over generations. For a recipe to make your own, see page 16.

Ghee
Clarified butter, which keeps for months in the refrigerator, or weeks in a cool part of the kitchen. It is available in supermarkets and Asian food stores, and gives a rich, buttery flavour to curry sauces as well as being used for frying. Cooking oil and butter may be substituted. To make your own ghee, see page 10.

Ginger
Choose roots with unwrinkled beige skin, and test for freshness by snapping off one of the nodules. The flesh should be moist, fragrant and a light yellow colour. Keep refrigerated to prevent dehydration; peel and then use in chunks, sliced, shredded, grated or crushed, as required. Crystallised and pink sushi ginger may replace fresh in an emergency, but squeeze-pack crushed ginger is better. Ground ginger is only very occasionally used in curry cooking.

Kaffir lime
A different fruit to the more familiar Tahitian lime. Most of its unique, intense fragrance is concentrated in the deep-green, knobbly skin, which can be peeled or grated for use. The leaves have a similar intense fragrance and are added whole, or very finely shredded, to curries. The leaves keep fresh for several weeks in the refrigerator (they can also be frozen): they will eventually dry out, but can still be used after rehydrating in hot water.

Kecap manis
A thick soy sauce sweetened with caramelised sugar. It adds a glossy, dark colour and sweet-salty flavour as a seasoning or garnish. Available in supermarkets as well as Asian food stores it will keep for many months.

CURRY SPICES AND SPECIAL INGREDIENTS

Lemongrass
Has a tapering, pale-green layered stem with long, willowy leaves; it is the compacted lower section that gives the distinctive citrus flavour. Before use, trim off top and bottom of the stem and discard outer leaves if they are dry and coarse; slitting or bruising the stem helps release its wonderful flavour. It's available fresh in Asian stores and supermarkets (the stems keep for 1–3 weeks in the vegetable crisper), or you can grow some at home (it likes moisture and heat). Avoid dried lemongrass if possible, but if this is all you can find reconstitute it in hot water before use. Bottled chopped lemongrass, treated with mild citric-acid marinade, is an acceptable substitute and keeps for months in the refrigerator.

Lentils and split peas
These dried pulses replace meat protein in a vegetarian diet, and are the basis of the side dishes known as dals. They keep indefinitely in a cool dry place. Don't salt the water when cooking dried legumes, as it toughens them and they will never completely soften.

Mushrooms
They appear in many curries, particularly in Thailand where oyster and straw (small, round mushrooms) are commonly used. Keep cans of these in stock, though fresh are increasingly available in Asian food stores and produce markets. The familiar button mushroom also features in Indian cooking.

Mustard
The spice seeds come in two forms, brown and yellow. Brown mustard seeds are the ones most commonly used, in spice mixes, and fried whole in ghee or oil as a garnish. Yellow mustard is more often used as a pickling spice.

Nigella (also known as kalonji)
A small black seed spice with a distinctive flavour somewhere between onion and cumin (for which reason it is sometimes called black cumin or wild onion).

Nutmeg
A spice best used freshly ground or grated; the hard oval-shaped pods can be broken into chips and ground in a spice grinder. Ground nutmeg should be bought in small quantities and kept tightly covered to retain its sweet fragrance.

Okra
A small, pointed vegetable with pale-green, slightly hairy skin, and many gelatinous seeds inside. A common curry vegetable, it can be replaced by green beans or sliced zucchini. Frozen sliced okra is usually stocked in Indian food stores, and can be used straight from the pack.

Onions
Used extensively in curry cooking, providing sweet flavour and also helping to thicken sauces. Common brown or white onions are used in Indian cooking, while Southeast Asian cooks prefer the smaller shallots, which have pink flesh and mild flavour. As shallots vary in size, it is difficult to give exact quantities in a recipe, but using more or less will not affect the result.

Palm sugar
Derived from sugar palms and other varieties, it comes in jars, blocks and logs. Like cane sugar it varies from pale to dark; the darker the colour, the stronger the flavour. It is crushed, grated or chopped for use. Raw or soft brown sugar can be used instead.

Paneer
A cottage-style, rennet-free pressed cheese that is popular in Indian cookery. It is available in supermarkets as well as Asian food stores, and can be frozen.

Paprika
Dried, powdered red capsicum, with a rich, earthy flavour. Sweet (mild) red paprika is used to boost the colour of red curries, while hot paprika can replace chilli powder in a recipe.

Pepper
Black and white pepper, and fresh or brined green peppercorns, are all used in curry cooking. Black pepper is an ingredient of garam masala and other spice mixes. White pepper features in dishes with light, creamy sauces, while sprigs of green peppercorns are a decorative ingredient in Thai green and jungle curries. Dry-roast peppercorns before grinding, to enhance flavour.

Saffron
An expensive spice, but a little goes a long way. A small pinch of red saffron threads (stigma) or powder is enough to add brilliant yellow colour, a unique and delicate fragrance, and distinctive taste to curry and rice dishes. Beware imitation saffron powder, which uses artificial dyes and has no flavour.

Sambal ulek/oelek
A potent blend of crushed red chillies and salt. Sold in jars, it should be refrigerated after opening and will then last for many months. Unsalted crushed red chilli is now also available, and can be used instead.

Shrimp paste
This foul-smelling ingredient, made from fermented, ground shrimps, is one of the most interesting but least understood flavourings in curry cooking. Like fish sauce, shrimp paste enlivens other flavours while adding its own complex, salty taste. Compressed shrimp paste goes by various names, including blacan (Malay) and trasi or terasi (Indonesian), while kapi (Thai) and nam rouc (Vietnamese) are softer, smoother pastes with a more refined flavour. The block version should be fried or roasted before use, to release its true flavour: enclose in a square of foil and cook on a hot grill, in the oven or a frying pan for a few minutes. Store in a tightly closed glass (not plastic) jar. No gain without pain – turn on the exhaust fan before you begin cooking with shrimp paste!

Snake beans (also known as long beans)
Tropical beans about 30 cm long, which come in two varieties: the darker green has a sweeter flavour, the pale green a tougher skin. They are interchangeable with each other in recipes, or with green beans.

Spring onions (also known as green onions)
An important ingredient in Southeast Asian curry cooking. The whites and paler green parts are used in curry pastes and sliced into sauces, while the bright-green tops are shredded or sliced as a garnish and to give a delicate onion flavouring to dishes. To store, wrap in damp paper towel and keep in the vegetable crisper.

Star anise
An elegant, star-shaped spice with an intense anise flavour and aroma. In curries, where it makes occasional cameo appearances, it can be replaced by fennel or caraway seeds.

Tamarind
Used in curries the way lemon juice is used in the west, to add a tart-sour flavour and to tenderise meat. Tamarind is sold in different forms: the simplest to use is tamarind concentrate or paste, which can be added directly to curries. Dried tamarind pulp, compressed into blocks, requires some attention before use: it must be soaked in hot water and the seeds and pith strained off. Lemon juice can be used as a substitute for tamarind.

Tomatoes
Provide texture and mild acidity in curry sauces, as well as helping thicken them. To use fresh tomatoes, place in boiling water for about 10 seconds or until the skin splits, and then peel, cut in half and scoop out and discard the seeds and juice, then finely dice the flesh. Canned tomatoes are perfectly acceptable in curry cooking.

Turmeric
A relative of ginger, this root with intensely red yellow flesh is what gives curries their vibrant yellow colour. Ground dried turmeric is an ingredient in most basic curry powders, and is used extensively on its own to add colour and a subtle flavour to curry sauces and rice dishes, where it can replace the more expensive saffron. Ensure ground turmeric is kept away from damp and heat, which can turn it mouldy. Fresh turmeric has become more readily available in Asian fresh food stores and even supermarkets: to use, peel and cut into chunks or slices, or chop to a paste. It keeps for several weeks in the vegetable crisper. One teaspoon of ground turmeric roughly equates with a 4-cm knob of turmeric root.

Vietnamese mint
(also known as Cambodian mint or rau ram)
Aromatic herb whose pointed, brown-marked leaves have a pungent, peppery flavour. It is available fresh in Asian food stores and will grow vigorously in a home herb garden.

Water spinach (also known as kangkong)
A spinach-like vegetable with long tapering leaves and hollow stems. It is popular in Asian cooking and is becoming more readily available, but you can use fresh English spinach or watercress instead.

Yoghurt
Creamy, natural yoghurt plays several roles in Indian curry cooking, as an acidulant for tenderising meats and as a thickener for curry sauces. Sour cream can replace it, with a squeeze of lemon juice added.

Conversions

(All conversions are approximate)

Oven temperatures

° Celsius	° Fahrenheit
150	300
180	360
190	375
200–230	400–450
250–260	475–500

Liquids

ml (millilitres)	fl oz (fluid ounces)
60	2
125	4
250	8
500	16
625	20 (1 pint)
750	27
1 litre	35

Spoon and cup equivalents

ml	spoons/cups (UK)
5	1 teaspoon
20	1 tablespoon
60	¼ cup
125	½ cup
250	1 cup

Weights

g (grams)	oz (ounces), lb (pounds)
30	1
60	2
90	3
125	4
250	8
375	12
500	16 (1 lb)
750	1⅔ lb
1 kg	2 lb

Index

A

accompaniments & side dishes 279–93
ajwain (carom) 296
almonds
  Lamb in saffron almond cream (shahi korma) 216
asafoetida 296
asparagus
  Cumin-spiced sweet potato with asparagus 37

B

Baked fish with spicy coconut crust 112
Balinese duck baked in banana leaves (bebek betutu) 206
Balinese vegetables 52
Balti curries
  accompaniments 2
  Balti lamb & zucchini curry 226
  Balti meat & mushroom curry 254
  characteristics 2, 122, 254
  garnishes 2
  Hot Indian (Balti) curry paste 13
  Prawn & vegetable Balti stir-fry 122
bamboo shoots 296
  Jungle curry of quail with bamboo shoots & choko 198
  Red Thai curry of chicken & bamboo shoots 160
  Thai beef & bamboo shoots in red curry 242
  Yellow curry of fish with baby bamboo shoots 97
Banana and onion raita 287
banana leaves 296
  Balinese duck baked in banana leaves (bebek betutu) 206
Bangladeshi curries 2
Basic curry powder 16
basil 6, 296
Basmati rice 280
  Buttery ghee rice 280
  Fruit and nut rice 280
  Gold and white rice 280
  Lemon and spice rice 280
  Saffron rice 280
beans
  long beans (snake beans) 303
  see also green beans
bean sprouts 296
beef
  Balti meat & mushroom curry 254
  Beef curry with eggplant & chickpeas 253
  Beef & pumpkin red curry 238
  Beef vindaloo 248
  Fast & fiery Madras beef curry 247
  Fast-cook Mussaman beef curry 241
  Fifteen-minute meat curry with tomatoes & peas 228
  Indonesian beef curry 243
  Kofta curry with chickpeas & tomatoes 231
  Penang beef curry with peanuts 244
  Sumatran beef rendang 250
  Thai beef & bamboo shoots in red curry 242
Beef stock 23
besan (chickpea flour) 297
black pepper 302
  Black pepper chicken (kozhi melagu) 179
  Black-pepper liver curry 276
breads
  Chapatis 291
  Parathas 293
  Puris 293
  Rotis 291
Breast of duck in fiery vindaloo sauce 200
buffalo meat
  Indonesian beef curry 243
bugs
  Thai sour orange curry of bug tails & vegetables 141
Burmese curries
  accompaniments 5
  Burmese curry of potato, cabbage & onion 48
  characteristics 1, 5, 25, 260
  garnishes 5
  Rangoon pork curry 260
Buttery ghee rice 280

C

cabbage
  Burmese curry of potato, cabbage & onion 48

304 INDEX

Cabbage with chilli & coconut 42
Nonya fish curry with eggplant, tomatoes & cabbage 113
Penang curry of eggplant, cabbage & beans 55
Calf's liver curry (masala kaleji) 275
candlenuts (kemeri nuts) 296
caraway 296
cardamom 296

cashews
Chicken curry with coconut & cashews 186
Hot Sri Lankan chicken with spinach & cashews 182
Sweet potato, paneer, pea & cashew curry 45

cassia bark 297

cauliflower
Cauliflower, tomato & pea curry 30
Kashmiri okra & cauliflower curry 32
Thai green-bean, cauliflower & peanut curry 29

chaat masala 297
Chapatis 291

chicken
Black pepper chicken (kozhi melagu) 179
Chicken in a buttery tomato curry with dried fruit & nuts (murghi baghdadi) 171
Chicken in creamy spinach sauce (saag murghi) 172
Chicken & crunchy peanut Thai curry 162
Chicken curry with coconut & cashews 186
Chicken curry with green peppercorns 192
Chicken curry laksa 187
Chicken koh-i-noor 174
Chicken with lime leaves (ayam limau purut) 185
Chicken tikka masala 168
Chicken & tomatoes in hot curry 196
Daljit's mild chicken curry with yoghurt 180
Grilled chicken & tomatoes in red curry sauce 164
Hot Sri Lankan chicken with spinach & cashews 182
Indian chicken on the bone 177
Malay chicken curry with red chillies & peas 191
Penang curry of chicken drumsticks & potatoes 167
Red Thai curry of chicken & bamboo shoots 160
Roast chicken & mango curry 194
Singapore chicken in coconut curry 176
Sri Lankan molee of chicken & vegetables 188
Thai green chicken curry 158
Thai red chicken curry with straw mushrooms 161

chicken livers
Malaysian chicken liver curry (karikering hati ayam) 197

Chicken stock 23

chickpeas 297
Beef curry with eggplant & chickpeas 253
Chickpeas with green chillies & tomatoes 77
Curried chickpeas with tomatoes & coriander 78
Kofta curry with chickpeas & tomatoes 231

chickpea flour (besan) 297

chillies
Cabbage with chilli & coconut 42
Chickpeas with green chillies & tomatoes 77
Coconut chilli sambal 284
fresh 297
Fresh chilli sambal 290
ground and flakes 297
heat of 298
Javanese padang curry of duck & red chillies 204
Malay chicken curry with red chillies & peas 191

Chinese cabbage
Prawns & Chinese cabbage in coconut milk 124
Tofu & Chinese cabbage in coconut curry 83

choko 297
Jungle curry of quail with bamboo shoots & choko 198

chutneys
Fresh mint chutney 286
Ginger & date chutney 288

cinnamon 297
cloves 297

coconut 297–8
Baked fish with spicy coconut crust 112
Cabbage with chilli & coconut 42

INDEX 305

Chicken curry with coconut
 & cashews 186
Coconut chilli sambal 284
Coconut, peanut & shrimp
 paste sambal 289
Coconut rice 283
Green-bean, tomato & coconut
 dry curry 26
Green vegetables in coconut
 41
Prawns & Chinese cabbage
 in coconut milk 124
Singapore chicken in coconut
 curry 176
Sri Lankan molee of chicken
 & vegetables 188
Tofu & Chinese cabbage in
 coconut curry 83
Vegetables in mildly spiced
 coconut sauce 58
coconut cream 298
coconut milk 298
coconut oil 107
coconut powder 298
compressed rice cubes 282
conversions 303
coriander 6, 298
Curried chickpeas with
 tomatoes & coriander 78
Lamb cutlets with green
 coriander sauce 219
Lentil dal with tamarind
 & coriander 86
crab
Crab stir-fried with curry spices
 136
Quick creamy curried crab
 meat 135
Crayfish in a creamy curry 138

Creamy mashed pumpkin
 payesh 36
cucumber
Kachumbar 287
Pickled vegetables 288
Simple raita 286
cumin 298
Cumin-spiced sweet potato
 with asparagus 37
Curried chickpeas with tomatoes
 & coriander 78
Curried cuttlefish 148
Curried minced lamb with peas
 (keema mattar) 223
Curried pumpkin 35
Curry laksa of seafood 154
curry leaves (kari leaves) 298
cuttlefish
Curried cuttlefish 148

D

daikon
Kachumbar 287
dal
Lentil dal with tamarind
 & coriander 86
Red lentil dal 85
Split-pea dal with spices 84
Daljit's mild chicken curry with
 yoghurt 180
dill 6
dried fruit
Chicken in a buttery tomato
 curry with dried fruit & nuts
 (murghi baghdadi) 171
Fruit and nut rice 280
Ginger & date chutney 288
dried shrimp 298
Malay pork, dried-shrimp
 & pineapple curry 268

duck
Balinese duck baked in
 banana leaves (bebek betutu)
 206
Breast of duck in fiery vindaloo
 sauce 200
Javanese padang curry of
 duck & red chillies 204
Roast duck red curry stir-fry
 with spring onions 203

E

eggplant 298
apple (ball) eggplants 298
Beef curry with eggplant
 & chickpeas 253
Eggplant in hot curry sauce
 72
Eggplant, onion & pea curry
 67
Malaysian lamb & eggplant
 curry 225
Nonya fish curry with eggplant,
 tomatoes & cabbage 113
pea eggplants 298
Penang curry of eggplant,
 cabbage & beans 55
Smoky eggplant yellow curry
 74
Spicy Sri Lankan eggplant 71
eggs
Egg & green vegetable
 vindaloo 91
Sambal eggs 88
Fast & fiery Madras beef curry
 247
Fast-cook Mussaman beef curry
 241
fennel 298
fenugreek 298–9

Fifteen-minute meat curry with tomatoes & peas 228

F
fish
  Baked fish with spicy coconut crust 112
  Goan mackerel in hot curry sauce 98
  Indonesian fish in tangy curry spices 107
  Kerala green curry of fish 100
  Malaccan pepper fish 104
  Nonya fish curry with eggplant, tomatoes & cabbage 113
  Spicy barbecued fish 108
  Spicy Malaysian fish curry 102
  Tandoori fish skewers 94
  Tandoori-baked whole fish 111
  Tangy curry of scallops, prawns & fish balls with spinach 133
  Yellow curry of fish with baby bamboo shoots 97
fish balls 299
fish sauce 299
Fish stock 22
Fresh chilli sambal 290
Fresh mint chutney 286
Fresh tomato and onion sambal 290

G
galangal 299
Game curry with Sri Lankan roasted spices 272
Garam masala 11, 16, 299
garlic
  Crisp-fried garlic 284
  pickled garlic 260

ghee (clarified butter) 299
  Buttery ghee rice 280
  making and storing 10
ginger 299
  Ginger & date chutney 288
Goan mackerel in hot curry sauce 98
Goan pork vindaloo 258
goat
  Young goat curry with potatoes 274
Gold and white rice 280
green beans
  Green-bean, tomato & coconut dry curry 26
  Penang curry of eggplant, cabbage & beans 55
  Stir-fried red curry of pork & green beans 265
  Thai green-bean, cauliflower & peanut curry 29
green curries
  Green prawn curry from south-western India 128
  Green Thai curry of mushrooms, peppers & zucchini 68
  Kerala green curry of fish 100
  Thai green chicken curry 158
  Thai green curry paste 18
  Thai green pork curry 266
  Thai green prawn curry 114
Grilled chicken & tomatoes in red curry sauce 164
gulai
  Indonesian gulai of lamb 222

H
heat of store-bought mixes 11
herbs 6

hot curries
  Black pepper chicken (kozhi melagu) 179
  Chicken & tomatoes in hot curry 196
  Eggplant in hot curry sauce 72
  Fast & fiery Madras beef curry 247
  Goan mackerel in hot curry sauce 98
  Hot Indian (Balti) curry paste 13
  Hot Sri Lankan chicken with spinach & cashews 182
  Mussels in hot red curry 142
  Pork diablo 256
  Spicy Sri Lankan eggplant 71
  Stir-fried red curry of pork & green beans 265
  see also vindaloo curries

I
Indian curries
  accompaniments 2
  Black pepper chicken (kozhi melagu) 179
  characteristics 1, 2, 25, 45, 172, 232
  Chicken & tomatoes in hot curry 196
  Fast & fiery Madras beef curry 247
  garnishes 2
  Green prawn curry from south-western India 128
  Hot Indian (Balti) curry paste 13
  Indian chicken on the bone 177

INDEX 307

Kerala green curry of fish 100
Mild Indian (korma) curry paste 14
vegetarian 25
Indonesian curries
accompaniments 5, 88
Balinese vegetables 52
characteristics 1, 5, 25, 107, 209, 250
garnishes 5
Indonesian beef curry 243
Indonesian fish in tangy curry spices 107
Indonesian gulai of lamb 222
Indonesian spinach & pumpkin curry 38
ingredients 6–7

J

jasmine rice 5
Javanese padang curry of duck & red chillies 204
jungle curries
characteristics 198
Jungle curry of quail with bamboo shoots & choko 198
Thai jungle curry paste 21

K

Kachumbar 287
kaffir lime 6, 299
Kashmiri okra & cauliflower curry 32
Kashmiri rogan josh 213
kecap manis 299
kemeri nuts (candlenuts) 296
Kerala green curry of fish 100

Khadai paneer (Paneer in spiced tomato sauce) 46

kitchen equipment 6
Kofta curry with chickpeas & tomatoes 231
korma curries
Mild & creamy lamb korma 210
Mild Indian (korma) curry paste 14
Prawn korma 119

L

laksa
Chicken curry laksa 187
Curry laksa of seafood 154
lamb
Balti lamb & zucchini curry 226
Curried minced lamb with peas (keema mattar) 223
Fifteen-minute meat curry with tomatoes & peas 228
Indonesian gulai of lamb 222
Kashmiri rogan josh 213
Kofta curry with chickpeas & tomatoes 231
Lamb cutlets with green coriander sauce 219
Lamb & lentil hotpot (dhansak) 232
Lamb in saffron almond cream (shahi korma) 216
Lamb-shank curry 234
Lamb with spinach 214
Malaysian lamb & eggplant curry 225
Mild & creamy lamb korma 210
Parsi-style lamb curry 220
Lamb stock 23
Lemon and spice rice 280

lemongrass 6, 300
lentils 300
Lamb & lentil hotpot (dhansak) 232
Lentil dal with tamarind & coriander 86
Red lentil dal 85
lime leaves
Chicken with lime leaves (ayam limau purut) 185
liver
Black-pepper liver curry 276
Calf's liver curry (masala kaleji) 275

M

Malaccan pepper fish 104
Malay chicken curry with red chillies & peas 191
Malay pork, dried-shrimp & pineapple curry 268
Malaysian curries
accompaniments 5, 88
characteristics 1, 5, 25, 209, 268
garnishes 5
Malaysian chicken liver curry (kari kering hati ayam) 197
Malaysian lamb & eggplant curry 225
Pork diablo 256
Spicy Malaysian fish curry 102
mango
Prawn & mango curry 127
Roast chicken & mango curry 194
masala
Chicken tikka masala 168
Pork ribs in hot masala 271

308 INDEX

Meatballs in mild & creamy curry sauce 237
mild curries
   Chicken in creamy spinach sauce (saag murghi) 172
   Crayfish in a creamy curry 138
   Daljit's mild chicken curry with yoghurt 180
   Meatballs in mild & creamy curry sauce 237
   Mild & creamy lamb korma 210
   Mild Indian (korma) curry paste 14
   Mushrooms & peas in mild curry 66
   Peas with paneer in mild curry sauce (mattar paneer) 40
   Prawns in mild cream curry 117
   Sri Lankan molee of chicken & vegetables 188
   Vegetables in mildly spiced coconut sauce 58
mint 6
   Fresh mint chutney 286
   Simple raita 286
Mixed vegetable curry 61
molee 188
   Sri Lankan molee of chicken & vegetables 188
mushrooms 300
   Balti meat & mushroom curry 254
   Green Thai curry of mushrooms, peppers & zucchini 68
   Mushrooms & peas in mild curry 66
   Thai red chicken curry with straw mushrooms 161
Mussaman curries
   Fast-cook Mussaman beef curry 241
   Mussaman potato & peanut curry 54
   Thai Mussaman curry paste 19
mussels
   Mussels in hot red curry 142
   Yellow Thai curry of stuffed mussels 144
mustard 300

N

Nasi goreng 283
nigella (kalonji) 300
Nonya dishes
   characteristics 1, 185
   Chicken with lime leaves (ayam limau purut) 185
   Indonesian gulai of lamb 222
   Nonya fish curry with eggplant, tomatoes & cabbage 113
   Nonya spiced pork & potato curry 262
nutmeg 300
nuts
   Chicken in a buttery tomato curry with dried fruit & nuts (murghi baghdadi) 171
   Fruit and nut rice 280
   Lamb in saffron almond cream (shahi korma) 216
   see also cashews; peanuts

O

okra 300
   Kashmiri okra & cauliflower curry 32
   Singapore curry of seafood & okra 152
onions 300
   Banana and onion raita 287
   Burmese curry of potato, cabbage & onion 48
   Crisp-fried onions 284
   Eggplant, onion & pea curry 67
   Prawn & onion vindaloo 120
   see also spring onions

P

Pakistani curries 2
palm sugar 300
paneer (cheese) 301
   Peas with paneer in mild curry sauce (mattar paneer) 40
   Paneer in spiced tomato sauce (khadai paneer) 46
   Sweet potato, paneer, pea & cashew curry 45
paprika 301
Parathas 293
Parsi-style lamb curry 220
pastes and powders
   Basic curry powder 16
   Garam masala 11, 16
   home-made 9
   Hot Indian (Balti) curry paste 13
   Mild Indian (korma) curry paste 14
   Roasted curry spices 14
   store-bought 9, 11
   storing 9
   Tandoori paste 13
   Thai green curry paste 18

Thai jungle curry paste 21
Thai Mussaman curry paste 19
Thai red curry paste 17
Thai yellow curry paste 20
Vindaloo paste 11

peanuts
Coconut, peanut & shrimp paste sambal 289
Chicken & crunchy peanut Thai curry 162
Mussaman potato & peanut curry 54
Penang beef curry with peanuts 244
Thai green-bean, cauliflower & peanut curry 29

peas
Cauliflower, tomato & pea curry 30
Curried minced lamb with peas (keema mattar) 223
Eggplant, onion & pea curry 67
Fifteen-minute meat curry with tomatoes & peas 228
Malay chicken curry with red chillies & peas 191
Mushrooms & peas in mild curry 66
Peas with paneer in mild curry sauce (mattar paneer) 40
Sweet potato, paneer, pea & cashew curry 45

Penang curries
characteristics (mild) 167
Penang beef curry with peanuts 244
Penang curry of chicken drumsticks & potatoes 167
Penang curry of eggplant, cabbage, & beans 55

pepper
black 301
dry-roasting 301
white 301

peppercorns
Chicken curry with green peppercorns 192

peppers (capsicum)
Green Thai curry of mushrooms, peppers & zucchini 68
pickled garlic 260
Pickled vegetables 288

pineapple
Malay pork, dried-shrimp & pineapple curry 268
Thai red curry pork with pineapple 259

pork
Goan pork vindaloo 258
Malay pork, dried-shrimp & pineapple curry 268
Nonya spiced pork & potato curry 262
Pork diablo 256
Pork ribs in hot masala 271
Rangoon pork curry 260
Stir-fried red curry of pork & green beans 265
Thai green pork curry 266
Thai red curry pork with pineapple 259

potatoes
Burmese curry of potato, cabbage & onion 48
Mussaman potato & peanut curry 54
Nonya spiced pork & potato curry 262
Penang curry of chicken drumsticks & potatoes 167
Singapore potato curry 56
Young goat curry with potatoes 274

prawns
Green prawn curry from south-western India 128
Prawns & Chinese cabbage in coconut milk 124
Prawn korma 119
Prawn & mango curry 127
Prawns in mild cream curry 117
Prawn & onion vindaloo 120
Prawn & vegetable Balti stir-fry 122
Red curry of prawns 116
Sri Lankan prawn curry 129
Tangy curry of scallops, prawns & fish balls with spinach 133
Thai green prawn curry 114

pumpkin
Beef & pumpkin red curry 238
Creamy mashed pumpkin payesh 36
Curried pumpkin 35
Indonesian spinach & pumpkin curry 38
puris 293

Q

quails
Jungle curry of quails with bamboo shoots & choko 198
Quick creamy curried crab meat 135
Quick-cook rice 282

R

raita
- Banana and onion raita 287
- Simple raita 200, 286

Rangoon pork curry 260

red curries
- Beef & pumpkin red curry 238
- Grilled chicken & tomatoes in red curry sauce 164
- Mussels in hot red curry 142
- Red curry of prawns 116
- Red curry of tofu & water spinach 80
- Red curry of vegetables 51
- Red Thai curry of chicken & bamboo shoots 160
- Roast duck red curry stir-fry with spring onions 203
- Scallops in red curry sauce 130
- Stir-fried red curry of pork & green beans 265
- Thai beef & bamboo shoots in red curry 242
- Thai red chicken curry with straw mushrooms 161
- Thai red curry pork with pineapple 259
- Thai red curry squid 147
- Thai red curry paste 17

rendang
- Sumatran beef rendang 250

rice
- Basmati rice variations 280
- compressed rice cubes 282
- freezing 280
- quantities 280
- Quick-cook rice 282
- steamed white rice variations 283
- Sticky rice 282

Roast chicken & mango curry 194
Roast duck red curry stir-fry with spring onions 203
Roasted curry spices 14

rogan josh
- Kashmiri rogan josh 213

rotis 291

S

saffron 301
- Gold and white rice 280
- Lamb in saffron almond cream (shahi korma) 216
- Saffron rice 280

sambal
- Coconut chilli sambal 284
- Coconut, peanut & shrimp paste sambal 289
- Fresh chilli sambal 290
- Fresh tomato and onion sambal 290
- Sambal eggs 88

sambal ulek/oelek 301
Sausage curry 277

scallops
- Scallops in creamy masala 132
- Scallops in red curry sauce 130
- Tangy curry of scallops, prawns & fish balls with spinach 133

seafood
- Crab stir-fried with curry spices 136
- Crayfish in a creamy curry 138
- Curried cuttlefish 148
- Curry laksa of seafood 154
- Quick creamy curried crab meat 135
- Singapore curry of seafood & okra 152
- Thai chu-chi seafood curry 151
- Thai yellow seafood curry 134
- Thai sour orange curry of bug tails & vegetables 141
- *see also* fish; mussels; prawns; scallops

serving sizes iv

shrimp paste 301
- Coconut, peanut & shrimp paste sambal 289

Simple raita 286

Singaporean curries
- accompaniments 5
- characteristics 5
- garnishes 5
- Singapore chicken in coconut curry 176
- Singapore curry of seafood & okra 152
- Singapore potato curry 56

Smoky eggplant yellow curry 74
snake beans (long beans) 265, 301

spices
- dry-roasting 182
- Roasted curry spices (Sri Lankan) 14

spice mixes
- chaat masala 297
- garam masala 11
- Spicy barbecued fish 108
- Spicy Malaysian fish curry 102
- Spicy Sri Lankan eggplant 71

INDEX 311

spinach
  Chicken in creamy spinach sauce (saag murghi) 172
  Hot Sri Lankan chicken with spinach & cashews 182
  Indonesian spinach & pumpkin curry 38
  Lamb with spinach 214
  Tangy curry of scallops, prawns & fish balls with spinach 133
split peas 300
  Split-pea dal with spices 84
spring onions (green onions) 301
  Fresh tomato and onion sambal 290
  Roast duck red curry stir-fry with spring onions 203
squid
  Thai red curry squid 147
Sri Lankan curries
  accompaniments 2
  characteristics 2, 45, 71, 182
  Game curry with Sri Lankan roasted spices 272
  garnishes 2
  Hot Sri Lankan chicken with spinach & cashews 182
  Roasted curry spices 14
  Spicy Sri Lankan eggplant 71
  Sri Lankan molee of chicken & vegetables 188
  Sri Lankan prawn curry 129
star anise 301
steamed white rice 283
  Coconut rice 283
  Nasi goreng 283
  Yellow rice 283

Sticky rice 282
stir-fries
  Crab stir-fried with curry spices 136
  Prawn & vegetable Balti stir-fry 122
  Roast duck red curry stir-fry with spring onions 203
  Stir-fried red curry of pork & green beans 265
  see also Balti curries
stock
  Beef stock 23
  Chicken stock 23
  Fish stock 22
  Lamb stock 23
  Vegetable stock 22
Sumatran beef rendang 250
sweet potato
  Cumin-spiced sweet potato with asparagus 37
  Sweet potato, paneer, pea & cashew curry 45

T

tamarind 302
  Lentil dal with tamarind & coriander 86
Tandoori fish skewers 94
Tandoori paste 13
Tandoori-baked whole fish 111
Tangy curry of scallops, prawns & fish balls with spinach 133
Thai curries
  accompaniments 1, 5
  characteristics 5, 25, 142, 198, 209, 301
  Chicken & crunchy peanut Thai curry 162
  garnishes 5

  Green Thai curry of mushrooms, peppers & zucchini 68
  Jungle curry of quail with bamboo shoots & choko 198
  Red Thai curry of chicken & bamboo shoots 160
  Thai beef & bamboo shoots in red curry 242
  Thai chu-chi seafood curry 151
  Thai green chicken curry 158
  Thai green pork curry 266
  Thai green prawn curry 114
  Thai green-bean, cauliflower & peanut curry 29
  Thai red chicken curry with straw mushrooms 161
  Thai red curry pork with pineapple 259
  Thai red curry squid 147
  Thai sour orange curry of bug tails & vegetables 141
  Thai vegetable yellow curry 62
  Thai yellow seafood curry 134
  vegetarian 25
  Yellow curry of fish with baby bamboo shoots 97
  Yellow Thai curry of stuffed mussels 144
Thai curry pastes
  Thai green curry paste 18
  Thai jungle curry paste 21
  Thai Mussaman curry paste 19
  Thai red curry paste 17
  Thai yellow curry paste 20
tofu
  Red curry of tofu & water spinach 80

Tofu & Chinese cabbage in coconut curry 83

tomatoes 302
- Cauliflower, tomato & pea curry 30
- Chicken in a buttery tomato curry with dried fruit & nuts (murghi baghdadi) 171
- Chicken & tomatoes in hot curry 196
- Chickpeas with green chillies & tomatoes 77
- Curried chickpeas with tomatoes & coriander 78
- Fifteen-minute meat curry with tomatoes & peas 228
- Fresh tomato and onion sambal 290
- Green-bean, tomato & coconut dry curry 26
- Grilled chicken & tomatoes in red curry sauce 164
- Kachumbar 287
- Kofta curry with chickpeas & tomatoes 231
- Nonya fish curry with eggplant, tomatoes & cabbage 113
- Paneer in spiced tomato sauce (khadai paneer) 46
- Tomato curry 64

turmeric 302
- Yellow rice 283

V

vegetables
- Balinese vegetables 52
- Egg & green vegetable vindaloo 91
- Green vegetables in coconut 41
- Mixed vegetable curry 61
- Pickled vegetables 288
- Prawn & vegetable Balti stir-fry 122
- Red curry of vegetables 51
- Sri Lankan molee of chicken & vegetables 188
- Thai sour orange curry of bug tails & vegetables 141
- Thai vegetable yellow curry 62
- Vegetables in mildly spiced coconut sauce 58
- *see also* particular vegetables

Vegetable stock 22

Vietnamese mint 302

vindaloo curries
- Beef vindaloo 248
- Breast of duck in fiery vindaloo sauce 200
- Egg & green vegetable vindaloo 91
- Goan pork vindaloo 258
- Prawn & onion vindaloo 120
- Vindaloo paste 11

W

water spinach (kangkong) 302
- Red curry of tofu & water spinach 80

Y

yellow curries
- Smoky eggplant yellow curry 74
- Thai yellow curry paste 20
- Thai yellow seafood curry 134
- Thai vegetable yellow curry 62
- Yellow curry of fish with baby bamboo shoots 97
- Yellow rice 283
- Yellow Thai curry of stuffed mussels 144

yoghurt 302
- Banana and onion raita 287
- Daljit's mild chicken curry with yoghurt 180
- Simple raita 286

Young goat curry with potatoes 274

Z

zucchini
- Balti lamb & zucchini curry 226
- Green Thai curry of mushrooms, peppers & zucchini 68

VIKING
Published by the Penguin Group
Penguin Group (Australia)
250 Camberwell Road, Camberwell, Victoria 3124, Australia
(a division of Pearson Australia Group Pty Ltd)
Penguin Group (USA) Inc.
375 Hudson Street, New York, New York 10014, USA
Penguin Group (Canada)
90 Eglinton Avenue East, Suite 700, Toronto, Canada ON M4P 2Y3
(a division of Pearson Penguin Canada Inc.)
Penguin Books Ltd
80 Strand, London WC2R 0RL England
Penguin Ireland
25 St Stephen's Green, Dublin 2, Ireland
(a division of Penguin Books Ltd)
Penguin Books India Pvt Ltd
11 Community Centre, Panchsheel Park, New Delhi – 110 017, India
Penguin Group (NZ)
67 Apollo Drive, Rosedale, North Shore 0632, New Zealand
(a division of Pearson New Zealand Ltd)
Penguin Books (South Africa) (Pty) Ltd
24 Sturdee Avenue, Rosebank, Johannesburg 2196, South Africa

Penguin Books Ltd, Registered Offices: 80 Strand, London, WC2R 0RL, England

First published by Penguin Group (Australia), 2009

10 9 8 7 6 5 4 3 2 1

Copyright © Penguin Group (Australia), 2009

All rights reserved. Without limiting the rights under copyright reserved above, no part of this publication may be reproduced, stored in or introduced into a retrieval system, or transmitted, in any form or by any means (electronic, mechanical, photocopying, recording or otherwise), without the prior written permission of both the copyright owner and the above publisher of this book.

Written by Jacki Passmore
Photography by Cliff Schaube
Cover and text design by Marley Flory © Penguin Group (Australia)
Typeset in Nimbus Sans Novus T Regular by Post Pre-press Group, Brisbane, Queensland
Scanning and separations by Splitting Image P/L, Clayton, Victoria
Printed and bound in China by 1010 Printing International Limited

Cataloguing information for this book is available from the National Library of Australia

ISBN 978 0 670 07254 5

penguin.com.au